Washington Irving

Washington Irving

THE DEFINITIVE BIOGRAPHY OF
AMERICA'S FIRST BESTSELLING AUTHOR

BRIAN JAY JONES

Arcade Publishing • New York

Arcade Publishing books may be purchased in bulk at special discounts for sales promotion, corporate gifts, fund-raising, or educational purposes. Special editions can also be created to specifications. For details, contact the Special Sales Department, Arcade Publishing, 307 West 36th Street, 11th Floor, New York, NY 10018 or arcade@skyhorsepublishing.com.

Arcade Publishing® is a registered trademark of Skyhorse Publishing, Inc.®, a Delaware corporation.

Visit our website at www.arcadepub.com.

10 9 8 7 6 5 4 3 2 1

Library of Congress Cataloging-in-Publication Data is available on file.

ISBN: 978-1-61145-354-6

Printed in the United States of America

For Barb,
who told me I could,
and Madison,
who wants to

Contents

Preface ix

1   Gotham (1783–1804)   1

2   Traveler (1804–1806)   28

3   *Salmagundi* (1806–1808)   51

4   Hoax (1808–1810)   77

5   Adrift (1810–1815)   102

6   Desperation (1815–1817)   127

7   Determination (1817–1818)   154

8   Sensation (1819–1821)   174

9   Rut (1822–1825)   201

10   Professional (1826–1829)   233

11   Politician (1829–1832)   264

12   Frontiersman (1832–1834)   290

13   Sunnyside (1834–1842)   316

14   Minister (1842–1846)   344

15   Icon (1846–1859)   380

Acknowledgments   411

Notes   413

Selected Bibliography   451

Index   455

Preface

Washington Irving was an American original. His life story is the kind on which America was built and thrives: a likable, average man does something no one has ever done before and becomes very, very famous. So famous that women swoon over him and adoring fans hang his picture on their walls. Newspapers track his every move. Politicians want to be associated with him. It's a story you might think you've read and heard countless times before, but this one is different—because it's the first.

The first American to earn a living by his pen, Washington Irving was America's first bona fide best-selling author. Unlike writers before him, he had no family wealth or personal estate to sustain him if he simply dabbled or wrote for pleasure. Irving had to write for a living. And write he did, churning out books, reviews, and articles for six decades, working with such regularity that he was sometimes accused of "bookmaking." Like many of today's best-selling authors, who publish books readers love but critics loathe, Irving wrote for the masses—and for profit, not for posterity. The fact that his work sold so well and so quickly surprised even him.

Consequently, Irving was the nation's first international superstar, even in the most modern sense of the word. He had talent, movie-star good looks, and a charm that endeared him to his audience. He was a friend to presidents and kings, artists and poets; admirers begged for his autograph or a piece of his blotting paper, while writers sought an encouraging word. Were he alive today, he would be a staple of gossip magazines and tabloids, as he frequented plays and operas, and danced and drank with the glitterati.

For all his success, Irving was a man in perpetual crisis—and here, too, he was an American original, frequently engaging in damage control to protect a carefully cultivated reputation. While the public saw a wealthy, eligible bachelor and gentleman, Irving's private life was often in shambles. Money was a constant concern, as irresponsible family members lost his earnings in a variety of poor investments and ill-advised schemes. He fretted over his health, and suffered from a herpetic condition that periodically laid him up for months. He struggled with writer's block, feuded with publishers, and sulked over criticism. Frustrated in matters of the heart, he never married and was, in all likelihood, a homosexual.

More than anything, Irving wanted to be loved by readers, cherished by friends and family, and successful in his chosen profession. And while his writing is an important part of his life story, it is only a piece of a larger and more complex portrait. Until now, Irving's body of work has always been better known than the man. A few of his stories and characters are so deeply ingrained in our culture that most people can relate the plot of "Rip Van Winkle" or "The Legend of Sleepy Hollow" without ever having read the original stories. Yet even those who have read the stories can rarely identify their author.

This new biography attempts to shift the focus from Irving's writings to Irving the writer. For this reason, I have deliberately left literary criticism and analysis of his oeuvre in the capable hands of others. Instead, this is the story of the man behind those stories. And what a character he is! Far more intriguing than any one of his literary creations. The Washington Irving in these pages is complicated and conflicted. He is the talented, charming, and easygoing man of letters he projected to the public—but he is also the privately petty, jealous, and lazy malcontent. That conflict was part of his considerable charm.

An elegant writer in print, Irving was a terrible speller. His letters are a mishmash of misspelled words and poor grammar, and his personal journals, which he believed no one else would read, were even worse. For the most part, I have chosen to leave his words and syntax intact, even in the endnotes, stepping in only when grammar or punctuation interfered with clarity. The words and sentiments, the very story, are Irving's own—the story of an American original.

Washington Irving

1

Gotham

1783–1804

My beloved island of Manna-hata!

—Washington Irving, *A History of New York*, 1809

WASHINGTON IRVING WAS A DUNCE.

That was the unfortunate assessment of Mrs. Ann Kilmaster, his kindergarten teacher, in 1789. Every day six-year-old Washington Irving was marched from his family's home on William Street around the corner to Mrs. Kilmaster's classroom on Ann Street in New York City. William and Sarah Irving hoped their youngest child would learn to read and perhaps begin to write under Kilmaster's watchful eye, but the young charge only exasperated his instructor.

As disappointed as Mrs. Kilmaster was, her frustration didn't begin to compare with the wrath of Washington's father. Zealous, hardworking, and utterly humorless, William Irving—the Deacon, as he was known—lorded it over his family of five sons and three daughters ranging in age from twenty-three-year-old William Jr. to six-year-old Washington. A strict Presbyterian, the Deacon tolerated neither idleness nor stupidity.

Born of solid Scotch stock in the Orkney Islands in 1731, the Deacon had initially earned his living at sea, working on an armed packet in the service of Great Britain. While running slants between England and New York, petty officer Irving met Sarah Sanders, the pretty granddaughter of an upright British clergyman. The two were wed in Plymouth, England, and migrated to New York two years later, arriving in Manhattan on July 18, 1763.[1]

By the time of the American Revolution, the Irvings had five children and a moderately successful business dealing mainly in wine, sugar, hardware, and auctioneering. The Deacon and his wife were staunch patriots, and British occupation during the war made New York an increasingly dangerous place for the Irving family. Concerned for their safety, the Irvings fled across the Hudson River to Rahway, New Jersey, and were fired on by British troops. As the war wound down, the family returned to a battle-scarred New York to reestablish the family business. By mid-1782, Sarah Irving was pregnant with their eighth child.

On the evening of April 3, 1783—the same week New Yorkers learned of the British ceasefire that effectively ended the Revolutionary War—Washington Irving was born in Manhattan. There had never been any doubt as to the child's first name. "Washington's work is ended," Sarah Irving said to her husband, speaking reverently of the hero of the American Revolution, "and the child shall be named after him."[2]

"The house in which I was born," Washington Irving remembered as an old man, "was No. 131 William-street, about half-way between John and Fulton streets. Within a very few weeks after my birth the family moved into a house nearly opposite, which my father had recently purchased; it was No. 128. . . . It had been occupied by the British commissary during the war; the broad arrow was on the street door, and the garden was full of choice fruit-trees, apricots, green-gages, nectarines, etc. It is the first home of which I have any recollection, and there I passed my infancy and boyhood."[3]

The house on William Street was large, but Washington never considered it spacious enough to provide an adequate distance from his father. The Deacon had "small sympathy with the amusements of his children," Washington's nephew and first biographer Pierre Munro Irving wrote forgivingly years later, "and lost no opportunity of giving their thoughts a serious turn."[4]

There was no room for frivolity in the Irving home. Religion was decidedly tedious; church in the mornings and afternoons, followed by lectures in the evenings at which the Deacon sang the closing hymn with pious tears streaming down his face. The Irving children listened to it all dutifully, but the Deacon's passion never persuaded. Recalling his religious upbringing decades later, Washington's bitterness still lingered: "When I was a child, religion was forced upon me before I could understand or appreciate it. I was made to swallow it whether I would or not, and that too in its most ungracious forms. I was tasked with it; thwarted with it; wearied with it in a thousand harsh and disagreeable ways; until I was disgusted with all its forms and observances."[5]

For the rest of his life, Washington recalled the Deacon and his lessons with derision: "When I was young, I was led to think that somehow or other everything that was pleasant was wicked."[6] Fortunately, there was a compassionate, mitigating presence in the house; his mother, Sarah, who taught him that what was pleasant could also be beautiful.

While Washington remained understandably skeptical of all things religious, he was nevertheless convinced that his mother was a saint. Apart from protecting him from his disapproving father, Sarah Irving understood that gentleness, even in a man, could be a strength, and she tolerated—perhaps even slyly encouraged—her youngest son's dreamy endeavors. Washington never forgot this; his mother remained both his solace and his inspiration for the rest of his life. "The purest and strongest affection that winds itself round the human heart," he wrote in his journals years later, "is that between the mother and the son." The Deacon may have hoped to save Washington's soul, but it was Sarah Irving who salvaged his spirit.

The abundance of brothers and sisters provided another buffer between the Deacon and his youngest son. All the Irving children were unusually close, despite the spread in their ages, and remained so for the rest of their lives. Washington was especially reverential of his brother William, viewing him as not only his oldest brother but a surrogate—and ideal—father figure.

New York's economy was thriving, thanks in no small part to the efforts of the Federalists and Alexander Hamilton, who argued forcefully that loyalist money was just as vital to the economy as that of their patriot neighbors. While never overtly political, the Deacon, along with sons William and Ebenezer, adhered to the Federalist party line, which catered to the interests of the merchant class. The Deacon's business was moderately prosperous, though the Irvings never became part of the powerful Federalist clique of businessmen that evolved into the New York aristocracy. Neither did another New York merchant, a German music shop owner with an interest in fur named John Jacob Astor. Astor ignored politics and went on to amass a fortune, while the Irvings remained solidly and reliably middle class.

Despite Astor's indifference, politics were becoming increasingly important in New York—so important, in fact, that following ratification of the Constitution in 1787, the Continental Congress designated New York as the temporary seat of the new American government. On April 23, 1789, as cannons boomed and music swelled, President-elect George Washington arrived in New York for his inauguration.[7] A week later, at New York's new Federal Hall, Washington stepped onto the second-floor balcony to take the oath of office. As fireworks lit up the skies above Manhattan that night, six-year-old Washington Irving was among the tens of thousands of dazzled bystanders.

Irving's Scottish nursemaid, Lizzie, was something of a presidential groupie, following the president doggedly over the next few weeks as he strolled among the shops on Broadway or made his way along the narrow streets to his residence on Cherry Street. Holding Irving aloft on her shoulders every time the president rode past, Lizzie was determined to catch the great man's attention.

Her perseverance paid off, for she finally cornered him in a shop, where she proudly presented Washington Irving to the bemused president. "Please your Honor," she appealed in her Scottish burr, "here's a bairn was named after you."[8] To her delight, the father of the nation placed his hand upon Washington's head, bestowing his blessing upon his namesake. Irving never forgot the moment. He recounted the story with little variation for the rest of his life, and as an old man had a small watercolor painting of the episode hanging in his bedroom.

Apart from his brush with the president, Irving had no memories of the political glitterati—Vice President John Adams, Congressman James Madison, the fiery partisans Alexander Hamilton and Aaron Burr, or Chief Justice John Jay—with whom he and his family mingled in their William Street business. That was largely because the political splendor lasted only a little more than a year. In 1790 the compromise brokered by President Washington and his inner circle that allowed the federal government to assume state debts as part of the new national economy also moved the seat of the national government from New York to Philadelphia. New Yorkers shrugged, and went on making money. Manhattan ceased to be a capital city, but was content to be a city of capital.[9]

The Deacon had every reason to be confident about the future, yet his youngest son had just been labeled a dunce by his frazzled kindergarten teacher. The Deacon growled, Sarah Irving made reassuring noises, but Washington escaped Mrs. Kilmaster's classes with a mastery of the alphabet and not much else.[10]

His new teacher, Revolutionary War veteran Benjamin Romaine, taught a classroom full of boys and girls in a schoolhouse on Partition Street, still scorched by the fires of the American Revolution. Over the next seven years in Romaine's classroom, Irving learned little more than how to read and write—he was such a dismal student that one fellow classmate later remembered him as "a sluggish and inapt scholar of great diffidence—what teachers call stupid." Yet Irving and Romaine grew to appreciate each other, recognizing in the other a similar good-natured, easygoing attitude. Romaine teasingly referred to Irving as "the General," alluding not only to his student's famous namesake but also his seeming inability to tell a lie, so frequently and willingly did Irving admit his role in any mischief or scuffle. He went largely unpunished for his part in any trouble not because he was a teacher's pet but because his delicate stomach made it nearly impossible for him to bear the sight of his classmates being disciplined. Romaine's punishments were somewhat severe, and he was not above a practice known as "horsing," in which ill-behaved male students were rigorously swatted on their bare backsides. When Romaine exposed the rear ends of the other boys in preparation for the whipping, it was all the nauseous Irving could do to stagger miserably out of the classroom with the girls.[11]

Outside the classroom, he cultivated his reading skills, paging through newspapers to read about battles, which he and brother John Treat, five years his senior, reenacted in their yard, pelting each other with gravel and fallen fruit. In these clashes, it was John Treat, not Washington, who served as the historian and storyteller. John narrated the details with such gusto—and with such an overbearing bias toward his own side—that Washington eventually quit playing. It was a lesson in storytelling that Irving wouldn't forget: never let your biases offend your audience.

Newspapers aside, Irving's tastes tilted toward adventure stories—the nineteenth-century equivalent of comic books and pulp novels. At age ten, he became engrossed in a 1783 translation of Ludovico Ariosto's *Orlando Furioso*, a lengthy epic poem featuring swordfights, quests for maidens, ghosts, and lamenting knights. By eleven, he discovered Robinson Crusoe and Sinbad the Sailor, sparking a lasting fascination with sailors and the navy, as well as marking the beginning of a lifelong love affair with travel.

Just as appealing to his sense of growing wanderlust was a twenty-volume collection of illustrated travel essays entitled *The World Displayed*, which Irving found among the otherwise solemn tomes in the Deacon's library. Each pocket-sized volume contained pieces by various writers from around the world, with the editorial assistance of a slumming Samuel Johnson. It was within these pages that Irving first encountered stories of ancient Spain and Mexico, two cultures that enthralled him. Sneaking a small volume out of his father's library at night, he read in bed by candlelight until the flame of his smuggled candle finally sputtered out. "I used to take the little volumes to school with me," Irving recalled sixty years later, "and read them slyly to the great neglect of my lessons." Romaine recalled stealing up behind his student and snatching the book from him, but the old soldier gave Irving credit for his choice of literature, asking merely that he refrain from reading the books in his classroom. There were other literary gems in the Deacon's study—it was here that the teenage Irving discovered Shakespeare, Chaucer, and Spenser—but *The World Displayed* made a far larger impact on Irving than would any of those masters.[12]

There was another important, albeit fleeting, influence in his life at this time: John Anderson, a thoughtful, artistic young man who was in active pursuit of Irving's sister Catharine throughout 1794 and 1795. Eleven-year-old Washington worshipped the elegant Anderson, who could sketch, paint, play the violin, and talk about literature, philosophy, and the theater. Anderson frequently escorted Catharine—"Kitty," he called her—on trips to visit her newly married brother William. Washington seemed to always show up just in time to take tea with them, and listened to their conversation late into the evening.

The young suitor seemed to have a genuine affection for Irving. "Washington Irving spent the afternoon with me," Anderson wrote in his journal in January 1794. "Gave him some of my drawing books to look over, and presented him with a small one; play on the violin for him. He stayed to tea. Shew'd him the copy of my old journals and let him read a part."[13] It is easy to see why Irving responded so strongly to Anderson—here was someone who encouraged his interests in art, music, and writing.

Anderson was an unsuccessful suitor—Catharine later spurned his advances and turned her attention to future husband Daniel Paris. But Anderson's influence on Irving was both permanent and prominent. The young man nurtured Irving's love and appreciation for drawing and painting, and encouraged a more active interest in music, though Irving's instrument of choice was the flute, not the violin. Listening to Anderson discuss literature, theater, or current events, Irving absorbed the basics of good conversation. And there were Anderson's journals, in which he laid out his thoughts, dreams, and plans—a habit Irving adopted and maintained for the rest of his life.

With school growing increasingly tedious, Irving began to wander around and beyond Manhattan. Broadway dead-ended on open fields beyond Reade Street, but new buildings were rapidly being erected around the city, ripe for exploration. When small outbreaks of yellow fever made some areas of the city inaccessible, Irving headed north, picking his way up the Hudson shoreline to hunt, swim, read, and investigate the villages and scenery beyond the city limits.

Irving was strongly affected by these sojourns into the countryside, remembering them warmly twenty years later:

> As I grew into boyhood, I extended the range of my observations. My holiday afternoons were spent in rambles about the surrounding country. I made myself familiar with all its places famous in history or fable. I knew every spot where a murder or robbery had been committed or a ghost seen. I visited the neighboring villages and added greatly to my stock of knowledge by noting their habits and customs, and conversing with their sages and great men. I even journeyed one long summer's day to the summit of the most distant hill, when I stretched my eye over many a mile of *terra incognita,* and was astonished to find how vast a globe I inhabited.[14]

Watching his youngest son returning alone from his excursions upriver, reading books out on the piers, or listening intently to adult conversation, the Deacon could only shake his head in bafflement. "My father dubbed me the Philosopher," Irving later recalled, "from my lonely & abstractd habits." If this nickname was given with affection, Irving scowled that it was completely inappropriate—"I was the least of a philosopher as a boy."[15] Philosopher or not, the solitary existence that so puzzled the Deacon came to an end one afternoon in 1797 in the parlor of William and Julia Irving, where fourteen-year-old Washington was reacquainted with William's brother-in-law, nineteen-year-old Tarrytown native James Kirke Paulding.

James Paulding and Washington Irving had met years earlier, shortly after the 1793 marriage of Paulding's sister to Washington's oldest brother. That had been, Paulding recalled, merely a "boyish acquaintance." Four years later, with a job at the United States Loan Office, Paulding had come to the city to stay. While he lived with his brother on Vesey Street, he spent a great deal of time visiting with his sister, where he again encountered Washington Irving. This time, Paulding wrote, the relationship "ripened into a solid friendship." It was one that would span seven decades.[16]

Despite their five-year age difference, the two young men were much alike. Paulding, like Irving, was the eighth and youngest child in an intensely patriotic family. Like the Irvings, the Paulding family had fled their home during the war and had been fired on by British occupiers. And like Irving, Paulding was an introspective boy who turned to books for solace. Poverty limited his access to very few volumes, but he managed to find in his uncle's library Oliver Goldsmith's *Citizen of the World*, which, Paulding said, "possibly gave a direction to my whole life."[17]

A strapping boy and largely self-taught, Paulding was regarded by neighbors as a slouch. "I lived pretty much in a world of my own creating," he admitted later. "My life at Tarrytown was weary and irksome. The present was a blank and the future almost a void." Fortunately, his brother stepped in and helped him land both a job and a place to stay in Manhattan.[18]

Something of a country bumpkin when he first arrived in the city, Paulding remembered being laughed at for walking down the middle of the street. Nonetheless, he and the urbane Washington Irving were quickly inseparable, and just as quickly discovered they had something else in common: a passion for the theater.

While attending the theater was easy for nineteen-year-old Paulding, for fourteen-year-old Irving it was no small matter. Unlike the employed Paulding, Irving was still in school; with no source of income, he had to scrape up the cost of admission however he could. When he could finally buy a ticket, he had to leave the performance early, to his annoyance, so he could be home by 9:00 P.M. for the Deacon's evening prayers. Once in bed, however, Irving would sneak out his bedroom window, leap onto the roof of the woodshed, and scramble down to the street to return to the theater in time to catch the afterpiece.[19] If caught, he was certain to raise his father's ire to new, awe-inspiring levels, for this was willful defiance of the Deacon, who not only expected his children to remain at home in bed after curfew but also intensely disliked the theater.

While it is easy to dismiss the Deacon's opposition as pious rhetoric, he did have reason to be concerned—the theater was a rowdy, bawdy, somewhat shady place. The action on stage was frequently drowned out by the audience, as the working class in the pits drank and smoked and talked back to the actors. The more active attendees in the tier of boxes often expressed their dislike for a performance or actor by pelting the stage with rancid fruit or nuts. Meanwhile, in the top balcony, prostitutes openly carried out their business, with the tacit approval of both management and the police.

For all this, Irving was willing to risk the Deacon's fury. While the offstage activities were entertaining enough, Irving was more absorbed by what took place onstage. He attempted writing a play at this time—nothing of it survives—but more importantly, he quickly became a keen and intelligent critic. For Irving, theater was always a topic he could discuss knowledgeably and tastefully.

While his evenings were occupied with the excitement of sneaking off to the theater, his days were still spent in the increasing dullness of Romaine's classroom. "Thot of running away & going to sea," Irving wrote flatly in one of his journals. Such a life, he surmised, offered not only adventure and romance, but also an attractive alternative to being under the Deacon's roof. For weeks, the teenage Irving prepared for life at sea by strictly adhering to what he called a "regimen," gagging down pieces of salt pork and sleeping on the hardwood floor of his bedroom. Suffice it to say, the call of the sea couldn't compete with such discomforts. "Hated pork," he recalled matter-of-factly, "and gave it up."[20]

To his surprise, he suddenly had to give up Romaine as well, as the schoolmaster decided to go into business in spring 1797, and closed the doors of his classroom for good. Irving was immediately placed in a "male seminary," under the baton of Josiah A. Henderson, where Irving sat with college-bound older students, but continually frustrated the efforts of Henderson to teach him Latin, or anything else. Six months later, he was enrolled in Jonathan Fiske's school, where he stayed only until March 1798, at which point the frustrated Fiske began tutoring him privately. On the sly, Irving took lessons in music, dance, drawing, and painting—all activities certain to inspire the Deacon's rage.

In the summer of 1798, there was a different and more serious kind of wrath to be avoided. Cases of yellow fever had been reported on the docks along the East River, close to the Irving home. Unlike the 1795 outbreak, which had been limited to a few isolated parts of town, this time the fever swept through New York like wildfire. The Irvings made the quick decision to abandon the city altogether, scattering the family among friends and relations upstate.

That decision likely saved Irving's life. While 1,600 residents were treated at the Quaker estate of Bellevue, some 2,000 New Yorkers—including twenty doctors and poor John Anderson—succumbed to the fever.[21] Meanwhile, fifteen-year-old Irving was safe with Paulding in Tarrytown, where they explored the eastern shores of the Hudson and hunted squirrels in the woods surrounding a nearby Dutch village called Sleepy Hollow.

Gable-end stone mansions squatted among gardens full of hollyhocks. Wrens nested in unraveling hats nailed to walnut trees lining the roads. In the afternoons Paulding's grandfather read aloud from his enormous Dutch Bible with gigantic silver clasps. It all appealed strongly to Irving, this throwback to quaint traditions and old styles, a place where "population, manners, and customs, remain fixed."[22]

And there were the old Dutch legends and local ghost stories. Villagers spoke in hushed whispers of the strange cries heard in the woods where the captured British spy John André had been hanged. There was the Woman of the Cliffs, who was seen near the river when a storm was blowing in. Most terrifying was the unnerving "apparition of a figure on horseback without a head." Irving listened to it all with shuddering relish.[23]

When the yellow fever burned itself out in Manhattan, it was time to return to the city—and to regular study sessions at home with Fiske, who was determined to prepare him for admittance to college, despite Irving's best efforts. Unfortunately, like Kilmaster, Romaine, and Henderson before him, Fiske was doomed to frustration and disappointment.

Irving's last formal teacher, Fiske finally threw up his hands and abandoned his charge in 1799. It was clear Irving was not destined to follow his brothers Peter and John Treat to Columbia University. At the age of sixteen, with his formal schooling completed, he had, by today's standards, little more than an elementary school education. He had learned little science, a smattering of history and geography, and no logic, theology, foreign languages, algebra, or higher math.[24] Even in an area of real interest to him—writing—he lacked discipline, with an erratic sense of spelling, grammar, and punctuation.

Although he was a scribbler as a student, a career as a writer likely never occurred to him. At that time, it was unheard of for anyone to make a living as a full-time, professional author. Benjamin Franklin, Thomas Jefferson, Thomas Paine—these gentlemen were lawyers, printers, politicians first, writers second. There was Charles Brockden Brown, a recent New York transplant who dabbled at novel writing, but he was considered more of a magazine writer and editor.

Considering his options for a career, Irving sought what he believed to be the path of least resistance. The law, he thought, appeared to have both the greatest promise of wealth and security and the least amount of labor-intensive work. Lawyers talked, argued, discussed, and socialized, all habits in line with his natural proclivities. And they weren't slaves to the countinghouse, trade winds, or political embargoes, three masters Irving had watched his father and brothers struggle with as merchants.

"As I had some quickness of parts I was intended for the Law," Irving said years later in a somewhat embellished version of events, "which with us in America is the path to honour and preferment—to every thing that is distinguished in public life."[25] This was likely only part of the story. The American Revolution had been fought as much in the courtroom as it had on the battlefield, and Irving had seen civic-minded lawyers like Burr and Hamilton amass fortunes as practicing attorneys. It was also the path his brother John Treat was taking with relative ease, though Irving hardly appreciated that the overachieving John made everything look simple.

To the bar it was, then. At age sixteen, Irving entered the offices of Henry Masterson to begin his study of the law. Although one son had already taken to the law, it remained a profession that did not meet with the Deacon's approval. Peter had also considered the legal field, but the Deacon's glare had sent him scrambling into medicine instead. In the Deacon's limited worldview, industrious young men in the new economy made money, not arguments. Washington dismissed his father's disapproval; the youngest Irving had long grown used to disappointing the Deacon.

Better, in the Deacon's eyes, were William Jr. and Ebenezer, who had chosen lives of business and commerce—and the late nineteenth century was certainly a good time for merchants in New York. American neutrality throughout the Napoleonic Wars benefited the economy; between 1795 and 1800, the value of American exports tripled.[26] The more well-to-do merchants set up homes on the west side of Manhattan, independent from their businesses, making it one of the most fashionable parts of town. With the influx of new money, lower Broadway became one of the city's wealthiest and most sociable areas.

Watching the upwardly mobile strolling on Broadway, Irving dreamed of making it big. "My anticipations of success at the Bar," he wrote, "how I would overwhelm the guilty—uphold the innocent—I would scarcely have changed my anticipation for the fame of Cicero."[27] He may have meant it, but he wasn't willing to do the necessary work to become a Cicero—his study habits hadn't changed a bit. It didn't help that Peter frequently dropped by in the early afternoon to gossip.

Twenty-seven-year-old Peter Irving was considered the most sociable and literary of the Irvings. He frequented the best drawing rooms and belonged to all the right clubs. He was vice president of the Calliopean Society, one of New York's early literary clubs. William Dunlap, the manager of the Park Theater, spoke highly of him and valued his opinions on acting, costumes, and sets.[28]

But Peter's star declined as he succumbed to the indolent habits he now encouraged in his youngest brother. Failing to live up to the promise of his potential—Peter was a doctor in title only; he never practiced—he was likely concerned that his younger brothers might outshine him. While the Irving children were all exceptionally close, brotherly competition always brought out the worst in Peter.

Peter was not threatened by William Jr. or Ebenezer, who had followed their father into a life of commerce. Younger brothers John Treat and Washington, however, were another matter. When John Treat flirted briefly with the ministry, a move Peter considered a deliberate attempt to curry favor with the Deacon, Peter's contemptuous fury was blistering. "Mind Jack," he mocked, "you must preach dashing sermons!"[29] Such brotherly sarcasm was more than John Treat could bear.

Washington, who resembled Peter both in looks and temperament, was easier to keep in check. He revered his older brother and sought his approval, so he was easily influenced to adopt Peter's indolent routines. While both had literary ambitions, each struggled, with varying degrees of success, against what Washington called "gentlemanly habits." The two spent their time together smoking cigars, discussing the theater, and avoiding work.

It didn't take long for Washington to decide he needed a break from his studies. In 1800, pleading ill health, he convinced his family to send him on a recuperative vacation up the Hudson to

Johnstown, where he would stay with his sisters Ann and Catharine and their families. Given its proximity to Albany, Johnstown was considered a cultivated place.[30] Irving could barely contain his excitement. Once on the Hudson River, he never looked back.

As his sloop coursed up the river and into the Highlands, Irving was overwhelmed by the sheer beauty of the scenery. Nothing ever spoke as loudly to his senses as the grandeur of the Hudson, the Catskills, and the Highlands.

> What a time of intense delight was that first sail through the Highlands. I sat on the deck as we slowly tided along at the foot of those stern mountains, and gazed with wonder and admiration at cliffs impending far above me, crowned with forests and eagles sailing and screaming around them; or listened to the unseen stream dashing down precipices; or beheld rock, and tree, and loud, and sky reflected in the glassy stream of the river. . . .
>
> But of all the scenery of the Hudson, the Kaatskill Mountains had the most witching effect on my boyish imagination. Never shall I forget the effect upon me of the first view of them predominating over a wide extent of country, part wild, woody, and rugged; part softened away into all the graces of cultivation. As we slowly floated along, I lay on the deck and watched them through a long summer's day; undergoing a thousand mutations under the magical effects of atmosphere; sometimes seeming to approach; at other times to recede; now almost melting into hazy distance, now burnished by the setting sun, until, in the evening, they printed themselves against the glowing sky in the deep purple of an Italian landscape.[31]

For Irving, there was no God in these regions, but there were plenty of goblins, ogres, witches, and pirates—and at every turn in the river, crew members and passengers traded local legends and ghost stories that sent shivers up his spine.

Whether this first trip to Johnstown had the desired effect on his physical health, Irving couldn't say—he was far more interested in its energizing effect on his spirit. Just as Walden stirred Henry David Thoreau or the Mississippi moved Mark Twain, the Hudson River would forever be Washington Irving's solace and stimulus: "To me the Hudson is full of storied associations, connected as it is with some of the happiest portions of my life. Each striking feature brings to mind some early adventure or enjoyment; some favorite companion who shared it with me; some fair object, perchance, of youthful admiration."[32]

It was with a heavy heart that Irving made the trip back to Manhattan and returned to Masterson's law offices. His time there was unremarkable; the only surviving documents attesting to his abilities as an attorney show his signature as a witness.[33] In the summer of 1801 Irving left Masterson for the law offices of the well-connected Henry Brockholst Livingston.

An outspoken attorney of pro-agrarian Jeffersonian politics, Livingston had survived an assassination attempt and had killed in a duel an angry Federalist who had punched him in the nose. Livingston was an amusing mentor, but Irving didn't have the opportunity to study under him for long. In January 1802, in gratitude for Livingston's efforts in the 1800 elections, President Jefferson appointed him to the New York Supreme Court.

Scrambling for a new post, Irving became a clerk to Josiah Ogden Hoffman, who had just resigned as New York's Federalist attorney general. It was a fortunate placement for he, but it wasn't Hoffman's professional guidance to which he responded so well; rather, it was to Hoffman himself, and especially to Hoffman's new young wife, Maria, and their four children.

Hoffman—whom everyone courteously referred to as "the Judge"—was one of New York's most gifted and respected attorneys. He was ambitious, but his success was partly due to marrying well. In 1789 he had married Mary Colden, of one of New York's most prominent political families.[34] Mary died in February 1797, leaving the Judge a widower at the age of thirty-one, with three young daughters and a son to care for. In August 1802 Hoffman married Maria Fenno, a vivacious twenty-one-year-old who, like Mary Colden, came from a formidable political family. Her father, journalist John Fenno, was an active and vocal Federalist who had established the anti-Jeffersonian *Gazette of the United States* with Alexander Hamilton in 1789.

The newlywed Hoffmans settled on Greenwich Street, and the Judge's young clerk immediately became a regular in their household. Irving admired Hoffman's connections and the ease with which he talked politics, and looked to him as a kind of surrogate father, with a smart but not too stern demeanor that—unlike the Deacon's—persuaded rather than intimidated. He also fell in easily with the Judge's four children—Alice Anna, the energetic eldest whom everyone called Ann; quiet Sarah, who went by her middle name of Matilda; Ogden, the only boy; and Mary, who was named after her biological mother. But it was Maria Hoffman who kept him coming back.

In his letters, Irving always called her "my dear friend," never the overly familiar "Maria." While their closeness in age and the amount of time Irving spent alone with her in the Judge's house may raise modern eyebrows, there is no indication that their relationship was ever inappropriate—Irving was far too respectful of Mrs. Hoffman, and the Judge likely would have destroyed Irving if anything improper had occurred. "She was like a sister to me,"[35] Irving said, and the two regularly enjoyed each other's company and correspondence. It was the first of many close relationships Irving would have with older (albeit in Maria's case, it was only by two years) nurturing, motherly women.

When it came to work, Irving was still a dawdler. In the summer of 1802, overplaying an illness, he convinced his employer and his family that he needed another retreat to Johnstown and the recuperative spas at Ballston Springs.

He reached his sister Catharine in Johnstown, traveling in relative ease by wagon along the turnpike, "but I was so weak," Irving wrote, "that it was several days before I got over the fatigue."

Like an errant employee who makes certain to cough when he calls in sick, Irving reported, "I have had a little better appetite since I have been up here, though I have been troubled with the pain in my breast almost constantly, and still have a cough at night. I am unable to take any exercise worth mentioning, and doze away my time pretty much as I did in New York. . . . However," he wrote with a near-audible sniffle, "I hope soon to get in a better trim."[36]

Irving traveled with his brother-in-law Daniel Paris to the spas at Ballston Springs, where his hacking cough was heard through the walls of their hotel. New York Supreme Court justice James Kent asked incredulously if it was really "young Irving who slept in the next room to me, and kept up such an incessant cough during the night?" When told that it was, Kent could only add in disbelief, "He is not long for this world."[37]

Suitably recovered, Irving was back in New York by autumn, sorting through the onion-skinned volumes in Hoffman's chambers, gossiping with Peter, and listening to the Judge and his colleagues discuss politics—especially the rise of that Federalist in Democrat-Republican clothing, the crafty New Yorker Aaron Burr.

After losing his bid for reelection to the Senate in 1797, Burr went on to wield considerable power in the New York state legislature, and helped steer all thirteen of New York City's seats to the Democrat-Republicans. "We have beat you by superior Management,"[38] Burr told defeated but impressed Federalist colleagues. It came as little surprise when the Democrat-Republicans nominated Burr to their 1800 presidential ticket with Thomas Jefferson.

The messy victory of the Jefferson-Burr ticket in 1801 helped sweep Federalists out of a number of key offices around the nation. As Jefferson's Democrat-Republicans worked to consolidate their power through changes in voting practices, the battered remnants of Hamilton's Federalists were screaming as loudly as they could from the sidelines. The war quickly, and typically, spread to rival newspapers. Political journalist James Cheetham carried the Democrat-Republican banner in his *American Citizen*, while Hamilton helped William Coleman establish the *New York Evening Post* as the Federalist's journalistic home base. Trying to walk the fine line between the two was the *Morning Chronicle*, a small daily newspaper established somewhat on the sly by Aaron Burr in October 1802, which was managed and edited by someone Burr considered literary as well as loyal: Peter Irving.

It was possible to be both a Federalist and a Burrite—the Irving brothers certainly were, as was Hoffman, who recognized Burr's Federalist tendencies, even if he didn't necessarily trust him. In one of the *Chronicle*'s first issues, Peter wrote that he hoped the *Chronicle* could make its way in "a world of turmoil and vexation" as "a fair and independent newspaper." With political tensions mounting, however, it didn't take long before the *Chronicle*'s political cannon fired at both the *Citizen* and the *Post*. While Peter claimed to be staking the middle ground, his self-proclaimed "fair and independent" commentary was blistering. Martin Van Buren, who knew a thing or two about smear campaigns, later remembered the *Chronicle* as "a stinging little sheet." It was within its pages that editor Peter Irving's nineteen-year-old brother Washington made his literary debut.[39]

"If the observations of an odd old fellow are not wholly superfluous," began a letter in the November 15, 1802, edition of the *Morning Chronicle*, "I would thank you to shove them into a spare corner of your paper." With this, Washington Irving, in his first published writing, proceeded to poke fun at the current trends in dress and fashion, training most of his criticism on young men and their "most studied carelessness, and almost slovenliness of dress," who are more interested in themselves than their unfortunate ladies who "undergo the fatigue of dragging along this sluggish animal." A second letter followed five days later, this time about the "strange and preposterous . . . manner in which modern marriages are conducted." The signature appearing in all capital letters at the end of each piece was not "Washington Irving," but the first of many pseudonyms Irving adopted throughout his literary life: "Jonathan Oldstyle."[40]

Irving wasn't doing anything new by writing under an assumed name. He was working in a tradition—an "old style"—that traced its roots in America as far back as the 1720s, when a young printer's apprentice named Benjamin Franklin had written similar letters to the *New-England Courant* under the name Silence Dogood. It is revealing that in his first published appearance Irving not only found comfort in a form of writing that was going out of fashion, but also adopted the persona of a wealthy, older gentleman bachelor. While the persona was a lark, it had a whiff of truth about it, for a well-heeled gentleman was exactly what Irving aspired to be. For this reason, Oldstyle's personality is sometimes difficult to pry away from Irving's own. While he attempted to write in an older, more experienced tone, there is too much whim and too little worldliness in Oldstyle's voice for the act to be entirely convincing.

Why adopt the pseudonym at all? Not privacy, for it was commonly known around New York that Irving was Oldstyle. Some have suggested that Irving, at nineteen, was uncomfortable speaking publicly in his own voice. Others have argued that his decision to combine the uncouth American first name of Jonathan with the more refined last name of Oldstyle was an intentional exercise in irony.[41]

The real answer is probably nowhere near as complicated or sophisticated. Irving likely had read similar ramblings attributed to "Oliver Oldschool" in *Port-Folio*, and saw the potential enjoyment one could derive from assuming another name and identity. Adopting a new persona appealed to his love of all things theatrical. He became Oldstyle because it was *fun*.

By his third letter, Irving discarded discussions of fashion and marriage—he had only a slight interest in the first, and no experience in the second—in favor of a topic he knew well, and which he could write about at length: the theater. In his December 1 letter, Irving dismantled *The Battle of Hexam*, a play he had likely seen at the Park Theater. One scene was so confusing, Oldstyle complained, that all he could do was scratch his head in bewilderment: "What this scene had to do with the rest of the piece, I could not comprehend. I suspect it was a part of some other play thrust in here by *accident*."[42]

On December 4 Irving turned his attention from the performance onstage to the audience, "who, I assure you, furnish no inconsiderable part of the entertainment." It was the longest piece he had written so far, and as Oldstyle grumbled about being pelted by fruit and nuts from the rowdy gallery, it was clear Irving wrote from experience:

> I can't say but I was a little irritated at being saluted aside of my head with a rotten pippin, and was going to shake my cane at them; but was prevented by a decent looking man behind me, who informed me it was useless to threaten or expostulate. They are only *amusing themselves* a little at our expense, said he, sit down quietly and bend your back to it. My kind neighbor was interrupted by a hard green apple that hit him between the shoulders.[43]

Elsewhere, spectators in the pit were spattered with hot wax from chandeliers; ladies in the boxes flirted instead of watching the play; and crowds in the gallery demanded the orchestra play drinking songs rather than the repertoire. Neither were critics spared, as Oldstyle wondered how they had the nerve to inform the public what to think of a play when they themselves spent the entire time playing cards with their backs to the stage. "They even *strive* to appear inattentive," he sputtered. By the fifth letter, all the flustered Oldstyle could do was offer suggestions for improving the theater, washing his hands of the entire matter in frustration.[44]

Irving and his Oldstyle letters were getting noticed. The public lapped it up, and *Chronicle* copublisher Aaron Burr was impressed, sending copies of the first five letters to his daughter Theodosia. Irving also had a fan in Charles Brockden Brown, editor of the *Literary Magazine and American Register*, who tried unsuccessfully to recruit Oldstyle to write for his publication.[45]

Good reviews aside, some of Irving's punches were landing hard among the theater crowd. William Dunlap, manager of the Park Theater, thought highly of Oldstyle, calling the letters "pleasant effusions," but grumbled that Oldstyle was provoking "excessive" irritation among his actors. Irving finally drew blood with his sixth letter on January 17, 1803, in which Quoz—a new character introduced as Oldstyle's friend—trained his fire on theater critics who took all the fun out of going to a play. "The critics, my dear Jonathan," Quoz said, "are the very pests of society . . . they reduce our feelings to a state of miserable refinement, and destroy entirely all the enjoyments in which our coarser sensations delighted." Five days later Oldstyle griped about the play *The Wheel of Truth*, knowing full well he would get a rise out of Coleman at the *Post* and Cheetham at the *Citizen*, who had been bickering publicly about the play's authorship and whether a certain character had been introduced solely to offend them.[46]

Sure enough, tempers flared, and on February 8, 1803, Irving coyly insisted he was "perfectly at a loss" over all the fuss. "My remarks hitherto have rather been the result of immediate impression than of critical examination," Oldstyle explained. Knowing that he had rattled both Cheetham and Coleman, Irving couldn't resist one final twist of the knife. "I begin to doubt the motives of our New-York critics," Oldstyle wrote, concluding that all the dithering over nothing has "awakened doubt in my mind respecting the sincerity and justice of the Critics."[47]

Irving's final Oldstyle letter didn't appear for another two months. He was tiring of the ruse, especially since he had exhausted his best material—the theater—and had to rely on current events for inspiration. Still, he could get a laugh. In discussing the practice of dueling, which had just been formally outlawed, Quoz recommended that duelists simply draw lots to see who gets to have a brick dropped on his head from a window. "If he survives, well and good; if he falls, why nobody is to blame, it was purely accidental."[48]

While Oldstyle marked Irving's first foray into print, he later looked back on the nine letters as "crude and boyish."[49] For modern readers, the letters offer not only a glimpse of a young Irving playing with convention and finding his voice, but also an accurate and humorous look at the theater of the time, with rowdy galleries, perplexed musicians, disjointed plays, self-important critics, and sensitive actors. Irving never quite stepped into the skin of Oldstyle as comfortably as he would later alter egos, but there were glimmers of his distinct voice, sense of humor, and wry irony. Plus, the exercise had proven that he could write. For much of 1803 Irving basked in the glow of public adoration for his Oldstyle letters. For the twenty-year-old frustrated lawyer, that was enough.

Scribbling as Oldstyle had provided Irving with an interesting distraction, but it was back to the dreaded law books again for the summer. Fortunately for Irving, another diversion soon presented itself—and this one was sanctioned by the Judge and his business partner and cousin, Thomas Ogden. Hoffman and Ogden were preparing a trip to the New York–Canada border to inspect their properties in and around Oswegatchie (now Ogdensburg) in St. Lawrence County, and meet with representatives of the Northwest Fur Company in Montreal. A law clerk, Hoffman thought, even a dabbler like Irving, could always be of some use on such a trip, helping in the witnessing and preparation of legal documents. The trip promised to be difficult, taking them across remotely populated areas with few inns and bad roads, but to Irving it sounded like a paid vacation. Of course he agreed to go.

Rounding out the party were Ogden's wife Martha and his twenty-one-year-old cousin Eliza; Maria and thirteen-year-old Ann Hoffman; the Judge's business partner Stephen Van Rensselaer; English merchant Thomas Brandram; and another gentleman Irving only referred to as "Mr. Reedy." On July 30 the company set off.

After thirty-nine hours of travel, they arrived in Albany, where the Judge and Ogden had business. Irving spent the next two days touring the surrounding area with the women, making side trips to the spas at Ballston Springs and Sarasota Springs. He was disappointed by both, mainly because they were dull and filled with pretentious guests. Ballston Springs in particular he found "intolerably stupid."

The company soon left by stagecoach for Utica, tantalizingly close to Johnstown; he dashed off on horseback to visit his sister Catharine. "I had just time to speak a few words to them all and eat something," he wrote, "when I had to remount and gallop to [rejoin] the party."[50] Several days after reaching Utica, the group set out for Oswegatchie, the final and most brutal leg of their journey. Amenities were scarce, and the road—clogged with burned roots, tree stumps, and downed trees—was so bad they often had to walk behind their wagons. Nonetheless, Irving passed the time reading *Romeo and Juliet* aloud with Ann Hoffman, and playing his flute in the evenings as Mrs. Hoffman sang. Next came eight days of pure misery. Soaking rain, lack of food, filthy lodgings, drunken wagoneers, and biting insects so tormented them that their arrival in Oswegatchie on August 16 could not have come sooner. But for Irving, the most entertaining part of the adventure was over. He spent the rest of the tour writing bonds and deeds for Hoffman.

The party returned to Manhattan that autumn. The trip had been a success not only for Hoffman and Ogden—who had laid out towns and surveyed lands that would make fortunes for their families—but also for their grumbling clerk. Irving had brought a journal on the trip in which he began experimenting with his writing. While he was more reporter than diarist, the Irving that emerges is all at once charming, shallow, generous, petty, elated, and depressed. He was also brutally funny, especially when deflating egos, including his own.

He had also proven himself a rugged traveler. He had paddled a scow in a rainstorm, subsisted on crackers and cucumbers, and plunged into a river after deer without a second thought. Irving had experienced the American frontier at its rawest, living close to the ground, and improvising according to each challenge that rolled his way. This unflinching adaptability proved to be one of his most valuable character traits. "I was at an age when imagination lends its coloring to everything," he later recalled, "and the stories of Sinbads of the wilderness made the life of a trapper and fur trader perfect romance to me."[51] Not every young man embraced the frontier with the same sense of romance as Irving. Some—like twenty-one-year-old Henry Brevoort Jr., who Irving met on the last stop in Montreal—approached it with a keen eye for possible business opportunities.

Henry Brevoort Jr. could trace his roots back to the early-seventeenth-century Dutch inhabitants of Manhattan. His family had been a staple in New York business for more than 150 years. His ancestors had a knack for purchasing large, valuable tracts of property; the Brevoort family still owned several significant pieces of land in New York, including productive farmland at the base of Fifth Avenue in Manhattan. Business, as well as an uncanny aptitude for successful speculation, was in Henry's blood. With his family wealth, reputation, and Dutch ancestry, Brevoort was New York royalty.

Such distinguished ancestry mattered little to Irving when he was introduced to Brevoort on the Montreal frontier, where he was speculating in the fur trade. What Irving saw was a charming, good-looking, smart young man who was adept at the art of conversation. Irving was strongly attracted to such types—it was John Anderson all over again—and the two young men struck up an immediate friendship. It was the beginning of the closest and most intimate relationship of Irving's life.

By winter Irving's legal obligations dragged at him, but the distraction of the pen was too much to resist. He wrote two more letters for the *Morning Chronicle* in late December, this time as "Dick Buckram." Buckram's voice was more refined than Oldstyle's, but not nearly as funny. Buckram lacked zip. If Irving needed fresh material to fuel his pen in earnest, Peter happily provided a new muse: politics.

In the spring of 1804 Aaron Burr—who had just been unceremoniously dumped from Jefferson's 1804 presidential ticket—was running for governor against Democrat-Republican Morgan Lewis. Peter Irving still toiled away in the pages of the *Chronicle*, trumpeting the policies of Burr and his allies and tearing into Jefferson's Democrats. Given the *Chronicle*'s prominence as Burr's primary mouthpiece, it didn't take long for James Cheetham to turn the wrath of his Jeffersonian *American Citizen* on Peter and the *Chronicle*.

Out of nowhere, a new pro-Burr newspaper, the *Corrector*, leaped to Peter's defense, scolding the *Citizen* for its "flagitious conduct." It was a shame that the *Corrector* had to jump into the fracas at all, sighed its editor Toby Tickler, "but the good of society requires its execution, and it shall be faithfully performed."[52] In truth, the enigmatic Toby Tickler was none other than Peter Irving himself, who had founded the *Corrector* in March 1804 as yet another cog in Burr's media machine. The *Corrector* was the harder-hitting of the two pro-Burr newspapers, not only ripping into his enemies but setting him and his allies up for the coming state elections. As editor of both papers, Peter was in the enviable position of attacking his detractors in one paper, then defending himself from counterattack in the other.

Washington was not a frothing fan of Burr, but he took the attacks on his brother personally, and Cheetham—whom Irving had poked fun at as Oldstyle the year before—always made him particularly angry. So when Peter approached his brother about helping find "persons of wit and genius" to lend their assistance in responding to Cheetham, Washington jumped at the opportunity to bring his own pen to the rapidly escalating fray.

While Washington had passion, he didn't have a firm grip on the politics; he relied on Peter and others to feed him the information he needed to score the correct political points. "They'd tell me what to write and I'd dash away,"[53] he said. The politics might have belonged to the Burrites, but the sting was all Washington Irving. The headline of Irving's first piece read:

BEWARE OF IMPOSTORS!!

TWENTY YEARS PRACTICE!!

JAMES CHEETHAM—QUACK-DOCTOR

Irving called Cheetham's writings "powerful promoters of sleep; if however, they are taken in too large quantities, they are apt to excite a nausea of the stomach. The patient will find it difficult to swallow them at first, they generally have to be crammed down the throat by force, and the patient beaten over the head with a club called *the Citizen*, if he refuses to take them."[54] There was nothing subtle in this satire. Irving and other New York journalists did much during the 1804 election to flog Cheetham and his candidates, but it did Burr no good. After an ugly three-day election, Burr lost the governor's race to Morgan Lewis. His political career flaming out— and careening blindly toward his duel with Hamilton later that year—Burr pulled the plug on the *Corrector* on April 26 after only ten issues. Irving, at the request of William Coleman, wrote a piece for the *Evening Post* ridiculing a Democratic parade celebrating the Louisiana Purchase, but the effort was no longer entertaining. He put away the pen.

It didn't matter. Twenty-one-year-old Irving had a reputation, however modest, as a writer and, perhaps just as important in New York circles, as an eligible bachelor. A female fan in Philadelphia cooed that he was "a gentleman of extraordinary merit and literary acquirements, whose head and heart are equally deserving of admiration and esteem."[55] Paulding and other male friends teased him about his relationship with his "mistress," Maria Hoffman—hadn't they disappeared into the Canadian wilderness together?—and what they perceived to be an increasing interest in Eliza Ogden.

But something else pulled Irving's focus from the pen and politics. Despite his jaunt into Canada with no seeming ill effects, the Irving family, especially William and Ebenezer, continued to worry about their youngest brother's health. Something needed to be done not only to strengthen Washington's body, but also to enrich and stimulate his somewhat idle mind. His brothers studied their company ledgers and determined they had adequate funds to bankroll this effort. Washington Irving was going to Europe.

2

Traveler

1804–1806

For my part I endeavor to take things as they come, with cheerfulness, and when I cannot get a dinner to suit my taste, I endeavor to get a taste to suit my dinner.

—Washington Irving to William Irving Jr., September 20, 1804

ᴵT IS WITH DELIGHT we share the world with you," William Irving told his youngest brother, "and one of our greatest sources of happiness is that fortune is daily putting it in our power thus to add to the comfort and enjoyment of one so very near to us all."[1]

They were generous words. Neither William nor any of the Irving siblings had been to Europe. In the early 1800s, only diplomats, sailors, and the wealthy traveled to Europe—and William, despite his success, was not a rich man. Washington's trip would be a drain on William's purse, yet he financed the trip willingly, with a genuine concern for his brother's well-being. William, whose knowledge and appreciation of Europe had been cultivated by years of reading, instructed Washington on the places and things he expected a cultured young man to experience, but there was no set agenda for Washington's journey. *Improvement*, both physical and intellectual, was the primary objective.

On May 19, 1804, twenty-one-year-old Washington Irving stood on a Manhattan pier before the ship *Rising States* and bade good-bye to his brothers, nervous yet excited at the thought of an extended absence from family. His knees wobbled as he boarded the ship. It was enough to catch the captain's disapproving eye— "There's a chap who will go overboard before we get across," he is said to have remarked.[2]

Watching the steeples of New York disappear beneath the horizon, Irving said, "It seemed as if I had left the world behind me, and was cast among strangers, without a friend, without a protector, sick, solitary and unregarded." Those feelings quickly dissolved, and Irving proved to be a robust traveler. The trip was " 'a lady's Voyage,' gentle and mild," and by the time *Rising States* docked in Bordeaux, France, and completed its required quarantine, New York was little more than an afterthought; Irving was ready to begin his European adventure. His first obligation, however, was to write William.[3]

Irving said that his letters were "the hasty sketches of the ideas that arise . . . I take no pains either to polish or correct them," but that wasn't entirely true. He kept meticulous notes in his travel journals, which he used as the basis for much of his correspondence. This involved copying eye-glazing amounts of minutiae—statistics, major imports and exports—directly from travel guides, then incor-porating the information into his letters to give his family the impression he had learned such details on his own. The ruse was a success, but the effort grew tiring and Irving privately admitted that while he felt "duty bound to give histories of my adventures . . . I detest the long tedious details into which it continually leads me." He was also careful to report any improvement in his well-being and omit the opposite.[4]

Capitalizing on family business connections, Irving roomed with Jean Ferriere, a local merchant and former mayor who lived in an elegant house with a good library. He and his wife spoke only French, so Irving engaged the services of an instructor to teach him the language ("very good," the locals told him, "but you must take a French *mistress* also"[5]). In time, he was conversing in French with moderate fluency.

Irving found Bordeaux pleasant enough, with good theaters

and elegant gentlemen's clubs where he could read newspapers and converse with sympathetic bachelors. But to his disappointment, locals were most interested in discussing business. In fairness, commerce was a serious concern throughout France; the ongoing war with England was making it difficult to earn a living, and Napoleon's maritime policies were putting a crimp on the economy of shipping towns like Bordeaux.

Despite Napoleon's heavy-handed politics, Irving admitted a grudging respect for the man, who had proclaimed himself emperor of France on May 18. "You may well suppose I am impatient to see this wonderful man, whose life has been a continued series of actions, any one of which would be sufficient to immortalize him," he wrote admiringly. He never saw Napoleon, but he witnessed firsthand the impact the little emperor's policies were having on his people, and Irving pitied the French for their politicians. Everything the French had obtained, Irving noted sadly, was "gradually stripped from them by a creature of their own creating."[6]

In early August, after several weeks in Bordeaux, he prepared to head south toward Montpellier on the French Mediterranean coast, "with no pilot," he told William, "but my own discretion."[7] His own discretion, however, left much to be desired. When he tried to leave Bordeaux, he ran into problems with his passport, and was forced to navigate the bureaucratic traps to prove his nationality and get his papers in order.

In 1804 there was no such thing as a passport photo. Instead of sitting for a photograph, as tourists do today, travelers in the early nineteenth century had their descriptions written into their passports. Once a traveler arrived in a province or country, authorities there would check the description against his appearance. Thanks to passport officials in France and Italy, we have a good idea of what Washington Irving looked like at age twenty-one. He was five foot seven, slim, with chestnut hair brushed forward at the temples. He had an aquiline nose, an oval face, a "middling" mouth and forehead, and smoky blue-gray eyes under dark eyebrows. Irving dutifully copied each passport description into his travel journals—and just as today's travelers complain about terrible passport photos, Irving, too, grumbled that his passport descriptions never did him justice.[8]

In a letter home, Irving bragged of his self-reliance: "I am to depend upon my own judgment and often to resort to my own resources for assistance and expedient; it will therefore call forth the powers of my mind, oblige me to rely upon my own exertions and I hope tend to forming that manliness and independence of character which it has ever been my ambition to acquire." In fact, Irving accepted help whenever he could. For his journey to Montpellier, he found it in a short, fat windbag from Pennsylvania known simply as "Dr. Henry," with whom he shared a carriage for the trip. Standing only five-four, Dr. Henry compensated for a lack of height with an enormous ego and even taller tales. He was more swindler than doctor, but Irving nonetheless thought him an ideal companion, "a most amusing character having much talk and a great deal of whim & eccentricity." He spoke several languages, and Irving noted that the little man took great pleasure in playing a "variety of characters" of different nationalities and occupations. "With a Farmer, he was a Wine merchant," Irving wrote in his journal, "with a Shoemaker, a Tanner; with an officer, he was formerly a captain in the American army; with others, a professor in one of the German colleges."[9]

While Dr. Henry was a constant source of comic relief, he also personified the Ugly American, arguing with porters, fighting with landlords, and groping young women. His exploits were cringe-inducing, but Irving relied on the diminutive doctor as an interpreter and protector. "While in travel with him," Irving said, "he continually saved me from imposition & extortion." They parted ways just before arriving in Montpellier, but not before Irving learned what he thought was a valuable lesson: "In traveling in France, it is absolutely necessary to be quarrelling all the while to keep from being imposed upon."[10]

After several days in the Montpellier heat, Irving attempted to leave for Marseilles, but his efforts were frustrated by more problems with his passport. "I had been continually mistaken on the road for an Englishman," he sighed to William. Given that the French were presently at war with the English, being regarded as an Englishman was potentially dangerous—especially since French authorities suspected every British traveler as a potential spy. After an unpleasant interview with a French undercover agent—asked what part of America he was from, Irving retorted dryly, "*North* America"—Irving was permitted to continue to Marseilles without further aggravation.[11]

The hassle was worth it. The town was charming, and the weather perfect. If he had any complaints, it was with the surprising abundance of "beggars, shoe blacks, fiddlers & peddlers." "The shoe blacks," an amused Irving noted, "thinking to gain our custom by speaking english, run after us in the street with their brushes & blacking crying 'Monsieur, monsieur, God dam, God dam, son de bish son de bish!'" He was also disappointed by the theater—he found the attire of their ballerinas "immodest."[12]

Apart from ballerinas, Irving had spent a good deal of time observing French women—and after two months in France, he remained, at best, indifferent to their charms. They lacked "that delicacy, that sentiment, that *je ne scai quoi*, which is common to our American females," he reported to Peter. He was equally disappointed by their looks. "I have hardly seen a lady since my arrival that I would call handsome," he told one male friend. While many were well-shaped and attractive from behind, he said, "She turns her face towards me—the charm is broken . . . I see a wide mouth, small black eyes, cheeks highly rouged and hair greased with antient oil and twisted from the forehead to the chin till it resembles the head dress of a Medusa!"[13]

Irving reluctantly abandoned Marseilles in early autumn, and hired a carriage for the three-day ride to Nice, where he planned to stay a few days before making the sprint across the border into Italy. The 120-mile trip wound along bad roads dotted with small taverns that charged exorbitant prices for terrible beds and even worse food—but Irving took it all in stride. "For my part," he told William proudly, "I try to take things as they come, with cheerfulness, and when I cannot get a dinner to suit my taste I endeavor to get a taste to suit my dinner."[14]

Catching sight of Nice shimmering on the Mediterranean among fig and olive trees, with the Alps rising just behind it, Irving thought the city perfectly "fruitful picturesque & romantic"—the ideal way to end his tour of France. "I felicitated myself with the idea that nothing remained but to step into a Felucca," he told William, "& be gently wafted to the classic shore of Italy!"[15]

If it had only been that easy. His passport continued to present problems. Compelled to appear before the mayor of Nice, Irving learned that he had been denounced—by whom, he didn't know— as an English spy! The stunned American pled his case, and the sympathetic mayor promised to call off the police, but still required a revised passport before he would allow Irving to leave.

Rattled, Irving fired off letters to various American officials, including William Lee, the American consul at Bordeaux, and Hall Storm, a family friend who was American vice consul at Genoa. He begged them to "reclaim" him as an American citizen and thundered away in righteous indignation at his predicament. "Is this the manner an American Citizen is to be treated by a people who pretend an amity for his country," he fumed, "to be interrupted in the peaceable pursuit of his lawful affairs, subjected to detention & examination of police officers to have the freedom of going from place to place denied him"?[16]

A letter from Storm vouching for his nationality provided a momentary glimmer of hope, but the secretary general at Nice, in a bureaucratic runaround, informed Irving that he also needed formal approval from the commissary general of Marseilles. "This is the infamous manner in which I am trifled with by these scoundrels," Irving seethed.[17]

He had been waiting for his papers in Nice for more than a month—"Little did I think of being *persuaded* by the police to defer my departure & take time to enjoy the climate & prospects of Nice,"[18] he wrote sarcastically—when the necessary documents finally arrived. Glowering but victorious, he was off in a felucca the next morning, bound for Italy. On October 20, after three days on a rough sea, he arrived in Genoa.

He was immediately greeted by Storm, and the twenty-three-year-old vice consul insisted Irving stay with him in one of the Italian palaces. "You cannot conceive the joy the rapture of meeting with a favourite companion in a distant part of the world," Irving wrote. For the next eight weeks, he and Hall attended the theater and spent most of their time dancing, singing, chatting, and socializing with Genoa's wealthy families. There was Madame Brignoli, who had a small private theater set up in one wing of her villa, and Mrs. Bird, daughter of the British consul, whose home was regularly filled with music and chatty female company. There was Lord Shaftesbury, a wealthy English prisoner of war suffering from a head injury who railed away at visitors as if still on the floor of Parliament. And there were various members of Genoese royalty, "a stupid set of beings without much talents or information," Irving thought, but who at least provided decent billiards tables and amusing conversation.[19]

As he listened to the Italian drawing-room chatter, Irving came to appreciate the liberties his own country afforded, where political dissent was openly discussed rather than violently oppressed. Yet, when he learned of the politically motivated duel between Alexander Hamilton and Aaron Burr that ended with Hamilton dead of a gunshot wound, he was disgusted: "My fellow countrymen do not know the blessings they enjoy; they are trifling with their felicity and are in fact *themselves* their worst enemies. I sicken when I think of our political broils, slanders & enmities."[20]

There was plenty in Genoa that would have appealed to any American abroad for the first time, but Irving paid only obligatory visits to the local sites; it was far more entertaining to fraternize with Hall and his Genoese circle. But all this socializing, he explained to William, was for a good reason: "I shall have a series of acquaintance through Europe that is exceeding difficult for an American to make, as our letters are generally to Merchants in the sea ports who are most commonly a tasteless interested set of beings. Perhaps no American has ever traveled in this country with similar advantages, and surely if traveling is necessary to polish the manners, this is the society most conducive to that end."[21]

He promised William he would leave Genoa as quickly as he could, but provided excuses for why he might be delayed. "At Leghorn and Pisa," he warned, "the quarantines are very long and all Tuscany is surrounded by Cordones, which it is impossible to pass without performing quarantines of two or three weeks." Further, "I should be exposed to innumerable difficulties & embarassments was I to attempt to pass thro Tuscany particularly as I am almost entirely ignorant of the Italian language."[22]

Lastly, he informed William he was in danger of exceeding his budget, and asked his brother to make more credit available. "I would rather forego the pleasure of seeing any part of Europe than run my family to expenses they cannot afford," he told William. All that he had been given so far, he said, he had only accepted because he knew it gave his *brothers* pleasure. "I well know the delight my brothers experience in contributing to the happiness of each other," he wrote ingratiatingly. To Washington's relief, William extended his credit without protest.[23]

With his pockets filled, a relieved Irving booked passage on the *Matilda*, an American ship bound for Messina on the northeastern coast of Sicily. As the *Matilda* sailed into the Mediterranean on Christmas Eve, Irving was nearly moved to tears by the sight of the sun winking off the snow-covered mountains on the Corsican coastline. The Roman gods were no longer there, he sighed to William: "In these dull *matter of fact* times, our only consolation is to wander about the haunts they once frequented and endeavor to make up by imagination the want of the reality. . . . Our imagination becomes tinctured with romance and we look around us with an enthusiastic eye that heightens every scene."[24]

Such pensive reflection, however, was short-lived; on December 29, as the unarmed *Matilda* neared the Isle of Planosa, it was fired upon by French pirates! The *Matilda* struck its American colors, and Captain Matthew Strong allowed the pirates to pull up along-side. Irving was disappointed the pirate ship was so small—"about the size of one of our Staten Island ferry boats," he grumbled—but he admitted he was terrified. "My heart almost failed me," he wrote, "a more villainous looking crew I never beheld."[25]

Captain Strong was taken aboard the pirate ship for a conversation, along with Irving as an unwilling interpreter. In what Irving called "some confused story," the pirate captain explained that his crew was merely patrolling the area to ensure no ships escaped quarantine at Leghorn. Unconvinced, Irving and Strong returned to the *Matilda*, where the pirate captain rummaged through the contents of Irving's trunks, pausing only to cock an eyebrow at a letter of introduction he was carrying to the governor of Malta. "They treated me with much more respect than before," Irving noted with some satisfaction.[26]

After several agonizing hours, the privateers departed, taking only two cases of quicksilver, some rum, and "about half of the provisions we had on board," Irving reported. To his lasting disappointment, nothing had been stolen from him, and the entire affair had been carried out more like a business transaction than a sacking. The pirates even had the gall to provide a receipt for the pilfered provisions, informing Strong the English consul at Malta would reimburse them for their losses. Still, the encounter was enough to give Irving nightmares. That night, he said, "I started out of bed with the horrid idea that their stillettos were raised against my bosom."[27]

On January 5, 1805, after thirteen days at sea, the *Matilda* docked at Messina, where they faced an adversary more fearsome than pirates, "one of the greatest torments of the seas," Irving wrote in mock horror, "the Health Office." After a quick inspection for signs of yellow fever ("The sage geniuses," Irving wrote haughtily, "imagined that it was possible to perceive whether people had the infection lurking in their veins by taking a hasty look at their neck & chests at ten or fifteen feet distance"), the Messina Health Office ordered the *Matilda* to sit in quarantine for twenty-one days.[28]

To Irving's frustration, he wasn't permitted to board other ships quarantined in the harbor, or mingle with their crews. No matter; he climbed up the masts of the *Matilda* to have shouted conversations with the seamen on board the American schooner *Nautilus*. Defying local health authorities, Irving took great delight in sailing around the harbor in a small boat, flouting quarantine by rowing as close as he could to other vessels. When he was spotted one afternoon trying to sneak a letter on board the *Nautilus*, Sicilian guards jumped into a longboat and chased him in a mad pursuit around the harbor, shouting at him in Italian. Irving laughed, pretending not to understand, but was eventually hauled defiantly back to the *Matilda*.

After the Matilda's release from quarantine in late January, Irving arranged to be on board the *Nautilus* when it departed for Syracuse. He spent a limited time exploring Messina; the town was still a shambles, not yet having recovered from a 1783 earthquake. Worse, a fistfight between an officer of the *Nautilus* and the mate on an English transport had ended with the Englishman dead and the Americans trying to avoid a sticky political inquiry. On January 31—after catching a glimpse of Admiral Nelson's British fleet coursing up the straits in pursuit of the French armada that had escaped his blockade at Toulon—Irving and the *Nautilus* slunk out of Messina.

A nine-day stay in Syracuse failed to convince Irving of the city's charms; after a week preyed upon by beggars, he finally pronounced the place "a miserable hole," though he was quick to point out the competence of the local opera singers. He eagerly played the tourist, visiting a cavern known as the Ear of Dionysus—where he risked his neck by being lowered over a precipice to test the cave's unique acoustics—and viewing the relics of nearby churches. "By the way," Irving wrote in his journal, after looking at yet another saintly pelvis, "these disciples must have been an uncommon bony set of fellows. I have seen no less than five thigh bones of St. John the Baptist, three arms of St. Stephen, and four jaw bones of St. Peter."[29]

He arrived by mule in Catania on February 12, just in time to take part in a celebration for Saint Agatha, the town's patron saint. Ever the skeptic of all things religious, Irving asked a local priest to explain the value of a patron saint who had permitted half the city to be consumed by a volcanic eruption in 1693. The priest replied that Agatha had allowed lava to cover only *part* of the city so the rest would see what miseries she had saved them from. Irving left the church in head-shaking disbelief. "Such is the flimsy manner in which the priests impose upon the credulity of this superstitious people," he wrote.[30]

Irving left Catania a week later, making the 130-mile trip west across Sicily to Palermo in five long, rainy days, "a detail of misery, poverty, wretched accommodation, and almost every inconvenience a traveler could suffer."[31] Things were better in Palermo, where Irving visited the opera and the theater, and continued to capitalize on his uncanny talent for snagging invitations to the most fashionable parties. One evening he spent drinking with the prince of Belmonte until two in the morning; the next in conversation with various nobles at the Palazzo Reale.

On March 7 Irving arrived in Naples, with Mount Vesuvius smoking heavily across the gulf. Despite the "apparent misery" and "vile exhalations" of the place, he liked Naples. He immediately found American companionship, attaching himself to two Virginians, a twenty-six-year-old attorney and agrarian named Joseph Cabell and Colonel John Mercer, a member of the U.S. Board of Commissioners who had been sent to France to settle legal claims under the Louisiana Purchase. Irving was particularly fond of Cabell—"a gentleman of whose talents information & disposition I cannot speak too highly." Cabell had considerable charm and merit as a traveling companion, but he also proved to be a bad influence on Irving, indulging and encouraging what Washington always referred to as his "gentlemanly habits."[32]

The three men visited the ruins at Pompeii and hired mules to take them up Mount Vesuvius, which Irving reported was "vomiting" smoke. He was captivated by the view from the top of the mountain—"a prospect the most lovely I ever beheld"—but was nearly overcome by fumes. He staggered down the mountainside to a local tavern, where he, Cabell, and Mercer recovered their senses by downing several glasses of wine.[33]

After more than two weeks in Naples, Irving was beginning to find the town too crowded and expensive. He was ready to leave, and on March 24 he and Cabell set out in a carriage for Rome. Three days later, under a driving rain, they entered the city's Lateran Gate. "To describe the emotions of the mind and the crowd of ideas that arise on entering this 'Mistress of the World' is impossible," Irving wrote. "All is wonder, restlessness, unsatisfied curiosity, eagerness and impatience."[34] After unpacking at their hotel, they learned three American gentlemen of Cabell's acquaintance were also in town, one of whom was an aspiring painter from South Carolina named Washington Allston.

Smart, good-looking, and hugely talented, twenty-five-year-old Allston had graduated from Harvard in 1800 and briefly studied art in Charleston, alongside miniaturist painters Charles Fraser and Edward Greene Malbone. In 1801 he and Malbone entered the Royal Academy in London, where they studied under the American neoclassical painter Benjamin West. Since 1804 Allston had been studying in Europe, mainly in Paris, but had recently come to Rome.

While Allston later became known by students and admirers as "the American Titian," in March 1805 he was simply an eager and gifted young man beginning his career as a painter and part-time writer. Irving adored him—indeed, was smitten by him. "There was something, to me, inexpressibly engaging in the appearance and manner of Allston," he wrote years later, describing the young painter in remarkably intimate terms: "I do not think I have ever been more completely captivated on a first acquaintance. He was of a light and graceful form; with large blue eyes, and black silken hair, waving and curling round a pale expressive countenance. Every thing about him bespoke the man of intellect and refinement."[35]

Irving wasn't the only one who succumbed to the young man's

charm and brilliance; Allston later counted Samuel Taylor Coleridge and Samuel F. B. Morse among his admirers. But this was something more. Beginning with John Anderson, Irving esteemed smart, talented, refined gentlemen in ways that transcended mere respect and admiration. He genuinely *loved* such men, craving, almost requiring, their constant companionship and approval. It is likely he had fallen in love with Washington Allston—and Allston may have reciprocated his feelings. "A young man's intimacy took place immediately between us," Irving said delicately later in his life, "and we were much together during my brief sojourn at Rome."[36]

Still, Allston was in Rome to work, so being with him meant tagging along while he visited the Villa Borghese, Farnese Palace, or Barberini Palace to look at paintings and sculptures. Irving watched Allston with slightly jealous awe, doing his best to mimic Allston's interest in art. Statuary bored him—"I no longer feel interested in them unless they have something more than antiquity to recommend them," Irving wrote impatiently—but painting stirred him. With the enthusiasm of a dilettante, Irving decided that painting, not literature, was his new passion. "Suddenly the thought presented itself," he recalled years later. "Why might I not remain here and turn painter?"[37]

According to Irving, Allston responded with enthusiasm, and the two planned their future as artists. "We would take an apartment together," Irving wrote dreamily. "He would give me all the instruction and assistance in his power, and was sure I would succeed."[38]

It was a plan—at least for several days. The two young men continued visiting palaces and museums, staring at landscape paintings and marble torsos. Better still, at least in Irving's opinion, were the dinners with artists like L. Caracciolo, who engraved the works of Claude Lorrain, or the visits to sculptor Antonio Canova's studio, where the artist made casts for statues of the Bonaparte family.

Then, just as quickly as the scheme had been hatched, it evaporated. Even Irving admitted his folly. "I believe it owed its main force to the lovely evening ramble in which I first conceived it, and to the romantic friendship I had formed with Allston," he wrote later. "I promised myself a world of enjoyment in his society, and in the society of several artists with whom he had made me acquainted, and pictured forth a scheme of life all tinted with the rainbow hues of youthful promise. My lot in life, however, was differently cast."[39]

Irving had flirted so briefly with the idea of an artistic life that he does not mention it in his letters to William. But he did tell William that after only eight days in Rome, he was bored. The Italian art of *conversazione* he found dull—"an Italian conversazione is a place where people meet to do anything else but converse," he complained—and he thought the city a shadow of its former glory. He believed he had exhausted all that Rome had to offer, though he was careful to couch his explanation in terms he thought William would understand: "To a man of fortune traveling for amusement or who has plenty of time to spare, it may be well enough to spend a couple of months in Rome; but to one whose object is improvement and who has to be economic of his time, a much shorter term will suffice."[40]

The truth was Cabell had talked him into accompanying him to Paris, ostensibly to attend a series of botany lectures, though the two likely had ulterior motives. Irving again justified his decision to quit Rome for Paris in the name of *improvement,* which he felt certain would resonate with William: "There will commence in May a course of lectures at the Garden of Plants in Paris, on botany, chemistry and different other branches of science by the most experienced and learned men. . . . The doors of knowledge are there thrown open and the different pursuits both useful and ornamental may be prosecuted with more facility and less expense than at any other city in the world." The route he and Cabell would be taking, he explained to William, would wind north through Loreto, then slingshot over to Bologna, thus avoiding all of Tuscany and bypassing Venice. "So much for my route," wrote Washington, "which I hope will meet with your approbation."[41]

It didn't. William immediately fired back, his irritation

obvious: "This day your letter, dated Rome, 4th April, was received, and afforded us both pleasure and mortification—pleasure to hear that your health is so completely re-established, and mortification to learn that you have determined to *gallop through Italy*. . . . And, as you propose to be at Paris to attend the lectures which are to commence in May, all Italy, I presume, is to be scoured through, (leaving Florence on your left and Venice on your right) in the short period of eight or nine weeks!"[42]

William wasn't fooled by Washington's explanation for leaving Rome so quickly; he knew his brother's predilections too well to be taken in by stories about botany and chemistry. He knew too well his brother's *real* motivation: "Good company, I find, is the grand desideratum with you; good company made you stay eleven weeks at Genoa, where you needed not to have stayed more than two, and good company drives you through all Italy in less time than was necessary for your stay in Genoa. I find no fault, however, with your stay in Genoa; your skipping through Italy, omitting to visit Florence and Venice, I cannot forget. But it is painful to find fault—especially when the evil is now without a remedy." Fortunately for Washington, William's response didn't reach him for months. For now, he had only a few days remaining in Rome, and he was determined to make the most of them. He saw the Sistine Chapel and the ruins of Tusculum, attended concerts, visited galleries, and participated in more *conversaziones*. And he continued to meet interesting people. Baron de Humboldt, the Prussian minister to the Court of Rome, introduced him to Madame de Stael, the strong-willed author of *Delphine*, who was in Italy researching her next book. "She is a woman of great strength of mind & understanding by all accounts," Irving wrote appreciatively.[43]

As Holy Week wound to a close in mid-April, Irving and Cabell departed Rome for the northeastern coast of Italy. Their journey from Rome to Paris—which took them across Italy, through the Alps into Switzerland, and across the French countryside to Paris—was indeed the gallop that William feared. Washington was in constant motion—on horseback, in a carriage, in a boat, or on foot—for the next forty days.

Their first destination of interest was 175 miles away at Loreto, a small hillside town just off the Adriatic Sea, whose main tourist attraction was, and still is, the Santa Casa di Loreto. According to legend, the Santa Casa was the house in which the Virgin Mary was born, which was miraculously transported by angels from Nazareth to Loreto. Irving dismissed both the site and story as "the greatest triumphs over human credulity that ever priestcraft achieved."[44]

Turning northwest along the coast, Irving and Cabell arrived in Bologna on April 22, just in time to attend the evening opera. Bolognese audiences, Irving noted in his journal, had no problem attending the same opera night after night, and cheered every song as if they'd never heard it before. The crowds were equally receptive to the ballet, though Irving was quick to point out that the loudest bravos came when a ballerina's skirts fluttered over her head.[45]

Four days later, they were bound for Milan, covering 140 miles on dangerous roads marked at intervals by crosses, where travelers had been murdered by bandits. ("One of the crosses appeared quite new," Irving shivered in his journal.) As the Alps began to rise into view, he and Cabell crossed the bridge at Lodi, where Napoleon had come under heavy artillery fire in his conquest of Lombardy nine years earlier, the divots of cannonballs still visible on the surrounding houses. The next evening, they arrived in Milan, a lively city of 140,000 residents. It was a city he fit into easily, as it was home to the impressive 3,600-seat La Scala opera house.[46]

While Irving thought the ballet he attended at La Scala "very pretty," he reserved most of his praise for the "magnificent" scenery. The Milanese had adopted a novel practice of hoisting their backdrops upward on ropes between scenes, rather than pulling them off sideways, a method, Irving noted, that was "preferable." As for the Milanese audiences, they were more refined than New York's boisterous Park Theater crowds; when an opera singer stepped forward to sing a well-known aria, audience members shushed one another. "The whole house is silent as a tomb," an impressed Irving wrote.[47]

After three days in Milan, Irving and Cabell engaged a carriage and mules to drive them to Sesto, at the southern end of Lake Maggiore. There they hired a boat to row them roughly thirty miles up to Locarno, just within Swiss territory at the lake's northern end. From there, it was a rougher and chillier ride through Bellinzona and up into the Alps, where the travelers crossed into Switzerland through the pass at St. Goatherd.

It was a chilly 41 degrees on the morning Irving and Cabell hired a boat to take them across the Lake of the Four Cantons into Lucerne. Irving struggled for the right words to describe the surrounding scenery. In an unusual fit of inspiration, he wrote a few lines of poetry:

> Upon the placid bosom of the Lake
> I lie and sweetly dream the Hours away.
> Anon a Vision of approaching Day
> Strikes on my Lids, and I awake
> To find 'tis but the Glimmering Ray
> Of the false dawn: And I again partake
> Of the Lethean Waters of the Lake,
> And sleep and dream throughout this night of May[48]

This was hardly Wordsworth, but it shows Irving beginning to experiment with other forms of writing. If he aspired to be a gentleman of letters, it was necessary to dabble at poetry.

Irving and Cabell stayed in Lucerne only long enough to hire a carriage to take them to Zurich, making the forty-mile trip in two quick days. So far, they had been traveling for twenty-six days, covering more than 650 miles. At Zurich, they finally took a little time to relax. The town, Irving said, seemed "almost to be built in the waters" of the lake, with little architecture of interest (it was more "designed for comfort than for elegance"). The hills surrounding the lake, however, were perfect for walking and for dabbling in his journals: "At a great distance the stupendous mountains of Glaris & Schwartz reared their fantastic heads above the clouds and sublimely terminated the prospect, offering the contrast of bleak winter to the luxuriant charms of spring. The rays of the declining sun slanting along the hills, gilding their tufted tops lighting up the spires of the village churches—& the white walls of the cottages and resting in bright refulgence on the snowy summits of the alps."[49]

On May 16, after three relatively peaceful days in Zurich, Irving and Cabell set out for Basel, where they took a stagecoach to Paris. Traveling with them were a French merchant and a young woman whom Cabell tried to woo when he believed Irving was asleep. The very much alert Irving heard every word. "At length my disposition to laugh became so strong," he wrote, "that I had to awake completely and interrupt one of the most amiable conversations that ever took place in a Dilligence. Cabell tried in vain to induce me to sleep again."[50]

The passenger seat was an ever-changing canvas of interesting characters. At Vesoul, they picked up an old musician inclined to drink too much; in Belfort, an anxious young Frenchman who screeched at every bounce of the carriage, convinced he would break his neck in an accident; at Troyes, a woman who constantly talked to her pug. Irving wrote it all down with delight, far more interested in his fellow passengers than in the towns outside his window. The journey, he told William, "was the most interesting and delightful I have made in Europe."[51]

By mid-morning of May 24, Irving caught his first glimpse of Paris. "The distant view of Paris is very fine," he wrote, "and like mariners after a long voyage, we hailed with joy our haven of repose."[52] After forty days and a thousand miles, they had arrived. Here Irving would stay for four months.

Paris brought out the very best and the very worst in Washington Irving. His first order of business was to engage a tailor and boot maker "to rig me out," he said, "*a la mode de Paris*." With its abundance of theaters, coffeehouses, parlors, French wines, willing women, and good conversation, Paris presented a gentleman of leisure with more distractions—and opportunities for trouble—than Irving ever thought possible: "There is not a place on the globe where the sensual pleasures appetites &c &c &c are more thoroughly studied and may be more completely gratified. . . . Every desire, wish, inclination—natural or artificial seems to have been completely investigated—to have been followed up to its source traced thro every turning twisting and ramification—and a thousand means devised both to incite and satisfy it."[53]

This was hardly an atmosphere conducive to self-improvement. Yet he had promised William he would study botany, and technically, he was as good as his word—his journal records his attendance at exactly one lecture. He then wrote William to make sure his brother knew he had lived up to his promise. "I have begun to attend a course of Lectures," he reported, then immediately offered a disclaimer: "Tho I do not expect to make any important proficiency in these studies, yet they serve to improve me in the language, and it is always well, to be acquiring information. I shall take a French master as soon as I get settled."[54] While Irving did buy a botany dictionary and scribbled some cursory, almost incoherent botany notes in his notebooks—perhaps another show of good faith to William—his interest had waned. The botany journal became a list of plays, and then an expense book. Irving wasn't the only one who had lost interest in the lectures. In early June Cabell, who had proposed the whole scheme in the first place, departed for Geneva.

Despite Cabell's early exit, Irving didn't lack American company. His old acquaintance Colonel Mercer—with whom he had tromped about on Vesuvius in Naples in March—was residing in Paris, and introduced him to a number of respectable Americans, including Nicholas Biddle, secretary to the French minister, Fulwar Skipworth, the American consul general, and John Vanderlyn, a young painter who was collecting casts for the American Academy of Fine Arts. Vanderlyn was struggling financially—the executor for his letter of credit had died, rendering it useless—so Washington appealed to Peter Irving to make inquiries to the academy on Vanderlyn's behalf, and sat to have his portrait sketched in chalk, for which he paid Vanderlyn in cash.

Vanderlyn's drawing of Irving at age twenty-two—the first known portrait we have of him—shows an elegant, handsome young man with an aquiline nose, thin, somewhat pursed lips, dark, heavy-lidded eyes, and sideburns curving down his cheeks. His curly hair is brushed forward, falling across his forehead—"A peculiarity," Pierre Irving points out, "not observable in any later likeness."[55] With his dark coat and a cravat tied neatly at his neck, the relatively average American male that had been described in his passport a year before now looked every inch the nineteenth-century European gentleman.

William tried to push his youngest brother toward Germany, but Irving wasn't interested. "I have thoughts of remaining in Paris till some time in September, as there is no place in Europe where a man has equal opportunities of improvement and at so little expense." Irving's idea of improvement likely remained at odds with William's expectations. Washington was having the time of his life—so much so that he couldn't bother to write about it. The journal entries became catalogs of theaters and gardens. Letters home slowed to a trickle, as Irving claimed he had "neither time nor inclination" to write lengthily. "I can only plead as an excuse that I am a *young man* and in *Paris*."[56]

As much as he enjoyed Paris, Irving was put off by what he regarded as a lack of earnestness on the part of the French. "A Frenchman can contradict you with the best grace imaginable, and even at the same time make you think he is complimenting you," he wrote. "Tho this politeness renders France extremely agreeable to the stranger, yet were I to become a resident I would willingly exchange half of it for a little plain sincerity."[57] By mid-September, the novelty was wearing thin; it was time to move on. On September 22, after gathering friends around him for one last celebratory dinner—at William's expense, of course—he left Paris in a diligence bound for the Netherlands.

Since his trip to Sleepy Hollow with Paulding in 1798, Irving had been infatuated with all things Dutch. Quaint Sleepy Hollow had been right out of a Flemish painting. As he moved along the paved road to Brussels, Irving had his first opportunity to observe the Dutch on their home turf.

"I look chiefly with an eye to the picturesque," he wrote, and even under a light rain, the surrounding countryside didn't disappoint. Sitting snugly among the tightly clipped orchards were well-kept cottages of brick and thatch. Peasants worked the fields with pipes clenched between their teeth, and children sang and tumbled over each other as they ran alongside the coach, pleading for money. Even Brussels was clean and well-scrubbed, with no sign of the beggars that so annoyed Irving elsewhere in Europe.[58]

He was less enthralled with the physical appearance of the Dutch, noting their "heavy tread and phlegmatic leaden features." But what they lacked in physical attractiveness, they more than made up for with their amusingly quirky behavior, which seemed to Irving to lean toward laziness and constant smoking. Watching Dutchmen in Delft, he noted with amusement that "Mynheer smoaks his pipe in the afternoon and dozes over his favorite canal whose muddy sluggish waters resemble his own stagnant ideas." And everyone, "even the porter," smoked.[59]

At Rotterdam, Irving booked passage for London, the last stop on his European journey. "Thank heavens my ramblings are nearly at an end," he wrote Peter, "and in a little while I shall once more return to my friends and sink again into tranquil domestic life." The excitement of travel had worn off; it had come to feel like an obligation. "I feel no more that interest that prompted me on first arriving in Europe to be perpetually on the hunt for curiosities and beauties," he told Peter. "In fact, the duty imposed upon me as a traveler to do so is often irksome."[60]

Upon arriving in London in early October, Irving had trouble finding lodgings. He believed, perhaps rightly, that he was being discriminated against because he was a foreigner, and it convinced him that his initial suspicions of the British were justified: "I thought myself surrounded by rogues and swindlers and felt that I was a foreigner among people who regard all foreigners with contempt and enmity. . . . I thought everyone eyed me with hostility, and perceived that I was a foreigner—and I expected every moment to experience some rudeness or vulgarity. My hands were half the time in my pockets to guard them from depredations, in short I was completely *on the alert*."[61]

To his surprise, the British turned out to be gracious hosts. "I have not suffered the slightest impertinence," he reported to William, "and my pockets, though very frequently exposed, have never been plundered." He eventually landed a suite on Norfolk Street, close to the coffeehouses and—no surprise—the theater. It was in the theater that Irving learned the news of Admiral Nelson's victory over Napoleon, and Nelson's death at Trafalgar. Only ten months earlier, Irving had seen Nelson's fleet coursing off the coast of Syracuse, in pursuit of the French fleet. Now Nelson was dead, the British victorious, and the war all but over. Still, the shouts of victory in the streets were subdued. "I can scarcely say which is greatest," Irving mused, "joy at its achievement, or sorrow for Nelson's fall."[62]

On January 18, 1806, Irving boarded the ship *Remittance*, bound for New York. "I hope to return to you untainted with the vices of Europe," he had written to one correspondent more than twenty months earlier, "and if neither wiser nor better, at least I hope I shall not be worse than when I set out."[63] He had recovered his health—there was no sign of the hacking cough or the fatigue that had so concerned his brothers two years before. Whether he was wiser—whether he had truly *improved* himself, as William hoped—was a matter of opinion.

It was true that Washington hadn't taken in many of the sights William had recommended. He had all but frittered away his time in Rome and had boomeranged off Sicily almost immediately after clearing quarantine. Florence, Venice, Germany, and Scotland he skipped altogether. Apart from a few obligatory strolls through museums and churches, he had forsaken many of the more intellectual pursuits in favor of theater and conversation.

Yet there was more to his trip than missed opportunities. Washington had traveled over 3,000 miles across Europe, covering five countries by diligence, mule, packet ship, carriage, fruit boat, horse, scow, and, when necessary, on foot. He had been harassed by police, chased by health officials, and attacked by pirates. He had experienced the theater in three of the finest cities in the world—Milan, Paris, and London—and socialized with nobility. He had frolicked in France, strolled Italian palaces, and walked the Alps. It's also possible that, while in Rome with Washington Allston, he had engaged in his first homosexual relationship. These were experiences that transcended the intellectual pursuits William had intended for him; they were life experiences that shaped the man and writer Washington Irving would become.

At the moment, Irving was going home to resume his legal studies—a "starving profession"—and the journey home was a long one. On March 2, 1806, after fifty-two days at sea, the *Remittance* landed at Paumanok, on Long Island, in the middle of a blinding snowstorm. Washington Irving was back in New York.

3

Salmagundi

1806–1808

The antient and venerable city of Gotham, was, peradventure, possessed of mighty treasures, and did, moreover, abound with all manner of fish and flesh, and eatables and drinkables, and such like delightsome and wholesome excellencies withal.

—Washington Irving, "Chap. CIX. Of the Chronicles of the Renowned And Antient City of Gotham," *Salmagundi*, issue 17, November 11, 1807

"I SHALL ONCE MORE RETURN to my friends and sink again into tranquil domestic life," Irving had written to his brothers shortly before his return to New York.[1] Once back in the city in March 1806, however, tranquillity was the last thing on his mind—and who could blame him? New York was just as changed, just as *improved*, as he. There were so many things a traveled man and aspiring gentleman could do in New York, especially if it kept him away from the tedious law books.

With a population creeping up beyond 60,000 residents, New York, like Irving, was growing more literary and sophisticated. New clubs, parlors, and public gardens had sprouted and flourished across the city. It had nineteen newspapers, eight of which were dailies. Painter John Trumbull had returned to New York to take over as director of the floundering American Academy of Fine Arts—the same organization that had left poor Vanderlyn in the lurch in

Europe—and had produced portraits of Alexander Hamilton, John Jay, and Peter Stuyvesant that hung in City Hall, alongside his portrait of George Washington.[2]

The very face of the city was changing. On Varick Street, work was under way on the chapel of St. John's, under the careful eye of architect John McComb. Eventually, St. John's 214-foot clock tower and steeple would make it one of the city's most recognizable—and audible—landmarks; its chapel bells could be heard as far away as the Battery and Greenwich. On the more fashionable Park Row, just around the corner from the Park Theater, the gigantic Dyde's London Hotel had recently opened, boasting a massive ballroom and advertising hospitality "in the true Old English Style."[3]

Money and philanthropy were also shaping the town. Isabella Graham and Joanna Bethune were laying the groundwork for the orphanage for working-class children they would soon open in Greenwich, while Quaker Thomas Eddy—with the help of philanthropist John Pintard and others—was organizing the New York Free School Society to eliminate poverty in children by endowing "habits of cleanliness, subordination, and order." John Jacob Astor, who came to personify wealth and industry in nineteenth-century America, was investing in New York land and properties, which would benefit both the city and Astor himself. In 1804 Astor had acquired Vauxhall Gardens on north Broadway near the Bowery. A year later he and John Beekman purchased the Park Theater, where a major renovation soon began under the guidance of its new manager, and Irving's friend, the actor Thomas Cooper.[4]

Broadway had solidified its place as the heart of the city. It was also its most respectable address—Astor had recently taken up residence there, as had various Livingstons and Roosevelts. From Bowling Green to the Park, Broadway was humming with both business and pleasure, as the wealthy and the fashionable—along with those who aspired to be both—swarmed among "large and commodious shops of every description . . . book stores, print-shops, music-shops, jewelers, and silversmiths; hatters, linen-drapers, milliners, pastry-cooks, coachmakers, hotels and coffee-houses."[5] With such distractions, the "tranquil domestic life" Irving had written of—along with his legal studies—was cast aside for rowdier pursuits. Like drinking.

Drinking to excess, both in private and in public, was not only accepted but encouraged—and Irving was happy to oblige. "It was almost treason against good fellowship not to get tipsy," Pierre Irving reported forgivingly, "and the senseless custom of compelling guests to drink bumpers, not unfrequently laid many under the table who never would have been led willingly to such excess."[6] However, Irving was never one to drink—or, for that matter, to do much of anything—alone. William's stern rebuke of 1805—"Good company, I find, is the grand desideratum with you"—was as true for Washington Irving in New York as it was in Europe. Within weeks of his return home, Irving fell in with a group of smart, literate, and extremely social young gentlemen he referred to as "the Nine Worthies," or—since membership often crept above nine—"the Lads of Kilkenny."

At the core of the Lads were, as one might expect, the always willing Paulding, who was still working as a loan officer and still living with Irving's brother William over on Greenwich Street, Henry Brevoort, who had settled back in the city, and a new addition to their inner circle, twenty-year-old Gouverneur Kemble, the son of a prosperous New York merchant and attorney. Other members included Kemble's younger brother, Peter Jr., Henry Ogden, Richard McCall, David Porter, and Peter Irving, who shared the Lads' love of literature, politics, and conversation. Also sitting in from time to time were the otherwise staid Ebenezer Irving and William Jr., who, despite his earlier admonition, appreciated intelligent company just as much as his younger brothers.

As the self-proclaimed ringleader of the Lads, Washington, that lover of pseudonyms, took great delight in assigning nicknames to each of his cronies: "the Doctor" for Peter Irving; "Sinbad" for Porter; Brevoort became "Nuncle"; Paulding, "Billy Taylor"; Gouverneur Kemble, "the Patroon"; and Peter Kemble, "Petronius." Ebenezer was dubbed "Captain Great-heart"; William, "the Membrane"; Richard McCall, the cryptic "Oorombates"; and Henry Ogden, "the Super-cargo." Secret identities were part of the fun to Irving, who, as the driving force behind the Lads, remained without a nickname. The nicknames not only provided the group with an internal intimacy but also protected the identities of the Lads when they reported their antics in correspondence.

Dining, conversation, and theater were the major engage-ments, made all the merrier by the copious amounts of alcohol con-sumed. After an evening at the Park Theater, the Lads would go around the corner to Dyde's Hotel to sing and drink cherry bounce or Madeira. If Dyde's was deemed too expensive by any of the group, they gathered instead at the porter house on the corner of John and Nassau streets to enjoy what they called "blackguard suppers."[7] Other times, they staggered home after an evening at Thomas Hodgkinson's Shakespeare Tavern at Nassau and Fulton.

Stories of their drunken exploits were legend among the group. After one evening of heavy drinking, a "half bewildered" Henry Ogden fell through an open grating in the street, landing in a sprawl in the darkened vault below. "The solitude," he said, "was rather dismal," until a number of other drunken wanderers fell into the vault with him, and "they had, on the whole, quite a pleasant night of it." Another evening an inebriated group of Lads spied an intoxi-cated gentleman sleeping in the gutter in front of Trinity Church. Through fogged eyes and muddled brains, they recognized Henry Brevoort's hat on the fellow's head, and dragged their passed-out friend back to his apartment and put him to bed—only to discover the next morning that the drunk they had lodged in Brevoort's chambers wasn't Henry Brevoort! The Lads laughed, but never learned how Brevoort's hat had ended up on the stranger's head in the first place.[8]

Best of all were the times at Mount Pleasant, Kemble's family mansion on the Passaic River in New Jersey, just between Newark and Belleville. Kemble had inherited the house and surrounding acreage from an uncle, and the property remained empty much of the time. Once the Lads descended on it, Irving soon provided another, more suggestive name: Cockloft Hall.

Here Irving, Kemble, and the Lads spent their afternoons drinking, playing leapfrog, and engaging in ill-advised activities. Once, while trying to knight Dick McCall with a sword, Peter Irving accidentally stabbed the young man in his posterior. As evening fell, they collapsed in drunken "general naps" on the antique chairs in the drawing room, or simply passed out on the lawn overlooking the river. The drinking, horseplay, group naps, and overall familiarity among so many young men certainly raises eyebrows today, and perhaps with good reason. Writing in 1867 of his uncle and the Lads, Pierre Irving dismissed their activities as "madcap pranks and juvenile orgies," an interesting choice of words for the discreet Pierre. Even Paulding's son and first biographer, William Irving Paulding, describes the relationship between the Lads somewhat delicately: "There is another noticeable thing. Of this society, four in particular, namely Washington Irving, Henry Brevoort Jr, Gouverneur Kemble, and James K. Paulding, became more closely bound in an unusual friendship. The relations which united this little group were of the most intimate. A confidence even beyond that of brothers existed among them; a confidence which, it was believed, was never violated under any circumstances, on any hand." Whether the Lads indulged in homosexual behavior at Cockloft Hall is not known. What is clear is that the summer of 1806 cemented the life-long friendships of Irving, Kemble, Brevoort, and Paulding.[9]

When not at Cockloft Hall, Irving was in Hoffman's offices, preparing for his bar examination. It was slow going, and at times the sheer tedium drove him into fits of silliness. It was far more entertaining to draw the green blinds on the office windows, loll in an armchair, and smoke cigars over the fire. A good smoke, Irving said, "made my blood circulate with greater vivacity, and to play about my heart with greater activity," though it didn't make him any more likely to work.[10]

Kemble didn't make things any easier, writing Irving funny letters from Philadelphia that completely diverted his focus. Dispatched by Hoffman one afternoon on an errand, Irving took one of Kemble's letters with him, reading it as he walked, and laughed so hard he continually stumbled into people. "I had completely forgotten the errand I was sent on," he told Kemble, "so I had to return, make an awkward apology to boss, and look like a nincompoop."[11]

Although the other Lads provided regular distractions, Irving reported that a few of their ranks—himself included—had temporarily peeled away from the group in favor of female companionship. "The Lads of Kilkenny are completely scattered," he told Kemble playfully, "and, to the riotous, roaring, rattle-brained orgies at Dyde's, succeeds the placid, picnic, picturesque pleasure of the tea table. We have resigned the feverish enjoyments of Madeira and Champagne, and returning with faith and loyalty to the standard of beauty, have quietly set down under petticoat government. . . . I am a new man, and am hasting with rapid strides towards perfection." Still, he couldn't resist mocking such domesticated behavior as emasculated or affected: "In a month or two, I shall become as modest, well-behaving, pretty-boy kind of a fellow as ever graced a tea party." And if the absent Kemble wanted his friends to sing his praises to the ladies at those tea parties, Irving informed him that he should let them know "in what light you wish to be held up, whether as a true Lad of Kilkenny, or a gentle prince prettyman."[12]

Irving's obvious confidence in his abilities as a conversationalist was well founded; one young lady compared him favorably against the rest of the Lads, noting that Irving was "better able to make a pun and has more small talk." And there were the stories he told about his travels in Europe, "which you know," the lady continued, "he makes go a great way."[13] The bar exam Irving hoped to take in August was continually postponed in favor of tea with young ladies, discussions on the theater with Thomas Cooper, or work with Peter on a translation of François Depons's *Voyage to the Eastern Part of Terra Firma*.

But even Irving couldn't keep putting off the inevitable forever. On November 21, 1806, the twenty-three-year-old stood for admittance to the bar, with Hoffman and attorney Martin Wilkins as his examiners. By Irving's own admittance, his performance was embarrassingly bad. "I . . . was admitted to the bar, more through courtesy than desert, for I scarcely answered a single question correctly," he wrote, "but the examiners were prepossessed in my favour." That was probably true, and for the rest of his life, Irving told a story of how his poor performance had earned him a certain distinction in the eyes of Hoffman and Wilkins. After quizzing Irving on the intricacies of the law, Hoffman appealed to Wilkins on behalf of his young clerk. "I think he knows a *little* law," Hoffman said. "Make it stronger, Jo," Martin replied, "*damned* little!"[14]

Fortunately, even damned little knowledge of the law was enough to earn Irving the title of "Esquire," and he was welcomed into the Wall Street offices of his brother John Treat, who likely knew what he was getting into. For the next decade, "lawyer" would be Washington Irving's formal occupation; not a bad one for a young gentleman with lofty ambitions, provided he had a proclivity for the law—which Irving assuredly did not.

Instead of the law, Irving devoted his attention to a much more attractive project, a literary scheme he and Paulding had cooked up over drinks. As Paulding later recalled, "one day in a frolicsome mood, we broached the idea of a little periodical merely for our own amusement, and that of the town, for neither of us anticipated any further circulation." The object of this self-published effort, Paulding explained, "was to ridicule the follies and foibles of the fashionable world," and generally poke fun at just about anything. The project sounded so amusing, in fact, that even William offered to contribute from time to time. (Peter, who seemed the more natural collaborator, declined to participate—his *Morning Chronicle* had folded in the fall of 1805, but inspired by Washington's stories of Europe, Peter had booked a European tour of his own, and would be leaving in January 1807.)[15]

Irving and Paulding located one other much-needed accomplice for their project: David Longworth, a local printer with a good sense of humor. Longworth fit in so well with the Lads that Irving almost immediately assigned him the Kilkenny nickname of "Dusky Davey."

On January 24, 1807, the first issue of their collaboration rolled off the press into the hands of unsuspecting New Yorkers—and exploded like a bombshell.

SALMAGUNDI

announced the all-caps title at the top of the cover page of their small, yellow-backed booklet. It was a word that was familiar to nineteenth-century readers as a cold dish made from chopped meat, anchovies, eggs, onions, and other ingredients—the equivalent of chef's salad today—but it could also mean a "hotchpotch" or "miscellany."[16] Either definition would do, but if readers were still confused by its meaning, the authors helpfully offered a more direct subtitle:

Or, the
Whim-Whams and Opinions
Of
Launcelot Langstaff, Esq.
and Others.

The opening remarks—mostly by Paulding, but with an assist from Washington—effectively set the tone for the series and directly stated its motives: "Our intention is simply to instruct the young, reform the old, correct the town and castigate the age; this is an arduous task, and therefore we undertake it with confidence. We intend for this purpose to present a striking picture of the town; and as every body is anxious to see his own phiz [face] on canvas, however stupid or ugly it may be, we have no doubt but that the whole town will flock to our exhibition."[17]

Paulding was right; New York had never seen anything like it. Readers snapped up copies faster than Longworth could print them, sending the first issue back to press seven times. The tone was defiant, yet playful; the authors cocksure of themselves, yet still regarding their readers with a wink: "Like all true and able editors, we consider ourselves infallible. . . . We are critics, amateurs, dillitanti, and cognoscenti, and as we know 'by the pricking of our thumbs' that every opinion which we may advance in either of those characters will be correct, we are determined, though it may be questioned, contradicted, or even controverted, yet it shall never be revoked."[18]

While Longworth's name showed up under the "Publisher's Notice," neither Paulding nor the Irving brothers ever appeared in *Salmagundi's* pages under their own names—an anonymity Washington Irving used increasingly, as it allowed him to take on different personas and write in different voices. In the first issue, Paulding played the part of Launcelot Langstaff, dispensing wisdom from his "elbow-chair," while Washington commented on the theater as "Will Wizard, Esq.," and wrote about fashion and dancing as "Anthony Evergreen, Gent." William made appearances in later issues as the poet "Pindar Cockloft" or as "Mustapha Rub-A-Dub Keli Khan," a Tripolitan ship's captain and New York prisoner initially created by Paulding to provide a foreigner's perspective on America.

Paulding and the Irvings produced *Salmagundi* at a remarkable pace, releasing the first five issues in a span of forty-six days. Public demand required each to go through multiple printings—no small task in 1806, as each reprinting had to be entirely reset by hand. While Irving and Paulding feigned nonchalance in the pages of *Salmagundi*—"we write for no other earthly purpose but to please ourselves"—its immediate success surprised them. "The sensation increased with every issue," Pierre Irving remarked; one issue allegedly sold eight hundred copies in a single day. "Though we had not anticipated anything beyond a local circulation," Paulding said later, "the work soon took a wide sphere; gradually extended throughout the United States; and acquired great popularity."[19]

While there was considerable entertainment to be derived from the pages of *Salmagundi,* speculation on the real identities of Langstaff, Wizard, Cockloft, and their cronies became something of a parlor game. "The public have already more information concerning us than we intended to impart,"[20] Langstaff wrote in the first issue, and New Yorkers were buzzing with curiosity. Irving and Paulding couldn't resist acknowledging the discussion in the third issue:

> This town has at length allayed the titillations of curiosity, by fixing on two young gentlemen of literary talents—that is to say, they are equal to the composition of a news-paper squib, a hodge-podge criticism, or some such trifle . . . but pardon us, sweet sirs, if we modestly doubt your capability of supporting the atlean burthen of Salmagundi, or of keeping up a laugh for a whole fortnight. . . . We have no intention, however, of undervaluing the abilities of these two young men whom we verily believe according to common acceptation, young men *of promise*.[21]

Actually, Irving did little to keep up the ruse. If he wanted to make a literary name for himself, he certainly had nothing to gain by keeping secret his part in the biggest literary event in New York.

Over the next thirteen months, from January 1807 to January 1808, Irving, Paulding, and Longworth—with periodic assistance from William Irving—produced twenty issues, comprising sixty-five different articles, commentaries, short essays, poems, and fake advertisements. Irving and Paulding eventually became enmeshed in the universe they had created in *Salmagundi,* populating it with its own characters—Ichabod Fungus, Diana Wearwell, and Dick Paddle—in an internal soap opera that revolved around the activities of the Cockloft family and Cockloft Hall.

With its tongue-in-cheek commentary on fashion, politics, society, and culture, *Salmagundi*—"Old Sal," as Irving sometimes called it—was neither a newspaper nor a pamphlet. More than anything, it was a nineteenth-century version of *MAD* magazine, and in 1807 no one had seen anything quite like it. Even today, the youthful cockiness and defiance—the sheer *attitude*—are still entertaining, although the nineteenth-century references are lost on modern readers. For the most part, Old Sal was simply funny gossip and silly stories—but every once in a while, the Lads' pens stung.

Thomas Jefferson, his Republicans, and his red pants bore the brunt of their attacks. Just as Oldstyle had taken his shots at competing newspapers and theater critics, Old Sal skewered anyone the Lads deemed quirky, stuffy, or downright pompous.

Sometimes they got the desired rise—and publicity—out of their targets. When William Irving criticized local poet and newspaperman Thomas Fessenden, the poet was not amused. "From one end of town to another, all is nonsense and 'Salmagund,'" Fessenden fumed in his newspaper. "America has never produced great literature—her products have been scrub oaks, at best. We should, then encourage every native sapling; but when, like *Salmagundi*, it turns out to be a bramble, and pricks and scratches everything with its reach, we naturally ask, why it encumbereth the ground."[22]

Other times—as in the case of *Port-Folio* publisher Joseph Dennie, whose "delicacy of nerves" Irving parodied—the recipient appreciated the joke. Dennie was a fan. *Salmagundi*, he wrote in a glowing review, "bears the stamp of superior genius, and indicates its unknown authors to be possessed of lively and vigorous imaginations, a happy turn for ridicule, and an extensive knowledge of the world."[23]

With such critical and popular accolades—not to mention multiple reprintings and rapid sales—Longworth encouraged Irving and Paulding to secure the copyright to their work. Incredibly, both authors refused, either out of naïveté or perhaps because they were *gentlemen* who couldn't bothered be with such trivial concerns as money. "We have nothing to do with the pecuniary concerns of the paper," they had written in the first issue, "its success will yield us neither pride nor profit."[24] When the authors balked, their publisher jumped. On March 6, 1807, Longworth secured the copyright to *Salmagundi*—an action that earned him the distinction of becoming the first of several publishers Irving would feud with about money over the course of his career.

Throughout 1807 Old Sal was Irving's main project. His duties in the Wall Street law firm largely neglected, the slack was taken up by the understanding John Treat. It cannot be said, however, that

Salmagundi was the only activity taking Washington's time and focus away from the law firm. In early 1807, after only four months in his brother's firm, Irving was already job hunting, pleading with the politically connected Hoffman to secure him any appointment that might be available under Governor-elect Daniel Tompkins. "Will you be kind enough to speak a 'word in season' for me?" he wrote Hoffman at Albany. "There will, doubtless, be numerous applicants of superior claims to myself, but none to whom a 'crumb from the table' would be more acceptable." Then the groveling began. "I can plead no services that I have rendered," Irving said truthfully, "for I have rather shunned than sought political notoriety. . . . I know that there are few offices to which I am eligible . . . your good word is all I solicit."[25]

Although Irving was not offered a position, he was still a regular in the Hoffman household. He stayed with the family when the Judge was away on business, acted as the surrogate head of the household, and wrote chatty letters to the Judge reporting on his family's activities. During Irving's absence in Europe, Mrs. Hoffman had given birth to a son, Charles, and Irving spent the early months of 1807 doting over the child. While in Europe, Irving had tried to keep tabs on Ann, asking one correspondent to "write me an account of her, and what effect the nunnery has had in altering & improving her—She promised to make a charming girl when I last saw her."[26] Sitting in the Judge's parlor, he wasn't disappointed; sixteen-year-old Ann was becoming a dark-eyed beauty who bantered with Irving more and more freely.

Despite her blooming charms, however, Ann Hoffman couldn't compete with Irving's newest female friend and correspondent, a vivacious young woman named Mary Fairlie. Attractive, witty, and a "declared belle," Mary was the daughter of Revolutionary War veteran Major James Fairlie, who, it was rumored, had distinguished himself by making George Washington laugh out loud.[27] Mary certainly had a similar effect on Washington Irving, and the two began a flirtatious correspondence in early spring 1807, just as Irving was basking in the initial glow of *Salmagundi*'s success.

"The Fascinating Fairlie," Irving called her, and he chattered, punned, and flirted with her like a smitten suitor. He filled his letters to her with eye-rolling jokes, self-deprecating humor, and dashes of erudition, making literary allusions that, more often than not, were incorrect. "The good folk of this city have a most wicked determination of being all thought wits and *beaux esprits*," Irving playfully wrote to Mary during a visit to Philadelphia, "and they are not content with being thought so by themselves, but they insist that every body else should be of the same opinion—now this in my humble opinion is the very Devil, as Chaucer says, and it has produced a most violent attack of puns upon my nervous system." It didn't matter that Chaucer had said no such thing—Irving was playing his role as the gentleman to the hilt. And if he couldn't impress her with his banter, he would flatter her in print. In the fifth issue of *Salmagundi*, he introduced a new character, "Miss Sophy Sparkle, a young lady unrivaled for playful wit and innocent vivacity, and who, like a brilliant, adds luster to the front of fashion." The portrayal was flattering and obvious; Irving was practically waggling his eyebrows at Mary from the printed page.[28]

Salmagundi had earned Irving a bit of repute in Philadelphia, an opportunity on which he was quick to capitalize. He spent a good deal of that spring in the city, and as he had noted in his letter to Mary Fairlie, the town was indeed brimming with "wits and *beaux esprits*." Even New Yorkers grudgingly admitted that Philadelphia was the place to be. The "intellectual centre of the nation," Henry Adams called it, matched only by Europe for its fashionable, literary company—and the Europeans agreed. "It would be no exaggeration to say, in numerous assemblies of Philadelphia it is impossible to meet with what is called a plain woman," wrote an admiring duc de Liancourt. "As to the young men, they for the most part seem to belong to another species."[29]

It was no wonder friends had difficulty prying Irving away. "I have so many engagements on hand," he told Mary, "—am so intolerably admired and have still so much money in my pockets that I really can fix no time when I shall return to my New York insignificance." New York was calling, and Irving dutifully obliged, but not before he made an impression on the Philadelphia ladies, some of whom tearfully begged him not to leave. "Half the people exist but in the idea that *you* will one day return," one female admirer told him. "When will pleasure return to these wretched beings? They have no philosophy, and ages will not reconcile them to the loss of your society."[30]

Irving's presence was needed in New York in late April. There was an election in Manhattan, and Judge Hoffman was standing as a Federalist candidate for a seat in the state assembly. Despite his earlier vow to "never meddle any more in politicks," Irving threw himself into the campaign with gusto, only to see Hoffman and his fellow Federalists drubbed by the Republicans after three days of elections and hard campaigning. "Never were poor devils more intolerably beaten and discomfited than my forlorn brethren the Federalists," Irving reported to Mary. "What makes me the more outrageous is that I got fairly drawn into the vortex and before the third day was expired I was as deep in mud and politics as ever a moderate gentleman would wish to be."[31]

Irving staked out a spot in the city's Seventh Ward, one of the rowdiest in Manhattan, where the election was marked by marches and demonstrations—"such haranguing & puffing & strutting among all the little great men of the day," Irving snorted. Votes in 1807 New York were certainly earned through campaign literature and speeches, but they were equally as likely to be purchased with alcohol, or scrounged up in the city's underbelly. Irving reported it all to the Fascinating Fairlie with a mixture of disgust and amusement: "I drank beer with the multitude, and I talked handbill fashion with the demagogues, and I shook hands with the mob—whom my heart abhorreth. . . . Oh my friend, I have been in such holes and corners; such filthy nooks and filthy corners, sweep offices and oyster cellars . . . faugh! I shall not be able to bear the smell of small beer or tobacco for a month to come." Even more shocking to Irving was the treatment of black voters, who were corralled and compelled to vote Federalist. "I almost pitied them," he wrote, "for we had them up in an enormous drove in the middle of the day waiting round the poll for a chance to vote. The Sun came out intolerably warm—and being packed together like sheep in a pen, they absolutely fermented." It hadn't been the Federalists' finest hour. "Truly," he concluded, "this serving ones country is a nauseous piece of business."[32]

Reading his letter in Boston, Fairlie—who was not only witty, but also Republican—couldn't resist giving Irving a good poke in the ribs. "How my heart joyed to hear of your defeat! Never did I receive a letter which gave me so much pleasure," she teased. "I cannot say, however, that this was unexpected, as I am too good a Republican to have thought of leaving New York without being perfectly sure of our victory."[33]

Irving may have fumed, but he was more loyal to conviction than party. His own politics were, by today's standards, progressively conservative, favoring business, nonregulation, and individual rights, while valuing older traditions—all convictions that appealed to a proper gentleman. If his political party drifted too far from his core values, Irving simply abandoned the party. He didn't lack for conviction, merely the stomach for the fight. His own political style was decidedly nonconfrontational, a trait that served him well.

Still, arguing about politics was always a good excuse for chatting with or writing Mary Fairlie, whose letters continued in the same playful vein. He was still talked about as one of the authors of *Salmagundi*, she told him. "A *cute* young man," she started one letter, knowing the stress on the word *cute* would shake up Irving, "asked me the usual question of 'who was the author of *Salmagundi?*' I told him that it was absolutely not *known*, but that you were shrewdly *suspected*; he said he thought so; that he had seen you in Italy; that the instant he saw the likeness of Launcelot in [*Salmagundi*] No. 8, he perceived it bore a strange likeness to you, indeed very striking." After teasing him with the mention of another young man, she reeled Irving back in. "I forthwith determined to have it [the likeness] set in pearl, and shall evermore wear it next to my heart, in token of the great love and kindness I bear the original!"[34]

Irving was just as flirty. "I have read of heroes and heroines of novels, when separated, looking at the moon at the same time and thus in a manner holding 'sweet converse' with each other," he wrote at the close of a May 13 letter. "I leave to these lovesick gentlefolk all such lunatic speculation as mere matters of *moonshine;* but I will improve upon their idea, and while writing to you, will fancy that you are the same time scribbling an answer."[35]

What Mary likely found most surprising about the letter was not the sentiment itself, but rather the postmark at the top of the first page: Fredericksburg, Virginia. "I did not so much as dream of this jaunt four and twenty hours before my departure,"[36] he explained to Mary, but he had been asked to come south to attend the trial of fellow New Yorker Aaron Burr, who had been indicted in early April on charges of treason and high misdemeanor.

Aaron Burr's lone term as Jefferson's vice president had unceremoniously expired on March 4, 1805. Since then, he had been a busy man, gazing at the newly acquired Louisiana Territory with an emperor's eye, and making plans. With its borders in turmoil, Burr believed Louisiana could be pried away from the United States with a minimum of force or fuss. He approached British minister Anthony Merry about providing him with $500,000 in cash and a British squadron that Burr could lead up the Mississippi. Merry made reassuring noises but no promises, leaving Burr to improvise a means for raising funds and forces on his own. The Burr conspiracy, as it was called, was under way.

Joining Burr in the plot was a fat, drunken blowhard named James Wilkinson, the commanding general of the U.S. Army whom Burr, as vice president, had managed to get appointed as governor of Louisiana. "Ambitious and easily dazzled, fond of show and appearance," French minister Louis Turreau described Wilkinson to Talleyrand. "General Wilkinson is the most intimate friend, or rather the most devoted creature, of Colonel Burr."[37] Burr had also found another willing accomplice in an Irishman named Harman

Blennerhassett, who offered Burr his island home on the Ohio River as a base of operations.

In no time, people were talking openly about the conspiracy—and the biggest mouth was Aaron Burr's! "He or some of his agents have either been indiscreet in their communications, or have been betrayed by some person in whom they considered that they had reason to confide," a nervous Minister Merry wrote to his government, "for the object of his journey has now begun to be noticed in the public prints."[38]

By January 1806 the conspiracy was so well known that even U.S. District Attorney Joseph Daveiss had caught wind of it, and warned President Jefferson. Jefferson dismissed Daveiss's concerns; he didn't take Burr and his swaggering seriously. Still, Daveiss had Burr hauled in front of a U.S. court in Kentucky several times to respond to charges that he was planning an armed expedition against Mexico, and instigating revolution in the western states and territories.[39] With Henry Clay serving as his counsel, the charismatic Burr was acquitted, to thunderous applause.

Over time, the details of the conspiracy leaked. According to one of Burr's coconspirators, the plan included an outrageous plot to kidnap the president, vice president, and president pro tempore of the Senate, seize public money in Washington and Georgetown banks, and burn all the vessels in the navy yard.[40] Burr put his plans in a coded letter to Wilkinson—the infamous Cipher Letter—then set out for the western frontier, openly badmouthing the U.S. government to anyone who would listen, and blustering and bullying accomplices as he tried to raise money and troops.

Despite Burr's confidence, Wilkinson was getting cold feet. He decided the best way to save his own skin was to blow the lid off the entire affair and plead his own innocence. On November 25, 1806, President Jefferson received a letter from Wilkinson that detailed the terms of the conspiracy and hung the entire affair around Burr's neck. Jefferson issued a warrant for Burr's arrest, and in early December Ohio militiamen captured most of Burr's boats and supplies at a Marietta boatyard. Nearly two months later, after a mad pursuit down the Mississippi, federal agents finally nabbed Burr. The disgraced vice president was dragged to Richmond, Virginia, for indictment and trial.

The U.S. attorney general, Cesar Augustus Rodney, and George Hay, his primary prosecutor, indicted Burr for treasonable acts committed under his direction at Blennerhassett's Island. For his defense, Burr engaged a team of legal heavy hitters, including über-loyalist John Wickham; Edmond Randolph, a former member of George Washington's cabinet; prominent Virginian Benjamin Botts; and Luther Martin, a formidable jurist who had helped write, but ultimately did not sign, the U.S. Constitution. Interestingly, Burr also requested the assistance of a rookie lawyer from New York named Washington Irving.

The precise nature of Irving's service to Burr remains tantalizingly unclear. Irving had no great legal reputation, and it's doubtful that his connections with Hoffman would have done Burr much good. However, Burr had been a fan of Irving's writing since the Oldstyle letters, when he had passed on clips from the *Chronicle* to his daughter, and likely appreciated the work Irving had done on his behalf in the pages of the *Corrector*. Perhaps Burr hoped that having Irving on hand as an official observer might result in some favorable press, but he never made his intentions entirely known, even to Irving. "Burr was full of petty mystery; he made a mystery of everything," Irving said. Even years later, Irving still had no idea why he had been sent for. "From some sounding of his, I suspected he wanted me to write for the press in his behalf," he recalled, "but I put a veto on that."[41]

Burr's trial began on May 22 in the Hall of the Virginia House of Delegates, crammed to capacity with gawkers and onlookers from all walks of life, with dusty frontiersmen jammed alongside nattily dressed southern gentlemen. The streets were packed with spectators hoping for a glimpse of Burr as he was bustled into the great hall for what they were sure would be "the trial of the century." The inns were so jammed that those without rooms simply slept in wagons or in tents by the James River. Through his connections, Irving had managed to land a room in the Eagle Tavern on Main Street at the base of Richmond's Capitol Hill.[42]

Amid the buzz, the two calmest people in the courtroom were Burr and Chief Justice John Marshall. Dressed entirely in black silk, his hair powdered, Burr was every inch the deposed emperor he had endeavored to be—and Irving, ever the romantic, felt sorry for him. "Though opposed to him in political principles," Irving admitted, "yet I consider him as a man so fallen, so shorn of the power to do national injury, that I feel no sensation remaining but compassion for him."[43]

By early June both sides were still arguing over definitions of treason—a critical matter, to be sure, but Irving found it boring. "You can little conceive the talents for procrastination that have been exhibited in this affair," he told Mrs. Hoffman. The prosecution was still waiting for its star witness—the blustery James Wilkinson—to arrive, but he was taking his time. "Day after day," Irving sighed, "have we been disappointed by the non-arrival of the magnanimous Wilkinson; day after day have fresh murmurs and complaints been uttered; and day after day we are told that the next mail will probably bring his noble self, or at least some accounts when he may be expected."[44]

The trial ground to a halt in anticipation, Irving wrote a bit testily, even as he took a jab at the southern mentality: "We are now enjoying a kind of suspension of hostilities, the grand jury having been dismissed the day before yesterday for five or six days, that they might go home, see their wives, get their clothes washed, and flog their negroes. As yet we are not even on the threshold of a trial, and if the great hero of the South does not arrive, it is a chance if we have any trial this term."[45]

On June 10 Wilkinson finally arrived, striding confidently into the courtroom amid a sea of important-looking aides.[46] "The first interview between him and Burr," Irving wrote Paulding, "was highly interesting, and I secured a good place to witness it."

Burr was seated with his back to the entrance, facing the judge, and conversing with one of his counsel. Wilkinson strutted into Court, and took his stand in a parallel line with Burr on his right hand. Here he stood for a moment swelling like a turkey cock, and bracing himself for the encounter of Burr's eye. The latter did not take any notice of him until the judge directed the clerk to swear Gen. Wilkinson; at the mention of the name, Burr turned his head, looked him full in the face with one of his piercing regards, swept his eye over his whole person from head to foot, as if to scan its dimensions, and then coolly resumed his former position, and went on conversing with his counsel as tranquilly as ever.[47]

Irving was impressed. "The whole look was over in an instant, but it was an admirable one . . . a slight expression of contempt played over his countenance, such as you would show on regarding any person to whom you were indifferent, but whom you considered mean and contemptible."[48]

Wilkinson, naturally, remembered the encounter differently, claiming that he had smugly "darted a flash of indignation at the little Traitor . . . [who then] made an Effort to meet the indignant salutation of outraged Honor, but it was in vain." Wilkinson's pomp did nothing to endear him to either the jury or the public. Popular sentiment, in fact, was beginning to lean toward the roguish Burr, who was treated like a rock star. He ushered visitors laden with gifts into the rooms Luther Martin had rented for him near the posh Swan Tavern—at least until complaints about preferential treatment required him to be moved to the new penitentiary outside town, where he continued to receive family and guests. Wilkinson, meanwhile, comported himself badly before the grand jury, and barely escaped indictment. Irving told Paulding that he had learned that the grand jury was "tired enough of his verbosity"—a rumor supported by jury foreman John Randolph, who called Wilkinson "the most finished scoundrel that ever lived."[49]

In the meantime, Irving was trying to conduct a little business with Paulding, who was working on the twelfth issue of *Salmagundi* in New York. Irving informed his friend that he had no time to write anything for this issue, but pressed his collaborator for any buzz he might have heard on issue eleven. "I wish to know all the news about our work, and any literary intelligence that may be in circulation," wrote Irving, who was always eager for his own reviews. Of more pressing concern was money. "What arrangement have you made with the Dusky for the profits?" Irving asked, perhaps oblivious to the fact that Dusky Davey now owned their discarded copyright. "I shall stand much in need of a little sum of money on my return."[50]

Irving was in no hurry to return to New York. Even as Burr was indicted on June 24 on charges of treason and high misdemeanor, Irving was drinking and ingratiating himself with Virginians on both sides of the issue. "I have been treated in the most polite and hospitable manner by the most distinguished persons of the place—those friendly to Colonel Burr and those opposed to him, and have intimate acquaintances among his bitterest enemies," he wrote. "The society is polished, sociable, and extremely hospitable, and there is a great variety of distinguished character assembled on this occasion."[51]

Following Burr's indictment, Marshall adjourned the court until Burr's trial on August 3—but Irving wasn't ready to leave. He was so busy socializing that he had nearly worn himself out, and any efforts to sneak away from parties to get to bed at a decent hour earned him playful reprimands from the young ladies. "I find I am declining in popularity from having resolutely and manfully resisted sundry temptations and invitations to tea parties—stew-balls and other infernal orgies which have from time to time been celebrated by the little enchantresses of this place," he told Kemble. And it was useless to try to think up excuses: "I tried my hand two or three times at an apology for my non attendance, but it would not do, my usual luck followed me; for once when I alleged the writing of letters, it was plainly proved that I was seen smoking a cigar and lolling in the porch of the Eagle, and another time when I plead a severe indisposition, I was pronounced guilty of having sat at a young ladies elbow the whole evening and listened to her piano."[52]

Compounding his problems, he told Mary Fairlie playfully, was that he had earned a reputation in Richmond "of being an *interesting young man*," which, he said, was an especially terrible thing to be in the Virginia summer heat. "The tender hearted fair ones think you absolutely at their command—they conclude that you must of course be fond of moonlight walks—and rides at day break, and red hot strolls in the middle of the day (Farenheits Themom. 98½ in the shade) and 'Melting hot-hissing hot' tea parties—and what is more they expect you to talk sentiment. . . . Twas too much for me." He was likely protesting too much, and it's doubtful that either Mary or Gouverneur Kemble had much sympathy for their young friend when he complained of having to "leave my beloved bed at sunrise to take a romantic walk along the canal."[53]

Exhausted and overheated, Irving was ready to head back to New York in early July. First, however, he wanted to see Burr, who was still lodged in the Richmond penitentiary. In his typical dramatic fashion, Irving reported that Burr was "confined by bolts & bars & massy walls in criminal prison . . . cut off from all intercourse with society, deprived of all the kind offices of friendship—and made to suffer all the penalties & deprivations of a condemned criminal." However, Burr's daughter Theodosia remembered things differently. "Since my residence here, of which some days and nights were passed in the penitentiary," she wrote, "our little family circle has been a scene of uninterrupted gayety."[54]

Despite his defiance in Marshall's courtroom, within the walls of the penitentiary, Burr had the appearance of a beaten man. Irving was never sorrier for the disgraced hero he had defended so rigorously in the pages of the *Corrector* in 1804:

> Burr seemed in lower spirits than formerly. He was composed and collected as usual; but there was not the same cheerfulness that I have hitherto remarked—He said it was with difficulty his very servant was allowed occasionally to see him. . . . I bid him farewell with a heavy heart, and he expressed with peculiar warmth and feeling, his sense of the

interest I had taken in his fate—I never felt in a more melancholy mood than when I rode from his solitary prison—such is the last interview I had with poor Burr—I shall never forget it.[55]

He never saw Burr again. Two months later the jury entered a verdict of "not guilty"—or, more accurately, "not proved to be guilty under this indictment by any evidence submitted to us."[56] Burr was also found not guilty of the misdemeanor count in October, but he never recovered his reputation. He retreated to Europe until 1812, then returned to America and ran a moderately successful law practice in New York until his death in 1836. Much later in life, when discussing his abilities as a lawyer, Irving always reminded his critics with a wink that he "was one of the counsel for Burr, and Burr was acquitted!"

Back in Hoffman's parlor at the beginning of August, Irving was hard at work on material for the next issue of *Salmagundi*. No new installments had been published since June 27, the longest break between issues yet. However, if he was worried the public had lost interest in Old Sal, he needn't have. The newest issue of the *Monthly Register, Magazine and Review of the United States* contained a laudatory review of *Salmagundi*: "This design is executed with so much spirit, wit, genius, elegance, and humour. . . . It seems superfluous to transcribe any passages from a book, which is undoubtedly, in the hands of every lover of merriment and gaiety; neither is it an easy task, to select from such an abundant assemblage of sportive excellence those periods, which might be deemed to stand pre-eminent for their keenness and brilliancy."[57] With the *Monthly Register* reminding any forgetful readers just how good *Salmagundi* was, Irving and Paulding released the thirteenth issue on August 14, 1807.

Two months later, on October 25, 1807, Washington Irving's father died at the age of seventy-six. Whether the Deacon had come to accept, or at least appreciate, the blooming talents and fame of his youngest son remains unknown. Nor did Washington ever write a word regarding his father's death. His passing does not appear to have put a visible crimp in Washington's schedule or style; a new installment of *Salmagundi*—number seventeen—appeared only two weeks later. Neither Irving nor Paulding could have realized it at the time, but this was the issue of *Salmagundi* that would earn their publication a permanent place in New York history.

Appearing in the November 11 issue was a piece Irving had written as Launcelot Langstaff, describing the library at Cockloft Hall. "It consisted of books not to be met with in any other collection, and as the phrase is, entirely out of print." Among those books was one particular volume—"a literary curiosity"—that gave Will Wizard a great deal of pleasure, and from which Langstaff now reprinted a chapter for his readers:

CHAP CIX.

OF THE CHRONICLES OF THE RENOWNED

AND ANTIENT CITY OF GOTHAM

Over the next few pages, in a mock history of New York, Irving related how "the thrice renowned and delectable city of GOTHAM did suffer great discomfiture, and was reduced to perilous extremity, by the invasion and assaults of the HOPPINGTOTS."[58] While Paulding and Irving had used the word "Gotham" in the pages of *Salmagundi* before—Paulding had made a passing reference to a musician, "a gentleman amateur in Gotham," as far back as issue two—Irving was the first to explicitly attach the name to New York, and to refer to its citizens as "Gothamites."

The word, which in Anglo-Saxon means "Goat's Town," came from a real English town in Nottinghamshire, near Sherwood Forest. According to English fable, the King's Highway would be built wherever the king set foot—and if the king walked through your town, the throne would take the land and construct a highway. To prevent King John from entering Gotham, its citizens pretended to be crazy, behaving so oddly that snickering scouts advised the king to steer clear of the town. "More fools pass through Gotham than remain in it," the English said, and New York readers grinned in appreciation.[59] The name caught on.

Hardly aware he had just created a brand name, Irving was blissfully carrying on a playful correspondence with seventeen-year-old Ann Hoffman, who was spending the winter with extended family in Montgomery, New York. His letters to Ann are intimate, though not quite as flirty as those he was writing to Mary Fairlie. Irving informed Ann that he had dreamed of her, and teased her about not writing back. "Surely you who can write with so little hesitation to your own family, should at least have kindness enough to believe that your letters would be received with equal pleasure and equal indulgence by one who regards you with the sincere affection of a brother." In short, Irving wrote, "The substance of all this preamble is simply *I wish you to write me.*"[60]

Ann and her sister Matilda probably *did* regard Irving more like a brother than an eligible bachelor, much less one of the most eligible bachelors in New York. In a letter to Ann urging her to return home so more young men will call on the two of them, fifteen-year-old Matilda Hoffman portrays Irving as nothing more than a consolation prize, though her broad brushstroke splattered poor Kemble as well. "If you have any compassion on me do come down. I hardly dare to stir out any longer I meet so many disappointed *beaux* I believe they think I keep you away that *I* may make conquests and therefore will not give me a chance, they have deserted our house entirely. Our old *stand bys* Gouverneur and *Washington*, and Mr. Bleeker *once* a week are the only people we see."[61]

Neither Kemble nor any of the other Lads had time for ladies at the moment. As the days turned colder, the Lads reunited and returned to their usual habits of excess. One evening Irving reported that the Lads descended on Kemble's house where they "remained two or three days, committed great devastation, & absolutely [ate] him out of doors." Meanwhile, in Philadelphia, Kemble's younger brother was keeping up the Lads' reputation by drinking so heavily,

Irving said, that they were prepared to "send orders in case his nose should catch fire to have it extinguished in the Delaware."[62]

Amid the winter frivolity, Paulding and the Irvings produced two more issues of *Salmagundi*, sending issue eighteen out on November 24—which contained one of Irving's finest pieces to date, "The Little Man in Black"—and issue nineteen on December 31, 1807. Though *Salmagundi* had lost none of its punch, and its authors remained as committed as ever to the project, they were growing increasingly frustrated with "Dusky" David Longworth. As is often the case with art, their disagreements weren't about the integrity of their mutual project, but about money.

According to Pierre Irving, the alleged source of the conflict between the authors and their publisher was not only over the one-shilling price Dusky had slapped on each issue, but also the limits on length that Longworth was now dictating.[63] While there is merit to that complaint, that was probably only part of it.

Despite their staggering refusal to secure *Salmagundi*'s copyright—at Longworth's behest, no less—once it was clear Old Sal was doing well, both Irving and Paulding wanted a piece of the profits that Longworth had legitimately secured. Paulding later complained that Dusky had bilked him and Irving out of as much as $15,000, about $250,000 in today's money. That was likely an exaggeration, but Paulding never admitted that the lost profits were due more to his and Irving's failure to secure their own copyright than to any duplicity on Longworth's part. "The publisher, with that liberality so characteristic of these modern Maecenases," Paulding grumbled, oozing sarcasm, "declined to concede to us a share of the profits which had become very considerable."[64]

Issue twenty of *Salmagundi* rolled off Longworth's presses on January 15, 1808. It was the final issue.

4

Hoax

1808–1810

Left his lodgings some time since and has not been heard of, a small elderly gentleman, dressed in an old black coat and cocked hat, by the name of Knickerbocker.

—Notice in the *New York Evening Post*, October 26, 1809

THE DEMISE OF *SALMAGUNDI* in January 1808, while disappointing to New York readers, was of little concern to Irving—"I was in hopes it would gradually have gone down in oblivion," he said with a shrug. He missed the regular outlet for the exercise of his pen, but for one of the few times in his life, inspiration wasn't a problem. Paulding, speaking as Launcelot Langstaff, had admitted as much in *Salmagundi*'s final issue: "It is not for want of subjects that we stop our career. We are not in the situation of poor Alexander the Great, who wept, as well indeed he might, because there were no more worlds to conquer; for, to do justice to this queer, odd, rantipole city, and this whimsical country, there is matter enough in them, to keep our risible muscles, and our pens going until doomsday." It was, in fact, the "queer, odd, rantipole city" that kept Irving's pen going for the next two years, though in ways no one could have anticipated.[1]

That New York would serve both as the muse and the subject of Irving's first real book and first national success was not surprising; that it was written at all, however, was remarkable. It was born of a grand idea that quickly groaned under its own weight and resulted in a series of frustrating false starts. It nearly sputtered out altogether when Irving made a critical decision about his future, before the literary prank was presented to the public—a lightning bolt of comedy and political satire written during his blackest hours.

The initial spark of inspiration came from an unlikely source—a rather turgid New York travel guide with the impressive title of *The Picture of New York; or, The Traveller's Guide through the Commercial Metropolis of the United States.* Published a year earlier by Dr. Samuel Mitchell, a well-known and admired professor of chemistry and zoology at Columbia University, the guide's practical value couldn't be denied. But the pompous nature of Mitchell's book, and the mundane topics he covered—topography, insurance companies, public health—was cause for much snickering among Irving and the Lads. It was a target ripe for parody—the Lads had already hooted at it in the pages of Old Sal—and Peter, newly returned from his European tour, approached his youngest brother about writing their own spoof of Mitchell's book.

Washington jumped at the project with relish, and he and Peter began compiling notes from all the appropriately obscure and suitably pretentious sources they needed to properly lampoon Mitchell and his book. "We laid all kinds of works under contribution for trite citations, relevant or irrelevant, to give it the proper air of learned research,"[2] Washington recalled. They scribbled outlines of possible chapters—Mitchell had begun his book with an account of the Aborigines, so the brothers were determined to trump the good doctor by beginning their book with a history of the world—but the joke was quickly smothered beneath the sheer weight of their research.

As the book swelled, Washington felt that they were writing the satire without any direction. Peter, meanwhile, seemed to think their burlesque, which he called *esta obra*—"that work"—was nearly complete. He was already counting on its certain profits. "I presume you must be aware *esta obra* must terminate for the present at the point at which I left it," Peter wrote. "It should, therefore, be completed without loss of time, and I entreat you either to whip your imagination into a gallop, or to leave it for an uncomplying jade, and saddle your judgment. If you do not, I shall have to give the thing such a hasty finish as circumstances may permit, immediately on my return—for my pocket calls aloud and will not brook delay."[3]

However, neither Washington nor Peter was in any rush to actually do the work when there were so many distractions worthy of their attention. Washington made side trips to visit friends in Philadelphia, and danced and drank too much at yet another "crazy party" thrown by Mary Fairlie, with whom he was still carrying on an arm's-length flirtation. To meet his many "drawing room demands," he ordered a new black coat and purchased a new horse. His pen essentially motionless, his legal practice neglected, he was once more falling back into his "gentlemanlike habits."[4]

Meanwhile, the Jefferson administration's recently passed Non-Importation Act and Embargo, which prohibited the importation of certain goods from Britain, was causing severe heartburn among New York merchants. Profits in the family hardware business were down, and Ebenezer's speculation in land grants had failed to pan out the way the family had hoped. The Irving brothers had always prided themselves on running a clean business—their father, the good Deacon, had made sure of that—but that didn't mean they were above a bit of subterfuge now and then. In late April 1808 Washington—with $9,000 in silver in his trunks—was dispatched by the family firm to conduct some business in Montreal.

The trip was designed to skirt the restrictions of the embargo. The Irvings hoped to convert their silver at a much more favorable rate than could be had in the United States. They weren't alone in adopting such tactics; illegal trade with Canada had become a constant source of frustration for President Jefferson. In fact, Brevoort, who was working for his brother-in-law John Jacob Astor in Montreal, seemed to have been openly involved in a covert business scheme. Washington laughingly referred to Brevoort as "our friend the smuggler."[5]

Typically, Irving took his time getting to Montreal; he made a side trip to Schenectady to visit a sick relative of the Hoffman family. There, he unexpectedly ran into Peter, on his way to visit their sister Ann Dodge, who was ill up in Johnstown. He asked Peter not to go to Johnstown, but to join him instead on his illicit adventure to Canada. Peter, never one to pass up an opportunity that might lead to a quick buck, agreed. By May 9 the brothers were at White-hall, near the southern tip of Lake Champlain. Drinking with other smugglers at their hotel, they waited for a favorable wind that would take their boat up the lake into Canada.[6]

This close to the border, Washington had a case of nerves, pet-rified he might get caught with his pockets full of smuggled silver. He wrote in a barely controlled panic to Brevoort, begging him to wait for him in Montreal and wailing that the "good folks at the line are so excessively strict that I dare not risk my silver across." He even considered abandoning the trip and getting what he could for his silver on the safer shores of Vermont. "I am afraid this will turn out but a lame business all round," he fretted.[7]

On May 10 the winds changed, and the brothers surged up Champlain by sloop, arriving in Montreal, unmolested, seven days later. Reunited with Brevoort, they carried out their transaction, then promptly traded business for pleasure. They spent the next two weeks dancing, drinking, and dining with Canadian belles and busi-nessmen.

By the beginning of June the Irvings were back in the United States, when they learned their sister Ann had died. It had been five years since Washington had seen Ann, and the loss hit him hard; she was only thirty-eight years old. "One more heart lies still and cold that ever beat towards me with the warmest affection," he wrote to Mrs. Hoffman, "for she was the tenderest, best of sisters, and a woman of whom a brother might be proud." He was even more upset that he had diverted Peter from his visit to Ann to romp with him in Canada. The brothers postponed their return to New York City to tend to their widowed brother-in-law and his five children in Johnstown. "Would to Heaven I had gone there a month ago," Washington sighed.[8]

Despite their successful Canadian expedition, the family business still suffered from the embargo, and Irving's pocketbook was emptying quickly. "I am sorry for the lowness of your purse, and might possibly bestow a sixpence in charity," his sister Catharine teased playfully, "but I fear you are not a deserving object."[9]

In August small help came in the form of an offer from bookseller Isaac Riley to translate one of the two volumes of the French work *A Voyage to the Eastern Part of Terra Firma; or, The Spanish Main during the Years 1801, 1802, 1803, and 1804*. Irving split the $300 commission with George Caines, who translated the other volume. The resulting hackwork, credited simply to "an American Gentleman," was a mess. When the books were published, one Boston critic remarked that the translator appeared to know very little French, and even less English. Amused, Irving mischievously informed Caines that he would take the blame for the poor French, so long as Caines took the heat for the ignorance of English.[10]

His pen reactivated, Irving revisited the unfinished burlesque. "I have been very free with my pen of late," he told one of the Lads, "and have written myself completely blank."[11] Yet *esta obra* only continued to bloat, an increasingly unwieldy work-in-progress.

Who could blame Irving for his lack of focus when there was Mary Fairlie to distract him?—especially since she had recently acquired a dance instructor who had taught her to kick up her heels in a manner even Irving thought approached immodest. Both Mary Fairlie and Ann Hoffman were trying at every opportunity to display their new dancing skills to Irving and his male friends. "Mary and Ann have been pestering Petronius [Peter Kemble] and myself with their abominable steps whenever we have been in their company of late,"[12] he wrote another bachelor friend with unconvincing exasperation.

Irving could walk the fine line between gentleman and rogue with remarkable acuity, and appears to have struck just such a balance one evening. Mary and Ann "insisted upon shewing us a new way of coming into a room, but we disappointed them by displaying an old way of going out—and actually made a safe retreat to our own homes." Ever the gentleman, he told Dick McCall with a wink that he had since "foresworn & abandoned their society," at least until the young ladies "regained their *understanding* (meaning a pun) . . ." The next lines are heavily inked out, the denouement obscured by a later, more discreet hand.[13]

Ann's athletic ability wasn't limited to dancing. That autumn, while she was attending a performance at the Park Theater, a cry of "Fire!" sent her leaping in a graceful arc from her box to the stage below. A perplexed Thomas Cooper escorted the shaken Ann to the wings, where she promptly fainted, but the gossip around town, Irving reported with amusement, was that Ann had intentionally leaped from her box into Cooper's arms. In truth, Cooper was far more interested in Mary Fairlie, while Ann was involved in an on-again, off-again relationship with Charles Nicholas, the man she would marry.

Irving had known Ann since she was twelve, when they had laughed and sung together on their trip to Montreal in the summer of 1802. While he was in Europe, it was Ann he always inquired after in his letters home. He had been part of her household, practically part of her family, for seven years. Now he was twenty-five, she nineteen. They seemed an ideal couple, with mutual interests in theater, books, parties, and conversation. By all accounts, she was a handful and a good catch—vivacious, witty, smart, and attractive. Yet here was Ann, preparing to marry another man, while Irving watched approvingly and without any visible indication, even in his most private journals, of any kind of regret.

Irving responded strongly to lively, independent women of character and substance. All his life, he would be drawn to smart, outgoing women like Ann and Maria Hoffman, Mary Fairlie, and Madame de Stael. To Irving, these were women with whom to flirt, spar, dance, and chat—but they weren't women one loved or married. Love and marriage were reserved for those who met a different and, in Irving's eyes, higher standard. Quiet, tender, and less aggressive, these women were more likely to look upon his face and tell him that everything was all right—in other words, they were more like his mother. Or Ann's younger sister, Matilda.

Irving himself could never pinpoint the exact moment, sometime in late 1808, that he had fallen in love with Ann's soft-spoken seventeen-year-old sister. Looking back years later, he imagined the romantic spark had been kindled following his return from Europe in 1806: "She came home from school to see me. She entered full of eagerness, yet shy from her natural timidity, from the time that had elapsed since we parted, and from the idea of my being a *travelled man*, instead of a stripling student—However, what a difference the interval had made. . . . I thought I had never beheld any thing so lovely—" This was romantic hindsight, tinted by time and distance. Only a year before, he had been writing playfully to Ann, castigating her for not responding to his letters, without ever mentioning or asking about Matilda. As late as June 1808, he was singing Ann's praises to Brevoort, telling him how "fair & beautiful as ever & full of fascination" she was. If his attention had shifted, Irving explained later, he could hardly be blamed, for even Ann was constantly explaining that "people began by admiring her, but ended by loving Matilda."[14]

"Matalinda dinda dinda," she called herself, and Irving adored her. Based on her surviving letters and the one remaining miniature portrait we have of her, Matilda Hoffman seemed to possess neither stunning intellect nor great beauty—a far cry from the vivacious women Irving socialized with. Pierre Irving wrote that while she was "not a dazzling beauty, she is described as lovely in person and mind, of the most gentle and engaging manners, and with a sensibility that mingled gracefully with a delicate and playful humor."[15]

Irving idolized—and idealized—Matilda. A look from her set his spirits soaring. "I would read to her from some favourite poet," he recalled in his journal some years later: ". . . when I came to some tender passage it seemed to catch my excited feelings I would close the book and launch forth into his praises and when I had wrought myself into a strain of enthusiasm. . . . Her fine eyes would kindle and beam upon me. . . . I would drink in new inspiration from them until suddenly [she] seemed to recollect herself—& throw them down upon the earth with a sweet pensiveness and a full drawn sigh."[16]

He had fallen in love with her. But despite his affection for Matilda, his intimacy with her family, and his good rapport with Judge Hoffman, he brought no real prospects to the relationship. His family's business was still struggling—a second trip to Canada in late 1808 had been unsuccessful—and his career as a lawyer was virtually nonexistent. Yet Irving clung to the belief that the law was his only real avenue for financial security and a future. It was a dreadful thought; but so, too, was that of having no prospects at all. He explained later, "I felt my own deficiency and despaired of ever succeeding at the Bar. I could study anything else rather than Law, and had a fatal propensity to Belles lettres. I had gone on blindly, like a boy in Love, but now I began to open my eyes and be miserable. I had nothing in purse nor in expectation. . . . I anticipated nothing from my legal pursuit," he concluded, disgusted with himself, "and had done nothing to make me hope for public employment or political elevation."[17]

To his further dismay, Peter had departed for Liverpool on January 1, 1809, to assist the slumping family business. Their abandoned *esta obra* was incomplete, rambling, and swollen, but Washington thought he might be able to salvage something from the wreckage. Still, writing wasn't the way a respectable gentleman supported his family; writing was a pastime, not a vocation. He needed not just a job, but a *career*, or he would have no chance of winning Matilda's hand.

"Young men in our country think it a great extravagance to set up a horse and carriage without adequate means," Irving later said wistfully, "but they make no account of setting up a wife and family, which is far more expensive."[18] He needed something, anything, to help him make money. He contacted Peter, who knew a thing or two about get-rich-quick schemes, and asked him to keep an eye out for opportunities in Liverpool or elsewhere. Nothing happened.

Judge Hoffman took mercy on the floundering suitor. Hoffman approved of Irving but, like a father, wanted to ensure Matilda would be provided for by any potential husband. Over the last seven years, Hoffman had treated Irving like a son, leaving the family in his care time and time again. But the Judge had also tutored and mentored the young man since 1802, and clearly understood Irving's dreamy nature and inclination toward laziness.

In the winter of 1808, Hoffman proposed a quid pro quo. If Irving applied himself to the law in earnest, proving that he could support a family, then Hoffman would give him a position in his own firm, and his daughter's hand with it. "Nothing could be more generous,"[19] Irving said, but it was a decision that needed serious consideration.

Irving had watched a number of his friends slowly amass wealth, which not only made them eligible bachelors but also enabled them to enjoy very comfortable lifestyles. He understood the value of marrying into one of New York's established, well-connected families, which the Hoffmans most decidedly were. Even Henry Brevoort—who came from a good family, had a knack for business, and seemed to need no help making his own way—had received from his brother-in-law John Jacob Astor a plum position managing Astor's affairs in Canada. Irving knew that building and maintaining the kind of life he wanted—indeed, was expected to lead, if he wished to marry Matilda—would require not just a job, but *work*, two things he hated.

The choice was his. Would he put his nose to the legal grindstone, cast his pen aside, and live a happy if rather ordinary life as a lawyer and man of business? Or would he refuse Hoffman's offer, relinquish Matilda's hand, and pick up his pen to take his chances as a writer?

The answer was obvious to Irving. He enjoyed writing and had a knack for it, but he also coveted financial security. He accepted Hoffman's offer—and hated every moment thereafter.

To his credit, while Irving always claimed that Hoffman had a better opinion of his legal capacity than he merited, he worked hard. "I set to work with zeal to study anew," he explained, "and I considered myself bound in honor not to make further advances with the daughter until I should feel satisfied with my proficiency in the Law."[20]

With the title of fiancé, he could visit Matilda with some impunity, and he spent more and more time at the Hoffman home. "We saw each other every day and I became excessively attached to her," Irving remembered. "The more I saw of her the more I had reason to admire her." Although *esta obra* was officially shelved for the moment, he scribbled at it in secret when staying at his mother's home a few blocks east of the Hoffmans', away from the Judge's watchful eyes. "I tried to finish the work which I was secretly writing, hoping it would give me reputation and gain me some public employment," he said later.[21]

Most of his time, however, was devoted to the hated law books, the bane of his existence. It proved more than he could bear. "It was all in vain," Irving said later, still shuddering at the memory of the moldy volumes. "I had an insuperable repugnance to the study—my mind would not take hold of it; or rather by long despondency had become for the time incapable of dry application. I was in a wretched state of doubt and self-distrust."[22]

Had Irving persevered, his life would have been very different. With his job at the firm, and Hoffman's wallet to sustain him, it is unlikely he would ever have turned to his pen in any meaningful way. He wouldn't have had the financial pressures that usually motivated him to write in earnest.

Despite all his hard work, Irving was fated to receive neither a place in Hoffman's business nor his daughter's hand in marriage. One evening in February 1809, Matilda Hoffman came home with a cold. "Nothing was thought of it at first," Irving said, "but she grew rapidly worse and fell into a consumption." The family, understandably, went into a nervous panic, and Irving tended to Matilda as the illness slowly and painfully wore her away. "I was often by her bed side and in her wandering state of mind she would talk with me," he remembered. "I saw more of the beauty of her mind in that delirious state than I had ever known before."[23]

Matilda was dying; the only question was how long she would linger. By late April, after a two-month illness, her death throes began. "Her dying struggles were painful & protracted," Irving wrote more than a decade later, still haunted by the memory. "For three day[s] & nights I did not leave the house & scarcely slept." By April 26 she was gone. "I was by her when she died," Irving wrote, "—all the family were assembled round her, some praying others weeping, for she was adored by them all. I was the last one she looked upon. . . . She was but seventeen years old when she died."[24]

Irving was destroyed. It was one of the most traumatic events he would ever face, and her death stayed with him for the rest of his life. During periods of hardship or uncertainty, his mind wandered back to those last moments with Matilda in the house on Greenwich. In one notebook, he scrawled, "1809 retd. Jany Peter gone," and on the line just below, "Mat died in April." In the German dictionary he purchased in London in 1816, he scribbled "M Hff died April 26, 1809 aged 17 yr 5 M." In one of his journals he wrote that Matilda "died in the beauty of her youth and in my memory she will ever be young and beautiful." His grief was profound: "She died. It seemed as if all the odour of life was exhaled. There was no longer joy under the sun—the world was blank & nothing was left worth living for."[25]

In the nearly two centuries since Matilda Hoffman's death, Irving scholars have struggled to determine her impact on his life and work. The more romantic biographers tend to throw Matilda's shadow over every moment of his life after 1809, using it to explain his lifelong bachelorhood and tendency toward sentimentalism in his work, while the more cynical believe that he overstated his attachment to Matilda, using it both as a crutch for sympathy and as an excuse to avoid the financial obligations of marriage. The truth, as always, is somewhere in between.

Irving was shaken to his very core by Matilda's death. It took him the better part of a year to really get over the loss, yet he *did* get over it. While sentimentalists would have us believe otherwise, the post-Matilda Washington Irving was neither celibate nor uninterested in marriage. He moved on to experience the highs and lows of love with various women—and men—again and again throughout his life. On the brink of fame, in London, he romped with a group of artistic young men, one of whom he likely was in love with, while at the very height of his success he proposed marriage to another young woman. Irving's perpetual bachelorhood was due mainly to his failure as a suitor rather than to any lack of interest in love or the institution of marriage.

Irving's possible homosexuality must also be considered. While it is clear from his journals and correspondence that he adored Matilda, he also "felt at times rebuked by her superior delicacy & purity, and as if I am a coarse unworthy being in comparison."[26] Her hand, with all its "superior delicacy," also promised the financial security he craved. As a popular young man who would all his life seek not only reputation but acceptance, it is not unlikely that Irving, as a closeted homosexual, would willingly enter into a marriage with a woman he may have idolized but didn't love, not only for the financial stability, but also to keep up the public appearance that he was straight. Once Matilda died, however, Irving the gay bachelor—perhaps literally—was off the hook for the rest of his life. He could simply claim, as sentimental biographers did for decades, that Matilda's death had so scarred him that it was impossible for him to ever marry another.

Irving, the master publicist, knew full well the value of a carefully cultivated public personality. While the private Washington Irving may have recovered from the death of his seventeen-year-old fiancée and gone on to woo others, the public Washington Irving— that writer of elegant, sometimes sentimental stories—mourned his first love for the rest of his life. Indeed, as he grew in age and fame, he surely knew that such a story—true love snatched from him by death's cold hand!—was good for his image, and he did nothing to publicly refute it. A romance novelist of the era couldn't have written a better story, and it was all true—or at least as true as the image-conscious Irving would allow.

Whatever his motivation later in life, one thing remains obvious: the first days after Matilda's death were extremely difficult. Irving was depressed and on the verge of a nervous breakdown. Not quite certain what to do with himself, he retreated 130 miles up the Hudson River to Kinderhook, the estate of his friend William P. Van Ness. He took the still unfinished *esta obra* with him.

Complaining that he "could not bear solitude yet could not enjoy society," he welcomed the relative calm and quiet at this old New York village, where Van Ness's uncle still preached in Dutch at the Claverack Dutch Reformed Church. Religion was no balm to Irving—the Deacon had seen to that—but he always took great comfort in picturesque rural settings, which the Van Ness estate exemplified.

Irving's true solace lay within the pages of *esta obra*. Over the past year, even as he had groaned over the law books in Hoffman's offices, he had continued to revise his manuscript extensively. As he read through his pages in Kinderhook, he realized that he had changed the tone of the work. *Esta obra* was no longer a mere burlesque on someone else's work; he had written it in a more humorous, satiric voice. It still needed work, but Irving believed he had found his way. Sequestering himself in Van Ness's farmhouse, he sat down to write.

"I now altered the plan of the work," Irving explained later. "Discarding all idea of a parody on the *Picture of New York*, I determined that what had been originally intended as an introductory sketch, should comprise the whole work, and form a comic history of the city."[27] Specifically, he decided to focus on the Dutch dynasty that had ruled the city in the seventeenth century. Throwing out everything that didn't pertain to the Dutch settlers, he began compressing the sheaves of notes, references, draft chapters, and false starts into a coherent narrative.

While writing distracted him from his grief, it didn't come easily. In a letter written to Brevoort ten days after Matilda's death, he complained that his mind was so languid that writing was nearly impossible. A week later, he reported that he was able to resume writing. While a "nervous fever" was causing his hair to fall out, he was beginning to feel more himself.

"My time here, though I pass most of it by myself," he wrote, "slips off very pleasantly—and I find so little want of amusement to while it away, that for two days I have scarcely been out of the house." He wasn't a complete hermit—he had befriended the local schoolmaster, Jesse Merwin, "a pleasant good natured fellow, with much native, unimproved shrewdness and considerable humour." Merwin dropped in on Irving for an hour each day, and Irving, always up for a good chat, "found much entertainment in his conversation."[28]

Between drafts of his mock history, he traded letters with Mrs. Hoffman, the one person he felt truly shared his grief. He was becoming increasingly comfortable, he told her in mid-May, with the "half Monastic" life he was leading at Kinderhook, and while he could not bear the thought of returning to the city, the act of writing was improving his spirits. "By constantly exercising my mind, never suffering it to prey upon itself, and resolutely determining to be cheerful," he wrote, "I have in a manner worked myself into a very enviable state of serenity & self possession, which is promoted by the tranquility of every thing around me."[29]

Things were indeed looking brighter at Kinderhook. The trees were in full bloom, and he had discovered a brook in a nearby meadow and a lake where he and Merwin passed countless hours fishing, usually unsuccessfully. He promised his mother he would return to New York to visit as soon as he could, but warned her that "if I return there immediately, I shall only get out of spirits and unable to do any thing."[30]

By the end of May, only a little more than a month after Matilda's death, he believed he was close to finishing his book. Both Brevoort and Paulding read through Irving's drafts, offering advice and encouragement. As he closed in on the end, Irving's nerves began to fray, and his anxiety was clearly visible to his friends. When one packet of materials went temporarily astray in the mail, he dashed off a panicky letter to Brevoort, berating him for addressing the package too cavalierly. "Why did you not drop me a line in the post office at the same time to let me know a pacquet was coming," he wailed. "As to directing it to be left at Hudson," he lectured, "you might as well say *the bank of the river*—I know not where to look for it, or whether it has been put ashore at Hudson or carried to Albany—Do write me immediately on the receipt of this." Meanwhile, he appealed to Paulding to read through the pages he had sent him as quickly as possible, then grumbled to Brevoort that Paulding would "be too minute & either be very long about it or tire himself out before he has got it half ways."[31]

Leaving Kinderhook for New York City in June proved to be as difficult as he had feared. "I must soon leave," he told Mrs. Hoffman, "but it will be necessity not inclination that will lead me. Life seems to flow on so smoothly in the country—without even a ripple to disturb the current, that I could almost float with the stream and glide insensibly through existence." Once back in the city, he contented himself with doing "*nothing*," except saying good-bye to his sister Sarah and her husband, Henry Van Wart, who were leaving to settle permanently in Birmingham, England, for Van Wart's business.[32]

By late summer he was putting the final touches on his book up at Ravenswood, the Hoffmans' family farm near Hell Gate. "My health has been feeble and my spirits depressed," he moaned to Peter, "so that I have found company very irksome, and have shunned it almost entirely."[33] Despite his dampened mood, his pen scratched on.

By late October the book was finished—or so he thought—and Irving trekked down to Philadelphia to secretly prepare it for printing. But he didn't stop revising—a habit that would annoy printers for the rest of his career—and, in a midnight marathon writing session, he wrote out an entirely new section, which he was determined to insert in the manuscript already at the printers. "Tomorrow I begin—by god," he told Brevoort on October 23, resolving to let the book go to press at last. He instructed Brevoort to "get Jim [Paulding] as well as yourself to prepare some squibs &c to attract attention to the work when it comes out."[34]

There was a good reason for the squibs, as well as the decision to print in Philadelphia, rather than in New York. The name on the title page of Irving's book, now called A History of New York, was not his own but that of Diedrich Knickerbocker, an old, wry, petulant Dutch historian created by Irving to serve not only as the narrator of his mock history, but also as its conscience and commentator. Knickerbocker was more than a pen name; for the first time, Irving had given one of his pseudonyms its own distinct personality and unique voice. Knickerbocker breathed with a life that was lacking in the old bachelor Jonathan Oldstyle or any of the various personalities Irving had assumed in the pages of Salmagundi, and Irving was determined—through a shrewd bit of advanced marketing—to make Knickerbocker just as real to his fellow New Yorkers. If he played it right, by the time his book was released in December, New Yorkers would have a vested interest in the old historian.

His plan depended a great deal on the "squibs" he had asked Brevoort and Paulding to prepare, a series of notices in the newspapers designed to catch the public's attention and whet its appetite for Knickerbocker's book. While the notices were Irving's idea, he left the details to Paulding and Brevoort. What the two young men delivered, and the buzz it created, was more than Irving could have hoped for.

"DISTRESSING," headlined a notice in the October 26, 1809, edition of the New York Evening Post. The single word was eloquent in its panic, and readers pored over the rest of the text, equally alarmed and intrigued:

Left his lodgings some time since and has not been heard of, a small elderly gentleman, dressed in an old black coat and cocked hat, by the name of *Knickerbocker*. As there are some reasons for believing he is not entirely in his right mind, and as great anxiety is entertained about him, any information concerning him left either at the Columbian Hotel, Mulberry-street, or at the office of this paper, will be thankfully received.

P.S. Printers of newspapers would be aiding the cause of humanity in giving an insertion to the above.[35]

The notice ran in several newspapers over the next few days, and concerned New Yorkers were on the lookout for the little man in black, certain that such a distinct-looking figure—for the cocked hat was already passing out of style by 1809—would be easy to spot. Yet no one reported seeing the gentleman until November 6, when a reader signing himself simply as "A Traveller" provided the following bit of information:

Sir,—Having read in your paper of the 26th October last, a paragraph respecting an old gentleman by the name of *Knickerbocker*, who was missing from his lodging; if it would be any relief to his friends, or furnish them with any clue to discover where he is, you may inform them that a person answering the description given, was seen by the passengers of the Albany stage, early in the morning, about four or five weeks since, resting himself by the side of the road, a little above King's Bridge. He had in his hand a small bundle tied in a red bandana handkerchief; he appeared to be traveling northward and was very much fatigued and exhausted.[36]

Irving's ploy was working. According to Pierre Irving, one New York City authority was so troubled by the thought of the old man wandering around the countryside that he contacted Wall Street attorney John Treat Irving to discuss the possibility of offering a reward for the safe return of Mr. Knickerbocker to the Columbian Hotel.[37] The notices had generated the kind of response a modern marketing firm could only dream of—but Irving and his collaborators weren't done yet.

The first two notices had effectively introduced the eccentric Mr. Knickerbocker to the public, and teased them with the mention of his small package wrapped in a red handkerchief. On November 16 it was time to give readers another taste:

To the Editor of the Evening Post

Sir,—You have been good enough to publish in your paper a paragraph about *Mr. Diedrich Knickerbocker*, who was missing so strangely some time since. Nothing satisfactory has been heard of the old gentleman since; but a *very curious kind of written book* has been found in his room, in his own handwriting. Now I wish you to notice him, if he is still alive, that if he does not return soon and pay off his bill for boarding and lodging, I shall have to dispose of his book to satisfy me for the same.

I am sir, your humble servant,
SETH HANDASIDE

Landlord of the Independent Columbian Hotel,
Mulberry-street[38]

New York was buzzing with anticipation. Would Knickerbocker return to the hotel in time to claim his book, readers wondered, or would Seth Handaside publish it to recoup the costs of Knickerbocker's room and board? What kind of book was it? Even those New Yorkers who suspected some sort of ruse—astute residents knew there was no Independent Columbian Hotel—wondered what the punch line of this rather elaborate joke would be.

Irving and his collaborators had brilliantly pushed the public to the edge of its seat, and it was in this atmosphere of anticipation that *A History of New York*—its official title was the somewhat wordy *A History of New York from the Beginning of the World to the End of the Dutch Dynasty by Diedrich Knickerbocker*—was finally published on December 6. But not before a final notice in the November 29 issue of the *Evening Post:*

LITERARY NOTICE.

Innskeep & Bradford have in the press and will shortly publish,

A History of New York,

In two volumes, duodecimo. Price three dollars.

Containing an account of its discovery and settlement, with its internal policy, manners, customs, wars, &c. &c., under the Dutch government, furnishing many curious and interesting particulars never before published, and which are gathered from various manuscript and other authenticated sources, the whole being interspersed with philosophical speculations and moral precepts.

This work was found in the chamber of Mr. Diedrich Knickerbocker, the old gentleman whose sudden and mysterious disappearance has been noticed. It is published in order to discharge certain debts he has left behind.[39]

Irving held his breath, waiting for the reaction. He needn't have worried; the public devoured it. Irving's masterful media gimmick had done the trick. But curiosity alone wasn't what kept the volumes moving off the stands in Broadway. As the prickly Knickerbocker, Irving wove a daring, magnificent story in his two-volume work. It was a performance unlike anything readers had seen from an American writer.

Irving opened his tale ambitiously, with a brief history of the world, an account of how the American continent had originally been populated, and a discussion of the ethics of the "right of Discovery," which entitled the discovering party to eject the native population from its own land. With this necessary justification out of the way, Irving followed the intrepid explorer Henry Hudson as he promptly, albeit accidentally, discovered the island of Manhattan, which the Dutch immediately colonized and dubbed "New Amsterdam."

In the next five sections, Irving explained how, in less than a century, the bumbling Dutch government, led by one colorfully inept governor after another, managed to lose their new colony. Irving played fair; his history was accurate as far as names and events were concerned. Even the obscure sources he cited—residue of the idea that had inspired the whole project in the first place—were, for the most part, genuine. The real tale was in the telling. His sense of humor as sharp as it would ever be, Irving led his readers on a romp through the administrations of three of New Amsterdam's seventeenth-century governors, and proceeded to lampoon nineteenth-century politicians.

Under Irving's pen, New Amsterdam's first governor, Wouter Van Twiller, became a sleeping, smoking, do-nothing administrator who presided successfully over his colony in spite of—perhaps because of—his laissez-faire approach to governing. Later his polar opposite, the busybody Peter Stuyvesant—the hero of Knickerbocker's narrative—fights not only with invading armies but also with his own people, and loses the colony not from inaction but because they want him to hand over the colony peacefully to the English. Stuyvesant complies, and retires in style.

Readers may have hooted at the antics of Van Twiller and Stuyvesant, but they roared the loudest at the exploits of William "The Testy" Kieft, a thinly disguised parody of President Thomas Jefferson. Just as modern readers would recognize references to Bill Clinton's libido or George W. Bush's garbled syntax, so 1809 readers picked up on the distinctly Jeffersonian traits displayed by Kieft: his red stockings, his penchant for waging war by proclamation, and his unusual scientific experiments, such as carts that went before the horse, or Dutch ovens that required no fire.[40]

For the Federalist Irving, the send-up was sincere, and he

unloaded like a Dutch blunderbuss, spraying his shot at nearly everything. Irving's Kieft is a scolder who loves to listen to himself talk, lecturing his enemies and his people in declarations "written in thundering long sentences, not one word of which was under five syllables." His policies, which "entangled the government . . . in more knots during his administration, than half a dozen successors could have untied," were justified by the bogeyman of "*economy*—a talismanic term, which by constant use and frequent mention, has ceased to be formidable in our eyes, but which has as terrible a potency as any in the arcane of necromancy." The humor could be subtle—such as when Kieft's policies inspired the birth of two new political parties—or heavy-handed: "How William the Testy enriched the Province by a multitude of good-for-nothing laws, and came to be the Patron of Lawyers and Bum-Bailiffs," the title of one chapter glibly states.[41]

While the timely political satire was part of the appeal to his audience, knowledge of 1809 politics isn't required for today's readers to enjoy *A History of New York*. Indeed, much of Irving's take on politics, politicians, and the political process has aged remarkably well. In his *History* Irving raged against politicians who talk but don't act, political parties that disagree with each other for the sake of disagreeing, wars fought through proclamation while generals strut, and governments that approve useless policies in the name of economy.

The book is hilarious—remarkable, considering Irving's state of mind when he completed it. There are moments of pure slapstick: fat messengers split their pants as they climb down from their horses; portly Dutch generals hurl vegetables at each other in battle and wrestle on the ground with the contents of their pockets spilling out; and battling governors fall elegantly into piles of cow manure.[42] At other times, the humor is impish, even crass, and Irving cackles from its pages like a schoolboy, such as when he robustly describes the Dutch ship *Good Vrouw*: "Like the beauteous model, who was declared the greatest belle in Amsterdam, it was full in the bows, with a pair of enormous cat-heads, a copper bottom, and withal, a most prestigious poop!"[43] And then there are moments of biting irreverence, as when Knickerbocker explains the origin of the name "Manhattan":

> The name which is most current among the vulgar (such as members of assembly and bank directors) is *Manhattan*—which is said to have originated from a custom among the squaws, in the early settlement, of wearing men's wool hats, as is still done among many tribes. "Hence," we are told by an old governor, somewhat of a wag, who flourished almost a century since, and had paid a visit to the wits of Philadelphia—"Hence arose the appellation of Man-hat-on, first given to the Indians, and afterwards to the island"—a stupid joke!—but well enough for a governor.[44]

This is some of Irving's most confident writing—and many readers and critics have rightly argued that *A History of New York* is the standard against which all of his subsequent works should be judged. It is Irving at his most irreverent, disrespectful, and rebellious—and for now, the twenty-six-year-old New Yorker was gleefully shouting from the rooftops.

His readers loved it. "It took with the public & gave me celebrity, as an original work was something remarkable & uncommon in America," Irving wrote years later, still surprised by its reception. "I was noticed caressed & for a time elated by the popularity I gained." Indeed, Irving's identity as Knickerbocker became one of the worst-kept secrets. As the *History* made its way across New England, down the Atlantic seaboard, and toward the expanding West, Irving was greeted as "Diedrich." "Wherever I went I was overwhelmed with attention," he wrote. "I was full of youth and animation . . . and I was quite flushed with this early taste of public favour." With his uniquely American book and his uniquely American voice, Irving became something else that hadn't been seen before: a true American celebrity.[45]

The few newspapers and magazines that reviewed books took

favorable notice: "The meager annals of this short-lived Dutch colony have afforded the ground work for this amusing book, which is certainly the wittiest our press has ever produced," hailed an anonymous reviewer in the *Monthly Anthology and Boston Review*, adding that, "if anything can be hoped from ridicule, the rash imbecility of those ignorant plagiarists, who have been for some years past carrying on war by proclamations and resolutions, might by this work be shamed into a retreat and concealment." Seconding the *Review*'s accolades, a Baltimore newspaper correspondent wrote, "If it be true, as Sterne says, that a man draws a nail out of his coffin every time he laughs, after reading Irving's book your coffin will certainly fall to pieces."[46]

History earned Irving considerable reputation and celebrity abroad. Sir Walter Scott, Irving's idol who would later become a close friend, compared him to Jonathan Swift—high praise indeed—and said his sides had been "absolutely sore with laughing" as he read it aloud to his friends and family. Both Lord Byron and Samuel Taylor Coleridge were fans, and Charles Dickens later told Irving that he had worn his copy out from carrying it around with him.[47]

Not everyone was so amused, however. Some Dutch readers—including Judge Hoffman's own mother—didn't appreciate the digs at their ancestors. "Your good friend, the old lady, came home in a great stew this evening," Mrs. Hoffman teased Irving as she related the incident: "Such a scandalous story had got about town—a book had come out, called a History of New York; nothing but a satire and ridicule of the old Dutch people—and they said you was the author; but from this foul slander, I'll venture to say, she has defended you. She was in quite a heat about it."[48]

One particularly offended Dutch frau even declared that, had she been a man, she would horsewhip Irving within an inch of his life. Delighted, Irving sought an introduction and, naturally, quickly won over his critic. For the most part, it was impossible for offended parties to stay angry once they fell under Irving's considerable charm. Visiting Dutch neighborhoods in Albany in early 1810, he reported that he had "somehow or another formed acquaintance with some of the good people . . . and have even made my way and intrenched myself strongly in the parlors of several genuine Dutch families, who had declared utter hostility to me." Looking back, Irving could only smile at all the fuss. "It was a confounded, impudent thing in such a youngster as I was to be meddling in this way with old family names," he said, "but I did not dream of offense."[49]

It wasn't long before New Yorkers embraced the name "Knickerbocker" as their own. With his flamboyant history, Irving had provided for New Yorkers not only a sense of their own heritage—New York was, until then, the only state in the Union that didn't have its own written history[50]—but also a sense of their own unique identity. Knickerbocker became emblematic of the city and the people; with his unshakable, unimpressed, irreverent attitude, he personified New York's very identity. To be a Knickerbocker, then as now, was to be a New Yorker.

In his introduction to the 1848 author's revised edition, Irving wrote of his delight not only at finding that people had embraced this "haphazard production" of his youth, but also at learning "its very name become a 'household word,' and used to give the home stamp to every thing recommended for popular acceptation, such as . . . Knickerbocker insurance companies, Knickerbocker bread and Knickerbocker ice."[51] Today the name is used by the city's professional basketball team, the New York Knicks.

Writing to Van Ness twelve days after unleashing Knickerbocker, Irving was relaxed and at ease, more concerned about what was playing at the local theaters than his own reviews. He was also flush with cash; the book earned him about $3,000, a tidy sum in 1809.

Basking in the glow of his newfound success, he had no immediate plans to follow up on it. Instead, in early 1810, he traveled to Albany where, at the urging of friends, he hoped to secure a political appointment to one of the clerkships available in the New York state courts. A year earlier, he had hoped to earn enough repute with his writing that he would be a shoo-in for a political appointment; now, he had not only published a phenomenally successful book, he also had the help of the well-connected Hoffman and his brother-in-law Daniel Paris, a member of the Council of Appointments.

The anticipated appointment never came, "mainly through the counterworking of some candidates for other offices," Pierre Irving later explained. Washington dismissed it with a shrug; he had been uncomfortable playing the patronage game—he compared himself and his fellow office seekers to "a cloud of locusts, [who] have descended upon the city to devour every plant and herb, and every 'green thing.'"[52] Besides, there was no need to look for a job: the family business had not only recovered, but was finally booming, and with his fame he remained a highly sought-after dinner guest and evening companion.

With financial pressures gone, Irving had no impulsion to keep writing. He was famous. Surely, if he couldn't find work, work would find him. Yet when publisher John Hall approached him about participating in a literary journal, Irving balked. "I do not wish to meddle with my pen for a long while," he wrote Hall. "The affectionate solicitude and extreme liberality of my brothers (who are engaged in commerce) have placed me beyond the necessity of using my pen as a means of support—and while they have admitted me to a share in the profits of regular business, I am left to the free indulgence of my own tastes & habits. Not being pressed therefore and hurrying into a random exercise of my talents, such as they are, I wish to proceed as cautiously as possible; and if my caution does not enable me to write better, it will at least preserve me from the hazardous error of writing a great deal."[53] The new American celebrity was determined, for now, to enjoy his fame and remain a man of leisure. The pen lay dormant for another nine years.

5

Adrift
1810–1815

My literary notoriety had made me an object of attention, I was continu-
ally drawn into Society, my time & thoughts dissipated and my spirits
jaded. I became weary of every thing and of myself.

—Washington Irving to Mrs. Amelia Foster, 1823

"I HAVE NOW NO PROSPECT AHEAD, nor scheme, nor air castle to
engage my mind withal," Irving sighed in a letter to Mrs. Hoffman in early 1810, "so that it matters but little where I am, and perhaps I cannot be more agreeably or profitably employed than in Van
Ness' library."[1]

He should have been so lucky. Such thoughts were attractive
but, he knew, unrealistic. His book was a success and he enjoyed a
national reputation, but Irving clearly did not believe his future lay
in his pen. As he struggled to come to terms with what his "real"
occupation would be, he also struggled to come to terms with himself. He was approaching thirty years old, and while he was by no
means having a midlife crisis, even by nineteenth-century lifespans,
he was fully aware that he was floundering.

Once again his brothers, who were always looking out for him,
rallied to his side. Peter and Ebenezer—who together had recently
set up a shipping business with offices in New York and Liverpool
specializing in "whitehead, glassware, Epaulets, Sword Knots, Sashes,
Hardware, &c"[2]—approached Washington about joining their firm

as a silent partner. By providing Washington with a fifth of their company's profits, the brothers hoped to provide their youngest with a regular source of income that would allow him to pursue his writing. Irving agreed, becoming the "and Company" of P. & E. Irving and Company in New York, and P. Irving and Company in Liverpool. Such financial security, however, only served to silence, rather than stimulate, Irving's literary muse. While Peter purchased and shipped in Liverpool, and Ebenezer made sales in New York, Washington simply killed time. "I cared nothing for money," he wrote later, "it seemed to come too late to do me good. I read a good deal at times, but I could not bring myself to write, I had grown indifferent to literary reputation."[3]

An opportunity found him in late June, when he was approached by Archibald Campbell, brother of Scottish poet Thomas Campbell, about publishing two of Thomas's poems, "O'Connor's Child" and "Gertrude of Wyoming," in the United States. Irving appealed to Ann Hoffman's new husband, bookseller Charles Nicholas, about underwriting publication of Campbell's poetry. Nicholas agreed, but on one condition: that Irving write an introductory biography of the poet.

It seemed the ideal setup, but Irving fliply regarded it as "uphill work." Archibald provided sparse biographical information about his brother, and it was all Irving could do to polish the rough notes he scribbled in his notebook into something readable. The result was a clunky, uninspired biographical sketch. While the piece was well received by the public, Irving groused that it had been "most horribly misprinted, with outrages on grammar & good language that made my blood run cold to look at them."[4]

He frittered away the rest of the summer with side trips to Philadelphia with the Hoffmans, sailing excursions with Brevoort, and parties at his favorite new hangout, Highland Grange, home of the boisterous Captain Frederick Philipse, "a true Lad of Kilkenny," Irving remarked approvingly.[5] Sitting 150 feet above the Hudson, Highland Grange offered a spectacular view of West Point directly across the river, and Irving spent countless mornings lounging on the lawn scribbling descriptions of the surrounding landscapes in his notebooks. Despite—or perhaps because of—his annoyance with his work on the Campbell biography, Irving continued to privately fine-tune his writing, searching for just the right turn of phrase:

> Morning—5 o clock—sky perfectly clear—Sun not up yet—a Soft mellow yellowish light over the landscape— perfectly calm—river like a glass. In some places almost black from the dark shadows of the mountains—in others the colour of the heavens—long sheets of mist suspended in mid air half way up the mountains—One large mass entirely shrouds the upper part of the mountain above buttermilk falls, and seem to droop into the water like a veil. Sound of the cattle bells from opposite shore—cocks crowing—roll of a drum from West point—Grass white with dew drops.[6]

The devotion to his craft didn't last long, however. With his brothers continuing to support him, there was little reason to take up the pen in earnest.

As it turns out, politics were about to occupy his time. That winter, stress was running high in the financial district over the direction the U.S. Congress was taking as it considered two pieces of legislation in which the merchant class had a vested interest.

The first bill was the Non-Importation Act, an act of legislative revenge against the British and French for their seizure of American ships, and for barriers the two nations had erected to impede American trade. A major cog in the machinery that would eventually propel the United States into the War of 1812, the legislation had been enacted by Congress in March 1809 to prohibit trade with France and England. But bungled diplomacy and crossed signals had resulted in trade being reopened, then closed again over the course of 1809 and 1810, much to the frustration of merchants, Congress, and President James Madison.

New legislation had been introduced, stating that trade would be resumed with both France and Britain until one of the two nations withdrew its offensive decrees—at which point the United States would cease trading with the other. No fool, Napoleon leaped at the offer, repealing a few offensive decrees, but hiding in the details of the agreement a trapdoor that allowed for the continued confiscation of American ships in all harbors of the French Empire. On November 10, 1810, Madison cluelessly issued a proclamation lauding France for removing its edicts, and demanded that Britain repeal its barriers to American trade by February 1811. With that deadline approaching, Madison fussed, Congress argued, and nervous merchants fretted in agony.

Compounding the problem was the expiring charter for the First Bank of the United States. The brainchild of Alexander Hamilton, the bank had been chartered by Congress in 1791, with responsibility for unifying national currency and shoring up debt from the Revolutionary War. A bank in name only, the First Bank was actually a private corporation whose profits passed to its stockholders. While New Yorkers watched the bank with an eye toward profit, it was viewed warily by western members of Congress who rightly believed it was interested only in granting favors to the privileged.

Worse, the congressional elections of 1810 and 1811 had not been kind to the mercantile class. The Jefferson administration's banner of agrarian reform was being waved by powerful new southern Republicans, including a remarkably committed delegation of South Carolinians, including freshman representatives John C. Calhoun, Langdon Cheves, and William Lowndes. The merchant class was on the defensive.

Given all this, Ebenezer and William thought it wise to send a representative to the nation's capital to keep tabs on Congress and act as a lobbyist for the family's business interests. The brothers hoped that Washington, with his natural social skills, would be an ideal lobbyist. They would be disappointed.

Irving arrived in Washington, D.C., on a cold January night, just in time to learn that First Lady Dolley Madison was hosting one of her famous "Wednesday Drawing Rooms" that evening at the

White House. Mrs. Madison's Wednesday-night sessions provided a regular opportunity for guests of different political parties—a new phenomenon in D.C. and the nation—to mix and press the flesh. It also gave chief executive and First Wallflower James Madison the opportunity to be seen and to make his case for the Non-Importation Act with congressmen and senators in a more relaxed setting. If there was ever an ideal opportunity for Irving to get inside information from both political parties, this was it. Unfortunately for the ever-patient Ebenezer and William in New York, the only party their youngest brother was interested in involved drinking, food, dancing, and conversation. "I swore by all my gods, I would be there—," Irving told Brevoort. "But how? was the question."[7]

A good question indeed, but Irving was never one to let lack of an invitation stand in the way of attending a good bash. He dressed for the evening in his most dandified manner—"pease blossoms & silk stockings, gird up my loins," he wrote Brevoort—then, utilizing the charm that had secured him invitations to the most fashionable drawing rooms of Europe, managed to attach himself to a group of guests invited to the evening's event, including a fellow New Yorker who offered to introduce him to Mrs. Madison. In no time at all, Irving "emerged from dirt & darkness into the blazing splendour of Mrs. Madison's Drawing room."[8]

Blazing it must have been. During Thomas Jefferson's administration, the room into which Irving now emerged had been used as the president's private sitting room. The use of such central rooms for this purpose was understandable, since the chief executive was known to greet guests in his slippers, but Dolley Madison would have none of that. She had converted the space into an elegant parlor and painted it a warm sunflower yellow, with drapes and furniture of the same hue. Here Irving shook off the cold D.C. evening and was "most graciously received" by Mrs. Madison and her sisters.

That evening's gathering—comprised largely of lonely congressmen and senators stranded in the city as the current congressional session stretched into the winter—had packed the suite with nearly two hundred guests. Irving happily dove into the throng—

"a crowded collection of great & little men of ugly old women and beautiful young ones"—as piano and guitar music encouraged guests to dance. Within minutes he "was hand and glove with half the people in the assemblage."[9]

Irving was enchanted by his hostess, and equally captivated by her two sisters. "Mrs. Madison is a fine, portly, buxom dame—who has a smile & a pleasant word for every body," he told Brevoort. "Her sisters, Mrs. Cutts & Mrs. Washington are like the two Merry Wives of Windsor." Compared with his outgoing hostess and her flamboyant sisters, the small, timid president paled in comparison. "As to Jemmy Madison—," Irving noted, unimpressed, "ah! Poor Jemmy! He is but a withered little apple-John—But of this no more—perish the thought that would militate against sacred things—Mortals avaunt! Touch not the lords anointed!"[10]

After his successful infiltration of the White House, Irving settled into respectable quarters for the rest of his stay in Washington, leaving behind his room in Georgetown for the home of John Peter Van Ness, a former New York congressman and the brother of his friend from Kinderhook, William P. Van Ness. John Peter, currently serving as major of militia in the District of Columbia, had opened his river-view home to several guests. Irving found the living arrangements quite agreeable, given that the boarders included two young ladies who delighted in gossip and gregarious conversation. "You see I am in clover—happy dog!—close Jacob!—& all that," Irving wrote with a wink.[11]

More relevant to the task at hand, the Senate had received a petition from the directors of the Bank of New York, "praying the renewal of the Charter of the Bank of the United States." But with both houses working in closed session late in the week, Irving could get his hands on very little information. Not that he was interested. "I am much too occupied & indeed distracted here, by the multiplicity of objects before me, to write with any degree of coherency," he wrote to Brevoort in early February. "I have become acquainted with almost every body here, and find the most complete medley of character I ever mingled amongst."[12]

The "medley of character" included a thirty-one-year-old Federalist congressman from Schaghticoke, New York, named Herman Knickerbocker, whom Irving delightedly referred to as "my cousin." Knickerbocker had not stood for reelection in 1810, and was serving as a lame-duck congressman as the current session of Congress sputtered to a close. Irving reported to Brevoort that they had become "two most loving friends" and that Knickerbocker was "overjoyed at the happy commencement of our family compact." Whether Irving had used Herman as inspiration for his own Knickerbocker is debatable. It seems unlikely that a young congressman would have served as the model for the crusty old historian, and Irving's report to Brevoort of his meeting with Knickerbocker makes it doubtful the two had been previously acquainted.

Irving maintained an active though apolitical social calendar, dining one night with Federalists, the next with Republicans—a savvy strategy for gleaning information on the pending legislation, had he any interest in doing so. But he was far more concerned with personalities than politics, and made the following observation in a letter to Brevoort in early February:

> You would be amused, were you to arrive here just now to see the odd, & heterogeneous circle of acquaintance I have formed. One day I am dining with a knot of honest, furious federalists, who are damning all their opponents as a set of consummate scoundrels, pandars of Bonaparte, &c &c, The next day I dine perhaps with some of the very men I have heard thus anathematized, and find them equally honest, warm & indignant—and if I take their word for it, I had been dining the day before with some of the greatest knaves in the nation—men absolutely paid & suborned by the British government.[13]

Irving's contacts were a veritable who's who of Washington, D.C. In the course of one week he dined at the Capitol Hill home of architect Benjamin Latrobe, shared a meal with the secretary of the navy, and attended a ball at the residence of Mayor Robert Brent.

And there were Mrs. Madison's levees and dances at the Van Ness mansion. "At all these parties you meet with so many intelligent people," Irving said with satisfaction, "that your mind is continually & delightfully exercised."

To his surprise and delight, Irving and the First Lady had become friends. Mrs. Madison admired the young man, more for his social and dancing prowess than his writing, and Irving spoke of her fondly for the rest of his life. As for the president, while Mrs. Madison herself once noted that her husband would stand in the middle of the room with no one to talk to, Irving was impressed by the president's skills as an active listener—"a most agreeable man in conversation." Yet looking back, Irving wondered, "What did he say. . . . I came to reccollect I had talked entirely myself." The president, in fact, was also a fan—"the president pronounced me a promising young man," Irving reported, "but that I talked too much."[14]

Another well-placed friend, Secretary of State Robert Smith, had even floated Irving's name with the president as a possible secretary to the American legation to France. "I make no doubt [the president] will express a wish in my favor on the subject," Irving told William confidently, "more especially as Mrs. Madison is a sworn friend of mine, and indeed all the ladies of the household and myself great cronies."[15]

Curiously, the appointment never materialized. While Irving was a relative newcomer to the political scene, he had a significant network in Washington and had obviously made an impression. Further, his reputation as the author of A History of New York certainly indicated he would be an ideal candidate for a secretarial position. Amid the head-scratching, there was some speculation that Irving was rejected outright by minister-designate Joel Barlow because Barlow had allegedly heard Irving criticize his epic poem The Columbiad. Not to worry, Irving told William, he already had a backup plan: "I shall pursue a plan I had some time since contemplated, of studying for a while, and then travelling about the country for the purpose of observing the manners and characters of the various parts of it, with a view to writing a work, which, if I have any acquaintance with my own talents, will be far more profitable and reputable than any thing I have yet written. Of this, however, you will not speak to others."[16] Nothing came of this contingency plan either. At the time, however, William had no reason to doubt his brother's resolve—after all, wasn't this the young man who had written a best seller while recovering from a severe depression?

In the meantime, there was, at last, activity on the bank issue. Senator William Crawford of Georgia introduced legislation on February 5 to renew the charter, and Irving reported its progress dutifully back to William. Things finally came to a head when the Senate deadlocked, and Vice President George Clinton cast the deciding vote to kill the charter bill. A week later the House of Representatives pushed the United States one step closer to war by passing the revised Non-Importation Act, and then adjourned on March 3. The 11th Congress wound to a close, as did Irving's services—such as they were—as a lobbyist.

For Irving, it was just as well. With the adjournment of Congress, Washington, D.C., was a ghost town. The absence of members meant a dearth of dancing, dinners, and social gatherings of any merit, which Irving found dreadful. "You cannot imagine how forlorn this desert City appears to me, now the great tide of casual population has rolled away," he complained to Brevoort. It was time to go home.[17]

The demands of the firm of P. & E. Irving and Company kept Irving busy throughout the spring, but whatever free time he had he spent at the theater and at evening tea parties. His old friend Cooper—who was actively courting Mary Fairlie—was performing with George Frederick Cooke in New York, and Irving attended their performances with considerable amusement. Cooke had a tendency to drink too much, and the audience once heckled him so belligerently during a curtain call that he rattled his sword at the crowd, telling them they were lucky it was only a prop. The audience only howled all the louder.[18]

In early May Irving moved out of his mother's house and in with Brevoort—an arrangement neither had much time to enjoy, as

Brevoort had at last secured a full-time position with John Jacob Astor. When Astor struck out for Mackinac, Michigan, he took Brevoort with him. Irving wouldn't lack company for long, however, as June marked the return of Gouverneur Kemble and his younger brother Peter from their tour of Europe. The Lads were back.

At this point, the new literary projects Irving claimed he was pondering were doomed—for the Lads, especially Peter Kemble, were up to no good. "Since his return, we have treated Peter, the late Prince Regent, with great contempt, and take all possible occasions to flout him and piss upon him," Irving wrote boorishly.

> I am convinced that there is nothing on earth so truly *despiseable*, as a great man shorn of his power. Peter however consoles himself by courting all the little girls in town, who are under Sixteen. . . . He has likewise become a notable leerer at buxom chamber maids and servant girls, and there is not a little bitch of a house maid that runs *proud* about the streets, but what peter has had the nosing of her—not that the little villain tups them all, but he is one of your little gluttons whose eyes are greedier than his belly, and where he honestly Rodgers one, he dishonors a dozen with his lascivious looks.[19]

Clearly, these were young men who needed something to do. Irving acknowledged as much. "I felt a degree of apathy growing upon me," he later wrote, "which was dismal."[20] And while young Peter Kemble continued to ravish random chambermaids—and consequently underwent treatment for venereal disease in the summer of 1812—Irving's attentions seemed to have fallen on Mrs. Jean Renwick, the mother of his friend James Renwick.

Whether Irving's relationship with Mrs. Renwick was sexual is debatable, but it is clear from the enthusiastic exhortations in his letters—an "excellent lady!" he gushes—that he adored her. A widow, and eleven years his senior, Jean Renwick still had the considerable charm she had shown at age fifteen, when she inspired poet Robert Burns to pen the lyrics to "When First I Saw Fair

Jeanie's Face" and "The Blue-Eyed Lassie." Indeed, Irving maintained the sort of playful, admiring relationship with her that he had with Mrs. Hoffman. While Brevoort, too, was a devotee, Irving's bubbling adulation was without equal. The two chattered playfully about politics, with Mrs. Renwick arguing her points so forcefully, Irving said, that "after three quarter of an hours fighting I was fain to sheer off with a broken heart and absolutely went supperless to bed." This was the kind of banter Irving excelled at, and the fact that Mrs. Renwick was a worthy adversary likely endeared her to Irving all the more.[21]

Distracted partly by business, but mostly by personal matters, Irving limited his literary output to revisions of his own work, as he focused on reprints and a second edition of Knickerbocker. In July an edition of *Salmagundi* appeared in London to good reviews, "much more favorably than I had expected," he told William. "On the whole . . . I think we came off very handsomely, and I can only hope the other critics may be as merciful."[22]

It was slow going on any new work. There were just too many interesting distractions, and Irving berated himself for his own inattention. "Pleasure is but a transient stimulus, and leaves the mind more enfeebled than before," he groaned to Brevoort. "Give me rugged toil, fierce disputation, wrangling controversy, harassing research, give me any thing that calls forth the energies of the mind."[23] Such hand-wringing was typical, especially when his conscience nagged at him to work—although it was hardly ever persuasive.

"Oh! Man, man, what a villainous compound of crudities art thou!" Brevoort wrote from Mackinac in mock sympathy. "One moment the mercury of thy soul sinks ten degrees below despair, and the next moment (from causes inscrutable) rises again, to the highest pitch of hope and enthusiasm."[24]

It was at this time that Brevoort began writing Irving of his adventures with Astor on the western frontier—more specifically, his impressions of the Native American tribes that he met along the way. Brevoort was incredibly sympathetic in his portrayal of the

Indians, and described their self-government with awe and admiration. He included in his letters copies of Indian orations, which he begged Irving to publish in the newspapers, as "they convey a faithful picture of their present and anticipated distresses."[25]

While Brevoort's letters reflect his employer's interest in the affairs of the Indians—the Non-Importation Act had also prevented Indian tribes from importing critical goods—Brevoort found it deplorable that the Native Americans should have grown so dependent on such goods in the first place. He also disapproved of the way tribes were treated by the westward-pushing United States, and told a story of an attempt to purchase a small parcel of Indian land, which was roundly rebuffed by the Indian Council. Under Brevoort's pen, Manifest Destiny took on a decidedly sinister tone: "They refused to sell on any terms for (said they) if we give you a spot the bigness of one of our feet, you will take up a handful of sand and scattering it as far as the winds blow, swear that the whole extent on which it has fallen is yours, therefore you shall not have it.—We caution you not to do as others of your Nation have done—to purchase our lands for a trifle of some drunken worthless individuals of our tribe, and make us all responsible for their acts."[26]

Irving, too, was sympathetic to the plight of the Indians, and had already lampooned their treatment by the American government in *A History of New York*. Brevoort's observations only reinforced Irving's already progressive, though still romantic, views on the Indians.

Brevoort also continued in his role as Irving's de facto literary agent, circulating copies of Knickerbocker among the frontier fur traders. "You contribute more to their merriment & pleasure than you probably would if you were here yourself," Brevoort told Irving. "One of the Traders swears you must have wintered among the Indians, for you appear to know them so well."[27]

The thriving fur industry soon forced Brevoort to make an extended business trip to Europe. The absence weighed heavily on Irving, and for the next twenty months he was practically heartbroken. "I have not been very well since your departure, and am completely out of spirits. I do miss you terribly," he wrote Brevoort shakily. Life, for the moment, was drained of vibrancy. "I dined yesterday with a small party at Mrs Renwicks and was at a tea party in the evening," he wrote, "and yet passed one of the heaviest days I have toiled through this long time."[28]

With the arrival of spring, however, Irving at last shook off the stupor that had paralyzed his pen throughout 1811. With renewed enthusiasm, he turned to the final polish on a new edition of *A History of New York*.

He had actually begun to revise the work almost immediately after its publication in late 1809. The first edition contained some careless printing errors, and Irving set to work correcting those errors and tweaking the text. Printing errors aside, the popularity of the first edition had made a second inevitable. For nearly three years the public had been awaiting the revised edition—*Port-Folio* of July 1812 reported with anticipation that "the ingenious author of Diedrich Knickerbocker, is said to be preparing a new edition for the press"—and Irving didn't disappoint. The new edition sold well, and Irving was paid a relatively generous sum for his work—$1,200, or about $16,000 in today's money, for a print run of five hundred copies.

He needed the money. On June 18 Congress formally declared war on Great Britain, and the War of 1812 hit the New York merchant classes particularly hard. Irving abandoned his apartment for a "snug retreat" in the hills opposite Hell Gate where he could read and perhaps start on a new work.

Perhaps. Instead, he spent two months at Hell Gate visiting friends, gossiping, and dining out. Much was happening in their social circle, and Irving did his best to keep up with the chatter. The Fascinating Fairlie had finally married Cooper on June 11, and Irving, his eyes emerald with jealousy, snorted to Brevoort that their marriage marked "the end of a dismal courtship and the commencement I fear of an unhappy union." In the same vein, he remarked nastily on the virtue of a mutual female friend who "has been acting very much the part of the Dog in the manger—she cannot enjoy her own chastity but seems unwilling to let anybody else do it."[29]

That fall another project landed in his lap. The second edition of *A History of New York* had caught the eye of a Philadelphia bookseller named Moses Thomas, who had recently purchased a literary magazine called *Select Reviews*. Thomas asked Irving if he would be interested in serving as its editor starting with the January 1813 edition. The content of *Select Reviews* consisted mainly of reprints of European works, and Irving's job—or so he thought—would be to choose and edit the works to be reprinted.

It seemed easy enough, and to sweeten the deal, Thomas offered Irving an annual salary of $1,500, the equivalent of about $20,000 today. Irving accepted, likely glad for both the work and the money, though he told Peter casually that he regarded it as "an amusing occupation, without any mental responsibility of consequence."[30] All very well, but they were words he would eat in due time.

Before his work for Thomas could commence, however, the family business beckoned again, and the youngest partner in the firm of P. & E. Irving was dispatched to Washington, D.C., for six weeks as part of yet another effort to lobby Congress on the still-feared Non-Importation Act. "Sick of the business in which I am engaged and Sick of Washington," Irving wrote irritably in November—yet he was protesting too much, for he continued to show up regularly at Mrs. Madison's levees and countless other parties.[31] In fact, he maintained such a rigorous social schedule and was in the company of so many prominent women that friends in New York teased that he must surely be getting ready to marry one of them. Paulding even carried the joke so far as to travel to Washington, D.C., where he demanded Irving allow him to attend his upcoming wedding. Irving took it all in rakish stride: "I have determined . . . to give as much countenance to this report [of my upcoming wedding] as possible and am resolved to become acquainted with the lady forthwith—that necessary preliminary not having as yet been attended to."[32]

He may not have had a prospect in mind when Paulding arrived, but he did miss an opportunity with one particularly eligible lady that set tongues wagging. He was to be set up with Baltimore socialite Elizabeth Patterson—better known as the former Mme. Bonaparte, before her marriage to Jerome Bonaparte was annulled by Napoleon. The two were to attend a social event at Mason's Island, the site of some of the district's most scenic and fashionable gatherings, and, as Irving said in relating the story, a "favourable opportunity . . . for sentiment & romance."

Unfortunately, the date never took place. As a rather embarrassed and disappointed Irving later explained, he had eaten dinner at the home of Congressman Henry Clay, drank too much wine, staggered home, and fell asleep in front of the fire, completely forgetting about his date until the next morning. Irving's faux pas was the cause of considerable snickering in D.C.'s social circles, but Irving maintained a sense of humor. "Do beg your mother for Gods sake to look out for some other lady for me," he appealed to Renwick in mock desperation, "I am not particular about her being a princess, provided she has plenty of money—a pretty face and no understanding." No worse for wear, Irving returned to New York in late December, ready to take up the reins of the *Select Review*, which he and Thomas rechristened the *Analectic* for its January 1813 launch.[33]

The *Analectic* was not the cakewalk he had originally envisioned. While Thomas had rigorously promoted the addition of Irving to his stable of talent, he had also advertised—without his new editor's prior knowledge—that Irving would be producing a series of biographies of naval commanders, a history of the events of America's maritime wars, and—Irving gasped—a British naval chronicle.

Irving was furious. The announcements had not only been made without his consent, but the production of new work was decidedly *not* what he had signed on for. He fumed to Renwick that he would not be "wickedly made the editor of a vile farrago—a congregation of heterogenious articles, that have no possible affinity to one another." He added that he had no idea his publisher would "have such a fools cap put on my head—and if they intended to interfere in the conduct of the work I should decline having any thing to do with it."[34]

The temper tantrum passed, and Irving got down to business, searching for articles of interest that could be reprinted—free of charge, of course, for there were no copyright laws to speak of—in the pages of the *Analectic*. Writing to Peter in Liverpool, he asked his brother to send any new works that might be of interest, and urged him to subscribe to any periodicals of importance from which he might pilfer. Meanwhile, Brevoort promised from Edinburgh that he would have any interesting journals and "old odd Books" forwarded to Irving. "All these are intended for the benefit of 'the Independent Columbian Review,'" Brevoort wrote, punning on the name of the fictional hotel from which Diedrich Knickerbocker had made his escape, "which I am happy to learn is soon to issue from Mulberry Street under the fostering care of Seth Handaside, Esq."[35]

With the help of his willing family and friends, Irving poached from the best, and his two-year run at the *Analectic* was far from the embarrassment he worried it would be. He reprinted works by and about Walter Scott, Thomas Campbell, and Lord Byron, whose booming poetic voice was quickly becoming a favorite of his. He also included German and Spanish tales and stories of Muhammad, topics that reflected his own blossoming tastes and interests. He provided a monthly column of "literary intelligence"—a gossip column that tracked the comings and goings of New York's artistic and literary young men, who were usually Irving's own friends—and encouraged reviews of other American writers. Paulding and Verplanck were also pressed into contributing regularly.

As it turned out, writing about naval heroes wasn't the unwelcome chore Irving had groaned about. Such work appealed to his romantic sensibilities, and he spent much of the war writing flag-waving essays about the heroes of the hour, churning out profiles of sailors like Captain James Lawrence or Commodore Oliver Perry.

These essays tilted toward the sappy and melodramatic—"The brave Lawrence saw the overwhelming danger," he wrote in the August 1813 issue, "his last words, as he was borne bleeding from the deck, were, 'don't surrender the ship!'"—but Irving regarded it as part of his patriotic duty.[36]

Naval biographies were one thing; literary criticism was another. Irving was not only a disinterested critic but a bad one, making vague observations of no real value or insight. He loved to gossip and criticize in the privacy of a drawing room or in his correspondence, but doing it publicly was something else altogether. He hated being publicly criticized himself. All his life he took even the most constructive criticism personally, and even the slightest word of disapproval sent him spiraling into a black sulk. He recognized his own weakness at writing such pieces—"I do not profess the art and mystery of reviewing, and am not ambitious of being wise or facetious at the expense of others"[37]—and abandoned the form altogether after leaving the *Analectic*.

He still missed Brevoort badly. "This making of fortunes is the very bane of social life," he wrote in early 1813, "but I trust when they are made we shall all gather together again and pass the rest of our lives with one another." He reported to his absent roommate that he was tired of living in the boardinghouse, and proposed that they "get a handsome set of apartments & furnish them" when Brevoort returned later in the year. Brevoort wrote back sympathetically: "You see my dear Wash, how much I long to fill the vacant chair on the opposite side of the well recollected Table in our private sanctuary, but let my remembrance fill all the vacancies in your heart as yours most truly does in mine."[38]

Brevoort traveled widely in Europe throughout 1813. Just as he had on the American western and Canadian frontiers, he continued to act as Irving's agent, putting copies of the revised *History of New York* and *Salmagundi* into the hands of literary acquaintances in Paris, London, and Edinburgh—including, Brevoort related in June, Irving's literary idol, Walter Scott. And Scott, Brevoort reported, had enjoyed the book enough to write an appreciative letter, which he enclosed for his stunned friend to read. Scott wrote:

> I beg you to accept my best thanks for the uncommon degree of entertainment which I have received from the most excellently jocose history of New York. . . . I am sensible that as a stranger to American parties and politics, I must lose much of the concealed satire of the piece, but I must own that looking at the simple and obvious meaning only, I have never read anything so closely resembling the style of Dean [Jonathan] Swift, as the annals of Diedrich Knickerbocker. . . . I beg you will have the kindness to let me know when Mr. Irvine [sic] takes pen in hand again, for assuredly I shall expect a very great treat which I may chance never to hear of but through your kindness.[39]

This was high praise from the writer Irving admired most, but it failed to spark the creative fire. Irving continued his duties at the *Analectic*, which was earning him a reputation as an editor—and not just in New York. He was approached by Philadelphia bookseller Joseph Delaplaine, who was collecting materials for his *Repository of the Lives and Portraits of Distinguished Americans*, and asked Irving for his portrait. A rather embarrassed Irving refused, and begged Delaplaine not to include him in the *Repository* at all. "I would rather that ninety nine should ask why I was *not* there," Irving explained, "than incur the possibility of one persons asking why I *was*."[40]

Both Irving and the *Analectic* were becoming more patriotic as the war continued. In late 1812, at a public dinner honoring the naval heroes Isaac Hull, Jacob Jones, and Stephen Decatur, the fanfare nearly moved Irving to tears. "I never in my life before felt the national feeling so strongly aroused," he wrote, "for I never before saw in this country so true a cause for national triumph."[41] As the war progressed and news of, first, surprising victories, then crushing defeats filtered into New York, Irving stepped up his rhetoric, and in one remarkable moment, scolded any fence sitters who might oppose the war to at least recognize that the reputation of the country, and every American citizen, was at stake:

> Whatever we may think of the expediency or inexpediency of the present war, we cannot feel indifferent to its operations. Whenever our arms come in competition with those of the enemy, jealousy for our country's honour will swallow up every other consideration. Our feelings will ever accompany the flag of our country to battle, rejoicing in its glory— lamenting over its defeat. For there is no such thing as releasing ourselves from the consequences of the contest. He who fancies he can stand aloof in interest, and by condemning the present war, is woefully mistaken. . . . If the name of American is to be rendered honorable in the fight, we shall each participate in the honor; if otherwise, we must inevitably support our share of the ignominy.[42]

This was hardly Tom Paine, but it was stirring enough. His own oratory, along with the feats of the naval heroes he was reading and writing of, was enough to get the frustrated sailor in him nagging once again. He was anxious to serve in any capacity, but his duties at the *Analectic* kept him rooted firmly on the sidelines.

Another Irving was actively serving his country, albeit in a somewhat different capacity. In the election of 1812 William Irving had run for Congress against Egbert Benson, a well-liked politician who had been one of New York's first congressmen and a former chief judge of the New York Court of Appeals. The popular he had won that election by only two hundred votes, but when he resigned his seat after only five months, William was easily elected to fill the vacancy. In January 1814 the oldest Irving was off to Washington to begin his term in the U.S. House of Representatives, where William and his Democrat colleagues held an easy majority over the Federalists.

The same month William left for Washington, Henry Brevoort returned to New York. As Irving had suggested, he and Brevoort changed their living arrangements. Rather than securing an apartment, they simply swapped one boardinghouse for another, moving into Mrs. Bradish's at 124 Broadway. In their common parlor, the two kept up on the latest news and gossip from various fronts, receiving regular visits from Stephen Decatur and his wife, and from Captain David Porter, a former Lad of Kilkenny who had led the naval forces at New Orleans, and whom Irving profiled in the *Analectic*.

Listening to Decatur and Porter talk of the war further stoked Irving's inner patriot. He reached his tipping point in late August 1814, when he learned of the British invasion of Washington, D.C., and the burning of the U.S. Capitol and White House. "The pride and honor of the nation are wounded," Irving declared, "the country is insulted and disgraced by this barbarous success and every loyal citizen would feel the ignominy and be earnest to avenge it."[43]

He was as good as his word. As New Yorkers hunkered down and raised fortifications on the heights of Brooklyn and Harlem, Irving joined the New York State Militia, becoming aide-de-camp to Daniel Tompkins, the governor of New York and a major general of the militia. Brevoort was also inspired to enlist, and received a commission as a first lieutenant in the "Iron Greys" artillery company.

It wasn't the navy, and it wasn't quite the heroic romance Irving likely envisioned when he enlisted—his duties consisted mainly of scribbling Tompkins's dispatches and notifying paymasters of the availability of payroll funds—but he liked it nonetheless. "I feel more pleased than ever with it," he wrote Brevoort in September. The job held a certain level of respectability, and as a colonel, Irving outranked most of his friends, including the uninterested Brevoort, who took frequent leave from his unit to pursue business opportunities in Vermont. Irving liked Tompkins, describing him as "absolutely one of the worthiest men I ever knew . . . with a greater stock of practical good sense and ready talent than I had any idea he possessed."[44]

Longing for a taste of military excitement and glory, Irving begged Tompkins for the opportunity to see a little action. That

September Tompkins obligingly dispatched him from Albany to Sackets Harbor, a sleepy village on the northeastern shores of Lake Ontario, where only months before stubborn American militia had repulsed an attack by British and Canadian troops. Fearing a renewed attack by land and water, Tompkins asked Irving to visit the front and assess the situation.

An eager Irving left Albany by stagecoach, then rode three long days on horseback through dense forest to Sackets Harbor. After huddling with officers, he believed that a British invasion was imminent, and called for reinforcements from the surrounding counties. Breastworks were thrown up, pickets were erected . . . and the anticipated attack never came. Disappointed, Irving plodded back toward Albany, regularly passing the reinforcements he had called into action, now making their way toward Sackets Harbor, where their services were no longer needed. Little suspecting this was the officer responsible for their deployment, the soldiers whooped in jest for Irving to about-face, telling him he was going the wrong way.[45]

Back in New York in late October, Irving sent a note to Moses Thomas, apologizing for neglecting his obligations as an editor while he carried out his military duties, then dropped a bombshell on his publisher: he was quitting in December—or, as he elegantly put it, "I shall have to give up all formal agency in the work after the close of the year."[46] He had no confidence in his abilities as an editor, little love for the role of critic, and he was growing increasingly disenchanted with the requirement that he produce original material.

Despite his deepening weariness of the editor's chair, Irving still had a knack for gauging the popular taste. In December 1814 he reprinted a poem called "Defense of Fort McHenry" by a Baltimore lawyer named Francis Scott Key, who had witnessed the event firsthand. Irving was a fan of such jingoistic sentiments, and enthusiastically endorsed the idea of Americans creating their own patriotic poetry, rather than merely rewriting or adapting British poems.

He found Key's lyrics especially inspiring, with their images of star-spangled banners and bombs bursting in air, and, in a prescient introduction to Key's poem, wrote that "their merit entitles them to preservation in some more permanent form than the columns of a daily paper."[47]

In the meantime, William Irving was doing his best in Congress to prop up the defenses of the country by working to ensure that an appropriate number of soldiers was called into service. "I think you were right," Washington wrote his brother supportively, after passage of a watered-down version of the militia bill, "to support any show of defence, though I regret that you were not able to effect any thing more substantially efficient." This ineffectiveness would come as little surprise to William's colleagues in the House of Representatives. A patient listener, William Irving is rarely recorded in the *Annals of Congress* as doing much more than taking his seat during a debate, though his final vote on legislation was almost always solidly with his Democratic colleagues. Indeed, while the eldest Irving brother was thoughtful, meticulous, and patriotic almost to a fault, he—like his brother Washington—shuddered at the thought of public speaking, a critical flaw in a congressman. However, William was a formidable conversationalist—another trait he shared with his youngest brother—and once spoke in a private discussion with such animation that Congressman William Lowndes of South Carolina grabbed him and fairly shouted into his face, "Why, in the name of God, will you not speak this way in the House?"[48]

In late December Washington's services as Tompkins's aide-de-camp ended unceremoniously when Tompkins, anxious to return to his gubernatorial obligations, departed for the legislative session at Albany. He entrusted his duties to a new commander, who simply dissolved the staff. It was an anticlimactic conclusion to an otherwise respectable stint, though Irving was disappointed he had never seen any real action. Sackets Harbor aside, he later joked that his most heroic moment in uniform had come when

Tompkins—never easy in the saddle—was thrown from his horse into a ditch, where Irving dutifully picked him up and dusted him off.[49]

Now that his term of service had expired, Irving considered enlisting in the regular navy. In January 1815 he began a trip down to Washington, D.C., where he planned to discuss his military options with William. He had gotten as far as Philadelphia when he learned that a number of publishers and booksellers had gone bankrupt, including Bradford & Innskeep, which dragged Moses Thomas—and the *Analectic*—down with it.

The mass bankruptcies were largely the result of the suspension of specie payments by United States banks. Business had been bad for almost everyone during the past year; on the back of one of his letters to Irving that fall, Brevoort had scribbled the names of fifteen collapsed businesses, writing at the top of the page in disbelief, "All failed within 2 or 3 weeks." However, the ruin of Bradford & Innskeep was considered especially shameful in Philadelphia, and both Bradford and Thomas were being maligned publicly for mismanagement. Irving believed Thomas to be largely blameless—he held Bradford responsible for the failure—but the result was the same: the *Analectic* was as good as finished.[50]

Irving was relieved. While he had given Thomas proper notice, the financial collapse of the magazine allowed him a relatively graceful escape. With other creditors knocking at Thomas's door, Irving generously refused to press for any money he was owed. "I promptly signed off whatever was due to me," he said, "because I thought him unfortunate & the victim of other peoples misconduct." He offered to provide Thomas with contributions free of charge should he get the magazine running again, but Irving vowed one thing for certain: he would "never again undertake the editorship of that or of any other periodical work."[51]

The experience had convinced him once again that living by the pen was not only impossible, but nerve-racking. "These failures," he told Verplanck, "I am afraid will sensibly affect the interests of literature and deter all those from the exercise of the pen who would take it up as a means of profit."[52] After settling his affairs, Irving might have continued his trip to the capital to join the navy had not the news of the Treaty of Ghent reached the United States on February 11, 1815. The war was over.

"I suppose this sudden news of peace has taken You all aback," Irving wrote on February 21 to Commodore Oliver Perry, the subject of one of his biographical sketches, and now a friend. "You however, of all men, have the least cause to regret it; having reaped a rich harvest of Laurels." If there was one person who regretted the peace, it was Irving. His military service had been "the first thing that roused and stimulated me," he wrote many years later, "but it did not last long; for peace took place, the forces were disbanded & I had nothing to do."[53]

Only Irving could find peace so depressing. With his military aspirations shelved and any further literary endeavors snuffed by the demise of the *Analectic*, he was in a funk. Still, his literary standing had risen because of the *Analectic*, and his fame was enough to secure invitations to the finest parlors and best parties around town. "My literary notoriety had made me an object of attention, I was continually drawn, into society," he wrote later. Yet the emptiness lingered. "My time & thoughts dissipated and my spirits jaded," he wrote flatly, "I became weary of every thing and of myself."[54]

At least there was still decent conversation to be had in the parlor he shared with Brevoort at Mrs. Bradish's, where Stephen Decatur and his wife were Irving's frequent guests. Like Irving, Decatur was suffering from blackened spirits. In January he had been forced to surrender his ship, the frigate USS *President*, to the British after a fierce firefight off the Atlantic coast—an action that resulted in a brief imprisonment and a loss of reputation. Decatur was looking for an opportunity to regain his good name—and that spring, as the disgraced commodore paced the floors of Irving's parlor on Broadway, he told Irving that such an opportunity had come his way. In March Congress authorized the deployment of naval power against Algiers—known as the Second Barbary War—and asked Decatur to command a fleet to the Mediterranean to suppress Algerian pirates. With Irving's eager encouragement, and against the wishes of his wife, Decatur accepted the post—and asked Irving to consider making the trip with him. After a hurried conversation with his brothers, Irving decided to go with Decatur, but only for as long as it took to shake off his "idle habits and idle associates & fashionable dissipation." Then, he promised, he would return home "to settle myself down to useful and honourable application."[55]

By May 18 Irving's bags were packed and stowed aboard Decatur's ship, ready for departure, when the news arrived that Napoleon had returned from exile at Elba. The U.S. government held Decatur in port while it sorted out its intelligence, and Irving—who feared that he was becoming a burden to Decatur—suddenly backed out. When Decatur and his fleet sailed for Algiers on May 20, it was without Irving.

With his bags still packed and his wanderlust raging, Irving was determined to go just about anywhere. He again consulted with his brothers, who generously agreed to bankroll a journey to Italy or Greece.

Irving went to visit his mother on Ann Street to say his good-byes. "I had a hard parting with my poor old mother," Irving remembered. "I was her favorite child & could not bear to leave her in her old days; but I trusted to return after a short absence, quite another being & then to settle down quietly beside her for the rest of her life."[56] He never saw her again.

On May 25 Irving boarded the ship *Mexico*, bound for Liverpool from New York. He would not return to the United States for another seventeen years.

6

Desperation

1815–1817

I think . . . that nothing but a prospect of a very considerable and certain gain should tempt you in any wise to link your fortunes with others, or place your independence of life and action in any wise in their control.

—Washington Irving to Henry Brevoort, August 23, 1815

THE MAY WIND WAS CHILLY as it filled the sails of the *Mexico*. As the ship coursed past the lighthouse at Sandy Hook and headed out into the Atlantic, Irving's thoughts lingered on the friends to whom he had failed to say good-bye. He had rushed off so quickly that he scarcely had time to bid farewell to his housemates at Mrs. Bradish's. He scribbled a hasty line to Henry Brevoort, apologizing for leaving "without taking you by the hand." He settled into his cramped quarters aboard the ship, and watched the Jersey shoreline recede below the horizon.

Typically, it didn't take long before he was fully engaged with his fellow passengers. "I do not believe," he wrote later, "that the same number of passengers were ever mewed up together for thirty days in dirty cabins and with equal deficiency of comforts, that maintained more unvarying harmony and good will toward each other." Irving dreamed of the tour of Europe he was planning to make, of the friends he would visit in London, and the theater he planned to attend.[1]

Politics was on his mind as well. That spring, Napoleon, who had spent the last year in exile, had marched on Paris and regained control of France. As Napoleon struggled with the political and constitutional issues of his government, European troops circled, ready to pounce. It was an international theater of the spectacular, and Irving—who had been fascinated by Napoleon since his first tour of Europe a decade before—could hardly wait to see how events would unfold. He couldn't reach Liverpool quickly enough.

To his disappointment, by the time the *Mexico* pulled into port in late June, Napoleon had been defeated at Waterloo by the Duke of Wellington. Descending the *Mexico*'s platform, Irving saw mail carriages decked with celebratory laurels rattling through the streets, carrying tales of Wellington's prowess and the bravery of the British soldiers in Belgium. Napoleon's Hundred Days were over; Irving had missed it.

Napoleon's armies had been defeated, but the deposed emperor remained at large. "I can do nothing but look on in stupid amazement," Irving sputtered to Brevoort, "—wondering with vacant conjecture—'what will take place next?' "[2]

He loitered for a week in Liverpool with his brother Peter, who he hadn't seen in seven years. While he reported back to the family that Peter lived comfortably and seemed "quite unaltered," in truth, he was worried about his brother's mental and physical health; the business was wearing him out. Peter suffered from erysipelas, a painful, burning skin infection. Confined to bed rest, he left the bulk of the business affairs to the firm's one elderly clerk. Washington sat with Peter in his quarters on Bold Street, tending to his needs as they caught up on seven years of gossip, thumbed through newspapers, and waited for any reports from arriving ships of the missing Bonaparte.

A week passed, and still the papers carried nothing new, so Irving departed on July 3 for Birmingham, where his sister Sarah and her husband, Henry Van Wart, resided. In the nine years since Irving had last seen her, she and her husband had filled their respectable house—"Castle Van Tromp," Irving playfully dubbed it—with five children. Here the lethargy that had overwhelmed him in New York was washed away by the laughter of his nieces and nephews. "It seemed as if my whole nature had changed," he told Brevoort, "—a thousand kind feelings and affections that had laid torpid, are aroused within me—my very blood seems to flow more warm and sprightly."[3]

In mid-July came news that Napoleon had surrendered. As the bells in Birmingham rang in celebration, Irving's heart went out to the fallen would-be conqueror. "In spite of all his misdeeds, he is a noble fellow," Irving said, "and I am confident will eclipse, in the eyes of posterity, all the crowned wiseacres that have crushed him by their overwhelming confederacy."[4]

After surrendering, Bonaparte had asked for the protection of English law, and the thought of this "noble fellow" supplicating himself at the feet of those "crowned wiseacres"—especially George, the prince regent of England, whom Irving called an "inflation of sack and sugar"—was reprehensible to him. Relating the situation to Brevoort, he groaned in disgust that "nothing shows more completely the caprices of fortune . . . than that, of all the monarchs of Europe, *Bonaparte* should be brought to the feet of the *Prince Regent*." It would have been far better, Irving thought, had Napoleon died in the field of battle than suffer such humiliations. "I am extremely sorry that his career has terminated so lamely," he snorted. For Irving, it was a decidedly anticlimactic ending to an otherwise satisfactory story.[5]

The British had cause to celebrate, but Irving thought they were too cocky. "English pride is inflated to its full distention by the idea of having Paris at the mercy of Wellington and his army," he said disapprovingly. Even in church, one parson worked himself into such a metaphorical lather about the overthrow of tyranny by the angels of Waterloo that Irving's eyes rolled skyward. "Every country curate and parish clerk now lords it over Bonaparte," he groaned.[6]

Lest the British get too full of themselves, there were still plenty of Americans in Liverpool who delighted in reminding their British hosts of the losses their kingdom had sustained in America during the War of 1812. "Let an Englishman talk of the Battle of Waterloo," Irving told Brevoort with some amused satisfaction, "and they will immediately bring up New Orleans and Platts-burgh—a thorough bred—thoroughly appointed [English] soldier, is nothing to a Kentucky Rifleman."[7]

Apart from the present English attitude, Irving was enthralled by England. "The country is enchanting," he told his mother, "and I have experienced as yet nothing but kindness and civility." Even the distinctly blue-collar Liverpool—where cockfighting, dog fight-ing, and bull baiting were the preferred forms of entertainment—didn't seem to irritate Irving, whose tastes were somewhat more refined. Walking the unpaved streets toward the warehouses of P. Irving and Company in Goree Dock, he easily made friends among the merchants, traders, hagglers, and shopkeepers.

There was no shortage of Americans on Liverpool's streets and docks; the Irvings' firm was only one of many that did business in the port town. Moving and storing goods was the city's primary source of revenue; it was practically one gigantic warehouse. With its docks on the western coast of England, Liverpool provided quicker and easier access to the Atlantic than London, making it a more desirable location for import or export. Besides the conve-nience, the city was also friendlier toward Americans than many other British cities—largely because it couldn't afford *not* to be.

It was with good reason that the inscription on the statue of Columbus in Liverpool's Sefton Park proclaimed that "the discov-erer of America was the maker of Liverpool," for the economic strength of the city hinged on its relationship with the New World. Trade with the young United States was profitable enough that an American Chamber of Commerce had been established in the city in 1801; and despite the political pressures of the Napoleonic wars, trade with the United States only continued to increase. When George III issued Orders in Council in January 1807 to prevent trade with Napoleon and his allies—the same orders that had con-cerned William Irving—the chamber, correctly guessing such orders might lead to war with the United States, pressed unsuccessfully for their repeal.[8]

As the chamber had expected, the War of 1812 hit merchants in Liverpool hard. By the time of Irving's arrival in 1815, Liverpool was a city working to recover from an economic crisis. As he strolled among the warehouses and beneath the dome of the new city hall, Irving had every reason to believe the future would be bright. He had confidence in Peter, who had overseen the business these past years, and the firm's clerk had been working to keep the books in order and the business solvent even as one wartime trade agreement after another forced the Irvings and other businesses to constantly improvise. Let Peter and the clerk attend to the business; he had other matters to attend to—like visiting friends in London.

Washington Allston, the painter Irving had admired in Rome in 1805, now lived in London's Fitzroy Square, near Regent's Park, which was fast becoming a fashionable address for artists. Irving quickly became a regular in Allston's quarters during the summer of 1815, where he also renewed his friendship with the American painter Charles Leslie. The three prowled London museums, theaters, and bookshops, where Irving was pleased to see that both *Salmagundi* and *A History of New York* could be found.

He also took the time to pay his respects at the Sydenham home of Thomas Campbell, the poet whose work Irving had promoted and steered through the New York press in 1810. To Irving's disappointment, Campbell was out, but he fell into a long conversation with the poet's wife, who lamented that her husband was suffering from a lack of inspiration. Walter Scott and Lord Byron wrote so much and so well, she informed Irving, that it intimidated her husband into a stupor.[9]

There were other friends visiting from America to keep Irving occupied. James Renwick had been traveling in England since spring. In late July the two met in Liverpool and set off on a whirlwind tour of Kenilworth, Warwick, and Stratford-on-Avon. Next was a short visit to Tintern Abbey, which Wordsworth had made famous in his 1798 poem. Irving was moderately impressed by the abbey, but less so by Wordsworth's poetic musings. Ever the sentimentalist, he never subscribed to the formal school of Romantic poetry led by Wordsworth, Coleridge, and Shelley. Byron was another matter, mainly because of his larger-than-life personality and the booming, confident poetic voice that told of love and adventure, but Wordsworth left Irving cold.

He was more anxious to walk the same grounds as *Henry IV*'s Owen Glendower and to visit the ring of castles erected by Edward I during his conquest of Wales—this better suited Irving's idea of romance. He marveled at Conway Castle, a most "sublime ruin," but was disappointed in the more famous castle at Caernavon. He and Renwick returned to Liverpool in mid-August, wrapping up what Irving regarded as a most successful and relaxing trip. Throughout, Irving had crammed his travel journals with observations of the countryside, the people, the inns, and the theaters they visited.

Sorting through the letters that had piled up in his absence, he learned of Stephen Decatur's victory at Algiers. Had he opted to travel with the commodore back in May instead of boarding the *Mexico*, he would have been in Algiers to witness the victory. He regretted his own missed opportunity, but he was pleased for Decatur. "He may now repose on his Laurels and have wherewithal to solace himself under their shade," he told Brevoort with satisfaction.[10]

He had been in England for three months, and while he felt more rested in mind and body than he had for some time, he was no closer to deciding what he would do for a living. The pressure was mounting. His friends in America were settling into lives and occupations, and were wondering when their dreamy friend might do the same.

In August Brevoort wrote that he had at last turned his on-again, off-again stint with Astor's Northwest Fur Company into a full-time job. Irving was pleased for his friend's opportunity—it was one that Brevoort used to increase his already sizable fortune—but warned him of the dangers of hitching his cart to another's horse unless he could be certain of his own success. "I think . . . that nothing but a prospect of a very considerable and certain gain should tempt you in any wise to link your fortunes with others," he cautioned Brevoort, "or place your independence of life and action in any wise in their control."[11]

It was some of the best advice he ever gave—and as he wrote those words, he must have wondered if he himself hadn't already made such a mistake. For as long as he could remember, he had linked his own fortunes—as well as his "independence of life and action"—with those of others, whether it was his brothers, Judge Hoffman, or Moses Thomas. So far, none of those links had assured him of "very considerable and certain gain"—and he was now more dependent upon such attachments than ever.

Still, he tried to remain optimistic about the fortunes of the family business. "Our business I trust will be very *good*," he told Brevoort almost too enthusiastically in August, "—it certainly will be very *great*, this year, and will give us credit, if not profit." Or so he had likely been convinced by Peter. "Notwithstanding that [P]eter has been an invalid and confined to the house almost continually since the Treaty of Ghent," he informed Brevoort, with proper deference to Peter, "yet he has managed to get through an immensity of business."[12]

Irving was beginning to wonder. The firm's lone clerk had suddenly and unexpectedly died, and Peter was still too incapacitated to assume his duties, so the burdens of the Liverpool office were slowly shifting to Irving's shoulders. Dutifully sorting through the books in their offices and warehouse in late summer, even a financial novice like Irving could see that things were a mess.

The War of 1812, with its diversion of capital from normal economic channels, had taken its toll on the merchant class, as had the increasing sense of American self-sufficiency, which had lowered the demand for imported goods from England. Winds blowing from the west had also stranded ships bound for America in their docks in Liverpool, their holds full of unsold goods. Times were tough, but during the relative economic calm of 1815, other shipping firms had recovered, or were beginning to. Something else was causing the firm of P. Irving and Company to flounder. As he turned over page after page in the business ledgers, Irving could see what the problem was. The problem was Peter.

Like Washington, Peter was a dreamer, not a businessman. And like his youngest brother, Peter had bounced from vocation to vocation until the family business had provided him with a financial safety net. Unlike Washington, however, Peter never applied himself to pursuing a vocation better suited to his more natural inclinations—whatever those might be—and chose instead to chase one get-rich-quick scheme after another. William and Ebenezer, who had better heads for business than any of the Irving men, certainly recognized that Peter was not an ideal partner for the family firm; perhaps they knew that the best way to keep an eye on him and curb his profligate ways was to keep him close, and keep him occupied with a steady job and a source of income.

It was a strategy that doomed their firm, as the business became another of Peter's speculative affairs. Hearing William testify before Congress in 1812 that there would continue to be a demand for English imports—a mistaken assumption, as it turned out—Peter smelled easy profit, and went on a buying spree, filling the cargo holds of ships in Liverpool with more goods than could possibly be moved, even under ideal economic conditions.

In late August Washington reported to Ebenezer—perhaps in a preemptive attempt to spare Peter the wrath of the stateside partners in the firm—that he had found his brother "comfortably situated . . . but not indulging in any extravagance or dash." He added a qualified defense that their brother was living like "a man of sense, who knows he can but enjoy his money while he is alive, and would not be a whit the better though he were buried under a mountain of it when dead."[13]

Watching Peter in their apartment on Bold Street, it was clear to Washington that his brother would be no help in getting things sorted out. Peter's skin condition was still raging, and he had developed rheumatism in both legs. In early September Irving sent his brother to soak in the medicinal baths at Harrogate, ninety miles away, while he began the long process of putting their business affairs in order.

Throughout September Irving calmly pored over the books and counted the crates stacked in the firm's waterfront warehouses. He found time to write letters, keeping Brevoort informed of the stream of mutual friends that filed through the port town, and following with interest the progress of Madame Bonaparte through England. Lest his mother worry, he wrote that he was "leading a solitary bachelor's life in Peter's lodgings and perhaps should feel a little lonesome were I not kept so busy."[14]

Busy was putting it mildly. Things piled up quickly, and as he dug ever deeper into the books, he realized he was in over his head. Neither his negligible skills as a lawyer nor his substantial aptitude for writing were of assistance; this was pure finance. In September he took a quick bookkeeping course to try to cope with the columns of numbers and accounts that swam before him. "Perfectly ignorant of every thing about business affairs, I came in and made them teach me," Irving recalled later. "It was all wrong; I turned away first one and then another; every thing was in confusion. As I began to learn the business, I saw the difficulties, the breakers ahead."[15]

By October his head was spinning, and he wrote a quick letter to Brevoort: "I will most certainly write to you amply when I have time, but for several weeks past I have been more *really* busy than I ever was in my life." One can only imagine. To Irving, who had barely escaped Benjamin Romaine's schoolhouse with a smattering of basic math, it must have been frustrating and exhausting. Indeed, his weariness was obvious in his letter to Brevoort:

> As I am a complete novice in business it of course takes up my whole time and completely occupies my mind, so that at present I am as dull commonplace a fellow as ever figured upon Change. When I once more emerge from the mud of Liverpool, and shake off the sordid cares of the Counting House, you shall hear from me. Indeed the present life I lead

is utterly destitute of anecdote, or anything that could furnish interest or embellishment to a letter—& my imagination is too much jaded by pounds shillings & pence to be able to invent facts or adorn realities.[16]

The unadorned realities facing Washington were unpleasant. Peter's expenditures had far exceeded their income, and Washington wondered whether the firm would be able to pay its autumn obligations. He advised Ebenezer, who was managing affairs on the American side, to remit continually until everything had been paid. Ebenezer and William, taking a break from his duties as congressman, frantically did their best to comply. Despite the gravity of their situation, the brothers hadn't lost their sense of humor. When William joked in one letter that he had to stop remitting at least long enough to take a breath, Irving teased him right back: "This was something like the Irishman calling to his companion, whom he was hoisting out of the well, to hold on below while he spit on his hands."[17]

The brothers paid their obligations as quickly as they could, but Irving could see that the money was running out. Swallowing his pride, he appealed to James Renwick, now touring Scotland, for guidance. To his surprise and relief, Renwick immediately provided the firm with a line of credit, making it possible for the brothers to pay the remaining balance, and asked for no collateral other than Irving's word. Because of Renwick's generosity—as well as hard work on the part of both Washington and Ebenezer—Irving believed the business had turned the corner sufficiently enough for him to enjoy the Christmas holiday.

He sprinted off to London to attend the theater, and still made it to the Van Warts' in time for Christmas. Peter had managed to make his way down to Castle Van Tromp from the waters at Harrogate, but he was confined to bed with rheumatism by the time Irving arrived. Washington must have sighed compassionately but regretfully at his brother's condition; the cares of business continued to be his alone.

"We have, in common with most American houses here, had a hard winter of it in money matters . . . and I have been harassed to death to meet our engagements," Irving wrote to Brevoort in March 1816. Yet he held out hope that the firm was, at last, on the road to recovery. "I have never passed so anxious a time in my life," he wrote, "but thank heavens we have weathered the storm & got into smooth water; and I begin to feel myself again."[18]

With money tight, he wondered if he could raise some income by preparing a new edition of A History of New York. He asked Brevoort to send him a copy of the American edition, and requested copies of the Analectic that contained his Indian sketches, with an eye toward writing a larger piece.

He sent Moses Thomas copies of English works the publisher could pirate for American editions, including Byron's "Fare Thee Well," "A Sketch from Private Life," and "Hebrew Melodies," which were all the rage in London that spring. Later he sent Christabel by Samuel Taylor Coleridge and The Antiquary, Walter Scott's sequel to Waverly—although at the time, Scott had not confessed to penning it. There was much speculation as to the author's identity, with many guessing it was Irving's friend Thomas Moore.

Irving returned to Liverpool in March, leaving the rheumatic Peter confined to bed rest in Birmingham. When he had sent Peter to Harrogate in September 1815, he never imagined it would turn into an extended absence of eight months. While sympathetic, Washington grew increasingly frustrated by his brother's continued poor health. He hoped Peter would recover so he could return to Liverpool and share the responsibility for the business.

Irving followed James Renwick's progress through Europe, and wrote to Renwick's mother that the burdens of business were so heavy that he barely had time for letters. "And when leisure does come," he told Mrs. Renwick, "I find every gay thought or genteel fancy has left my unhappy brain and nothing remains but the dry rubbish of accounts—Woe is me! How different a being I am from what I was last Summer, when the Laird [James Renwick] and

I went forth Castle hunting among the Welsh mountains."[19] He was burning out.

It was about to get worse. In May Ebenezer notified Washington that the spring market had not lived up to expectations. The brothers worried over their ability to meet new obligations. Renwick's line of credit was exhausted; their money was gone. Washington, who had worked so hard over the past nine months—learning bookkeeping, keeping creditors at bay, and going hat in hand to friends for money—began to despair.

The first sign of collapse appeared in his May 9, 1816, letter to Brevoort—written four days after receiving Ebenezer's bad news:

> I am here alone, attending to business—and the times are so hard that they sicken my very soul. Good god what would I give to be once more with you, and all this mortal coil shuffled off of my heart.
>
> My dear Brevoort what would I not give to have you with me. In my lonely hours I think of the many many happy days we have passed together and feel that there is no friend in the world to whom my heart turns so completely as it does you—For some time before I left New York I thought you had grown cold and indifferent to me—I felt too proud to speak frankly on the subject but it grieved me bitterly. Your letters have convinced me that I was mistaken, and they were like cordials to my feelings.[20]

This was, understandably, despair and loneliness, but was it something more? By 1816 Irving, who was thirty-three years old, had known thirty-four-year-old Brevoort for thirteen years, having met him in Montreal in 1803. Since then, each had traveled extensively, caroused with women, and dabbled in business. But they also lived together, on and off, for many years and dutifully corresponded with each other when they were apart. Separation from Brevoort was always particularly hard on Irving—when Brevoort departed for Europe on business in 1810, Irving had pined away for weeks in their rooms on Broadway.

Irving was most at home among a close-knit circle of male friends. In that respect, he was no more unusual than other nineteenth-century gentlemen, who joined exclusive clubs and disappeared into drawing rooms in the evenings to smoke cigars and drink brandy. Even the intimacy and foppishness Irving and Brevoort displayed in their letters was not all that unusual for nineteenth-century correspondence.

But Irving's relationship with Brevoort was very different; no one ever occupied a place in Irving's heart in quite the same way. He had adored Matilda Hoffman, but his feelings for Brevoort were more intimate. The letters the two exchanged were more heartfelt, the expressions of affection more intense, especially on Irving's part. That Irving loved Brevoort is certain; whether those feelings were as deeply reciprocated is debatable. What is undeniable is that they shared an attachment, a familiarity of feeling, unequaled in any other relationship Irving had his entire life. It was obvious from the tone of his May 9 letter that Irving could play the rejected suitor when he perceived he was being snubbed: "I thought you had grown cold and indifferent!" Such hurt feelings only intensified later, when Irving feared he would lose Brevoort to marriage.

For now, Irving was stuck in Liverpool, without Peter's company, watching the money slowly trickle away. Brevoort graciously arranged for a loan to Ebenezer to help meet the mounting obligations, but it was never enough.

As the situation worsened, the Irving brothers drew closer. Irving worried for himself, but he was even more concerned about Ebenezer, who, unlike Peter or Washington, had a family to support. "The difficulties he must experience give me more uneasiness than any thing else," he confided to Brevoort in July. "I hope he may be able to surmount them all, and that we may work through the present stormy season without any material injury." His brothers had looked out for him for much of his life; Washington felt he was at last repaying some of their generosity with the sweat of his own brow. It pained him that they couldn't make things right for Ebenezer, no matter how hard they worked. Peter had seen to that with his overspending, though the brothers never censured him outright for their woes, blaming instead the war, the winds, or the market . . . anything but each other.

The loneliness of the burden was overpowering, as Washington sat up nights in Peter's empty apartment, writing letters urging Ebenezer to continue remitting by any means necessary and wondering how he was going to do it without any cash. "I have been harassed and hagridden by the care and anxieties of business for a long time past that I have at times felt almost broken down in health and spirits," he wrote despairingly to Brevoort.[21]

Peter finally hobbled back to Liverpool in June, and Washington gratefully retreated to Birmingham for an extended stay. "Peters return to Liverpool enabled me to crawl out of the turmoil for a while," he told Brevoort, "and I have for some time past [been] endeavoring to renovate myself in the dear little circle of my sister's family."[22]

Unfortunately, writing remained a chore. He scratched lamely at A History of New York—at this pace, the revision would take two years to complete—and flipped through the pages of his journals for inspiration, but the words refused to flow. "My mind is in a sickly state and my imagination so blighted that it cannot put forth a blossom nor even a green leaf," he wrote wearily. "Time and circumstances must restore them to their proper tone."[23]

When that time or what that circumstance might be, he wasn't sure—but he was becoming increasingly certain that it wasn't going to happen while he was in England. He wanted to go home, but waved off requests from friends in New York for specifics. "I must wait here a while in a passive state, watching the turn of events, and how our affairs are likely to turn out," he wrote enigmatically in July in response to Brevoort's queries. "I will make no promises or resolutions at present, as I know they would be like those formed at Sea in a storm, which are forgotten as soon as we tread the shore." He said only one thing for certain: "all my ideas of home and settled life centre in New York."[24]

In late July he left Birmingham to meet Peter for an excursion through Derbyshire. Traveling always made him feel better. As they ventured into the countryside, Irving relaxed for the first time in months.

Irving enjoyed watching people as much, if not more, than he enjoyed the scenery. At an inn in Buxton, he delighted in observing three "queer old ladies" who were so difficult that even a pastor called them "damned ugly bitches." He stared in fascination at the assortment of English noses and chins that passed by. "I no longer wonder at the english being such excellent caricaturists," he wrote Brevoort with amusement, "they have such an inexhaustible number and variety of subjects to study from."[25]

He worried at first whether Peter was fit enough to travel— nothing frustrated him more than a fellow traveler who couldn't keep up—but his mind was put at ease when his brother easily descended the 110 steps into the Speedwell mine, while Washington and the son of their tour guide traded turns blowing tunes on the fife. They climbed the hills in Castleton near Peak Cavern, with its impressive forty-two-foot arched entrance that Daniel Defoe had once unofficially dubbed "The Devil's Asshole in the Peak."[26] Irving could barely contain himself when he described their visit in a letter to his mother, though he couldn't bring himself to write the name of the archway.

Near Bakewell, he took careful notes on medieval Haddon Hall, copying the inscriptions on its bow windows and adding detailed notes on people and scenery. In Dovedale, a sudden cloudburst forced Irving and his fellow tourists to seek shelter in a nearby cave, where they picnicked and traded stories to pass the time. As thunder rumbled overhead, an old woman in the group told a story about a ghost she had seen when she was a girl of twelve. "The ghost was on horseback," Irving scratched in his journal, "without a head but with bright spurs. He used to haunt their neighborhood."

When the trip ended, an energized Irving returned to Birmingham, leaving Peter in Liverpool. Writing to his mother in October, he reported that Peter "is in good health at present, though I think he is more delicate in Constitution than he used to be." As for himself, he "never was heartier and am only afraid of growing *too fat*." He must have felt he had at last put his worries behind him, with Peter back in what was his proper and rightful place at the head of the Liverpool office.[27]

A sudden financial downturn in late autumn sent Irving galloping frantically back to Liverpool to assist his brother. "My heart is torn every way by anxiety for my relatives," he wrote in near panic to William. "My own individual interests are nothing. The merest pittance would content me if I could crawl out from among these troubles and see my connections safe around me."[28]

Though things continued to be shaky, he still believed they would soon have the business turning a profit again, and wrote to Brevoort in early December that he was "now confident that my Brothers in N[ew] York will be able to weather the storm and spread their sails cheerily on the return of fair weather. I shall not let present difficulties give me any uneasiness."[29]

Actually, there *had* been one bit of business that caused him considerable anguish that autumn. In December 1816 he learned that James Renwick had married Brevoort's sister Margaret Ann; earlier in the year, James Paulding had announced his engagement to Gouverneur Kemble's sister, Gertrude. Irving must have felt his circle of bachelor friends beginning to fray, but that wasn't what was worrying him. What bothered him most was the rumor that Henry Brevoort might also be getting married.

Trying his best to contain his black mood, Irving had written Brevoort a supportive letter in July encouraging the marriage. He would miss the links that bind together bachelors, he had explained to Brevoort, but said he would regret asking his friend to miss out on an opportunity "which would give you so large an accession of domestic homefelt enjoyment."[30]

As it turns out, Brevoort had no intention of marrying—at least not yet—and Irving's relief when he learned of the news that winter was obvious. Unable to contain himself any longer, he poured out his feelings to Brevoort. The brave face he had put on in his earlier letter had been a mask, he told his friend; he was actually selfishly pleased that Brevoort would not be forsaking him for a wife:

> You will smile when I tell you that, after all the grave advice I once gave you about getting married, I really felt regret on fancying, from the purport of one of your letters, that you had some serious thoughts of the kind; and that I have indulged in selfish congratulation on finding nothing in your subsequent letter to warrant such an idea . . . if I am doomed to live an old Bachelor, I am anxious to have good company. I cannot bear that all my old companions should launch away into the married state and leave me alone . . . it is a consoling and a cherished thought with me, under every vicissitude; that I shall still be able to return home, nestle comfortably down beside you, and have wherewithal to shelter me from the storms and buffetings of this uncertain world.[31]

Brevoort's response, if any, to this rather presumptuous missive is unknown. Most of Brevoort's letters to Irving at this time have been conveniently lost. He likely regarded it as more of the same from his highly strung friend, and appreciated the candor, even if he couldn't return the sentiment. Nor does he seem to have resented Irving's remarks, as the two continued in their correspondence as if nothing out of the ordinary had transpired.

Peter managed to make it to Birmingham in time for Christmas dinner, and then returned to Liverpool just after the New Year, allowing Washington to continue his self-imposed domestic exile with the Van Warts. He merrily played his flute for his nieces and nephews to dance to. "They are but pigmy performers," Irving wrote to Brevoort in January 1817, "yet they dance with inimitable grace, and vast good will, and consider me as the divinest musician in the world: So thank heaven I have at last found auditors who can appreciate my musical talents."[32]

On February 23 Irving returned to Liverpool, a town he had begun to loathe, to assist Peter. The days passed slowly, and his spirits continued to sag. He was too busy even to socialize. "I have been a month in Liverpool—and count the days as they lag heavily by," he wrote Brevoort. "Nothing but my wish to be with Peter and relieve the loneliness of his life would induce me to remain an hour in this place . . . the good folks here are both too busy and too dissipated to be social, and a Stranger who has not business to employ his time will find it a dead weight on his hands."[33]

To employ his time, Irving was slowly revising A History of New York, and asked both Allston and Leslie in London if they would provide artwork for engravings for the new edition. Both agreed. By mid-April Allston had completed his drawing, and asked Irving to come to London to see it.

Irving declined the invitation. He had learned his mother was seriously ill, and was determined to return home to tend to her. His friends were stunned. "Your sudden resolution of embarking for America has quite thrown me, to use a sea-phrase, all a-back,"[34] wrote Allston. Thomas Campbell, still trying to shake the lethargy his wife had told Irving of in 1815, sent Irving a long, desperate letter—along with the printed sheets of the first two volumes of his new work, Specimens of British Poets—begging him, once he was stateside, to see if he could get the work published in America.

Allston's disbelief and Campbell's pleading met with silence. Irving's mother had died on April 9, 1817, probably around the time Irving learned of her illness. Irving was shocked into silence; letters went unanswered for some time, until he finally responded to Allston in late May to inform him that he would not be returning to America. "I have been much discomposed since last I wrote to you by intelligence of the death of my mother. Her extreme age made such an event constantly probable, but I had hoped to have seen her once more before she died, and was anxious to return home soon on that account. That hope is now at an end—and with it my immediate wish to return, so that I think it probable I shall linger some time longer in Europe."[35] As for Campbell's project, Irving forwarded the manuscript to Brevoort, who had no luck finding any takers.

Looking back years later, Irving was still distraught that he had not had the opportunity to bid his mother a proper farewell. "She died without a pang," he wrote. "She talked of me to the last, and would not part with a letter which she received a few days before from me."[36] He guiltily admitted that he was glad his mother did not live to see him and his brothers fail at business, failing to consider that she would have been overjoyed to witness his later successes.

Rains in Liverpool flooded the Mersey, turning the streets into muddy canals that required boats to move from house to house.[37] Irving's moods swung from one extreme to the other. The debts continued to pile up, and he wandered zombielike through the firm's warehouses, dutifully counting crates and goods, penciling in the ledgers, watching the winds, and tending to Peter. Liverpool had become his prison, and the business—and Peter—remained his burden.

As he had done in 1809 when weighed down with grief over the death of Matilda Hoffman, Irving searched for solace in his pen. For the sake of his own sanity, he needed to write. Inspiration was difficult. He was exhausted, worn down by the troubles of business. Things were worse, he told Brevoort, not better. "The cares and sorrows of the world seem thickening upon me," he wrote in anguish, "and though I battle with them to the utmost and keep up a steady front, yet they will sometimes drag me down."[38]

His spirits lifted slightly in June when he met another young American, a South Carolinian named William C. Preston, who was on his way to study law at the University of Edinburgh. Their meeting was accidental; while passing through Liverpool, Preston fell ill, and Irving—who likely had a reputation as a nurse because of the constant care he provided for Peter—was asked by the American consul at Liverpool to tend to the young man.[39]

Irving agreed to the charge, and was taken to the rooms of the twenty-three-year-old Preston, who drifted in and out of consciousness with a high fever. Irving cared for the young man for days, and when Preston's fever broke, he saw at his bedside "a small gentleman dressed in black." "I am your countryman Washington Irving," the gentleman told the groggy Preston matter-of-factly.[40]

Preston proved to be an agreeable companion—so agreeable that Irving later asked him to accompany him on a trip to Wales and a long tour of Scotland. He appreciated Preston's sense of humor, his devoted patriotism, and the long stories he told of the Carolina frontier. For Preston's part, he was in awe of Irving, whom he admired for his quick wit and strong opinions. He admitted later that he looked up to his countryman, eleven years his senior, who seemed "to exercise a large influence over me, especially in restraining the exuberance of my national and natural temper."[41]

It is through Preston that we have one of the most personal looks at Irving at this moment in his life, worn down by the burdens of tending to a failing business and an invalid brother. Looking back on his time with Irving in Liverpool years later, Preston described Irving as a "man of grave, indeed a melancholy aspect, of very staid manners, his kindness rather the offspring of principle and cultivated taste than of emotion. There was an unfailing air of moderation about him, his dress was punctilious, his tone of talking, soft and firm, and in general over subdued, until a natural turn would occasionally run into humour, and laughable delineation of character or events." It was likely a fair description, for Irving had at this time almost completely removed himself from society, which to him was the worst kind of agony. "I am living like a hermit," he told Brevoort, "passing my time entirely at home, excepting now and then I take a walk out of town for exercise. . . . This is a singular contrast to the life I once led, but one gets accustomed to every thing, and I feel perfectly contented to keep out of sight of the world and indeed have at present no relish for society."[42]

Irving may have thought he was the only one who felt the pressure and embarrassment of a failing business, but he wasn't the only member of the family courting bankruptcy. While Irving regarded the Van Wart home an untouchable sanctuary, Henry Van Wart was, in truth, working hard to hold on to Castle Van

Tromp. He had made the same mistake that Irving had advised Brevoort against in 1815, and had linked his fortune to that of another—in this case, the firm of P. Irving and Company. Peter's overspending had serious consequences; Van Wart was facing financial ruin.

In late June 1817, Van Wart met with creditors to see if he could settle his debts. The meeting must have been rather heated, for immediately afterward, one particularly irritated creditor, a William Wallis, issued a circular denying he had called Van Wart a swindler in the meeting—and added for good measure that when he had met Van Wart in the streets of Birmingham, Van Wart had threatened to pull his nose. A third circular issued in late July described Wallis's son going to Castle Van Tromp and horsewhipping Van Wart![43]

Irving was homesick in Liverpool, and Brevoort's letters, updating him on all the local gossip, only made him lonelier. He begged Brevoort to put off a trip to Canada and cross the Atlantic instead. "The obstacles are merely ideal—," he pleaded, "Three weeks would land you in England—Profit might be combined with the visit." Brevoort resisted, and continued to pressure Irving to come home. Irving finally told him in July that he had no intention of returning "for a year at least," as he remained Peter's sole means of assistance and company. He did, however, indicate that he was looking at a means of supporting himself. "I have a plan which, with very little trouble, will yield me for the present a scanty but sufficient means of support, and leave me leisure to look round for something better."[44]

Irving was nervous about his plan—so much so that he kept it secret from Brevoort. "You would probably consider it precarious and inadequate to my subsistence," he wrote cryptically, "—but a small matter will float a drowning man and I have dwelt so much of late on the prospect of being cast homeless and penniless upon the world; that I feel relieved in having even a straw to catch at."[45]

The "straw" was a rather ambitious plan to use the loopholes of the vague and nearly nonexistent international copyright law to his advantage. Irving wanted to establish himself as the middleman between American and British publishers; by providing American publishers with a prepublication copy of a British publisher's work—and vice versa—he would help both secure a nearly simultaneous copyright of their works on both sides of the Atlantic. This would prevent unauthorized reprints of British works in America, and American works in Britain—something writers and publishers desperately wanted. Irving knew his way around the delicacies of copyright law. He had poached many British works in the pages of the *Analectic* and regularly shipped key British titles off to Moses Thomas in Philadelphia so the publisher could print pirated editions in the United States. According to his plan, Irving would put pirates out of business—and have publishers pay him to do it. Thomas had already agreed to pay him an annual salary of $1,000 for his services.

As tenuous as the scheme may have sounded, it seemed more stable than either the family business or living by his pen. Writing was something to be done only *after* he had a real job to pay the bills. As he had said to Brevoort in a recent letter, "I have a plan for immediate support—it may lead to something better."

What that "something better" might be he wasn't sure, though he hoped it might involve writing. He had picked up the pen again, and during a stay in London in the summer of 1817, he was feeling his way once more, writing out rough notes for essays on scenes of British life. The June heat meant the well-to-do had departed the city for summer estates and cooler climates, and Irving strolled the deserted streets, filling the pages of his journals with random observations of London's citizens and sights.

His journals from the time are a mess of incomplete phrases, short paragraphs, and brief notes on topics he thought deserved further exploration—but every once in a while, the real Irving winks out from between the rougher lines. "A *meer scholar*," he wrote in one journal as he watched university students coming and going, "is an intelligible ass, or a silly fellow in black, that speaks sentences more familiarly than sense . . . he speaks latin better than his mother tongue, and is a stranger in no part of the world but his own country."[46]

Irving made a trip to Sydenham to present his copyright proposal to Campbell. He found the poet at home, revising the *Specimens of British Poets* that Brevoort had failed to find a publisher for in America. Campbell listened carefully, then suggested that Irving discuss the proposition with his own London publisher, John Murray. Campbell provided Irving with two letters of introduction that proved to be among the most valuable he would ever receive. One was to Campbell's friend Walter Scott in Scotland; the other was the formal letter of introduction he needed to enter the illustrious drawing room of publisher John Murray in London.[47]

On the afternoon of August 16, 1817, Irving stood nervously outside Murray's door on Albemarle Street, Campbell's letter in hand. Meeting Murray marked the beginning of one of the most important relationships in Irving's professional life, though not for reasons he was there to discuss that evening. As he stood looking at the brass plate with Murray's name and house number, he was slightly intimidated by the thought of approaching the man—this was essentially a job interview, and he didn't want to blow it.

Irving had good reason to be intimidated. In 1817 John Murray—born John Murray II in 1778—was one of the most powerful and respected publishers in Great Britain. Printer's ink ran through his veins. His father, the first John Murray, had founded the publishing house in 1768 to moderate success, but died in 1782 at the age of forty-eight. When the younger Murray entered the firm at seventeen, it was as a full partner. Murray learned the trade from his father's principal assistant, Samuel Highley, who changed the thrust of the business from publishing to bookselling. Murray dissolved their partnership in 1804, turning the House of Murray into both a bookseller and a publishing house.

Murray's tastes ran largely toward travel, medicine, and philosophy, but he recognized quality in other genres when he saw it, and in 1808 he had secured the copyright to the fourth part of Walter Scott's poem *Marmion*, marking the beginning of a long and mutually profitable friendship with Scott. He also published the poetry of Isaac D'Israeli, a lifelong family friend whose son Benjamin eventually became prime minister.

Murray was a shrewd businessman, and in 1803 he had entered into a partnership with Constable & Company in Edinburgh to copublish titles. The partnership with Constable resulted in coownership of the *Edinburgh Review*, a publication of literary criticism that could be not only brutally abusive in its reviews but equally abusive in its pro-Whig/anti-Tory rhetoric. In 1808 the Tory Murray severed his ties to Constable, and sold his shares in the *Edinburgh Review*. In 1809 Murray teamed with Scott to launch the *Quarterly Review*, a competing literary magazine that also served as the "voice of Constitutional Toryism."

Murray's ear for poetry resulted in an enormous coup in 1812, when the House of Murray became the first publisher of Lord Byron's *Childe Harold's Pilgrimage*. Its success took both Byron and Murray by surprise; at one trade dinner, Murray presold 7,000 copies of the third canto in one day. Murray wisely catered to the eccentric Byron, shopping for Byron's favorite tooth powders in London, introducing him to Walter Scott, and providing him with all the latest literary gossip. The House of Murray continued to build a regular stable of writers; besides Byron and Scott, Murray published Thomas Campbell, Thomas Moore, and Jane Austen.

In 1812 Murray moved his offices from Fleet Street to London's chic Mayfair District, purchasing outright the lease, copyrights, and stock of a retiring bookseller at 50 Albemarle Street. It quickly became one of the most fashionable addresses for literary men and women in London. Every afternoon, from 2:00 until 5:00, Murray presided over a drawing room that could be filled on any given day with writers, publishers, editors, politicians, or actors. In the evenings he hosted smaller, intimate dinners that often lasted well into the night.[48]

One attendee once remarked that there were three unwritten criteria to gain admittance to Murray's parlor: one had to be an author, a Tory, and patronized by the aristocracy. Irving was definitely the first, but neither of the remaining two. He was, however, an American, and to Murray, that was enough to compensate for the other shortcomings.

Irving knocked on the door, and presented Campbell's letter of introduction to the servant who answered. The letter was a good one, and within moments he was ushered to the first floor, and into the presence of John Murray II. At thirty-nine years old, Murray had thinning hair, brushed forward as was the fashion, a fine nose, and full, pursed lips. He was blind in his right eye—when he was a child, a writing instructor had accidentally run a penknife through it. The Prince of Booksellers smiled and offered Irving his hand.

Irving was led into the famous drawing room, where portraits of Byron, Campbell, and Scott stared down from the walls. Murray showed off his library, which the bibliophile in Irving itched to touch, and talked to him of Thomas Moore's poetry. They settled into a discussion with the guests in the drawing room that after-noon, among them George Canning, a former secretary of foreign affairs under William Pitt and a regular contributor to the *Quarterly Review*, and John Barrow, secretary to the admiralty, who promoted British exploration of both the Arctic and the Northwest Passage. By 5:00 it was clear Irving had met with Murray's approval. The drawing room patter he had learned and honed in Europe—as well as his own considerable charm and interests—had served him well. He had passed the first test. He was invited to dinner that evening.

The dinner guests included Isaac D'Israeli, who spoke of his latest researches in the British Museum; William Brockedon, a young artist just returned from Italy; John Miller, an English pub-lisher with a specialty in American authors; and Walter Hamilton, author of *The East India Gazeteer* and several other Asiatic studies. Irving spoke easily with D'Israeli, whose poetry was familiar to him, and was particularly taken with Hamilton, who chattered amiably.

After dinner, the party retired with glasses of port to the upstairs sitting room, where Murray showed Irving one of his letters from Byron—"written with some flippancy," Irving told Brevoort later—in which the poet promised to deliver the fourth canto of

Childe Harold as quickly as possible. Murray sometimes talked too much, especially when he'd been drinking—one correspondent wrote of "Murray's leaky lips"—and as he discussed Byron with Irving, he complained about lost profits due to the pirating of Byron's work in America.[49] That was the opening Irving needed, and he quickly explained his antipiracy scheme to Murray. The publisher agreed that such an idea had merit and agreed to discuss it at greater length with Irving later.

The party broke up close to midnight, and Irving lingered in the rain on Murray's steps, anxious to discuss his project. Murray waved him away with a smile, telling him to "keep an eye out for my advertisements in the papers and write to me whenever I have anything that might be of interest for republication in America."[50] It was enough. Irving left encouraged.

"I made the acquaintance of Murray the Bookseller, who you know is a most valuable acquaintance to a stranger, as by his means considerable access is gained to the literary world,"[51] Irving wrote excitedly to Brevoort. His future, he thought, was looking brighter. Ideally, his arrangements with Murray and Thomas would provide him with a steady flow of income.

That summer, Allston took Irving to visit his friend and mentor Samuel Taylor Coleridge. Irving was unimpressed and slightly confused by the great poet. "I was surprised by his volubility," he later wrote of Coleridge. "He walked about, in his gray hair, with his right hand over his head, moving the thumb and finger of his right hand . . . over his head, as if sprinkling snuff upon his crown."[52] Coleridge's *Biographia Literaria* had been published recently, and Irving was as uninspired by Coleridge's poetry as he was by Wordsworth's. He found it too vulgar, too coarse, too full of colloquialisms.

Irving spent most of August 1817 in London. The city was nearly deserted, the theaters closed for the season. He had scribbled the beginnings of a number of short stories in his journals, which he had every intention of working on—but after his self-imposed hiatus from society in Liverpool throughout the spring, the invitations he received to dinner and parties proved irresistible. He befriended actor John Kemble, who owned the Covent Garden Theatre, and spent more time with Allston and Leslie.

They were pleasant enough diversions, but the best was yet to come. A pilgrimage to Scotland—the land of his forefathers and of his literary father, Walter Scott—was, he thought, just what he needed for both inspiration and relaxation. Campbell's letter of introduction to Scott was safely stowed away in his rooms on Cockspur Lane. It was time to use it.

7

Determination

1817–1818

Man must be aspiring; ambition belongs to his nature. He cannot rest content but is continually reaching after higher attainments and more felicitous conditions. To rest satisfied with the present is a sign of an abject spirit.

—Washington Irving, Journals, 1817

"I HAD A LETTER of introduction to him from Thomas Campbell, the poet," Irving recalled of his visit to Walter Scott, "and had reason to think, from the interest he had taken in some of my earlier scribblings, that a visit from me would not be deemed an intrusion."[1]

Irving could thank Henry Brevoort for Scott's earlier interest. In 1813, while traveling in Scotland, Brevoort had passed a copy of *A History of New York* to Scott, who had enjoyed the book enough to write Irving an appreciative letter. Since then, it had been Irving's dream to meet his idol.

On August 21, 1817, Irving boarded the smack *Lively* in London, and sailed up the eastern British coastline bound for Berwick-upon-Tweed in Northumbria. With the ship barely out of port, he began writing in his journals, filling pages with colorful descriptions of the ship, the shoreline, and his fellow passengers. The notes were more polished now, the observations of a writer, not of a mere tourist. Four days later, the *Lively* docked in Berwick, where Irving discovered the next coach leaving for Edinburgh wouldn't depart for another two days. Too excited to wait, he leaped into the nearest available carriage, and arrived in Edinburgh eight hours later.

He had asked William Preston, who was attending law school at the University of Edinburgh, to meet him in town, but was unable to locate his friend upon his arrival. Undaunted, Irving dove eagerly into the sights of Edinburgh by himself. With smoke rising from the chimneys of the houses between the old and new parts of town, and the shadows playing on the nearby castles, he found the town charming—"It far surpasses all my expectation; and, except Naples, is, I think, the most picturesque place I have ever seen."[2] Scott's Abbotsford home was in Melrose, near Selkirk, about forty miles southeast of Edinburgh. Irving longed to be on his way, but a stretch of bad weather detained him in Edinburgh for several days.

Irving made the most of his time there, dining with Mrs. Renwick's brother, Francis Jeffrey, editor of the powerful *Edinburgh Review*, the magazine that had given poor Murray such fits back in 1808. Over dinner, he and Jeffrey agreed that the mysterious author of the *Waverly* novels was, indeed, Walter Scott.

Like his Tory counterpart John Murray, Francis Jeffrey was a talker. He had strong opinions on just about everything—his reviews could be scalding—and Americans did not escape his notice. He was particularly tart regarding American women, who he thought were "brought into company too early—[which] makes them flippant and ignorant." While Irving bit his lip around Jeffrey and even found him amusing, Brevoort was not a fan. "His foible is an unceasing effort to act the high finished gentleman," Brevoort had written contemptuously to Irving in 1813; "consequently he is blessed with such an immaculate degree of taste as to contemn every thing in the world both moral & physical." Brevoort's final word on Jeffrey was cutting—"I would not give the Minstrel for a wilderness of Jeffreys"—but Irving found him pleasant enough company.[3]

Irving met with Murray's Scottish agent, William Blackwood,

who asked if he would consider contributing to the magazine he had established to compete with the *Edinburgh Review*. Using a letter of introduction from John Miller, the bookseller he had met at Murray's, Irving made the acquaintance of Murray's former publishing partner, Archibald Constable, who also asked Irving to contribute to a new magazine. Irving was suddenly a hot commodity, though in the end he would write for neither magazine. He did, however, reach an informal agreement with both to act as their middleman with the American market—an arrangement that resulted in Thomas publishing an edition of *Rob Roy* in Philadelphia, but does not otherwise seem to have profited either Blackwood or Constable.

It continued to rain, but after four days in Edinburgh, Irving could wait no longer—he *had* to see Scott. Squeezing into a mail coach bound for Selkirk, he wondered nervously how he would be received by his idol. As the two later learned, Irving and Scott had much in common. Both had trained as lawyers, and both had experienced early fame from their writing before achieving iconic stature later in their lives. Both wrote out of necessity when money was tight, and both were fiercely protective of their reputations. Like Irving, Scott wrote under thinly veiled pseudonyms, as he had done with the recently published novel *Waverly*.

The Walter Scott that Irving had read and admired was not yet the Sir Walter Scott of *Ivanhoe*, *Rob Roy*, or *Kenilworth*—those novels all came later, as would the baronetcy. At the time of Irving's visit to Abbotsford in 1817, Scott's fame and reputation were built not upon his talents as a Romantic novelist but on his considerable skills as a Romantic poet.

As a young man in Edinburgh, Scott had been formally trained as a lawyer, but found the pull of the pen too strong to resist. He began dabbling in his early twenties, first translating German works, then eventually writing his own poetry. Within a few years, he had experienced moderate success with *The Minstrelsy of the Scottish Border,* a collection of Scottish ballads.

Shortly after marrying in 1797, Scott established his own press to print and publish his poems. Its first product, the poem *The Lay of the Last Minstrel*, was a huge hit with readers and critics alike. Subsequent works were also enormously successful, especially *Lady of the Lake* and *Marmion*, yet the revenue generated by Scott's poetry wasn't enough. The press bogged down in financial troubles.

To bail it out, Scott turned to his pen with the deliberate intention of writing a money-making novel. The result was *Waverly*, his first foray into fiction, and it sold well. Yet Scott was rather embarrassed by the need to turn to novel-writing and asked Murray to publish it anonymously to protect his hard-earned reputation; he preferred to be known as the poet who had penned *Lady of the Lake*.

The identity of the anonymous author was the subject of considerable debate. Even as it became generally known that the enigmatic voice belonged to Scott—and that his association with novel-writing was not going to harm his reputation—he still asked that subsequent novels, such as *Rob Roy*, be attributed to "The Author of Waverly," just to keep the transparent ruse going.

Irving's coach clattered to a stop in front of the gates at Abbotsford, and he excitedly presented Campbell's letter of introduction, asking the attendant if it would be agreeable for Mr. Scott to receive him. The servant retreated to the house, and Irving held his breath for the answer. As dogs yelped in the distance, he feared for a moment that Scott might not be at home. He could see the mansion some distance below the road on a hillside rolling down toward the Tweed River.

To his delight, here came Scott, walking slowly up the hill toward the front gate. A spry forty-six-year-old, he was twelve years Irving's senior, but his limp—the result of childhood polio—fooled one into thinking he was older. Writing of their initial meeting at Abbotsford years later, Irving never forgot his first sight of the man: "He was tall, and of a large and powerful frame. His dress was simple, almost rustic. An old green shooting coat, with a dog-whistle at the buttonhole, brown linen pantaloons, stout shoes that tied at the ankles, and a white hat that had evidently seen service.

He came limping up the gravel walk, aiding himself by a stout walking-staff, but moving rapidly and with vigor."[4]

Scott shook Irving's hand warmly, and invited him to breakfast with his family. Irving tried to beg off, saying that he had already eaten, but Scott would have none of it. "Hout, man," Scott said in his deep Scotch burr, "a ride in the morning in the keen air of the Scotch hill is warrant enough for a second breakfast." It was all the encouragement Irving needed; he spent a pleasant morning with Scott and his wife, Charlotte, their daughters, Sophia and Ann, and their sons, Walter and Charles.

After breakfast, Scott tapped Charles to take Irving on a tour of the ruins of Melrose Abbey—from which Scott pilfered stone for his house—while he stayed behind to work on *Rob Roy*. To make up for his absence, he promised to personally escort Irving the following day to the same Dryburgh Abbey that had been described in the poetry of Robert Burns. Irving's head spun. "I found myself committed for a visit of several days," he wrote, "and it seemed as if a little realm of romance was suddenly opened before me."

That afternoon, Scott himself, ever the good Scottish laird, provided Irving with a walking tour of Abbotsford, its grounds, and the surrounding neighborhood. At the time of Irving's visit in 1817, the estate spanned more than a thousand acres, with a number of houses within its boundaries. Scott had purchased the core of his property in 1811, and continued to buy up surrounding parcels of land and adjoining farms each year. Parts of the property butted up against Cauldshield's Loch, which, like any proper Scottish loch, was rumored to have its own sea monster, though Scott reported with some disappointment that he had yet to see it.[5]

In 1812 he had built a small villa that he named Abbotsford, in recognition of the nearby ford where abbots had crossed the river to reach Melrose Abbey. Scott was constantly extending the small house, adding four new rooms in 1816, building the ruins of nearby castles and abbeys into its walls, transforming the original farmhouse into the feudal manor Irving had seen from the front gates. Even as the two men walked the property, hammers were flying.[6]

Although Irving was presently the only guest in the house, Abbotsford often swelled with visitors, as friends, admirers, and the merely curious stopped by to gaze at the writer of *Marmion*. Charlotte Scott once remarked that Abbotsford was "a hotel in all but name and pay," and its bedrooms were occupied so frequently that Scott had advised the inns at Melrose and Selkirk to be prepared for guests who either could not be accommodated or were not expected at the estate.[7]

Despite his limp, Scott was a strong walker, and he steered his guest to the hills overlooking the Tweed, where Irving expressed surprise at the barrenness of the landscape that Scott had described so lovingly in his poetry. The two talked of their mutual friend Campbell, and Scott remarked that it was a pity the man did not write more, little suspecting that Campbell was far too intimidated by him to write quickly or often. "Campbell is, in a manner, a bugbear to himself," Scott harrumphed knowingly. "The brightness of his early success is a detriment to all his further efforts. He is afraid of the shadow that his own fame casts before him." He might have said the same of Irving.

Irving shared an intimate dinner with the writer's family that evening, listening to Scott talk colorfully of dogs, his neighbors, and the Scottish character. After dinner, Sophia sang Scottish border songs, much to her father's delight and approval, and Irving stayed up late into the evening chatting with, but mainly listening to, his idol. At evening's end, he retired, giddy, to his quarters, finding it impossible to sleep.

He awoke early to find Scott already up and about, giving orders to the masons and carpenters who were banging noisily about Abbotsford's grounds. Scott regaled Irving over breakfast with endless stories of local color, spinning one tale after another in inimitable style. He and Irving read over proofs of *Rob Roy*, then took another stroll around the countryside, poking through the remains of a Roman camp. The following day the two set out to visit the ruins of Dryburgh Abbey, a still impressive structure that had been decimated in the sixteenth century. Again Scott pointed out all the local landmarks and scenery, but Irving was paying no attention to the scenery; he was completely focused on Scott. He loved to listen to the man talk, and preferred their walks in the countryside to tours of local sights.

Caught in a sudden rainstorm one afternoon, Scott wrapped his tartan around himself and pulled Irving under the cover of a thicket. Motioning for Irving to sit beside him, he draped the tartan around Irving's shoulders, literally taking his young admirer under his wing. It was a gesture Irving never forgot.

Leaving proved difficult; his three days with Scott were the happiest he had spent since his arrival in England two years prior. Scott walked Irving to his carriage, and warmly took his hand. "I will not say farewell," Scott said, "for it is always a painful word, but I will say, come again . . . come when you please, you will always find Abbotsford open to you, and a hearty welcome."[8]

"I came prepared to admire him," Irving wrote of Scott later, "but he completely won my heart and made me love him." We can only imagine how much this visit meant to Irving; the great man actually *liked* him. "It was if I were admitted to a social communion with Shakespeare, for it was with one of a kindred, if not equal genius," Irving gushed later. "Every night I returned with my mind filled with delightful recollections of the day, and every morning I rose with the certainty of new enjoyment. The days thus spent I shall ever look back to as among the very happiest of my life; for I was conscious at the time of being happy."[9]

His affection was reciprocated; Scott was genuinely fond of Irving. "When you see Tom Campbell," Scott said to one correspondent, shortly after Irving's departure, "tell him, with my best love, that I have to thank him for making me known to Mr. Washington Irving, who is one of the best and pleasantest acquaintances I have made this many a day. He stayed two or three days with me, and I hope to see him again."[10] It was the beginning of a long and warm personal and professional friendship.

Returning to Edinburgh, Irving was reunited with Preston, and the two set out for an extended tour of Scotland that lasted for weeks. The weather was ideal, warm and sunny, and the two traveled "in every variety of mode—by chaise, by coach, by gig, by boat, on foot, and in a cart." They explored the haunts of Macbeth, rolling through Birnham Wood and Dunsinane, and visited the castle in Linlithgow where Mary Queen of Scots had been born. Irving also took special care to steer them through Stirling Castle, where Scott had set part of *Lady of the Lake*.

Travel always invigorated him, and he began writing regularly, the words flowing much more easily as he sat in the shadow of a Scottish castle or watched the sun glitter on the Clyde. His writing was more experimental, the phrases more finely tuned, and the people and places more fully and artfully described. Irving scribbled, as he usually did, in short bursts, with phrases separated by dashes. At times, even the most routine activities were painted vividly, even elegantly, in Irving's deliberate prose: "Tuesday morning—waiting for Steam boat—seated on a rock at the foot of Dunbarton castle—Hazy warm day—Sun just struggling thro the haze—tide low—beach grey—stones & seaweeds—Coal smack floating lazily in—hear now & then the creaking of the yards & hum of the boatmans song who is pacing his deck with folded arms . . . birds singing from the rocks over my head. [H]um of large blue flies about me—tokens of lingering Summer."[11]

At other moments, he indulged in rambling ruminations on life and love that seemed addressed to himself, a lifelong habit: "Man must be aspiring; ambition belongs to his nature. He cannot rest content but is continually reaching after higher attainments and more felicitous conditions. To rest satisfied with the present is a sign of an abject spirit."[12] Such self-examination was starting to resonate, for at this time Irving was clearly aspiring to something more than the role of frustrated businessman. The notebooks contain intriguing hints of plots, characters, and snatches of sentences that would appear in later works. The essay that became "The Widow and Her Son" was born in the 1817 notebook, among lines that could have easily described Irving's relationship with his own mother: "The purest & strongest affection that winds itself round the human heart is that between the mother & the son:—she will sacrifice all her comforts for him—she will love & cherish him in adversity—in disgrace—when all the world beside cast him off she will be all the world to him—"[13]

There is the whiff of a novel in these pages, as Irving scratched out a vague and disjointed outline of a story involving a southern belle named Rosalie and her husband, Frederick. The larger plot is now lost, but there seemed to have been a coy meeting, a rescue from a fire, a fight, a reconciliation, a marriage, and then—in a sudden, jarring entry in the notebook—Rosalie's death. Irving was experimenting with formats and with his voice. He may have figured that if Walter Scott could write a novel out of necessity, he might, too.[14]

As the Scottish excursion came to an end, Irving wrote Scott a letter of thanks and farewell, obviously agonizing over every word, as his notebooks reveal a first draft full of deletions and rewrites. The final version was warm, sincere, and appropriately self-deprecating: "Surrounded as you are by friends among the most intelligent and illustrious, the goodwill of an individual like myself cannot be a matter of much importance yet I feel a gratification in expressing it, and in assuring you that I shall ever consider the few days I passed with you and your amiable family as among the choicest of my life."[15] This was no overstatement. Irving's visit to Scott had been the highlight of his trip, and his friendship with Scott was one he treasured for the rest of his life.

Irving and Preston returned to Liverpool in late September. It had been a most satisfactory trip; his only real gripe was with Preston. While Irving was notoriously lazy at times, he took his traveling seriously, and Preston's proclivities for sleeping late and taking carriages when they could be walking was particularly galling to him. "The journey has been a complete trial of Preston's indolent habits," he had written to Peter in exasperation from Edinburgh. "I had at first to tow him along by main strength for he has as much alacrity at coming to anchor and is as slow getting under way as a Dutch Lugger."[16] Despite Preston's flaws as a traveler, Irving liked him and was sad to see the young man depart for London.

With Preston gone, there was no excuse not to return to the daily drudgery of P. Irving and Company. While he had Peter to keep him company and help with the work, his high spirits from the Scottish excursion disappeared quickly. His brother William, who understood his youngest brother's misery only too well, was pulling all the strings available to him as a member of Congress in an effort to secure for Irving an appointment as secretary to the United States Legation in London. Friends and family alike were promoting Irving as the most desirable candidate for the position, and William had even approached House Speaker Henry Clay to personally discuss the appointment.[17] Washington was grateful for the intervention, but told Brevoort that he doubted he would receive the appointment. He was right.

Time in Liverpool dragged on. Irving focused more intently on the essays he was writing in his assorted journals, and in his spare moments urged Campbell to publish a series of lectures the poet had written and delivered on poetry and belles lettres.

And then there was his work as the middleman between American and British publishers. To Murray he wrote official-sounding letters, vapidly explaining the intricacies of international publishing to London's master publisher: "If it is your wish to secure a participation in the profits of the American republication [of Byron's *Childe Harold*] in the way I suggested when I had the pleasure of seeing you in London, I would advise you not to lose time, as ships sometimes loiter in port and days may be lost here even after the work is sent."[18] He informed Murray that Moses Thomas was sending him a package of materials that had recently been published in America, and advised Murray to publish them quickly if he wished to secure their British copyrights.

Murray must have groaned when he opened the crate from Thomas; inside was a distinctly mediocre assortment of books, although William Wirt's *Sketches of the Life and Character of Patrick Henry* was probably the diamond in the rough. Murray declined, without comment, to publish any. When Irving asked Murray if he might send along Byron's *Childe Harold*, Canto IV, it appears that Murray did so, as an American edition appeared in Philadelphia in 1818. It was no wonder, then, that Irving and Thomas were excited about the prospects of effectively being Murray's American copublisher. So far, the advantages were decidedly one-sided.

Any pleasure Irving may have taken in his business dealings with Murray and Thomas evaporated in early October with news from America that cut Irving to the core. On September 20, 1817, Henry Brevoort married Laura Elizabeth Carson of South Carolina.

Irving was stunned. While Brevoort's letters from this time are missing, it is obvious from Irving's reaction that Brevoort had not informed him of his intentions, perhaps dreading the potential fallout. To his credit, Irving's response was not the near hysterics of 1816, but rather a sad, understated acceptance:

> I am almost ashamed to say that at first the news had rather the effect of making me feel melancholy rather than glad. It seemed in a manner to divorce us forever, for marriage is the grave of Bachelors intimacy and after having lived & grown together for many years, so that our habits thoughts & feelings were quite blended and intertwined, a separation of this kind is a serious matter—not so much to you, who are transplanted into the garden of matrimony, to flourish & fructify and be caressed into prosperity—but for poor me, left lonely & forlorn, and blasted by every wind of heaven— However I dont mean to indulge in lamentations on the occasion. Though this unknown piece of perfection has completely usurped my place, I bear her no jealousy or ill will; but hope you may long live happily together, and that she may prove as constant & faithful to you as I have been.[19]

Shortly after Irving posted this letter, Brevoort abruptly broke off their correspondence for several months—and Irving let the newlywed know that his silence had not gone unnoticed: "I cannot consent to be so completely forgotten. I don't mean to complain for

I know it is the nature of things and what we poor Bachelors must make our minds up to—but only do the thing decently and let me down as easy as possible. I wrote to you some time last winter . . . you have never acknowledged receipt of that letter. I hope it arrived safe and that you did not, in some sudden *fit of jealousy* suppress our correspondence."[20]

The mutual snit eventually blew over—perhaps each knew the other simply needed a good sulk. Their relationship had changed in unstated ways, but they had too much in common, too many shared experiences. The two resumed their warm, sincere correspondence and deep friendship, and continued to seek each other's guidance, solace, and support.

Stewing over Brevoort's marriage that fall, Irving's mood was suitably dark, though in a letter to Mrs. Hoffman in November, he indicated that he was still hoping to "find wholesome fruit springing out of trouble and adversity."[21]

Back in the States, William Irving, that most astute of men, saw the writing on the wall regarding the future of the family business. He stepped up his appeals to Henry Clay and others about political posts for both Washington and Peter. Writing to Ebenezer in December 1817 from Washington, D.C., where he had just taken his seat in the 15th Congress, William assured him he was working hard to secure something—anything—for their brothers in Liverpool. "I have not been inattentive to the situation of brothers Washington and Peter," he wrote firmly. "I have had two conversations with Clay on the subject. He stands ready to aid in anything that can be suggested. . . . You may rest assured that I will do my best. I need no pressing on my head, for my mind is full of the subject. I think on it night and day."[22]

Once again, the sought-for post fell through. Washington thanked William for his efforts, but said—perhaps too proudly—"I should not like to have my name hackneyed about among the office-seekers and office-givers at Washington." Instead, he told his brother, "I would rather that all consideration should be given to helping up poor Ebenezer and Peter, and let me take care of myself.

I feel excessive anxiety on Ebenezer's account, with such a numerous family to support, and I scarcely feel less on Peter's, who is brought down at a period of life when a man begins to crave ease and comfort in the world."[23]

As for his own situation, he told William that he did not require much to live and would much rather see his brothers successful and finally be "relieved from this cloud that hangs over us all." He was done playing businessman. "I certainly think that no hope of gain, however flattering, would tempt me again into the cares and sordid concerns of traffic," he declared.[24]

More important, he hinted that he was ready to strike out on his own. Firmly, but cryptically, he told William, "I give you this general assurance, which, I trust, will be received with confidence, and save the necessity of particular explanations, which it would be very irksome for me to make. I feel that my future career must depend very much upon myself, and therefore every step I make at present, is done with proper consideration. I look forward to a life of loneliness and parsimonious and almost painful economy."[25] The underlying implications of this letter were enormous. He gave his brothers no details, other than the pledge that he intended to be his own man and that no matter what happened, he knew what he was doing.

P. Irving and Company came to an end in the winter of 1817. Washington and Peter gave the ledgers a final look and realized they were finished; the business couldn't be saved. There was no other option but to declare bankruptcy.

The formal notice of the firm's bankruptcy appeared in the *Times* of London on February 2, 1818, and in the *Liverpool Mercury* on February 6, 1818. Henry Van Wart appeared again before his commission in Birmingham on February 13, 14, and 28, 1818; notice of his bankruptcy and that of the Irvings had appeared together on February 9, 1818, in *Aris's Birmingham Gazette*. There it was, for all to see. Theirs was among more than 1,300 bankruptcies filed that year. Appearing before their commission in Liverpool, with creditors, commissioners, and fellow debtors coming and going,

Washington and Peter could only watch in humiliation as the assignee pored over their books, determining how their assets would be divided.[26] The brothers made their last personal appearance before their commission on March 14. Their fate was now in the hands of the commissioners.

On April 30 Irving wrote Brevoort from Liverpool that he and Peter were "waiting here for the final settlement of our concerns; our certificates are going the round for Signature after which Peter will sail for New York." In the meantime, Irving was pacing the floors in their Bold Street rooms, still tinkering with *A History of New York*, conjugating verbs in the German he was trying to teach himself at Scott's urging, taking flute lessons, and fine-tuning the essays in his journals. Even Peter had returned to writing, translating Charles Nodier's *Jean Sbogar*, which had been published in Paris earlier in the year as *Giovanni Sbogarro, A Venetian Tale*. All things considered, Irving told Leslie, "we get through the day without a moment hanging heavy on our hands. I feel perfectly contented and in fact I do not think my time ever passed away more completely to my satisfaction."[27]

The Irvings' certificates were filed on May 25, 1818. "I am happy to inform you that we have had our Certificates duly signed and they have only now to go through the Lord Chancellor's hands," he wrote in relief to Brevoort. The firm was finally relieved of its obligations on June 22, 1818. The nightmare that had begun in 1815 was over.[28]

The bankruptcy finalized, Irving was briefly tempted to return home, but informed Brevoort that he was determined to remain in England for a while longer. He continued to ship British books to Thomas for him to publish in America, using Brevoort as his middleman to collect and remit payments—a system that seemed to work well enough.

He kept his writing close to his chest; so close, in fact, that when Thomas suggested he consider taking up the pen again, Irving dismissed the idea. "I notice what you say on the subject of getting up an original work but I am very squeamish on that point," he wrote. "Whatever my literary reputation may be worth, it is very dear to me, and I cannot bring myself to risk it by making up books for mere profit." Meanwhile, he was continuing to teach himself German, hoping to tap German literature and culture for literary inspiration. He reported to Brevoort with some satisfaction that he now knew enough to "read and *splutter* a little."[29]

In late June Irving returned to Birmingham, where he was delighted to learn that Henry Van Wart had already begun to recover from bankruptcy. "I am happy to say," he reported to one correspondent, "that Van is *full of business and business of the right kind*, and is in high spirits."[30]

It was hot that summer; one English newspaper reported temperatures as high as 116 degrees.[31] In the relative cool of Castle Von Tromp, Irving continued to guide the new edition of *A History of New York* toward production, mainly through directives to Allston and Leslie. The drawings the two had completed for the new edition were being engraved, and Irving managed their printing with care. Allston was particularly pleased with the quality of the engravings, and apologized to Irving that such work was going to cost more. Irving not only paid for the more expensive engraver, but asked that the engravings be printed on the finest French paper.

Something much more exciting, however, was about to occupy his time. Irving had moped about Castle Van Tromp, his mood somber, his flute quiet. Van Wart watched him staring at the blank sheets of paper in his room, head in his hands; he understood from his own experiences the humiliations of bankruptcy, but also appreciated Irving's tendency to brood. Determined to raise his brother-in-law's spirits, Van Wart pulled Irving aside one evening and spoke to him of New York, the theater, and Sleepy Hollow. The two laughed at the stories and memories, until Irving suddenly bolted from the chamber and fled to his room, slamming the door behind him. His pen scratched and flew all night long, filling sheets of paper with his barely legible handwriting, the words coming almost faster than he could get them down.

In the morning, he was still hunched over his desk while the house awakened, dressed, and breakfasted. As the family dined, Irving emerged from his room, manuscript in hand, flushed but showing no signs of exhaustion, despite having worked all night. It had all come back to him, he explained excitedly to the family—the conversations about Dutch New York and Sleepy Hollow had brought back his inspiration and his energy; he felt like a man waking from a long sleep. Sitting at the breakfast table, he read the Van Warts the opening chapters of what he had written all through the night, the tale of another man who had suddenly awakened from a long sleep: Rip Van Winkle.

Rip came in nearly finished form on his first draft. Irving's satisfaction must have been immense as he tucked the manuscript into his trunk, where it sat with nine near-complete essays. He was becoming more and more certain of what he wanted to do. Resolved, he notified Thomas that he was canceling their arrangement to act as an intermediary between the American and British markets, refusing the rest of his salary and telling him that he did not believe the arrangement had been as productive for Thomas as they had anticipated.[32]

Irving packed his bags and left for London in the middle of August, determined to earn his living by his pen. His journals were filled with half-finished essays, turns of phrase that appealed to his ear, plot outlines for stories, and long notes to himself. His mind was a jumble; it had been a long year.

Arriving in London, he received word that Allston was preparing to leave for America and rushed in panic to the artist's rooms in Fitzroy Square. They were empty. Frantic, he located Leslie, who told him that Allston was visiting Coleridge. Irving galloped out to Hellgate to meet him, pleading with Allston to remain in London, and trying to convince him he would be more successful and better appreciated in England than in the United States.

It was no use. Allston's mind was made up; he was going to Boston to open his own studio. "As he drove off in the stage and waved his hand to me," Irving said, "my heart sank within me and I returned gloomy and dispirited to my lodgings." Allston's departure was a severe blow to Irving. He had adored the painter since their brief time together in Rome in 1805, and Allston had nearly replaced Brevoort in his heart. "He was the most delightful, the most lovable being I ever knew," Irving sighed many years later, "a man I would like to have had always at my side—to have gone through life with; his nature was so refined, so intellectual, so genial, so pure."[33]

His absence had a similarly devastating effect on Leslie, who also seemed to have had more than friendly feelings for Allston. Leslie and Irving turned to each other for solace. Two years later, with his own marriage approaching, Leslie expressed his gratitude to Irving for carrying him through this particularly lonely time: "You came to London just when I was losing Allston, and I stood in need of an intimate friend of similar tastes with my own. I not only owe you some of the happiest social hours of my life, but you opened to me a new range of observation in my art, and a perception of qualities and characters of things which painters do not always imbibe from each other."[34]

Besides Leslie, Irving became attached to another American painter, Gilbert Stuart Newton, the nephew of the American portrait painter Gilbert Stuart. Newton and Irving soon moved into rooms together on Langham Place. "I often look back with fondness and regret to the times we lived together in London in a delightful community of thought and feeling," Irving later wrote of his time with Newton, "struggling our way onward in the world, but cheering and encouraging each other. I find nothing to supply the place of that heartfelt fellowship."

Rounding out Irving's small circle of friends—as he had done in New York, Irving referred to his group as the Lads, with nicknames for each—were the "highly animated" Peter Powell, who was quite a bit older than the others, with a larger-than-life personality that more than compensated for his near-midget stature, and William Willes, an Irish landscape painter who was a student at the Royal Academy.[35]

Scholars have scratched their heads at this nearly inseparable group of young men, wondering if there was perhaps something more going on. Given Irving's strong attachments to Brevoort, Allston, and Newton, as well as the strong expressions of need and love in their correspondence with each other over the years, it is not unlikely that some element of the homoerotic may have linked the men.[36] Regardless, the group cut an impressive picture of talented and handsome young men that would have been very much at home in London's artistic community.

Irving walked the streets of London more deliberately now, filing away information in his notebooks for future use, wandering in thought through Westminster Abbey and taking page after page of notes in the British Museum. The writing frenzy that had seized him in Birmingham had subsided in London. He told Brevoort that he was "nervous and debilitated," which produced a "great depression of Spirits."[37] The darkness was beginning to close in.

He sorted through the essays he had completed. No cohesive theme bound them together; turning them into a novel would be difficult. But just as Irving had inspired Leslie's art, so had living among artists inspired Irving as a writer. These essays were like a series of sketches—a sketchbook, as it were.

He read with mixed emotions of the birth of Brevoort's son, and at last put the finishing touches on the new edition of *A History of New York*. He was very pleased with the art he had received from Allston and Leslie, and the quality of the engravings surpassed his expectations. He covered the costs of printing the new plates out of his own pocket, paying an impressive one hundred pounds schilling, or about $11,000 today, which left his purse, as he said understatedly, "dry." He shipped them to Ebenezer in October, and asked that Moses Thomas be allowed to publish the new edition. In the same letter, there is a cryptic reference to a sealed packet he had sent to Ebenezer earlier, which he now informed his brother he could destroy. "I have nothing now to leave my brothers but a blessing," Irving wrote, "and that they have whenever I think of them."[38]

His brothers thought of him as well. Both Ebenezer and William had been working hard on his behalf since the unsuccessful appeals to Clay months before. In November Irving received the following letter from William, sent from New York in late October 1818:

> I added a postscript to a letter of Br[other] Ebenezer to you, written a few days ago. The purport of the letter was to inform you that Commodore Decatur informed me that he had made such arrangements, and such steps would further be made by the Navy Board, as that you will be able to obtain the office of first Clerk in the Navy Department, which is indeed similar to that of under secretary in England. The salary is equal to 2,400 Dollars per annum, which as the Commodore says, is sufficient to enable you to live in Washington like a prince. The Secretary of the Navy has resigned, and as harmony in that department is wished, the President wishes that the new one may meet with their approbation. The have been looking round for a suitable person, and they are resolved to make it a *sine qua non* with him, whoever he may be, that the present chief clerk, who has rendered himself particularly obnoxious to all the fine spirits of the Navy, shall be dismissed; and they have determined to secure the birth for you, until your answer can be obtained. It is a birth highly respectable—Very comfortable in its income, light in its duties, and will afford you a very ample leisure to pursue the bent of your literary inclinations. It may also be a mere stepping stone to higher station and may be considered at any rate permanent.
>
> If you think it will suit, you will return immediately. . . . My dear brother, how happy I will be to see you all in a comfortable way once more. It will take the only load remaining from my heart.[39]

For years Irving had sought the relative stability of a political appointment, going hat in hand to Albany in 1810, hearing his name bandied about, without success, in Washington in 1811, and then, in early 1818, having the secretaryship of the American Legation dangled before being snatched away. Now here was a plum, his for the taking, with minimal responsibilities, which would give him the opportunity to use his social skills to make the contacts he needed for his writing or, as William put it, some even "higher station."

William had pulled considerable strings—approaching first Clay, then Decatur—and had managed to find this exceptional post in the navy. It was an ideal opportunity, yet the letter must have sat heavy in Irving's hands.

Had the same arrived fourteen months earlier, before the visit to Scott, or even six months prior, before the all-night writing session that produced Rip Van Winkle, Irving's decision—and American literature—might have been very different indeed. But now, despite the unfinished sketches in his notebooks, the uncertainty of his endeavor, and the certain disappointment of his brothers, which was perhaps the heaviest weight of all, he was finally resolved.

"Flattering as the prospect undoubtedly is, which your letters hold out," he explained to Ebenezer later that month, "I have concluded to decline it for various reasons, some of which I have stated to William. The principal one is, that I do not wish to undertake any situation that must involve me in such a routine of duties as to prevent my attending to literary pursuits."[40]

He remembered his advice to Brevoort. He would not link his fortunes with others. He would earn his own way with his pen.

The answer to William was no. It was all or nothing.

8

Sensation

1819–1821

I am astonished at the success of my writings in England, and can hardly persuade myself that it is not all a dream. Had any one told me a few years since in America, that any thing I could write would interest such men as . . . Byron, I should have as readily believed a fairy tale.

—Washington Irving to John Murray II, October 31, 1820

Ome has lost its charms to . . . [Peter] and Washington," William Irving wrote sadly to Ebenezer. "It is as well to accommodate the heart to its loss, and to consider them, as to all but epistolary correspondence, dead to us."[1]

As terrible as having no job, no money, and no prospects might be, nothing depressed Washington more than the thought that he had disappointed William. He spent the next several weeks brooding and second-guessing his decision, so upset he could barely pick up his pen.

"Fancy, humor—all seemed to have gone from me," he said. "I had offended the best brothers a man ever had; given over the chance Providence seemed to have opened, and now my writing-hand was palsied; a more miserable, doubting creature than I was in the two following months can hardly have lived." He didn't even have Peter to commiserate with. Citing only "confidential business," Peter departed for France in early January. He, too, had refused assistance from William, waving aside an offer of a post for settling claims under the Treaty of Spain in favor of chasing get-rich-quick schemes in Europe.[2]

As always, Irving sought relief in the company of friends, plunging into London's social scene with Newton, Leslie, and other American expatriates. American minister Richard Rush was a constant companion, and decidedly more reputable than another friend, the actor and playwright John Howard Payne, who was working hard to stay one step ahead of his creditors. Irving and his Lads dined at the York Chop House with John Allan, a Richmond tobacco merchant traveling in London with his foster son, Edgar Poe, or with Colonel Thomas Aspinwall, just beginning a nearly forty-year stint as United States consul in London. Between tours of the surrounding countryside and shows at the Drury Lane Theatre, Irving's writing hand finally steadied. Through late January and early February 1819, the draft sketches in his trunks were revised and polished. Suddenly, five essays were ready.[3]

On March 1, 1819, Irving handed a package to the captain of the ship *Rosalie*, leaving for New York on March 11. "This letter is accompanied by a small parcel containing some manuscript for publication," Washington wrote Ebenezer. "It will form the first number of a work to be continued occasionally should this specimen meet with sufficient success."[4] He directed Ebenezer to secure its copyright and make arrangements with Moses Thomas for immediate publication. With business out of the way, Washington—who still feared his brothers disapproved of his career choice—launched into a long defense of his decision to refuse William's job offer. He was sending his manuscript, he told Ebenezer, "more for the purpose of showing you what I am about, as I find my declining the situation at Washington has given you chagrin. . . . It would have led to no higher situations, for I am quite unfitted for political life. . . . It is a mistake also to suppose I would fill an office there, and devote myself at the same time to literature. I require much leisure and a mind entirely abstracted from other cares and occupations, if I would write much or write well."[5] No longer satisfied to rest on the laurels he had earned as Oldstyle or Knickerbocker, Irving closed on a bold note, sounding like an independent adult for perhaps the first time in his thirty-five years:

> I have but one thing to add. I have now given you the lead-ing motive of my actions—it may be a weak one, but it has full possession of me, and therefore the attainment of it is necessary to my comfort. I now wish to be left for a little while entirely to the bent of my own inclination, and not agitated by new plans for subsistence, or by entreaties to come home. . . . Do not, I beseech you, impute my lingering in Europe to any indifference to my own country or my friends. My greatest desire is to make myself worthy of the good-will of my country. . . . I am determined not to return home until I have sent some writings before me that shall, if they have merit, make me return to smiles, rather than skulk back to the pity of my friends.[6]

At the same time, Irving appealed to Brevoort for assistance, tapping his friend to act as his literary agent and business man-ager—one of the smartest career decisions Irving ever made. "If the work is printed in NYork," he implored Brevoort, "will you correct the proof sheets, as I fear the Mss: will be obscure and occasionally incorrect, & you are well acquainted with my handwriting."[7]

It had been nearly ten years since Irving had dazzled the public with *A History of New York*. "I feel great diffidence about this reap-pearance in literature," he confessed to Brevoort. "I am conscious of my imperfections—and my mind has been for a long time past so preyed upon and agitated by various cares and anxieties, that I fear it has lost much of its cheerfulness and some of its activity."[8]

He was more anxious in his letters to Ebenezer. "Do not show the Mss. to any one, nor say any thing about it," Washington begged. "Write to [Moses] Thomas *confidentially*. It is better to awaken no expectations."[9]

Reading Washington's letter and manuscript in mid-April, Ebenezer shared his brother's uneasiness. The voice in the essays, while clear and confident, *was* different from Washington's earlier tone. Despite his brother's pleas for discretion, an uncertain Ebenezer held a private reading in his parlor for Brevoort, Renwick, and a few others before sending the manuscript to Moses Thomas. After a hoarse Ebenezer finished reading aloud the final sentence, there was stunned silence; then, the room erupted in applause. Ebenezer, relieved, burst into tears.[10]

In London Washington was oblivious to its reception. As Ebenezer and Brevoort attended to the manuscript in New York, Washington paced the floor nervously in Leslie's flat. Given the time it took for correspondence to cross the Atlantic, he wouldn't know until late summer how his essays had been received. All he could do was wait.

And still he kept writing. On April 1 Irving sent Brevoort a packet containing another four essays. Irving also indicated he wasn't above pandering to the masses, and asked Brevoort to let him know "what themes &c would be popular and striking in America." Another four essays were dropped in the mail, in duplicate, to John Treat and Brevoort on May 13. "I hope by the time this arrives some of them may be in print & the question settled whether they are profitable," he told John Treat.[11]

While the copyright for the first installment had been secured, it hadn't yet appeared in print. Strapped for cash, Washington asked Brevoort for a loan of $1,300—about $20,000 today—against any future profits he might secure on publication. If his work landed with a thud, Irving was finished—and he knew it. "My fate hangs on it," he told Brevoort, "for I am now at the end of my *fortune*."[12]

On June 23 an octavo-sized volume—about six by nine inches—entitled *The Sketch Book of Geoffrey Crayon, Gent.* went on sale simultaneously in New York, Boston, Baltimore, and Philadelphia. The paper quality was first rate, and the typeface was attractive. Henry Brevoort had done his job well.

Brevoort had balked at publishing *The Sketch Book* through the financially struggling Moses Thomas, but found a willing publisher in a Greenwich Street printer with the serendipitous name of Cornelius S. Van Winkle. Two thousand copies of the first installment had been printed, and the price on the volume was relatively steep—75 cents, or about $11 today, for ninety-three pages—but Irving had mandated both the print run and the price. "A large edition must be struck off," he told Ebenezer, "and the price must be pretty high. If it is known to be my work I presume it will have a quick sale."[13] Irving's name appeared nowhere on the book, but there was little doubt that Geoffrey Crayon, Gentleman, and Washington Irving, Esquire, were one and the same. Just to be safe, Brevoort was working to make sure readers saw right through Irving's latest pseudonym.

Irving had included a "Prospectus" at the beginning of the volume. The sentiment was straight out of *Salmagundi,* but the tone was less defiant: "The following writings are published on experiment; should they please they may be followed by others. . . . Should his writings, however, with all their imperfections, be well received, he cannot conceal that it would be a source of the purest gratification . . . it is the dearest wish of his heart to have a secure and cherished, though humble corner in the good opinions and kind feelings of his countrymen."[14]

His countrymen were more than willing to oblige him. There were five essays in the first installment, and the public responded enthusiastically to the first four: "The Author's Account of Himself," in which Irving introduced Geoffrey Crayon; "The Voyage," detailing Crayon's ocean voyage to England; "Roscoe," Irving's tribute to an English writer and historian he had met in Liverpool; and "The Wife," a sentimental piece in which the new wife of an impoverished gentleman teaches her husband that money can't buy happiness. But it was the final tale in the volume, "Rip Van Winkle"—a tale "found among the papers of Diedrich Knickbocker," Crayon claimed—that readers loved best, and kept the volume selling briskly.

The response from critics was equally encouraging, though Irving had Brevoort to thank for his first positive reviews. Just three days after the book's release, Brevoort placed an anonymous review in the *Evening Post,* lauding *The Sketch Book* and letting readers know that it was Irving's work: "The graces of style; the rich, warm tone of benevolent feeling; the freely-flowing vein of hearty and happy humour, and the fine-eyed spirit of observation, sustained by an enlightened understanding and regulated by a perception of fitness—a tact—wonderfully quick and sure, for which Mr. Irving has been heretofore so much distinguished, are all exhibited anew in the Sketch Book, with freshened beauty and added charms."[15]

It was a bit excessive, but even critic Gulian Verplanck—who had earlier complained that Irving was wasting his talents on the "coarse" Knickerbocker[16]—publicly admitted that he too was a fan. "It will be needless to inform any who have read the book, that it is from the pen of Mr. Irving," Verplanck wrote. "His rich, and sometimes extravagant humour, his gay and graceful fancy . . . betray the author in every page; even without the aid of those minor peculiarities of style, taste, and local allusions, which at once identify the travelled Geoffrey Crayon with the venerable Knickerbocker."[17] Positive notices continued to roll in. "When the first number of this beautiful work was announced," one American reviewer gushed, "it was sufficient to induce an immediate and importunate demand, that the name of Mr. Irving was attached to it in the popular mind."[18] Geoffrey Crayon was a hit. Back in London, Irving fretfully paced the floor, distracting himself by reading rough drafts of Payne's play *Virginius*, awaiting the latest news from Brevoort.

The longer Brevoort remained silent, the more nervous Irving became. When he received a letter in early July in which Brevoort expressed his own high opinion of Irving's five essays, Irving only became more agitated. He didn't want Brevoort's opinion; he wanted to know how his work had taken with the *public*. He also worried that his perilous financial position had forced him into print before he was ready, and that his work had suffered for it. "Had I been able to save but a pittance from the wrecks of our concerns, so as to keep me above the fear of a positively empty purse," he told Brevoort, "I should have felt more ease of mind and been able the better to have matured my plans."[19] That was doubtful; just as the need for financial stability had, at least in part, driven Irving to pen

A History of New York, impending poverty spurred Irving to write *The Sketch Book.* Nothing in his life would ever spark his pen into action quite as quickly as an empty pocketbook.

By July 28 Irving at last had a copy of the first installment of *The Sketch Book.* "The work is got up in a beautiful style," he told Brevoort appreciatively. All he required now was assurance that the effort had been worthwhile. "My spirits have revived recently and I trust, if I receive favourable accounts of the works taking in America, that I shall be able to go on with more animation."[20]

On July 31, as Irving watched the mail for reviews, Van Winkle's presses churned out two thousand copies of the second installment of *The Sketch Book.* Again, Brevoort had taken steps to ensure the work was released to good press, placing another flattering review in the August 3 *Evening Post.* It was unnecessary—the strength of the essays ensured the success of the second volume.

Priced at 62½ cents, the second volume featured four essays: "English Writers on America," Irving's magnanimous call for a ceasefire of "the literary animosity daily growing between England and America"; "Rural Life in England," a fond description of English countryside and character; "The Broken Heart," a story about a young Irish woman who wasted away "in a slow but hopeless decline" following the death of her true love; and "The Art of Book Making," a humorous piece in which literature is created as easily as a cook might make a stew.

Readers leaned toward the syrupy "The Broken Heart," while critics preferred "English Writers on America." Irving had walked a fine line on the latter, favorably comparing British writers to their American counterparts, but the writing was so elegant, even patriotic, that readers with staunchly anti-British sentiments—like Paulding—were impressed.

That same week Irving finalized his manuscript for another installment of *The Sketch Book,* sending Ebenezer four new essays: "The Mutability of Literature," in which Crayon discusses evolving literary tastes with a talking book; "John Bull," a tip of the hat to English character and custom; "The Inn Kitchen," a description of the hospitality Irving enjoyed during his 1805 tour of the Netherlands, which set up the final piece, "The Spectre Bridegroom," a ghost story—or is it?—with a happy ending.

Despite his earlier buoyancy, Irving was sinking into a depression. "I send the present number with reluctance," he wrote, "for it has grown exceeding stale with me, part of it laid out by me during a time that I was out of spirits and could not complete." Yet two weeks later, he sent Brevoort a new sketch, "Rural Funerals," describing English funeral traditions, and asked that it be inserted in place of the more irreverent "John Bull," fearing volume four would otherwise have "too great a predominance of the humorous."[21]

Irving gave Brevoort considerable leeway in preparing the book for publication, instructing him only to "look sharp that there are not blunders and tautologies" that might garble it. "I will not apologize to you for all the trouble I give you," he told Brevoort, "for there is something delightful to me in the idea that my writings are coming out under your eye and that you in a manner stand godfather to all my children. I feel as if it is a new tie that binds us together." Their relationship had suffered through mood swings, silent treatments, and bruised feelings over the past few years, but with these words, Irving assured Brevoort that all was forgiven. *The Sketch Book* was the offspring of their renewed friendship.[22]

In the second week of August—about six weeks after *The Sketch Book*'s American debut—came the news from Brevoort that Irving had been waiting for: *The Sketch Book* was a hit! Irving replied in measured tones. "The favourable reception it has met with is extremely encouraging, and repays me for much doubt & anxiety."[23] However, until he actually had copies of the critics' reviews in his hands, he wasn't going to let the news go to his head—at least not yet. Besides, he was bothered by something else Brevoort had mentioned in his letter: some were protesting that Irving's books were too expensive.

Irving bristled at the complaint. "If the American public wish to have literature of their own," he scolded, "they must consent to pay for the support of authors."[24] Prices on later issues varied from 62½ cents to 87 cents, but Irving never wavered from his view that he was worth it. The public, despite its grumbling, seemed to agree; each installment of The Sketch Book sold out and went back for multiple reprintings.

His copyright secure in America, Irving focused on protecting himself from any British publisher who wished to pirate his work. "I am fearful some [British] Bookseller in the American trade may get hold of it," Irving told Henry Van Wart, "and so run out an edition of it without my adapting it for the London public—or participating in the profits."[25] If Irving wanted to protect his copyright in Britain, he would have to find a British publisher himself.

As he considered his options, his writing slowed. Sketches he hoped to have published by Christmas lay unfinished on the table in his room in September. Even an invitation to attend the baptism of the Van Warts' newest child—christened Washington Irving Van Wart—was declined, as Irving insisted he had to be in London at the very moment a copy of the second volume of The Sketch Book arrived, so he could whisk it off to a potential publisher.

The long-awaited parcel arrived on September 9. Brevoort had enclosed multiple copies of the first two installments of The Sketch Book, as well as the positive reviews from Verplanck, the Evening Post, and others. "They go far, far, beyond my most sanguine expectations and indeed are expressed with such peculiar warmth and kindness as to affect me in the tenderest manner," Irving said of his reviews.[26] Despite the applause, he was always the first to see his glass as half empty. "Reading . . . some of these criticisms this morning have renderd me nervous for the whole day," he confessed to Brevoort. "I feel almost appalled by such success, and fearful that it cannot be real—or that it is not fully merited, or that I shall not act up to the expectations that may be formed . . . now that it is so extravagantly bepraised I begin to feel afraid that I shall not do as well again."[27]

It was a strangely prescient concern. For now, Irving basked in the glow of his well-earned literary triumph, and he congratulated

Brevoort for guiding the volumes to press in such an elegant manner. Brevoort downplayed his involvement with his usual aplomb.
"I am truly delighted to find you were pleased with the style of your
reappearance," he wrote. "I think you fully entitled to it."[28]

The third installment of *The Sketch Book* appeared in mid-
September, this one containing some of Irving's most English
pieces. Readers admired "A Royal Poet," a romanticized description
of the literary King James I; "The Country Church," in which Irving contrasted the quiet integrity of the nobleman with the offensive flashiness of the nouveau riche; and "The Boar's Head Tavern,
East Cheap," a detective story in which Crayon tries to find the
tavern of Shakespeare's Falstaff. But once again, it was the sentimental "The Widow and Her Son," in which an old woman tends
to her dying son, that took with the public. If Irving wanted to
know which pieces were resonating with readers, it was hanky-
wringers like this one or "The Broken Heart," which even Lord
Byron claimed had made him weep!

Copies of the first two volumes of *The Sketch Book* were being
passed around in London, particularly among more refined readers,
who grudgingly conceded that this American upstart could write.
"Everywhere I find in it the marks of a mind of the utmost elegance
and refinement," the English historian William Godwin wrote to a
literary friend, "a thing as you know that I was not exactly prepared
to look for in an American."[29]

Writing in the *North American Review*, American critic
Richard Henry Dana argued that "elegance and refinement" was
exactly what was wrong with *The Sketch Book*. While Dana admitted to being an admirer, he preferred the punch of Knickerbocker to
the grace of Crayon. Where Knickerbocker was "masculine—good
bone and muscle," Crayon was "feminine—*dressy*, elegant, and languid."[30] Dana's view, however, was in the minority.

Where the British literati saw elegance, British publishers
smelled easy profit. As Irving feared, his work was being reprinted in
England without his consent—or payment. The most offensive pirate
was the London *Literary Gazette*, which published long excerpts

from *The Sketch Book*. Fuming, Irving sent the *Gazette* a cease-and-desist letter, informing the paper that he planned to publish a British edition himself. While the paper had no legal obligation to do so, it honored Irving's request. Fearing that others might not be as gentlemanly, Irving scrambled to find a suitable British publisher. "I accordingly took the printed numbers which I had received from the United States, to Mr. John Murray, the eminent publisher, from whom I had already received friendly attentions," he recalled, "and left them with him for examination, informing him that should he be inclined to bring them before the public, I had materials enough on hand for a second volume."[31]

Since Irving's initial meeting with Murray in 1817, the House of Murray had continued to produce a steady run of literary best sellers, due largely to Murray's ear for poetry. He had recently scored a major coup with the publication of the first installment of Byron's poem *Don Juan*, which was so popular that Murray had to barricade his doors against overeager booksellers, passing copies of the book through the dining-room windows instead. In the wake of such success, Murray could afford to be choosy about his projects. For several days, Irving heard nothing as Murray carefully read the first two volumes of *The Sketch Book* and talked it over with his business associates.[32] The unbearable silence was broken on October 28.

Murray's answer was no.

Irving was disappointed, but determined. If he couldn't interest Murray, he would try Murray's former publishing partner, Archibald Constable. Constable had reprinted portions of *The Sketch Book* in his *Edinburgh Magazine and Literary Miscellany*, and Irving believed he might be interested in the English rights. But Irving was so nervous about approaching Constable that he appealed to Walter Scott to plead his case. "I feel that I am taking a great liberty in making this request," he told Scott, "but indeed my situation here is so peculiarly insulated that I do not know to whom else I can apply."[33]

Scott was characteristically magnanimous in his response. "I assure you nothing will give me more pleasure." Constable, however, also declined—and no one was more disappointed than Walter Scott. Their friendship aside, Scott had been a fan of Irving's writing since *A History of New York*, and he was even more impressed with *The Sketch Book*. "It is positively beautiful," he said.[34]

Having struck out twice, Irving decided to publish the book himself, using profits from the American edition to pay all British publishing expenses. He entered into an agreement with John Miller—whom he had met in Murray's dining room during his 1817 visit—to publish a thousand copies of *The Sketch Book* under Miller's Burlington Arcade imprint. "It is certainly not the very best way to publish on one's own accompt," advised Scott, who knew a thing or two about the perils of self-publishing. However, "I am sure of one thing," he told Irving warmly, "that you have only to be known to the British public to be admired by them."[35]

New installments of *The Sketch Book* continued to roll off Van Winkle's American press with determined regularity. The fourth appeared in bookstalls on November 10, 1819. The fifth was released in the United States on the first day of 1820, missing its intended publication date by about a week—for this volume was comprised entirely of Christmas stories. While a number of other stories in *The Sketch Book* were better known, none would have a greater impact on American culture than these four Christmas essays.

Irving had visited the topic before. In his 1812 revision of *A History of New York*, he had inserted a dream sequence involving "the good St. Nicholas . . . riding over the tops of the trees, in that self-same wagon wherein he brings his yearly presents to children," introducing readers to a figure others would eventually dress up as Santa Claus.[36] In *The Sketch Book* Irving described a Christmas gathering at the manor of the eccentric Squire Bracebridge. Moonlight glints off fresh snow, yule logs crackle in the fireplace, and Christmas greens and holly berries decorate windows. Stagecoaches arrive at rustic manors filled with antique furniture, where children sing Christmas carols and well-dressed couples dance, play games, and tell ghost stories. And then there was the food, something Irving excelled at describing: tables groan under the weight of ham, turkey, roast beef, and mince pie; tankards of beer gush with foam; and guests toast their host with mugs of wassail, ladled from a gigantic silver bowl, reflecting the flickering light of fat Christmas candles.

Charles Dickens later fine-tuned the Christmas story, but Irving had laid the foundation. Americans embraced Irving's vision of Christmas as their own, marking the revival of a holiday that had been banned in parts of the country for the excessive drinking and fighting it spurred in the populace.

Irving spent his winter working with John Miller to steer the first British edition of *The Sketch Book* toward its February publication date, and trying to convince John Howard Payne that he wasn't angry with him. In early 1820 Payne's reputation was in shambles, largely due to financial problems. A precocious child and gifted actor, he had written a play, edited a weekly theater newspaper, and made his New York public stage debut, all before the age of eighteen. Handsome, with a shock of black hair, a strong voice, pleasant manners, and a dry sense of humor, Payne had fallen in easily with Irving, Paulding, and Brevoort during his North American tour in 1809, and had corresponded regularly with Irving and the Lads as he traveled the eastern seaboard. Now, eleven years later, with a tour of Ireland, a Drury Lane premiere, and successful acting jobs in London behind him, Payne hoped to embark on a literary career as a playwright and poet.

He wasn't having much luck. Payne's attempt at managing the Sadler's Wells theater was a bust, and he was evicted from his rooms at the end of 1819. With his creditors in pursuit, he took to freeloading off his friends, begging for loans while he tried to find backers for his plays. In some ways, it was an existence that mirrored Irving's own reliance on the goodwill of family and friends to sustain him as he pursued a writing career. Yet he had the audacity to lecture the twenty-eight-year-old Payne for not having a career or sustainable income.

"I once did think you were acting inconsiderately and unjustifiable, in depending upon the casual assistance of others, without having any laudable object or definite pursuit," Irving harangued. He told Payne he could forgive such behavior, since he understood that Payne was "busily employed when others considered you idle, & that your difficulties had been occasioned by the faithlessness of others, not by your own imprudence."[37] It was a stunning rebuke, coming from someone who, until very recently, had a similar reputation for idleness and lack of direction.

The British edition of *The Sketch Book*, which included the first four installments of its American counterpart, landed in London bookstalls on February 16. As he had in the first American volume, Irving included a self-deprecating introduction: "The following desultory papers are part of a series written in this country, but published in America. The author is aware of the austerity with which the writings of his countrymen have hitherto been treated by British critics; he is conscious, too, that much of the contents of his papers can be interesting only in the eyes of American readers."[38] In this, he was wrong. The British loved Geoffrey Crayon, and Irving was lauded by British readers and critics with the same enthusiasm as in America.

A month after the publication of the first British edition, the sixth installment of *The Sketch Book* was released in the United States. "John Bull," which had been cut from the previous two issues, at last made its appearance, as did "The Pride of the Village," another weepy piece about true love lost, then found again, too late to save the life of a heartbroken young maiden. But it was the third story—which Irving had outlined at the Van Warts' two years earlier—that everyone agreed was his finest. It was "The Legend of Sleepy Hollow," and it propelled Irving from a mere man of letters into an international superstar.

"It is a random thing,"[39] Irving modestly called it, but "The Legend of Sleepy Hollow" was confident, cocky, and funny, much more in the vein of the rambunctious Knickerbocker than the elegant, inoffensive Crayon. Blending nuggets of Dutch customs,

WASHINGTON IRVING | 188

stories, and characters with dashes of German folklore, Irving's "Sleepy Hollow" was less about plot than mood. The story practically invented the spooky autumn atmosphere against which we now expect good Halloween tales to be set. And the characters were more vivid than any others Irving would ever create: the brash but likable Brom Bones, the plump but desirable Katrina Van Tassel, the gawky schoolmaster Ichabod Crane—Irving's nod to Jesse Merwin, who had kept him company at Kinderhook in the summer of 1809—and, always lingering in the background, the Headless Horseman.

"In my opinion [it] is one of the best articles you have written," Brevoort wrote to Irving in April 1820. "It unites all the excellencies of your old & new manner of writing." It was no wonder British critics were hailing Irving as the finest British writer America had produced. "I think you will become a great favourite in England," Brevoort said, "nor should I be surprised that they lay claims to you; proving their rights by your name & the purity of your style." Brevoort's assessment was dead-on. "[Irving] seems to have studied our language where alone it can be studied in all its strength and perfection," wrote a reviewer in the English *Quarterly Review*, "and in working these precious mines of literature he has refined for himself the ore which there so richly abounds."[40]

Such accolades and the sales they inspired couldn't save publisher John Miller, who, under his arrangement with Irving, received none of *The Sketch Book*'s profits. In early April 1820 Miller went broke, taking his Burlington Arcade printing house—and the unsold copies of *The Sketch Book*—down with him. It was a potential disaster, unless Irving could find another publisher willing to purchase the remaining stock and continue publication. Fortunately, Walter Scott was in London to receive his baronetcy. "I called to him for help, as I was sticking in the mire," Irving explained, "and, more propitious than Hercules, he put his own shoulder to the wheel."[41]

"Murray has taken it in hand," Irving proudly reported to Brevoort on May 13, 1820. Scott—now Sir Walter—had been as good as his word, and had convinced his publisher to buy the rest of Miller's stock. Even more encouraging, Murray wanted to publish a second volume.[42]

Suddenly, the publisher who earlier had determined there was no profit to be made from Irving's work was demanding that Irving produce more of it. The pressure was immense. "The manner in which the work has been received here, instead of giving me spirit to write, has rather daunted me for the time," he admitted to Brevoort. "I feel uneasy about the second volume, and cannot write any fresh matter for it."[43]

Such pressures aside, however, there were definite advantages to being Murray's author. His fashionable drawing room was now open to Irving, giving him access to the British literati and the best of European society. "Old D'Israeli is a staunch friend of mine," Irving told Brevoort, his head spinning. "This evening I go to the Countess of Besborough's, where there is to be quite a collection of characters, among whom I shall see Lord Wellington, whom I have never yet had the good luck to meet with."[44]

There was a rising demand for his likeness, so Irving commissioned Newton to paint his portrait. "It is considered an excellent likeness, and I am willing that it should be thought so," Irving told Brevoort, "though between ourselves, I think myself a much better looking fellow on canvas than in the looking-glass."[45]

On June 28 Irving shipped another packet to Ebenezer, this one containing "Little Britain," a picturesque stroll through the heart of old London; "Stratford-On-Avon," Irving's tribute to Shakespeare; "Westminster Abbey," a contemplative tour of the famous building; and "The Angler," a character sketch of the English naturalist Izaak Walton. They comprised the final volume of *The Sketch Book*. The pressures from Murray to complete the essays had worn him out. "I have had so much muddling work," he told Ebenezer, "that I have grown tired of it, and have lost all excitement. I shall feel relieved from a cloud, when I get this volume printed and out of my sight."[46]

With the final four sketches in hand, Murray was ready to go to press immediately with the second British installment of *The Sketch Book*. The burnt-out Irving, eager to be done with it, agreed to a July publication date, which was significantly earlier than that of the seventh and final American volume scheduled for the fall. The second British volume contained all the material from issues five, six, and seven of its American counterpart, as well as three additional essays—the American Indian sketches "Philip of Pokanoket" and "Traits of Indian Character," which Irving had originally written for the *Analectic* in 1814, and a short original piece, "L'Envoy," in which Irving thanked his British readers for their indulgence.

The Sketch Book was complete. Readers loved the stories and essays in *The Sketch Book,* but they adored its author. Geoffrey Crayon was well-read, well traveled, and clever—the kind of person you longed to chat with, dine with, or sit with at the theater. Elegant, self-deprecating, and never one to make himself more interesting than his stories, Crayon, readers were convinced, *was* Washington Irving. Crayon represented everything Irving would have *liked* to have been. In fact, Irving so successfully blurred the line between author and pseudonym that the polished, erudite, confident Geoffrey Crayon became the public persona of the nervous, unfocused, insecure Washington Irving—one Irving would cultivate and protect for the next forty years.

Knickerbocker's rough-and-tumble baritone was probably closer to Irving's real voice than the more measured tenor of Crayon. It wasn't a coincidence that the sketches Irving had written as Knickerbocker—"Rip Van Winkle" and "The Legend of Sleepy Hollow"—were the best and most memorable of *The Sketch Book*. Stepping back into Knickerbocker's black suit always seemed to bring out the finest—and the most *fun*—in Irving's writing. Yet Brevoort was right when he pointed out that "Sleepy Hollow" had seemed to unite Irving's old and new styles of writing. It had Knickerbocker's verve and Crayon's elegance. The *real* Washington Irving was neither Geoffrey Crayon nor Diedrich Knickerbocker; he was both—gruff yet graceful, blustering yet charming, crass but classy. And where Crayon made it all look easy, Knickerbocker knew it was hard work. The cultivated Crayon may have become the public personality, and Knickerbocker the private workhorse, but it was Irving alone who had earned the success and reputation. With *The Sketch Book,* he had guaranteed his legacy.

And still *The Sketch Book* sold. Murray was so astounded by its success that he offered to work with Irving on a comprehensive two-volume collected works that he would pay for himself. Incredibly, Irving—who was in a hurry to leave for Paris with Peter and no longer interested in managing his British business affairs—simply offered to sell Murray the British copyright outright. Like Dusky Davey before him, Murray knew a good deal when he saw one, and purchased the copyright for 250 guineas, about $20,000 today. A pirated version of *A History of New York* had appeared—at this point, almost anything with Irving's name sold—and as the Irving brothers sprinted to Southampton to catch their ship for France, Murray promised to bring out an elegant edition of *Knickerbocker* to drive the pirated volume underground.

After eighteen months of hard work, Washington was tired and had little interest in the passing scenery or writing in his journal. However, both he and Peter were intrigued by the steamboats they saw churning along the Seine near Le Havre. The boats belonged to a businessman named Edward Church, who mentioned that he was hoping to establish a regular service between Le Havre and Rouen, and asked the Irvings if they might be interested in investing. Impressed, they told Church they would think about it.

Arriving in Paris, the brothers were greeted by American minister Albert Gallatin, who hailed Washington as America's most celebrated author. Irving settled comfortably into lodgings on rue Mont Thabor, spending his afternoons in conversation—either in English or his competent French—at Galignani's, the city's most fashionable bookshop and reading room. He became better acquainted with John Jacob Astor, and met Thomas Wentworth Storrow, an American businessman with a talent for finance and a love of literature, who had lived in Paris with his family since 1815. It should have been a quiet and comfortable existence, but

Peter was restless; Church's offer to speculate in steamboats had intrigued him.

After driving the family business into the ground in 1817, and watching his translation of *Giovanni Sbogarro, A Venetian Tale* fail when it was published in 1819, Peter had no prospects and, to the annoyance of William and Ebenezer, remained vulnerable to dubious schemes promising easy money. Washington was sympathetic; he had suffered with Peter through the humiliation of bankruptcy, and understood the strong urge to pursue the path of least resistance or, better yet, let others take care of him. Perhaps Washington felt slightly guilty that his own literary dreams had been realized, while Peter's had withered. "Peter has now been living on hopes, and very feeble ones, for two or three years," Washington told Brevoort.[47] Whatever the cause, if owning part of a steamboat business would put Peter back on his feet, then Washington—who had been the benefactor of brotherly generosity many times over—was willing to finance it.

"I only want money enough to enable me to keep on my own way and follow my own taste and inclination,"[48] Irving told Brevoort in 1819. Since then, he had profited greatly from *The Sketch Book*. He made between $500 and $600 on each of the seven installments of the American edition alone. With the money he was earning from the British edition, Irving's income amounted to about $5,000, nearly $80,000 today.

It was likely no coincidence that $5,000 was precisely the amount Peter asked Washington to invest in the steamboat endeavor. Peter promised he would raise a matching $5,000. He was convinced the project would be a success, and as always, his brother's word was all Washington needed. Without hesitation, Washington wrote over all his profits from *The Sketch Book* to Peter.

"Peter and myself have taken part in an enterprise for navigating the Seine by steam," Irving wrote to Brevoort on September 22. His hope, he explained, was that Peter would run the steamboat business as his full-time occupation, while Washington devoted himself entirely to literature. He also informed Brevoort that he was writing to William to request another $5,000 on Peter's behalf, and urged Brevoort to use his influence with William "to prevent my brothers from disappointing us in this business . . . it behooves them to back [Peter] like true brothers."[49]

Washington approached William delicately, assuring his oldest brother that Peter's scheme was "a most promising mode of turning a small amount of money . . . to large account." If it was a matter of cash flow, he said, William could sell all of Washington's remaining literary copyrights—an astounding proposition. Whatever William decided, Washington wrote, "I trust you will all exert yourselves to launch him [Peter] fairly in this enterprise, which he seems to look upon as his last cast. I have therefore done the best I could to serve him; and if the steamboat business fails and all that I advance is lost, my only regret will be on his count."[50]

William's written reply has been lost, but it is not difficult to imagine his response to such a spurious project. "They have decided not to give it their support," Brevoort wrote flatly. He also hinted that Washington would do well not to ask him to serve as an intermediary with William again. "I have felt some rude intimations on this subject which I would rather dispense with in the future."[51]

Washington was hurt, but he tried to be understanding. "They have acted as they thought for my interest," he sighed. "I am confident they do it out of zeal for my interest, but a man may be killed even by kindness."[52] Despite William's refusal to loan Peter the money, Washington was still required to cover the amount he had obligated to Church. All he had to show for his work as Geoffrey Crayon was a partial share in Church's steamboat business, which he handed over to his brother. Peter was officially in the steamboat business, albeit just barely; Washington, however, was broke.

As if on cue, John Murray contacted him and begged him to accept 100 guineas as a bonus for the profits he was generating. Irving was outselling even Lord Byron, who told Murray that "Crayon is good!" and claimed to know entire passages of *The Sketch Book* by heart.

Murray was willing to eat crow for his earlier refusal to publish the writer who was now his most successful author. His experiences with the eccentric Byron had taught him how to soothe bruised egos, and Murray knew he had in Irving one he would have to continually massage. If he had underestimated Irving's value before, he now admitted he had made a mistake. "I am convinced I did not half know you," Murray wrote generously, "and esteeming you highly as I did, certainly my esteem is doubled by my better knowledge of you."[53]

The letter had the desired effect. "I have just received your letter of the 26th, which has almost overpowered me with the encomiums it contains," Irving replied. He could scarcely believe his own success, he told his publisher: "I am astonished at the success of my writings in England, and can hardly persuade myself that it is not all a dream. Had any one told me a few years since in America, that any thing I could write would interest such men as . . . Byron, I should have as readily believed a fairy tale."[54] He told Murray he would gladly take the 100 guineas the publisher had offered. It wasn't $5,000, but for the moment, it was enough.

Meanwhile, Leslie was at work on a new portrait of Irving, and the image-conscious author was adamant that Leslie not paint him in clothing "that might in a few years appear stupid." No Venetian cloaks, or "capes & corners & angles," Irving directed; rather, "let the costume be simple & picturesque, but such a one as a gentleman might be supposed to wear occasionally at the present day."[55]

Irving was burnishing his public image as a cultivated gentleman—and was doing such a masterful job of it that many British readers continued to express disbelief that Crayon was American. Literary conspiracy theorists among the British argued that Crayon was actually none other than "The Author of Waverly," Sir Walter Scott! One well-read English fan—Lady Lyttleton, the daughter of Earl Spencer—was convinced that Crayon's voice was so "new and peculiar" that there was no way The Sketch Book could have come from Scott's pen, and she appealed to American minister Richard Rush to confirm that Crayon was really the American writer Washington Irving. Amused, Rush relayed Lady Lyttleton's request to Irving for an answer—and could barely wait to see how he would respond.[56]

Irving was charmed and flattered by the question. "You may assure her that it was written entirely by myself," he told Rush. "The doubts which her ladyship has heard on the subject seem to have arisen from the old notion that it is impossible for an *American to write decent* English."[57] Delighted with his reply, Lady Lyttleton invited Irving to spend Christmas with her family at their country seat near Wimbledon. Irving declined her offer, opting to stay in Paris for the winter to write.

He didn't accomplish much. In December he met the Irish poet Thomas Moore, who was in Paris trying to sort out a botched government business affair that had left him nearly as broke as Irving. "A charming, joyous fellow," Irving called Moore, "full of frank, generous, manly feeling." Moore thought Irving "a good looking and intelligent-mannered man." The two were immediately inseparable, touring the rooms where Marie Antoinette had been confined in her final days, or discussing Byron in Moore's home on the Champs Elysées.[58]

The British edition of *The Sketch Book* sold out, the new edition of *A History of New York*—with Leslie's much-delayed illustrations—was selling briskly, and Irving was the darling of British readers and critics alike. "Geoffrey Crayon is the most fashionable fellow of the day," Leslie told him from London. "I am very much inclined to think if you were here just now, 'company would be the spoil of you.'"[59] Friends were urging Irving to write more pieces for *The Sketch Book*, or follow it up with a new work as soon as possible. But the pressure was too much; inspiration wouldn't come. And he was in debt, still on the hook for his steamboat speculation.

Irving's mood darkened. When Brevoort made the mistake of engaging in a bit of good-natured ribbing over whether he intended to remain in Europe or renounce his country altogether, Irving's response was scalding: "I am endeavoring to serve my country— Whatever I have written has been written with the feelings and published as the writing of an American—Is that renouncing my Country? How else am I to serve my country—by coming home and begging an office of it . . . If I can do any good in this world it is with my pen." Brevoort was used to such mood swings. "I did not intend to give you pain by interrogating you on the subject," Brevoort replied evenly, "and so, for the future, let it rest."[60]

It was Moore who inspired Irving to write again. In the spring of 1821, while chatting about Irving's Christmas essays from *The Sketch Book*, Moore suggested Irving use Squire Bracebridge, his family, and his manor as the setting for "a slight thread of a story on which to string his remarks and sketches of human manner and feelings." Ten days later Irving showed Moore 130 pages of a hand-written manuscript. "Amazing rapidity," an impressed Moore wrote in his diary.[61] It was a start.

Weeks later, as rain soaked Paris, Irving complained to Brevoort of "chills & damps which destroy all the sunshine of my mind."[62] It wasn't the rain that was dampening his mood and imagination, it was poverty. Peter's steamboat project continued to siphon away Washington's money. He needed to generate some income quickly. For Irving, the only way to do that was to keep writing.

"I have a Mass of writings by me," Irving told Brevoort in April, "which, so soon as I can bring them into form and prepare them for publication, will I trust produce me something very handsome in *cash down* in England." Once again, financial pressure was reanimating Irving's pen—and this time, he was willing to bank on his reputation. "Any book I should now offer for sale *good or bad*, would be sure to find a ready purchaser at a high price among the Booksellers," he told Brevoort—but until he finished his new manuscript, he begged Brevoort for a loan of $2,000 to pay off his final obligations to Church. "I trust my next work will fairly relieve me from all further embarrassment of the kind," he assured his friend.[63]

Brevoort, naturally, obliged. "I am happy to understand that by this arrangement your mind will be disengaged from pecuniary matters and exclusively devoted to literature," he told Irving. "The explanation you have given of your future ability to discharge these advances is perfectly satisfactory; I can, without inconvenience, wait until your means will enable you to do so at your leisure."[64]

And wait he did. With financial pressures off, Irving's interest in his manuscript—which he called *Bracebridge Hall*—waned. While he insisted that the strain of writing was so vexing that he could no longer enjoy society or leisure, in truth, he was finding plenty to do. He and Campbell continued to frequent Paris's most fashionable reading rooms and parlors. To Irving's delight, the rascally John Howard Payne—now back in his good graces—abandoned London for Paris.

It had been nearly a year since publication of the second volume of the British *Sketch Book,* and Murray was anxious to learn what his best-selling author had in mind for an encore. "Draw upon me for a hundred pounds, of which I beg thy acceptance," Murray wrote in June, knowing that the offer of money would lure a response out of Irving, "and pray tell me how you are and what you are about."[65]

As expected, Irving rose to the bait. "In compliance with your request I have drawn on you for an hundred pounds," he wrote Murray in early July. He admitted to having been "distracted" by engagements in Paris, but promised to have something for his publisher shortly. "I have scribbled at intervals," he said, "and have a mass of writings by me, rather desultory, as must be the case when one is so much interrupted." By mid-June Irving was comfortable enough with his progress on *Bracebridge* to read aloud parts to Moore. "It is amusing," Moore confided in his journal that evening, "but will, I fear, much disappoint the expectations his Sketches have raised."[66]

While reports of Napoleon's death at St. Helena set French parlors chattering in July, Irving decided he was bored with the Continent and returned to London. He arrived just in time to stand on the steps outside Westminster Abbey with Newton and Leslie, craning their necks to see the coronation procession of George IV file past them. Sir Walter Scott, who had witnessed the ceremony with Murray from within Westminster Abbey, was quick to tease Irving for not using his name to his advantage. "Hut man!" Scott twitted, "You should have told them who you were and you would have got in anywhere!"[67]

Murray was relieved to have his new cash cow back in London, and continued to nag Irving for new work. Irving moved in with Newton on Marlboro Street, where he hoped to concentrate on fine-tuning *Bracebridge Hall*. Instead he spent most of his time moaning about "monotonous and commonplaced" London. His only real amusement arrived in August in the form of an honorary degree from Columbia University in New York, which Irving, in an understatement, called "unexpected." All he really wanted to do was retreat to the warmth of Castle Van Tromp in Birmingham.[68]

Adding to his misery, word came from Peter that the steamboat business was failing. If Peter was looking for sympathy, he didn't find it in Washington, who had relied on Brevoort's generosity to be able to put the whole rotten affair behind him. "I am sorry they are not more productive," Washington wrote, "I do not calculate on any proceeds from that quarter, so that you need not feel solicitous with me." Meanwhile, he told Peter, "I have a variety of writings in hand, some I think superior to what I have already published; my only anxiety is to get them into shape and order." That proved more challenging than he had hoped. Reading over his manuscript with Leslie, the painter thought parts of the work so promising—especially an extended piece called "Buckthorne"— that he suggested Irving expand the sketch into a novel.[69]

The pressures were mounting. His nerves fraying, Irving left London with Leslie in early September, bound for Birmingham. Along the way, they made stops in Oxford, Warwick, Kenilworth, and Stratford-on-Avon, where Irving—who usually struggled with the muse—was surprised to find literary inspiration. After a rainy night at a country inn, Leslie spoke to him about "the stout gentleman" they had seen the night before. "Irving remarked that 'The Stout Gentleman' would not be a bad title for a tale," Leslie later recalled, "as soon as the coach stopped, he began writing . . . and went on at every opportunity."[70] The story was bundled into Irving's still incomplete manuscript, as were the random notes he jotted in his journal as he and Leslie walked through the medieval manor Haddon Hall in Derbyshire.

Arriving at Castle Van Tromp, Irving finally collapsed. He spent the next four months in Birmingham on the cusp of a nervous breakdown. "I have been so much out of health as to prevent my doing anything of consequence with my pen," he told Ebenezer in late September. By October his legs were so inflamed he could barely walk, and his right hand was covered with boils that made it impossible for him to write. He begged friends in London not to let the increasingly agitated Murray know where he was.

Things were about to get worse. On November 1 Irving received a letter from Ebenezer informing him that William Jr. was dying of tuberculosis.

William's health had been in decline for some time. As far back as September 1819, Brevoort had mentioned that William seemed to be "literally bent downward, with at least a dozen gratu-itous years"; in June 1821 he had thought William "infirm, and his spirits sadly depressed & broken." While he never said so, Brevoort likely believed that William's decline had been hastened by his constant worrying about Washington and Peter. Certainly, the last three years had strained Washington and William's relationship, with Washington first refusing the government post William had worked so hard to secure, and then squabbling with William over money for the steamboat venture. "[William] retains his old habit of burthening himself with a world of unnecessary cares and vexa-tions," Brevoort told Washington in 1819, and Brevoort spent the last two years delicately trying to reconcile the two brothers. "Your Brother William appears to be apprehensive that neither you nor the Doctor [Peter Irving] are sufficiently aware of the zeal which he has shewn in the promotion of your interests," Brevoort wrote. "I think some acknowledgement of your sense of his goodwill & kind disposition would give him great satisfaction."[71]

It was too late. As William lay dying an ocean away, Washington could only regret what had been said and unsaid. "Brother Williams situation, I perceive, is hopeless," he told Ebenezer. "I had been persuading myself that there was a reaction in his system . . . but the tenor of all the letters from New York puts an end to all hopes of the kind. I cannot reconcile myself to the thought."[72]

Still he could not bring himself to write William. "Give my most affectionate remembrances to Brother William," he told Ebenezer. "I would write to him, but cannot trust my feelings, whenever the thought of him comes over my mind, I feel my heart and eyes overflow."[73]

They were loving words, but William never read them. On November 9, 1821, William Irving Jr. died in New York. He was fifty-five years old.

9

Rut

1822–1825

No man in the Republic of Letters, has been more overrated than Mr.
Washington Irving.

—*New-York Mirror*, September 24, 1824

$\mathcal{T}$HE DEATH OF WILLIAM IRVING in December 1821, Washington wrote, was "one of the dismallest events that ever happened to me." Given their seventeen-year age difference—and Washington's own strained relationship with the Deacon—William was like a surrogate father to the youngest Irving. The Deacon's death in 1807, Washington dismissed without much comment; the death of his mother a decade later had been harder, but there had still been William to take care of him. With William gone, Washington felt parentless for the first time in his life. Worse, he felt partly responsible for William's deterioration. "He died of a rapid decline," Washington said later, "brought on I am convinced by the acute anxiety and distress of mind he had suffered."[1]

Irving spent a difficult winter in Birmingham. His legs were so inflamed and swollen that he could no longer stand or walk, and lesions and blisters on his hands made writing impossible. Given his symptoms, it is likely that he suffered from the rare skin condition erythema multiforme. While the condition is generally more prevalent among neurotic or nervous types, erythema multiforme is also associated with certain forms of the herpes simplex virus. In most

cases, the disease simply runs its course; until then, Irving's symptoms—and his physicians—were making him miserable. With their
endless prescriptions, the doctors, he reported, "have made a complete job and I may say *Job* of me; excepting that I have not his
patience."[2]

Apart from prodding physicians, he also had John Murray nagging him to complete his latest work. Glumly, Irving returned to
London in late December, and worked steadily on his book for the
next six weeks.

"I forward you a parcel, containing the first volume of *Bracebridge Hall, or The Humourists, a Medley* in two volumes," Washington wrote Ebenezer on January 29, 1822. "I had hoped to have sent
both volumes, but I have not been able to get the second volume
ready." Murray had pushed him to his limit, and he was exhausted.
"I have fagged until the last moment," he told Ebenezer. "My health
is still unrestored. This work has kept me from getting well, and
now my indisposition on the other hand has retarded the work."[3]

The manuscript he enclosed was a mess, but Washington was
so eager to secure the copyright to *Bracebridge* on both sides of the
Atlantic that he was willing to rush an unpolished American edition into print. Meanwhile, as the manuscript made its way across
the ocean, he had time to refine the text for the British edition.

Irving had recently been approached by American publisher
Charles Wiley for help in securing the British copyright for a book
he had just published, a Revolutionary War–era espionage novel
called *The Spy*, written by a thirty-two-year-old New Yorker named
James Fenimore Cooper. Irving limped over to Albemarle Street to
confer with Murray on Cooper's behalf.[4] It was the beginning of a
professional relationship between Irving and Cooper that would
swing between warm and frigid over the next four decades.

Murray declined to publish *The Spy*, a decision that annoyed
Irving. "[Murray] is precisely the worst man that an American work
can be sent to," he fumed to Wiley. "He is surrounded by literary advisers, who are prejudiced against any thing American."[5]
Undeterred by the bad news, Cooper sent Irving a note of thanks,

and asked for Irving's help in securing the British copyright for a new manuscript he had completed. This time, Murray was more impressed, and at Irving's behest agreed to publish Cooper's novel *The Pioneers*, the first book of the Leatherstocking Tales.

Despite his irritation with Murray over *The Spy*, Irving stayed loyal to the Prince of Booksellers, even as he was wooed by other publishers for the rights to his next book. Irving had shipped the second volume of *Bracebridge Hall* to Ebenezer in late February, and Henry Colburn—whom Irving regarded as one of the most fashionable publishers in London—offered him a thousand guineas for the British rights. But Irving didn't want to disappoint Murray. "He should have my second even at a less price than the one offered to me by [Colburn],"[6] Irving declared—and Murray nearly did.

On March 12 Irving brought his manuscript to Murray. With the American edition looming, Irving needed a commitment from the publisher quickly. As he skimmed the pages, Murray asked Irving his price for the British copyright. Without blinking, Irving requested 1,500 guineas.

"Fifteen hundred?" Murray gasped. "If you had said a thousand guineas . . ."

"You shall have it for a thousand," Irving interjected, anxious to secure a deal. "My friends thought I ought to have had more for it," he told Peter later, "but I am content."[7] In the United States, however, Irving insisted on retaining his American copyright, which prompted some grumbling from Moses Thomas, who hoped to purchase it outright on terms similar to Murray's.

On May 21 the first volume of *Bracebridge Hall* was published in the United States; the British edition two days later. Irving's and Murray's copyrights were secure on both sides of the ocean, but at the cost of a muddied first American volume. Despite Ebenezer's efforts to clean up the manuscript, *Bracebridge* was so replete with garbled punctuation and misspellings that parts of the book were practically unreadable.

Not that it mattered. Irving was rightly convinced his reputation was secure enough in the United States to risk a somewhat slapdash first volume. It was the English he was trying to impress. It was partly for this reason that the stories in *Bracebridge* have a decidedly English slant. Until Diedrich Knickerbocker's cameo appearance late in the second volume, there was no sign of Irving's less refined, and more natural, American voice. *Bracebridge* was Geoffrey Crayon's show.

Despite efforts then and now to locate the "real" Bracebridge Hall, Irving based his portrayal on no single place, but built his manor house as an amalgam of different locations: Haddon Hall, which he had toured with Leslie; Aston Hall, an impressive home near the Van Warts; Brereton Hall in Cheshire; and, perhaps the most important influence, Walter Scott's Abbotsford. While Squire Bracebridge was no Walter Scott, there were hints of Scott in the eccentric Bracebridge. Bracebridge's advice to his sons "to ride, to shoot, and to tell the truth" was the same advice Irving heard Scott give his own son at Abbotsford.[8]

As Moore had suggested, Irving used Squire Bracebridge, his family, and his home as the framing device to tell more than fifty short stories. The result was a random, somewhat disorienting mix of styles and settings. It was *The Sketch Book* all over again, although a lesser incarnation. Despite its flaws, readers loved *Bracebridge Hall*. Murray easily recouped his investment, making about £980 (roughly $120,000 today) on the four thousand copies sold in Britain. Most critics were forgiving, even as they criticized Irving's tendency to be syrupy or, of all things, *indecent*, as he snickered at a character's underwear or fixated on women's breasts. As Irving feared, his own reputation had set expectations high, and some reviewers weren't sure he had lived up to them. "We took up the book predisposed to admire," one said, "but a perusal, we are compelled to say, has in some measure shaken our faith."[9]

Fortunately, just as he had with *The Sketch Book*, Irving won over the feared Francis Jeffrey and his *Edinburgh Review*. "We have received so much pleasure from this book," Jeffrey gushed, "that we think ourselves bound in gratitude . . . to make a public acknowledgement of it." Yet Jeffrey was careful to put Irving on notice: "Though we, and other great lights of public judgment, have decided that his former level has been maintained in this work with the most marvelous precision, we must whisper in his ear that the millions are not exactly of that opinion; and that the common buz among the idle and impatient critics of the drawing room is that, in comparison with the Sketch Book, it is rather monotonous and languid." Such humbugging aside, Irving was relieved. The strain of completing *Bracebridge* had worn down his health and his patience with Murray, but the public reception made it all worth it. If Irving/Crayon had been considered en vogue after *The Sketch Book*, then *Bracebridge Hall* cemented his celebrity. "The success of my writings has given me ready access to all kinds of Society," he told Brevoort. "And I have been the rounds of routs, dinners, operas, balls & blue stocking coteries. I have been much pleased with those parties in which rank & fashion and talent are blended." Such a whirlwind schedule took its toll. The inflammation on his legs—his "cutaneous complaint," he called it—still bothered him, and he announced to Brevoort his intent to visit Aachen, Germany, to soak in its hot sulfur springs.[10]

Unfortunately, recovering his health took longer than anticipated, as Irving spent several weeks experimenting with various cures. The baths at Aachen did nothing. At Wiesbaden, the water was too hot, while in Mainz, the fumes of the dry vapor baths nearly caused him to pass out. Compounding his misery, he was suffering from a massive case of writer's block. Contemplating a *Sketch Book*–type project about Germany and its legends, he couldn't get in the proper mood to write. "I read considerably, but do not pretend to write," he told Sarah from Mainz, "and my mind has complete holiday so that it will be some time before I get another work under way."[11]

By early September his legs had recovered sufficiently for him to travel to Heidelberg. The sixty-mile trek sent him down the scenic Bergstrasse at the foot of the Odenwald Mountains, and as he snacked on freshly picked grapes and drank newly pressed wine, he thought he had never enjoyed himself more. After only a few days in Heidelberg, he declared himself healthy enough to take long walks and scramble among the ruins of nearby castles. He felt so good, in fact, that he declined an invitation from Thomas Moore to join him in Paris for the winter. "I was so much delighted with what I had seen of Germany," he told Moore later, "that on recovering sufficiently to venture again on long journeys, I set out in quest of adventures."[12]

Off he went, exploring the Rhine Valley, the Black Forest, Strasbourg—where he was pleased to see a French translation of *The Sketch Book* in a bookshop—and the fields of Blenheim before finally making his way to Munich. With its libraries, theaters, operas, and galleries, Munich held Irving's attention for nearly a week. "I do not know when I have enjoyed traveling more," he told Moore. "The only drawback on all this pleasure is that I am burning the candle at both ends all the time. I am spending money, and my pen is idle—."[13]

It was also getting colder; it was time to choose a place to winter where he could relax, read, and, hopefully, find the motivation and imagination to get his idle pen moving again. Tracing his finger down the blue line of the Danube on his map, Irving decided either Salzburg or Vienna was worth a look.

He was disappointed in both cities. Salzburg he abandoned after only two days, and it took only a month before he proclaimed Vienna "extensive, irregular, crowded, dusty, dissipated, magnificent, and . . . disagreeable."[14] As a last resort, he turned toward Dresden. "It is a more quiet and intellectual city than this," he told his sister, "a place of taste, intellect, and literary feeling; and it is the best place to acquire the German language."

While Dresden's reputation as the fashionable capital of the Kingdom of Saxony was secure well before Irving's arrival in 1822, the city was still recovering from the Napoleonic Wars. King Frederic I had allied himself with Napoleon, and had suffered for it, watching his kingdom raided, sacked, torn in half, and eventually absorbed into Prussia. But Irving's instincts about its feasibility as winter quarters were justified. It was definitely a place of "taste, intellect, and literary feeling." The city of 50,000 was on the rebound, with a thriving theater and opera district, numerous museums and libraries, picturesque scenery, and an active social element that revolved mainly around the activities of the court.[15] Irving made himself at home in the Hotel de Saxe, overlooking Neumarkt Square, where he stayed for the next seven months. They were among the happiest—and most heartbreaking—of his life.

His literary reputation had preceded him. "There are German translations of my works just appearing, and my writings and myself are topicks in the little literary papers which abound in Germany," he reported. "This has made me an object of Blue stocking curiosity and instead of quietly taking a post of observer in society I have to talk—and to fight my way through tough conversations with the aid of bad French and worse German." Fortunately, he had the help of John P. Morier, a friend from Washington, D.C., who was serving as the British envoy extraordinaire to the court of Saxony. Morier steered Irving into the inner circle of Dresden's diplomatic society, and in late December accompanied Irving on his first of many conversations with King Frederic and the royal family. "When the King entered . . . I was introduced & he spoke to me very flatteringly about my works," Irving wrote in amazement.[16]

Through Morier, he met Barham John Livius, a hack writer and dramatist who was attempting to do in Dresden what Payne was doing in Paris: translate and adapt foreign-language plays for the London stage. Livius was trying to acquire the rights to Carl Maria von Weber's opera *Der Freischütz*, which had premiered to great success in Berlin in 1821. In the meantime, he spent much of his time with his cousin Mrs. Amelia Morgan Foster at her residence in Courland Palace, just two blocks from Irving's hotel. On December 19 Livius invited Irving to join him and the Fosters for dinner. Irving returned for dinner again on Christmas Eve, and soon became a regular in the household.

The Foster household, as Irving soon discovered, was a hub for

English society in Dresden. The wife of a wealthy and well-connected Englishman, Amelia Foster had arrived in Dresden in 1820 to provide a European education for her two daughters, Emily and Flora, and three younger sons. Fluent in German and Italian, the Foster women were well-read, charming, and beautiful. By the time of Irving's arrival in late 1822, eighteen-year-old Emily was being actively courted by various prominent Germans, Italians, and Englishmen—and now here was a famous American trying to catch her eye. Emily was intrigued; she confided in her diary that the thirty-nine-year-old Irving was "neither tall nor slight, but most interesting, dark, hair of a man of genius waving, silky, & black, grey eyes full of varying feeling, & an amiable smile."[17]

In a way, it was the Hoffman household all over again. Like Maria Hoffman, Amelia Foster was close to Irving's age, yet Irving's feelings for her bordered on matronly adulation. Just as he had in the Hoffman residence more than a decade before, he made himself at home among the family, amiably chatting up the mother while keeping an eye on one of the daughters. With so many young and aggressive suitors around, he had to find creative ways to earn Emily's favor.

As luck would have it, he learned the Foster family was fond of putting on amateur theatricals, usually under the direction of aspiring director/producer Livius. For the theater-loving Irving, it was an ideal opportunity. In no time, Livius had them rehearsing an adaptation of his own opera, *Maid or Wife*, in which Irving was Emily's leading man. Irving also set to work adapting *Three Weeks after Marriage*, a comedy in which Emily took the role of Lady Rackett, and he played her husband—another convenient bit of casting.

At this point, Livius finally acquired the rights to adapt *Der Freischütz*, and he asked Irving to help him prepare it for the London stage. Irving was still learning German, but he had seen the play performed several times, and thought he could help with the songs until he was more comfortable with the language. Between his work with Livius and the amateur theatricals, Irving had little interest in writing. Not that he was complaining. "Though I have done noth-ing with my pen, and have been tossed about on the stream of soci-ety," he told Peter, "yet I console myself with the idea that I have *lived into* a great deal of amusing and characteristic information which, after all, is perhaps the best way of studying the world."[18]

Most of his *living into* was done at the Fosters' Courland Palace residence, as Irving dined with the family almost daily and spent evenings "reading & gossiping, until near one oclock." He was becoming increasingly interested in Emily Foster. Though Irving was always careful in his journals never to give away too much, his discreet entries nevertheless raised the eyebrows of a later reader— possibly Pierre Irving, or the author himself—who erased a number of entries involving Emily Foster. It was perhaps an attempt to pre-serve the image of Irving as too devoted to the memory of Matilda Hoffman to ever woo or love another woman, for the erasures, when comprehensible, are telling. "E . . . of heart—Dance with her," reads one nearly invisible entry on February 11; the next day, a similarly effaced message can be seen: "Ask E to give me a subject for a poem."[19]

Emily was coy, though similarly reserved, in her journal. She was probably more curious than romantically interested, but she did, at times, neglect some of her other suitors in favor of this older, famous American who behaved like an elegant Englishman. Through his constant attention, entertaining conversation, and careful casting of their theatricals, Irving was convinced he was vanquishing all other suitors.

He wasn't. It's likely Emily was being delicate with Irving's feel-ings, for she had clearly picked up on his need for praise and accep-tance. "Mr. I. is in want of constant excitement & support, interest & admiration of his friends seem the very food he lives on," she wrote in her journal. "He is easily discouraged & excited."[20] Even Flora recognized the insecurity beneath Irving's otherwise confident, gentlemanly demeanor, as well as his tendency to despair: "His countenance varies with his mood. His smile is one the sweetest

I know; but he can look very, very sad. . . . He judges *himself* with the utmost severity, feeling a deep depression at what he fancies are his shortcomings, while he kindles into enthusiasm at what is kind or generous in those he loves."[21]

Irving didn't stray far from the Fosters; "Dine at Mrs. Fosters" was a regular entry in his journal throughout March. Writing was all but impossible; he was too preoccupied. "I am merely seeing and hearing, and my mind seems too crowded and confused a state to produce anything," he told his sister. To Leslie, however, he was more animated on the subject: "I have done nothing with my pen since I have left you! Absolutely nothing!"[22]

As the end of March approached, Irving believed Emily was responding positively to his efforts. On March 24, following a morning of rehearsals for their latest amateur play, he walked along the Elbe with Emily and her mother, then attended a party at their home that, he noted in his journal, "ends pleasantly." Four days later, on Good Friday, he spent the evening with the Fosters, and before turning in for the evening, made an entry in his journal that was later almost forcefully rubbed out. "Early part of day triste," Irving wrote, which he frequently used to describe gloomy weather, but "Emily delightful."[23]

His confidence was up, as was his nerve. On March 31 he recorded in his journal—in yet another entry that has been almost completely obliterated—that he had gone to the Fosters for a party that evening, but had gone home "very much . . ."[24] Here the erasure makes the rest of the entry completely unreadable. It is likely that the deleted word is "depressed," or something of a similar sentiment—for it is likely that on this date he proposed marriage to Emily Foster, and found his proposal did not meet with the desired reaction.

Emily probably did not refuse him outright. She likely asked for time to consider his offer, for Irving remained close by for the next month, waltzing with her on his fortieth birthday, and watching her warily. Publicly, he and Emily remained warm to each other, but the strain of keeping up appearances was obvious in an April entry in Emily's journal: "Irving is amiable & amusing. I must not yield to capricious coldness fits." For much of the month, she was conveniently unwell or nursing a headache when Irving called on her.[25]

Irving could only wait and brood. Despite his "amiable & amusing" facade, his spirits were sinking. "Endeavor to write poetry but in vain—," he recorded on April 14, in another rubbed-out entry, "determining not to dine today at Mrs F Think of leavg Dresden." The tension must have been palpable, yet in late April, as Irving put the finishing touches on *Der Freischütz,* Emily seemed to warm to him again. "E in good spirits & listens delightfully," reads a scrubbed April 18 journal entry. By April 20 she was "in good spirits . . . and very agreeable" (erased), on the twenty-first, "much better" (also effaced), and on the twenty-seventh he was writing a poem in preparation for her nineteenth birthday on May 4.[26]

Then, in late April there was an angry confrontation. Rumors of Irving's marriage proposal had been whispered around Dresden drawing rooms, but when it was mentioned at a party she and Irving were attending, Emily exploded. "That report that I am to marry 'certo signore autore'—begins to annoy me," she wrote testily in her journal. When Irving entered the room, other guests discreetly filed out, "to leave me," Emily continued, "a *tete-a-tete* with him[.] I was quite angry."[27]

What was said remains unknown, but the confrontation wrecked Irving. His journal entry for that day was brief, but curious. No mention was made of the argument, yet its absence screamed from five terse etceteras and twelve angry, decreasing horizontal lines:

Study at home all morning—[c]all at Livius—Take Italian lesson at Mrs F—Dine there—with Livius—read French in the Evg.—call at Lowensterns—then at Livius—&c &c &c &c &c[28]

For the next two days, Irving avoided the Fosters. At the end of his self-imposed separation, he acknowledged in his journal that the time away had done him good: "Returnd home in very good spirits determind to see society and gather myself up."[29] But he had also unburdened himself by writing, perhaps at Mrs. Foster's request, a lengthy, cathartic letter, which he now presented to Mrs. Foster and Emily.

It was a letter unlike any Irving ever wrote. Composing it during an emotional and nervous crisis, he exposed his soul for perhaps the only time in his life. "It was left with us under a sacred promise that it should be returned to him," Flora Foster remembered later, "that no copy should be taken; and that no other eyes but ours should ever rest upon it."[30] The letter was so dear to Irving, in fact, that he kept the surviving pages in a locked box for the rest of his life, in a package marked simply, "Private Mems."

Over the course of nineteen rambling pages—three of which

are missing—Irving described his childhood, his love and grief for Matilda Hoffman, his struggles at a career, and the still smarting humiliation of bankruptcy, as he tried desperately to address concerns Mrs. Foster may have expressed about his lifelong bachelorhood, his moodiness and mental condition, and his plans for the future:

> You wonder why I am not married . . . I became involved in ruin. It was not for a man broken down in the world to drag down any woman to his paltry circumstances, and I was too proud to tolerate the idea of ever mending my circumstances by matrimony. My time has now gone by. . . . You want to know some of the *fancies* that distress me. . . . While at Dresden I had repeated feelings since I entered upon the world, which like severe wounds and maims in the body, leave forever after a morbid sensitiveness, and a quick susceptibility to any new injury.

Despite this "morbid sensitiveness," Irving asserted—after a long explanation of personal, financial, and artistic difficulties—that his outlook on life was generally positive, sometimes to a fault: "Indeed I often reproach myself with my cheerfulness and even gaiety at times when I have real cause to grieve. Whatever you may think of me, the natural inclination of my mind is to be cheerful; but I have had so many shadows thrown across my path; I see so much doubt before & sorrow behind me; I see every enjoyment hanging on so transient and precarious a tenure, that I cannot help sometimes falling into dejection."[31]

The letter ends on a down beat, breaking off in mid-sentence just as Irving began to discuss his family obligations. It is impossible to know what sentiments and confessions may have been on the three missing pages, but it is clear that he had informed Mrs. Foster—either in the missing pages or in person—that he would no longer pursue Emily's hand. As Flora Foster later recalled: "He has confessed to my mother, as to a true and dear friend, his love for Emily, and his conviction of its utter hopelessness. He feels himself unable to combat it. He thinks he must try, by absence, to bring more peace to his mind. Yet he cannot bear to give up our friendship—an intercourse become so dear to him, and so necessary to his daily happiness. Poor Irving!"[32]

Heartbroken, Irving resolved to leave Dresden. "He sometimes thinks he had better *never* return," Flora wrote. "That would be too sad." Irving lingered in town long enough to attend Emily's nineteenth birthday party, delivering to her mother the verses he had composed the day before the altercation. "If . . . they would give her any pleasure—Slip them into her scrap book," he wrote politely, "if not slip them into the stove that convenient altar."[33]

On May 19, as Irving bid the Fosters good-bye for a tour of Silesia and Bohemia, it wasn't clear if he would come back. "Mama suspects he meant not to return," Emily recorded in her journal, "he said he had thought of it—but that he would, he could not help it— We stood on the balcony by moonlight and talked of heaven." Irving's journal entry was more tight-lipped: "Evg. Pass at Mrs. F—take tea in open air—moonlight evg.—talk of stars &c."[34]

Irving's tour started well enough, as he drove through neat country villages and traipsed through the Giant Mountains. But he was an emotional mess, and the letters he wrote regularly to Mrs. Foster were rambling and confused: "When I consider how I have trifled with my time, suffered painful vicissitudes of feeling, which for a time damaged both mind and body—when I consider all this, I reproach myself that I did not listen to the first impulse of my mind, and abandon Dresden long since. And yet I think of returning! Why should I come back to Dresden? The very inclination that draws me thither should furnish reasons for my staying away." With time on his hands, Irving conducted some image-related business, fussing about a portrait he was having engraved for mass production in America. "I wished it to supplant the likeness already engraved for my country," he wrote, "in which I am made to look like such a noodle, that if I really thought I looked so I would kick myself out of doors." He still couldn't bring himself to write. "I think if I could get my mind fully employed upon some work it would be a wonderful relief to me," he sighed. By mid-June he was ready to return to Dresden, against his better judgment. "I ought to be off like your bird," he told Mrs. Foster, "but I feel I shall not be able to keep clear of the cage. I wish I liked you all only half as much as I do." He was back by June 26, sporting a new, albeit temporary, mustache and a determination to leave Dresden for good.[35]

The decision had actually been made for him, for the Fosters had decided to return to England at the end of July. Irving was determined to winter in Paris, but agreed to accompany the family as far as Rotterdam. On July 30 he rode down the Oube River with the Fosters until their steamboat entered open water, then boarded another boat to take him to Brielle. "As he looked up to us, so pale & melancholy," Emily wrote of their good-bye, "I thought I never felt a more painful moment, such starts of regret, a little self-reproach and feelings too quick to analyze." Irving tried manfully not to betray his emotions, but leaving the Fosters and Dresden rattled him. "Oh, Dresden, Dresden!" he said. "With what a mixture of pain, pleasure, fondness, and impatience I look back upon it."[36]

Irving slunk to Paris. Almost immediately, he dispatched a number of letters to Peter—still struggling with his steamboats at Le Havre—to assure him that he was preparing to work on a new book that would earn them both plenty of money. "We shall then be independent of the world and its chances," he told Peter.[37]

Preparing to write was one thing; actually writing was another. Irving still suffered from the massive case of writer's block that had kept his pen still for nearly a year. He began to have nightmares that depressed him and drained his energy. "I am aware that this is all an affair of the nerves," he told Peter, "a kind of reaction in consequence of coming to a state of repose after so long moving about, and produced also by the anxious feeling on resuming literary pursuits."[38] The unfinished Buckthorne novel, removed from *Bracebridge Hall* at Leslie's urging, was still in his trunk; yet the inspiration to finish didn't come.

He found some solace in the home of Thomas Storrow on rue Thevenot. Storrow, the son of a British army officer, had settled in Paris in 1815 with his wife and four children, and the family welcomed Irving into their home as one of their own. To his delight, he also had real family in France; his nephews Henry and Irving Van Wart, aged seventeen and sixteen respectively, were studying in Paris. Irving took them under his wing, bringing them along to dinner parties and going for walks on the Champs Elysées.

And there was John Howard Payne, who persisted in adapting French plays for the London stage, despite appeals from Irving to pursue a different line of work. Payne was living in rooms above the Salon Littéraire of the Palais Royal, basking in the success of an opera he had premiered in London in May, *Clari, the Maid of Milan*, with its still-famous song "Home, Sweet, Home." This time it was Payne who had a business proposition for Irving: if Irving helped him adapt A. V. P. Duval's play *La Jeunesse de duc Richelieu*, Payne would split any profits with him down the middle. Irving agreed to help, but on the condition that his name would not appear on the final product.

It wasn't Buckthorne, but it spurred his pen anew. In October Irving sublet rooms in a spacious apartment Payne maintained at 89 rue Richelieu, which the latter had crammed with furniture from a cottage he rented in Versailles. Here Irving could work on *Richelieu*, as well as *Azendai* and *Married and Single*, two more collaborations Payne had talked him into. It was hack work, but it was still work. If it was done right, Irving thought he might make a living at it. With Payne's encouragement, he was now determined to become a playwright—and suddenly, inspiration struck. "While dressing think of subject for play," he wrote in his journal on October 23, "Shakespeare as a young man." His pen scratched an outline for three acts. He was on his way, or so he thought.

Later that month Payne left for London, taking with him copies of *Richelieu*, *Azendai*, and *Married and Single*, which he hoped to peddle to Charles Kemble, the manager of the Covent Garden Theatre. Irving remained behind to manage their mutual business affairs, which, to his annoyance, amounted mostly to holding Payne's French creditors at bay.

In early November Irving began adapting *La Jeunesse de Henry V*. He changed its setting from France to England to better suit British tastes, and renamed it *Charles II; or, The Merry Monarch*. Peter visited to provide some much-needed company and assistance—he could translate from the French—and moved into a spare room in the rue Richelieu apartments. Within days, Peter was deep in conversation with the ironically named Mr. Goodsell, who was trying to convince the Irvings to speculate in an experimental flax machine. Money was an issue again.

Washington's mood soured. Payne sent news that Kemble might purchase *Richelieu*, but complained so much about money and future prospects that Irving came unglued. "When there is the necessity for whining and croaking—," he snapped, "wait until the plays are damnd, and then you may whine and be damned too." He sent Payne a draft of *Charles II*, reminding his coauthor to keep his name off it. As his own money grew tighter and Payne's debtors continued to call, Irving urged his friend to simply dispose of the remaining plays *"precisely as your own interests & emergencies may dictate."*[39]

Irving was out of money, and out of patience. In December he forced himself to work on his German *Sketch Book*, but to no avail. "Try this morning to write on German work," he noted in his journal on December 11, "but find it impossible." It was the same the next day. "Full of doubts as to literary prospects," he wrote.[40] The nightmares began anew.

It had been eighteen months since the publication of *Bracebridge Hall*, and Murray was understandably anxious. "I am perfectly ready for you," Murray wrote his absent author, "and the sooner you take the field, the better." Irving swallowed hard; he had nothing to show Murray. So he did the only thing he could do to keep the publisher off his back: he lied. "I do not like to make promises," he responded on December 22, "but I think I shall be able to furnish you with a brace more volumes of the *Sketch Book* in the course of the spring. I am already far advanced in them." As a contingency plan, he proposed adapting *Arabian Nights*. "I can be working at them in the intervals of more original writing," he told Murray.[41]

In early 1824 a pirated copy of *Salmagundi* appeared in London, and the French publisher Galignani offered Irving the opportunity to publish an authorized edition of Old Sal. "It is full of crudities and Puerilities and I had hoped would have remained unnoticed & forgotten,"[42] Irving told Murray. Yet, ever mindful of his reputation, he realized that if the public were to see Geoffrey Crayon in his younger, less refined days, it was better to publish a version he had sanitized himself. He agreed to revise not only *Salmagundi* but also *A History of New York* for Galignani.

Payne sent word that Charles Kemble had agreed to purchase both *Richelieu* and *Charles II* for two hundred guineas—he also purchased *Der Freischütz* from Livius—but the novelty of being a playwright had worn off. Irving told Payne to keep the money and to withdraw their unsold manuscripts from consideration; he was quitting the playwriting business altogether. "The experiment has satisfied me that I should never in any wise be compensated for my time & trouble,"[43] he told Payne.

Murray refused to acknowledge Irving's *Arabian Nights* suggestion; his readers wanted Crayon, not rehashed Persian tales. Irving quickly finished his revisions to *Salmagundi* for Galignani, but creating new Geoffrey Crayon stories for Murray proved far more challenging. The clock was ticking; his self-imposed spring deadline, he told Leslie in February, "obliges me to make the most of what I have in hand & can soonest turn to account." He strained to finish the Buckthorne piece, breaking it into a series of shorter stories about writers, booksellers, agents, and actors. "It had grown stale with me," he explained to Leslie.[44]

Irving was "very much out of spirits," frequently waking in the middle of the night and unable to get back to sleep. Then, on February 15 Thomas Medwin, Percy Shelley's cousin, read to him the journal of a painter who had been abducted by robbers near Rome.

"He relates an anecdote or two which excite me," Irving recorded in his journal, "return home and & commence."[45] The pen was back in action.

Rising at five, sometimes four in the morning, Irving wrote at a speedy clip, at one point completing seventy-five handwritten man-uscript pages in five days. The restless John Murray gently, but firmly, leaned on him to finish, and even provided financial incen-tive to spur his pen, offering 1,200 guineas for the manuscript sight unseen. By March 25 Irving was comfortable enough with the pieces he'd finished to promise Murray a complete manuscript by mid-May. "I think the title will be *Tales of a Traveller, by Geoffrey Crayon, Gent.*," he told his publisher.[46]

As for Murray's 1,200-guinea incentive, Irving acknowledged that such an offer was "a liberal one and made in your own gentle-manlike manner." However, "I would rather you would see the Mss: and make it *fifteen hundred*." He assured Murray that those who had read his pages so far "think the work will be the best thing I have written."[47]

Satisfied, Murray backed off—and Irving's pen suddenly went dry. "Out of spirits—distrustful of my work," he wrote.[48] Instead he sat for a portrait—his image remained in demand—and looked for new apartments. He sent letters of encouragement to Payne in Lon-don, read James Fenimore Cooper's new novel *The Pilot*, and learned of Byron's April 19 death.

The fog lifted in early May, which proved fortuitous: Murray was advertising *Tales of a Traveller* for publication that summer. After some hectic writing, Washington sent the manuscript of the first volume to Peter for copying on May 17. A week later he trav-eled to London, where he planned to oversee production of *Trav-eller* and edit his proofs, even as he worked on material for a second volume.

Irving arrived in London at six-thirty on the evening of May 28, and went immediately to the Covent Garden Theatre to catch the second performance of his and Payne's *Charles II*. As prom-ised, Payne had ensured Irving's name appeared nowhere on the program, merely acknowledging a "literary friend."[49] Irving watched the performance in a box seat with Payne and a young widow Payne was wooing named Mary Shelley.

Calling on Murray the following evening, Irving was delighted to learn the publisher would pay 1,500 guineas for *Traveller*. Murray had never even asked to see it. Now it was a mad sprint to the finish—and as Irving would soon find out, no book of his would be so plagued with problems as it moved toward publication.

Irving spent ten days visiting the Fosters at their estate in Brickhill, as he reviewed proofs, made extensive revisions, and wrote new pieces, which was certain to drive his typesetter mad. While he enjoyed his reunion with the Fosters, the intimacy of 1823 was gone; he was a welcome friend and houseguest, but that was it. For one, Mr. Foster was now a presence, and his mundane talk of road paving was a far cry from the amateur theatricals Irving had staged with the Foster women in Dresden. The family was also more actively pious than Irving liked, and he was uncomfortable with their open displays of devotion. When an animated conversation between the Fosters and various evangelicals ended in a call for prayer, Irving's eyes rolled skyward—"All kneel down and pray," he wrote caustically in his journal, and down he went, Flora Foster said later, "with an impatient gesture, and almost a shudder," onto his knees.[50]

In late July came word from Murray that Irving hadn't written enough to fill two octavo-sized volumes. As the proofs rolled off the printing press, he scrambled to fill the gap, lengthening some stories and hastily writing several new ones. "Vile Book work," he groused to his journal.[51]

On August 4 he had a long meeting with Murray to discuss a problem that had arisen when the publisher shared Irving's proofs with William Gifford, the stuffy editor of Murray's *Quarterly Review* and a longtime friend. In a dither, Gifford had written to Murray demanding changes in Irving's manuscript. The priggish Gifford had a number of complaints, but his biggest objection was that Irving had the nerve to "ridicule our provincial clergy, an exemplary body of men of whom he is completely ignorant." Out of deference to Gifford, Murray requested Irving modify his manuscript.

It was the first time Irving had faced censorship, and his reaction is telling: the private Irving complained, but the public Irving complied. Irving wrote Murray a long, mollifying letter, apologizing for any offense, however unintentional. His portrayals of clergymen, he said, were based on personal experience, but he told his publisher with a tinge of sarcasm that he would make the requested changes and would be more careful in the future "not to venture too far even when I have fact on my side." He obediently inserted a too-sweet parson and his family into his work, then griped privately in his journal that he was "marring the story in compliance with the critique of Gifford."[52]

Irving was tired of the whole mess. He stayed in London only long enough to take in a few more theater performances, sitting in a private box at the Haymarket Theatre on August 10 with Mary Shelley and two other ladies, then collected his payment for *Tales of a Traveller* from Murray. On a rainy Friday the thirteenth, Irving left for Paris.

"I never have had such fagging in altering, adding, and correcting," he told Moore, "and I have been detained beyond all patience by the delays of the press. Yesterday, I absolutely broke away [from London], without waiting for the last sheets. . . . From the time I first started pen in hand on this work, it has been nothing but hard driving with me." He asked Moore for his thoughts on *Tales of a Traveller* after its publication—unless, of course, Moore didn't like it, in which case Irving advised him to keep his mouth shut. "I am easily put out of humor with what I do," he wrote sheepishly. It was just as well; Moore was unimpressed with *Traveller*. "Rather tremble for its fate," he confided in his journal.[53]

On August 15 Irving arrived in Paris. Peter remained in the rue Richelieu apartments, but Washington retired to new quarters in the quieter nearby village of Auteuil. Here, close to the Storrows, he waited for word on the reception of *Tales of a Traveller*. For the first time, he had confidence in his writing. "For my own part, I think there are in it some of the best things I have ever written," he told his sister Catharine. "They may not be so highly polished . . . but they are touched off with a freer spirit, and are more true to life."[54]

On August 25, 1824, Murray published the two-volume *Tales of a Traveller by Geoffrey Crayon, Gent.* Simultaneously, Moses Thomas released *Traveller* in the United States in four installments. The book sold rapidly; Irving's name alone was enough to keep copies moving. While Geoffrey Crayon, in his preface, "To the Reader," claimed that writing the book "was no difficult matter," Washington Irving had labored hard over nearly every word. This time the strain showed. And the critics—who had been waiting for the well-spoken Crayon to finally stutter—pounced.

"I have been miserably disappointed," wrote John G. Lockhart in a blistering review in *Blackwood's Edinburgh Magazine*. The *United States Literary Gazette* agreed. "On the whole, we are not satisfied with these tales. Some of them, indeed, are quite respectable as productions of the light kind of literature, but . . . the public have been led to expect better things." The *Westminster Review* thought that Crayon's usually elegant voice had become ingratiating. "He would strike his best passage in fear of losing the next invitation to dinner he may expect from Grosvenor Square." Such an accusation must have stung, given that Irving, at Murray's request, had removed language that had been deemed offensive or inappropriate.[55]

What hurt Irving most, however, was that reviewers didn't just trash the work, they rebuked him as well. "It is high time that Mr. Irving should begin to ask of himself a serious question," Lockhart wrote in a schoolmasterly tone. "'What is it that I am to be known by hereafter?' . . . nearly twenty years have passed since his first and as yet his best production, 'the History of New York,' made its appearance. He has most certainly made no progress in any one literary qualification since then."[56] Perhaps the most withering assessment came from the American side of the Atlantic. "No man in the Republic of Letters," the *New-York Mirror* pronounced, "has been more overrated than Mr. Washington Irving."[57]

Irving was panned for the first time in his career, and the criticism cut him to the quick. Any thoughts he may have had of returning to America were abandoned under the weight of *Traveller*'s failure; there was no way he could return home under such a black cloud and what he was certain was a soiled reputation. "Feel dejected," he confided in his journal after reading yet another negative review. He suffered from stomach cramps and insomnia, and began studying Spanish to keep himself occupied when sleep wouldn't come. "Full of doubts of Success of my work," he wrote groggily.[58]

His spirits chilled as Paris grew colder. "An indifferent night—," he jotted in his journal in November, "awoke very early: depressed, dubious of myself & public." He wrote a letter to Catharine full of regret at his chosen path in life, and urged his sister not to let her own children hone their imaginations at the expense of more practical activities.[59]

By December he was feeling so sorry for himself that he couldn't even manage a few encouraging words to another aspiring writer, his eighteen-year-old nephew, Pierre Paris Irving— Ebenezer's oldest son, who sent his famous uncle copies of a small periodical to which he was contributing. Washington responded with a treatise on the hazards of a literary life, dripping with self-indulgent world-weariness: "I am sorry . . . to find you venturing into print at so early an age, as I consider it extremely disadvantageous. . . . The article you wrote in the periodical work for instance was very clever as to composition, and was all that could be expected from a writer of your age. . . . I hope, however, your literary vein has been but a transient one, and that you are preparing to establish your fortune and reputation on a better basis than literary success."[60] It is perhaps little wonder that Pierre Paris Irving eventually became a clergyman.

In a December letter to Brevoort, Irving provided a frank but rambling assessment of his strengths, weaknesses, and aspirations as a writer:

> I should like to write occasionally for my amusement, and to have the power of throwing my writings either into my portfolio, or into the fire. I enjoy the first conception and first sketching down of my ideas; but the correcting and preparing them for the press is irksome, and publishing is detestable. . . . I fancy much of what I value myself upon in writing, escapes the observation of the great mass of my readers: who are intent more upon the story than the way in which it is told. For my part I consider a story merely as a frame on which to stretch my materials.[61]

When it came to the critics, however, he couldn't bring himself to admit that he cared about what they had to say: "The fact is that I have kept myself so aloof from all clan ship in literature, that I have no allies among the scribblers for the periodical press. . . . However, as I do not read criticism good or bad, I am out of the reach of attack. If my writings are worth any thing they will out live temporary criticism; if not they are not worth caring about."[62]

Despite his glumness, Irving had reason to be pleased as he looked back on 1824. He had written *Tales of a Traveller;* had issued revised editions of Knickerbocker and Old Sal for Galignani; and had seen his play, *Charles II*, open to acclaim in London. Not a bad year—but overshadowing it all were the poor reviews of *Traveller*. His last journal entry for the year was suitably contemplative and self-pitying: "This has been a dismal day of depression &c and closes a year part of which has been full of sanguine hope; of social enjoyment; peace of mind, and health of body—and the latter part saddened by disappointments & distrust of the world & of myself; by sleepless nights & joyless days—May the coming year prove more thoroughly propitious."[63]

Unfortunately, worries over money made for a sleepless January 1825, and Irving was starting to lose patience with Payne, whose debtors, Irving told the playwright, "continually threaten to seize the furniture; and make my residence in the apartment very uncomfortable." Further, he had been paying Payne's debts out of his own pocket and was no longer confident he would be reimbursed. In the end, though, he couldn't bring himself to completely give up on the wayward playwright. "If I cannot assist you with money, I am ready at any time to assist you in your endeavors to make money," Irving wrote, "—and after all that is the best assistance that one friend can render another."[64]

He approached John Murray about writing a life of Cervantes, and continued to pitch his idea to adapt *Arabian Nights*. Both suggestions met with silence from Murray, who was no doubt regretting the 1,500 guineas he had invested, sight unseen, in *Traveller*. It was a mistake Murray would not make again. With his proposals ignored, Irving struggled for inspiration. "Thinking over project of American Work," he wrote on February 5, though "low spirits" prevented him from writing anything.[65] Instead he read the papers, attended the opera, and dined with Peter. As for Peter, his steamboat venture finally imploded in March, and he skulked to Castle Van Wart to look for new projects in which to invest other people's money.

Irving's spirits brightened with the coming of spring. Learning that his earlier comments to Pierre Paris Irving had soundly discouraged the young man, he insisted that he had been taken out of context. His remarks "were rather meant to warn you for the future, not to censure you for the past." His point, he stressed, had been to encourage his nephew to forsake "idle society" for good books and hard work. "Do not be impatient to enter in society & to make a figure in drawing rooms," Irving wrote. "A man can seldom figure to any purpose until he has acquired the knowledge & experience of years."[66] It was good advice, though Irving wouldn't have followed it himself at age nineteen.

In late April he dusted off the play about young Shakespeare he had outlined in 1823, and hoped inspiration would come. It didn't. "Wrote two or three pages," he grumbled in his journal, "but was not in mood—could not summon force & spirit."[67] Writer's block had taken hold.

Three days later came the meltdown.

On a drizzly Friday morning, Irving tried briefly to write, but felt such an "unconquerable lassitude" that he collapsed on his sofa, his eyelids heavy. "Unrefreshed feeling," he noted, "as if I had not slept enough." He walked to Galignani's to sort through the newly arrived stack of English and American newspapers. In the pages of the *New-York Mirror* was a scalding review of *Tales of a Traveller*: "It is suggested that Mr. Washington Irving's new work would sell more rapidly if the Booksellers would alter the Title, and call it 'STORIES FOR CHILDREN' by *a Baby Six Feet High*, instead of Tales of a Traveller." Irving was furious. "*It is hard to be stabbd in the back by ones own kin when attacked in front by strangers,*" he scrawled angrily in his journal. "No matter—," he continued in vengeful tones, "my countrymen may regret some day or other that they turnd from me with such caprice, the moment foes abroad assailed me."[68]

"To me," he told Brevoort years later, "it is always ten times more gratifying to be liked than to be admired; and I confess to you, though I am a little too proud to confess it to the world, the idea that the kindness of my countrymen toward me was withering, caused me for a long time the most dreary depression of spirits and disheartened me from making any literary mentions."[69]

"Intolerably heavy and torpid all Evg & day," he recorded on May 5. Days later, he was scribbling angrily at his "project of American work." He labored over them, on and off, for nearly a year, producing pieces on American behavior, character, education, and national prejudices. Given his mood, it's likely these essays reflected his bitterness with American critics and disenchantment with American readers. He later destroyed them, perhaps recognizing that such a vindictive appearance in print might irreparably damage his reputation.[70] At the moment, however, the exercise was cathartic.

He continued to be concerned about Peter, still sulking in Birmingham, and was determined to do whatever he could to ensure his brother's financial independence, even if it meant carrying Peter on his back. Washington's money from *The Sketch Book* had been all but consumed by the steamboat venture, and while *Bracebridge Hall* had sold well, the relative failure of *Tales of a Traveller* had forced him to rely on his past profits. But he was running out of money; if he meant to support Peter, he would have to earn enough for both of them, and quickly. Once again, Peter had ideas on how Washington might make that happen.

On his brother's advice—with the help and encouragement of an American businessman named George Myers and a shadowy acquaintance referred to only as "Mr. Jones"—Washington agreed to speculate in a Bolivian copper mine. It was a shaky proposition from the start, but he was confident he had at last found a regular source of income for Peter, and purchased fifty shares in the mine at £23 per share, for a total cost of about $100,000 today. "[Myers] has received letters . . . from his partner in America giving the most satisfactory accounts of the mine," Washington told Storrow. "Altogether, the intelligence is very encouraging." It was also wrong—and Washington soon saw his earnings from *Bracebridge* and *Traveller* sucked down an unproductive hole in South America.[71]

As much as Irving regretted the loss, he never questioned Peter's judgment. Just as William and Ebenezer never blamed Peter when their Liverpool offices had collapsed under his mismanagement, Washington never held him responsible for gambling away his literary profits on one ill-advised scheme after another. "Brotherhood," Washington said later, "is a holy alliance made by God and imprinted in our hearts, and we should adhere to it with religious faith. The more kindly and scrupulously we observe its dictates, the happier for us."[72] Fortunately for Peter, the Irving brothers always put blood ahead of bankruptcy.

Even though he had picked up a stalker of sorts, who took

great delight in mailing Irving his bad reviews, his spirits were reviving. But a July 31 offer from Archibald Constable—now reconciled with John Murray after a fifteen-year estrangement—to produce a biography of George Washington sent him into a panic. "It would require a great deal of reading and research," he told Constable, "and that too much of a troublesome and irksome kind. . . . I feel myself quite incapable of executing any idea of the task. It is one that I dare not attempt lightly. *I stand in too great awe of it.*"[73] The suggestion was shelved—for now.

In early August John Howard Payne arrived in Paris for a meeting with Stephen Price, a talent agent Irving had recommended as a potential business partner. Before meeting with Price, Payne pulled Irving aside to have a frank conversation over dinner.

For more than a year, Payne had been actively pursuing Mary Wollstonecraft Shelley, the attractive twenty-seven-year-old author of *Frankenstein* and the widow of poet Percy Bysshe Shelley. Following Shelley's death in Italy in 1822, Mary had returned to England to be near her father, the novelist and anarchist William Godwin, to write, and to care for her young son. Her friends encouraged the single mother to socialize more, and sometime in mid-1824, Mrs. Shelley—as nearly everyone referred to her—became acquainted with Payne.

For a while, the two traded casual letters and invitations, drinking tea in her rooms in Kentish Town, and strolling on the Strand. Within no time, Payne had fallen in love with her, singing her praises in long, fawning letters. Flattered yet nervous, Mrs. Shelley kept the playwright just at arm's length. "I know how entirely your imagination creates the admired as well as the admiration," she told Payne. In such a fashion the two had continued to see each other for the past several months.[74]

None of this was news to Irving. He had met Mrs. Shelley several times, and had even seen her and Payne together in May 1824, as they sat in their box at Covent Garden for a performance of *Charles II*. But there was more. In late June Payne had been invited to dinner at the Godwin home in Gower Place. As he walked Mary back to Kentish Town after dinner, they had a frank conversation in which Payne learned that Mrs. Shelley had developed something of a crush on Irving. "She said you had interested her more than any one she had seen since she left Italy," Payne told Irving, his eyes emerald with jealousy, "that you were gentle and cordial, and that she longed for friendship with you. I rallied her a little upon the declaration, and at first she fired at my mentioning that she talked as if she were in love. Upon her reply, I answered, 'What! Would you make a plaything of Mr. I[rving]?' "[75]

Mary shyly asked for copies of any of Irving's letters—"Irvine" she called him—that Payne might have on hand, and Payne grudgingly obliged, handing over a dog-eared pile, along with a cover note declaring he would end his one-sided pursuit of her. "I have given way to an absurdity," he huffed, "and have only myself to blame."[76]

Mrs. Shelley made reassuring noises. "Your letter gives me pain," she told the rejected suitor. However, she admitted, "W.I.'s letter pleases me greatly. I shall be glad to see Irvine's letters, and the handwriting . . . will become as clear to me as Lord Byron's letterless scrawl. As to friendship with him—it cannot be—though everything I hear and know renders it more desirable. How can Irvine—surrounded by fashion, rank, and splendid friendships—pilot his pleasure bark from the gay press into this sober, sad, enshadowed nook?"[77]

Dutifully, Payne continued sending Irving's letters to her even as he prepared to leave for Paris for his meeting with Stephen Price. Mrs. Shelley maintained a friendly correspondence with Payne, and joked that her relationship with—indeed, she teased, her plans to *marry*—her "favorite I[rving]" was not proceeding as quickly as she had hoped. "Methinks our acquaintance proceeds at the rate of the Antediluvians, who, I have somewhere read, thought nothing of an interval of a year or two between a visit. Alack! I fear that at this rate, if ever the Church should make us one, it would be announced in the consolatory phrase that the Bride and Bridegroom's joint ages amounted to the discreet number of 145 and 3 months."[78]

The following day, a blushing Mrs. Shelley sent a follow-up note to Payne, asking him to speak well of her to Irving. "Tho' I am a little fool," she wrote, "do not make me appear so in Rue Richelieu by repeating tales out of school—nor mention the Antediluvians."[79]

Payne gave Irving a parcel containing his correspondence with Mrs. Shelley, along with a note stating his intention to step aside and allow Irving to pursue what the playwright clearly thought was a golden opportunity. "I do not ask you to fall in love," Payne said, "but I should feel a little proud of myself if you thought the lady worthy of that distinction, and very possibly you would have fallen in love with her, had you met her casually—but she is too much out of society to enable you to do so."[80]

One can only speculate what might have happened had Irving and Mary Shelley created literature's first transatlantic power couple. Irving, however, while likely amused, wasn't interested. "Read Mrs. Shelley's correspondence before going to bed,"[81] he noted in his journal that evening—the only words he ever wrote regarding the entire affair. He handed the correspondence back to Payne without comment.

His summer continued without incident, though he still hadn't found the urge to write much of anything. "I have nothing ready for the press, nor do I know at present when I shall have, my mind having been rather diverted from composition of late," he told Murray, whose silence had discouraged Irving from any further work on his proposed life of Cervantes. Irving said he was reading about Spanish history and the Moors, and taking in "air and exercise" instead of society—which, of course, wasn't true.[82]

He regularly checked with Storrow on the status of his Bolivian mines to see if there was any hope of disposing of them advantageously. There wasn't. "I regret to hear the Bolivars are so low—," he sighed. "I had hoped to realize something from them to pay current expenses—it seems as if all my attempts to strike a little ahead are defeated."[83]

Irving wasn't the only one suffering financially. A wave of bankruptcies that had started in August was building into a tidal wave in London. On October 31 Irving learned that the banking firm of Welles & Williams had collapsed, taking down a staggering £400,000 in obligations with it, including a guarantee of £2,000 Irving had recently extended on Peter's behalf. Between the Bolivar mines and the collapse of Welles & Williams, Washington teetered on the brink of poverty, as did Ebenezer and the Van Warts. It was Liverpool all over again, and Irving plunged into despair. "Feel a want of confidence in myself in case of misfortune," he recorded in early November, "—do not feel the same vivacity of thought & feelings as formerly."[84]

Concerned that his copyrights might be dragged into the current business woes, Washington asked Ebenezer to place all his literary property in the hands of John Treat or Brevoort—then had a nightmare the following night in which his house burned down, and all his manuscripts with it. "I am now not worth six pence!" he had screamed in his dream.[85] He was a wreck.

As before, financial need spurred his pen into action, however slowly. He settled into lodgings in Bordeaux's rue Holland for the winter, and revisited his American essays. On December 2 he told Storrow that he was hoping to have something ready for publication soon. "When I once See a little capital of manuscripts growing under my hand," he said with some optimism, "I shall feel like another being and shall be relieved from a thousand cares and anxieties that have haunted my mind for a long time past."[86]

The American essays, which had helped him vent his frustration following *Traveller*'s poor reception, now served a similar therapeutic purpose, helping calm his nerves and build his confidence in the wake of economic collapse. By Christmas Day he probably surprised even himself when he wrote that "for some time past, indeed ever since I have resumed my pen, my mind has been tranquil. I sleep better and feel pleasanter."[87]

With his investments failing and future finances uncertain, Irving knew he had to keep writing to sustain himself. "I find there is nothing to be gained in looking beyond the pen," he told Storrow, "I believe I must content myself with driving my quill in a garret instead of coining the treasures of Mexico & Peru."[88]

Interestingly, it was among the treasures of Spain where Washington Irving sought—and found—his next inspiration and fortune.

10

Professional

1826–1829

I have principally been employed on my Life of Columbus, in executing which I have studied and laboured with a patience and assiduity for which I shall never get the credit.

—Washington Irving to Henry Brevoort, April 4, 1827

𝒯HE LETTER FROM THE AMERICAN MINISTER to Spain seemed too good to be true.

President John Quincy Adams's newly appointed minister, a thirty-five-year-old Bostonian named Alexander Hill Everett, had met Irving during the summer of 1825 in Paris. The two had enjoyed each other's company, and before leaving for Spain, Everett invited Irving to visit Madrid, even offering to formally attach him to the Spanish embassy for protection. Irving had declined, but in early January 1826, on a whim, he wrote Everett from Bordeaux, asking if his invitation was still open.

Everett's response arrived on January 30. Not only did the offer still stand, but Everett also had a potential literary project for him: the Spanish writer and scholar Martin Fernández de Navarette was preparing to publish the journals of Christopher Columbus, and Everett wanted to know if Irving would be interested in translating the documents into English. Everett suggested that such a translation might be sold to interested publishers.

Everett had shrewdly appealed to Irving's purse, and the offer was tempting. The investment in the Bolivian copper mine was a disaster, and his personal finances remained tight. As for the proposed project, Irving had undertaken similar work before, translating plays like *Richelieu* from French into English. It seemed to be easy money. "The very idea of it animates me," Irving wrote to the minister. "There is something in the job itself that interests and pleases me, and will assist to compensate me for my trouble." To Storrow, however, he was markedly less reserved. "A job has suddenly presented itself which seems like a godsend. This thing has come upon me so suddenly that it has thrown me quite in a flurry."[1]

In the meantime, Irving wrote to Leslie in London and asked the artist to approach John Murray, to see if he—or any other publisher, for that matter—would be interested in acquiring the Columbus translation, sight unseen, for 1,000 guineas. Irving apologized for the bother; Leslie and his wife were friendly with the Murrays, and Irving knew that his request could put Leslie in an awkward position. But Murray hadn't responded favorably to his letters lately, so he thought a more personal appeal was necessary. For good measure, he dropped a note to the publisher, assuring him that his project was sure to be "very interesting . . . I hope it will be a work to tempt you."[2]

And still there was Payne and his long, tiresome letters from London to deal with. A bit of good news had come from the wastrel playwright in early January, when Payne informed him that *Richelieu* would finally be performed at London's Covent Garden Theatre in February. But the play bombed badly, running only six performances. Worse, Payne had given Irving a writing credit, tacking a failed play onto Irving's résumé immediately on the heels of the hated *Tales of a Traveller*. Fortunately, most readers and critics took scarce notice of *Richelieu*.[3]

On their arrival in Madrid, Washington and Peter were welcomed by Minister Everett into the tight circle of English-speaking diplomats. Everett introduced the brothers to American consul Obadiah Rich, who lived with his family in a large, rambling house in the old section of Madrid near the Prado. Rich also served as archivist of the American legation, and his residence—a fusion of home, library, and museum—was a bibliophile's dream. Rich had one of the finest libraries in Spain, and perhaps *the* finest private collection when it came to Spanish history. Everett thought Rich's home the ideal place for the Irvings to rent rooms.[4]

He was right—"I have never been more pleasantly situated," Washington told Leslie. Not only did it have a remarkable library, but there was a beautiful courtyard garden where he could stroll for inspiration. The place was quiet, especially compared to his rooms in Paris, where the noise of horse-drawn carriages and loud late-night theatergoers had sometimes made it impossible to sleep or think. Irving thought Rich, a Massachusetts native and Harvard graduate, "a most excellent and amiable man."[5]

After settling in at Rich's, Irving visited Navarette for a look at the materials he would be translating. Navarette handed over the first two volumes of his forthcoming *Coleccion de los viages y descubrimientos, que hicieron por mar los Espanoles desde fines del siglo XV*, a massive five-part history of Spain that he was writing at the request of King Ferdinand.

Irving's heart must have sunk—Everett had misunderstood. The journals of Columbus were only *part* of the document Irving was to translate. Navarette had another nine hundred pages of rare Columbus-related manuscripts that he had plumbed from the closely guarded archives of the Spanish government over the past thirty years. It was a treasure trove of important, if obscure, papers, but it definitely wasn't what Irving had expected to translate.

Then news came from Leslie that Murray wouldn't purchase a Columbus translation without seeing it first. "It might be interesting or it might be dry," Leslie explained on Murray's behalf, "he therefore cannot make any arrangement until it is done."[6] Murray wasn't about to repeat the mistake he had made with his blind purchase of *Tales of a Traveller*.

The publisher was having other difficulties. Economic problems in London had been far-reaching, and the recent financial collapse had dragged down a number of publishers, including Murray's friend Constable. "They are all just now in so great a panic, occasioned by the recent failures here," Leslie told Irving. Murray had survived, but was trying to diversify by establishing a daily newspaper, the *Representative*, a Tory-leaning publication he had set up mainly as a mouthpiece for his friend Benjamin Disraeli. It occupied so much of Murray's time in 1826 that he neglected his correspondence with Irving for most of the year—and got an earful for it.[7]

Back in Madrid, a disappointed Irving spent the next month taking long walks in the overgrown gardens of the Buen Retiro, or strolling in the tree-lined Prado, the most fashionable location in Madrid. He continued to study Spanish, and toured museums and galleries. "Weary and out of order," he reported.[8]

Pope Leo had declared 1826 a Jubilee year, so the theaters were closed ("I never felt more out of humor with popery," Irving grumbled), and remained so for several months, forcing Irving to seek his diversions elsewhere. He enjoyed the company of Everett and his wife, and befriended the Russian minister, Pierre D'Oubril, and his family. Other days, Irving was content to browse Rich's library, though inspiration continued to evade him. "Exceedingly listless & dispirited part of the day," he wrote fussily.[9]

He was beginning to regret that he had ever seen Navarette's volumes. "I fear there is nothing to be done with it," he told Storrow. "They . . . are almost entirely made up of Documents which none but a historiographer would have an appetite to devour or Stomach to digest." That wasn't true; Irving knew how to sort through dense and esoteric papers—he had done it for *A History of New York*. Turning Navarette's volumes over in his hands, he knew the information the historian had compiled was useful, even if technical or academic. "Excellent materials for a work, but which in their present form would repel the general class of readers," he admitted to Leslie. "I am in hopes of making a work that will be acceptable to the public."[10]

Rich later claimed credit for encouraging Irving to write a life of Christopher Columbus. Irving was slow to embrace the idea, but once he did, he worked at a frantic pace. Sitting in Rich's library, he began as early as 5:00 A.M. and wrote steadily into the evening. For the first time, he treated writing like a real job, maintaining a regular schedule and producing a certain number of pages daily. "I had no idea of the Nature of the task when I undertook it," he later said. "Indeed had I seen it in the light in which I behold it at present, I should have been diffident of undertaking it at all." Despite his intense work schedule, Irving was no hermit. Writing, when it flowed, energized him, and most evenings he found time for walks and good company. "The people here are greatly pleased with him," remarked an impressed Everett.[11]

In early May he spent three days with Peter and the Everetts at the royal palace in Aranjuez, about thirty miles south of Madrid. It was an exclusive invitation that Irving could hardly refuse, yet he remained remarkably disciplined, spending part of each day taking notes or writing. Returning from Aranjuez on May 6, his rigorous pace resumed immediately. "Rise at ½ past 4," read one journal entry from this time, "write at Columb all day . . . write before going to bed. 29 p[ages]."[12]

On May 22 he attended his first bullfight—the *toros*, he called them—an entertainment that became his guilty pleasure. The spectacle, with its blend of formality and managed chaos, resonated with his sense of pageantry; and the bloodshed made it all seem that much more romantic. "I did not know what a bloodthirsty man I was till I saw them at Madrid," Irving recalled later. "The first was very spirited, the second dull, the third spirited again, and afterward I hardly ever missed. 'But the poor horses,' someone interposed. 'Oh, well, they were very old and worn out, and it was only a question whether they should die a triumphant death or be battered a few years longer.' "[13]

In mid-June Irving completed the first draft of his Columbus biography. "I am absolutely fagged and exhausted with hard work," he told Storrow. Looking through his seven hundred handwritten pages, he was uncertain of its quality. "It is so much in the rough that I have not as yet shewn it even to my brother," he wrote. "One person I am sure of not pleasing . . . is myself."[14]

For the next month, he continued reading and researching, poring over any titles in Rich's library that he might have missed, rereading Navaratte's two volumes, and reviewing his own manuscript. "Study all day," he wrote in his journal,[15] though his evenings were reserved for strolls in the Retiro, dining with friends, or attending the theater or bullfights. An even more welcome distraction presented itself on June 24, with the arrival of his twenty-four-year-old nephew, Pierre Munro Irving.

Pierre, the fourth of William Irving Jr.'s eight children, had recently passed the bar and was making a tour of Europe before setting up a practice in New York. His reunion with Washington owed more to luck than planning. Arriving in Madrid, Pierre had approached Minister Alexander Everett about a new passport—and a delighted Everett steered Pierre to his uncle, still huddled in Rich's library. "I found him in the midst of books and manuscripts," Pierre recalled, "full of the subject on which he was engaged, and in excellent spirits."[16]

Irving was delighted with the young man. Pierre was more than just family; he was surprisingly good company. "He has stuff in him to make a valuable man," Washington said appreciatively. For the next three weeks, Pierre was his constant companion. Despite the presence of family, Washington soon fell into a funk in which he was "incapable of work." Pierre thought he knew why: his uncle's mysterious stalker—the one who had barraged him with copies of his bad reviews following *Tales of a Traveller*—was at it again. "He adverted with deep feeling to the cloud which had been thrown over him by the persevering malignity with which all sorts of disagreeable things had been forwarded to him from America by some secret enemy," Pierre recalled.[17]

Such literary terrorism was certainly part of it, but Washington also fretted about money. To his embarrassment, he was forced to borrow from friends in Madrid and draw regularly on Storrow. Until he published another work, he subsisted only on his prior earnings, most of which were tied up in the failing Bolivian mines. "I must drive my pen hard," he confessed to Storrow, "to make up for these drawbacks."[18]

He was as good as his word. On July 11 he plunged into his second draft of Columbus. The following morning, he put Pierre in a carriage for France, where he had arranged for him to stay with the Storrows for the next leg of his European tour. With Pierre gone, the reprieve, such as it was, was over.

Hard at work, he found his insomnia returned. Staggering from his bed at 4:30 or 5:00 A.M., he would go for a walk with Peter, then return to Rich's for breakfast before finally settling in to write all afternoon. On one of their morning walks, Washington spoke of the history of Granada—specifically the events leading up to its conquest in 1492 by Ferdinand and Isabella and the defeat of the Moorish king Boabdil—as the possible subject of his next book.

By late August Irving believed he was close enough to finishing his second draft of Columbus to put it aside and begin another project. For several weeks he worked exclusively on a history of Granada, with the same intensity as he had on Columbus. Still, he was determined not to be antisocial; there were bullfights, operas, state dinners, daily walks in the Retiro, visits to court, and even a brief trip to the crumbling remains of the Escurial in mid-October.[19]

Money continued to be an issue. Many of the drafts he had drawn on Storrow hadn't been covered yet by either Ebenezer or Van Wart. Irving was mortified, and assured Storrow he would settle his account once he published . . . well, *something*. "Unluckily none of my literary matters are in sufficient forwardness to be pressed into present service," he apologized. "For a few weeks past I have neglected Columbus to run after a new subject."[20]

Irving worked exclusively on Granada for several more weeks before he returned full-time to Columbus in mid-November. He wrote to Murray, asking the Prince of Booksellers whether he thought the project sounded promising.[21]

As 1826 wound down, Irving had good reason to be pleased with all that he accomplished. It had been "a year of the hardest application & toil of the pen I have ever passed," he wrote; how-ever, "I feel more satisfied . . . with the manner in which I have passed it than I have been with these of many gayer years, & close this year of my life in better humor with myself than I have often done."[22] He was up by six on the morning of January 1, 1827, to work on Columbus.

If Irving was enthusiastic about his project, there was one per-son who was not. From the very beginning, Thomas Storrow had expressed serious reservations about the Columbus biography. In Storrow's opinion, the project was cost-prohibitive—Irving was investing more time and effort than Storrow believed Irving would ever recoup financially. Further, Storrow believed Irving was taking a chance with his readers if he expected to pass off the easygoing Geoffrey Crayon as the author of a serious biography.

Irving *was* taking a chance, but he had enough confidence in the work to politely dismiss Storrow's concerns. "I am sorry that you do not seem to think highly of my literary undertaking, and that you doubt whether Columbus will repay me for my trouble," he told him. "It is too late now to demur upon the subject. The work is nearly finished. It has cost me, for the time I have been employed upon it, an excessive deal of labour; if it fails to interest the public I shall be grievously disappointed." Storrow's doubts cast a momen-tary pall over the project, and for several days Irving sank into an unproductive rut. "Triste indisposed to work," he scrawled across the top of three days' worth of journal entries.[23]

Fortunately, Murray wrote to him—for the first time in nearly a year—with good news: he was interested in Columbus, and wanted to see the manuscript. He also apologized for not correspond-ing regularly, explaining that the *Representative* had taken up most of his time along with most of his money. Disraeli had proved a skit-tish collaborator, and had backed out of the project, leaving Murray in the lurch. Consequently, the newspaper only lasted until July 1826, at a personal loss to Murray of £26,000, about $3 million today. He managed to stay afloat by sharply reducing the number of titles he published. Irving's track record was enough to keep him interested, but his problematic finances demanded he see anything before agreeing to a deal. Two days after receiving Murray's letter, Irving wrote to Pierre in Paris, asking him to go to London to steer Columbus through production. Time was of the essence, he stressed to his nephew, especially if he was to work with Ebenezer to coordinate the near-simultaneous publication of the book in the United States.[24]

Suddenly, things went impossibly wrong. Irving's journals are vague, but in late January, during one of his conversations with Navarette, the senior historian must have said something that made Irving nervous about his project. Irving clearly believed he had missed something important—so important, in fact, that he started rewriting his manuscript from scratch.

Irving seems to have lost confidence in his narrative tone. He was writing an academic work that nonacademics would find accessible, and he was probably rightly worried about balancing his usual elegant tone with a scholarly one. He began to have bad dreams, "fearful the work was not well enough written."[25] He later admitted to Everett that "Columbus had more slovenliness of style in one stage of its preparation than any work I ever wrote; for I was so anxious about the verity of the narrative and had to patch it together from so many different materials, that I had not time to think of the language."[26] He was a nervous wreck; he barely slept. "Write from early 3 oclock to dinner time," began one exhausted entry. "Sleep 2 hours. Write from 6 till 8. Pass hour & half at rich's write a little but go to bed at ½ pa 10. wake at 2. write till breakfast time."[27]

Irving abandoned any hope of publishing by spring, and told Pierre to forget about going to London. "It is a kind of work that will not bear hurrying," he told his nephew, "many questions have been started connected with it which have been perplexed by tedious controversies, and which must all be looked into. I had no idea what a complete labyrinth I had entangled myself in when I took hold of the work."[28]

To the still skeptical Storrow, he wrote:

I am affraid, after the discouraging speeches you made about Columbus, to say that I am yet labouring at it. . . . You have no idea what a laborious and entangling job it is. There are so many points in dispute. I have fagged night and day for a great part of the time, and every now and then some further document, throwing a different light on some obscure part of the work has obliged me to rewrite what I had supposed finished. . . . I want to finish the work on many accounts. I want to produce something that will give satisfaction to the American public, I want to make a little money badly.[29]

He was "excessively wearied" and "extremely depressed," but the work continued.

Irving's work ethic impressed at least one new arrival in Madrid, a twenty-year-old professor and aspiring poet named Henry Wadsworth Longfellow. A native of Portland, Maine, Longfellow had graduated Phi Beta Kappa from Bowdoin College in 1825, and had shown such promise that the school offered him a professorship in modern languages, on the condition that he travel in Europe for additional language study. Arriving in Madrid, Longfellow never forgot his first glimpse of Irving laboring over his manuscripts. "He seemed to be always at work," Longfellow said. "One summer morning, passing his house at the early hour of six, I saw his study window already wide open." Despite his frantic writing schedule, for the months Longfellow was in Madrid, Irving made an effort to socialize frequently with the young man. Longfellow was delighted with the time and attention. "He is one of those men who put you at ease in a moment," he said warmly of Irving.[30]

To Irving's embarrassment, his money troubles persisted, and he was growing increasingly resentful—and jealous—of successful investors, referring to them derisively as "money-grubbers." Bitterly, he groused to Ebenezer that Brevoort had managed to avoid bankruptcy during the recent financial upheavals precisely because he, too, had become one of the hated money-grubbers.

Irving had nothing of substance to back up such an accusation—Brevoort had, in fact, suffered financially due to a number of bad investments—but Irving flung the charge at his friend in frustration. To support his allegation, he pointed out that he hadn't received a letter from Brevoort in nearly two years, and that the silence confirmed Brevoort had forsaken friendship in the name of profit. Of course, Irving hadn't bothered to write Brevoort to sort things out, but that was beside the point. Washington Irving was mad at Henry Brevoort—and Ebenezer delicately informed Brevoort of the one-sided spat.

Brevoort was stunned, and more than a little angry. On January 1 he wrote a long letter to Irving to plead his case. He rightly pointed out that he had received few letters from Irving over the same time period, yet "never did I permit any unkind construction of your seeming neglect to cross my mind. Nor was it possible that any neglect of the kind could weaken the deep foundation of my attachment to you—an attachment which as I hope for mercy, I have never felt towards any other man."[31] As for the "money-grubbing," Brevoort bristled at the charge. "Whoever it was that informed you, that my mind was absorbed & debased by money-making pursuits, was guilty of uttering a base falsehood. The repetition of so gross an aspersion, although disbelieved by you, appears irreconcilable to my conception of the disinterested f[rien]dship that has invariably existed between us." And yet, Brevoort was willing to give his friend the benefit of the doubt, and extended a generous olive branch: "I trust I have said nothing more than was strictly necessary to my own defence; but if I have said aught to offend your feelings, I hope you will overlook it & remember that this the only instance of discord that has ever arisen between us.—Let us then my dear Irving begin the new year by a renewal of kind and affectionate recollections & by frank and frequent interchange of our sentiments."[32]

Irving received the letter in mid-February, and waited nearly two months to respond. Finally, on April 4, the day after his forty-fourth birthday, he wrote back, composing one of his most revealing letters since the nineteen-page confession he had written to the Fosters. He apologized for the money-grubbing charge, claiming he had spoken "from feelings deeply grieved by your apparent neglect," and admitted that bad reviews and his mysterious mail stalker were making him hypersensitive even to imaginary slights.[33]

He was more wounded, he explained, by the constant assaults on his patriotism from critics who asserted that he had kowtowed to British sensibilities at the expense of his American heritage. "Do not let yourself be persuaded therefore that time or distance has estranged me in thought or feeling from my native country, my native places, or the friends of my youth," he told Brevoort. "The fact is that the longer I remain from home the greater charm it has in my eyes, and all the colouring that the imagination once gave to distant Europe now gathers about the scenes of my native country."[34]

Finally, he admitted that he feared Storrow might be right—that after all his hard work on his Columbus biography, readers wouldn't give the book a chance. "I have principally been employed on my Life of Columbus, in executing which I have studied and laboured with a patience and assiduity for which I shall never get the credit," he wrote sulkily. "How it will please the public I cannot anticipate. I have lost confidence in the favourable disposition of my Countrymen and look forward to cold scrutiny & stern Criticism; and this is a line of writing in which I have not hitherto ascertained my own powers."[35]

The rift between Washington and Brevoort—if there had ever really been one—quietly closed. "I need not assure you that it has removed from my mind every cause of complaint," Brevoort responded with relief, "& I beg that the warmth with which I expressed myself on the subject may be forgotten."[36] All was forgiven.

The Columbus manuscript continued to swell, and Irving apologized to Murray that the book he had sworn was "nearly ready for the press" in the winter of 1826 was still unfinished in the spring of 1827. "I make no promise about when it shall be forwarded," he told Murray, "lest I should disappoint both you and myself." By July 29 he had enough of Columbus completed, and neatly copied, to forward to London. However, the package wasn't going to John Murray.[37]

Eighteen months earlier, Irving had asked Charles Leslie to shop Columbus to Murray or any other interested publisher. Irving preferred Murray, but if the Prince of Booksellers rejected the manuscript, Irving was prepared to take it elsewhere. To properly circulate his book, however, Irving needed an agent. His first choice, Pierre M. Irving, was no longer an option—the young man had returned to America. There was always Leslie, but Irving had already pestered the artist once, and didn't want to put him in the middle of a potentially difficult business transaction, especially given the condition of the British publishing market. He needed a shrewd negotiator with a good head for business—and among Irving's circle of London friends, the person who fit that description best was the American consul, the Harvard-educated attorney Colonel Thomas Aspinwall.

Irving provided Aspinwall with the first nine of his eighteen "books" on Columbus—about 750 handwritten pages—as well as two letters for his agent's use. One was an official-sounding business letter for Aspinwall to present to interested publishers, with the proposed terms of the agreement Irving was seeking. The other was a confidential document for Aspinwall, detailing just how far Irving was willing to go in his negotiations. Irving rightly believed he had written a book that would earn its publisher profits for years to come, and he wasn't going to part with it on the cheap. "If the work is successful it must remain in regular demand and is not like a work of the imagination, which may be thrown aside on a change of public taste," he told Aspinwall. "As a literary property, therefore, it would in such case be more valuable than all my other writings."[38]

At Irving's direction, Aspinwall offered Columbus to Murray first, asking the publisher to either purchase the British copyright outright for a relatively hefty 3,000 guineas (about $300,000 today), or to publish the work on shares, in which Irving's cut would be based on the number of copies sold. "In publishing on shares,"

Irving admitted privately to Aspinwall, "I take my chance of its ultimate success or failure, and am willing to do so rather than part with the copyright at a lower rate."[39] Murray asked for time to consider his options—and kept silent for the next month.

The wait was unbearable. Irving set to work on the remaining half of his manuscript, but even as he completed the work on August 19, there was still no word from Albemarle Street. Unknown to Irving, Murray had asked poet Robert Southey, a longtime friend and contributor to the *Quarterly Review*, for his opinion on Irving's manuscript. Southey took his time reading it—hence the delay—but what he saw didn't impress him. "There is neither much power of mind nor much knowledge indicated in it," the poet told Murray. Still, Southey conceded that Irving had shown "a great deal of diligence employed upon the subject" and that the book was "likely to succeed."[40]

That was enough for the Prince of Booksellers. In September he informed Aspinwall that he would purchase the British copyright to *Columbus* for the 3,000 guineas Irving had requested, paying £300 up front, and the rest in regular installments over the next two years.

Irving was delighted. "I am heartily glad Murray has acceded so handsomely to my terms," he told Aspinwall. "I should not feel satisfied in dealing with any other publisher. I am accustomed to him. I have a friendship with him, and I like the truly gentlemanlike manner in which he publishes."[41]

He was also highly satisfied with Aspinwall. "He seems to have been very wary," wrote Newton, who had followed the negotiations closely, "and to have gained great credit with Murray as a sharp bargainer." Irving was inclined to agree—and when Aspinwall asked for a commission of £78, about 2½ percent of the price he had negotiated, Irving enthusiastically paid him an even hundred. "You have done wonders," he told Aspinwall gratefully. "I never could have made an arrangement in any degree as good had I been on the Spot."[42]

Securing an English publisher had been Irving's most worrisome task, but he still had quite a bit of work ahead of him. He was also working with Ebenezer and Brevoort to find an American publisher and coordinate a simultaneous American release. Meanwhile, the book needed a preface, there were revisions to be made, and Irving was working hard on the "illustrations"—what readers today would call an appendix—that would comprise almost an entire volume.

Unfortunately, he no longer had Rich's library at his disposal—the consul had recently quit Madrid and moved to London to open his own bookstore. Washington and Peter glumly transferred to a house on Plazuela de Santa Cruz, just southeast of the Puerta del Sol in the heart of Madrid. While Irving found countless resources available at the King's Library, the Jesuits' College, and at Navarette's, he missed Rich's library almost as much as he missed Rich. But he kept working, finishing his preface and jotting down notes on Columbus, as well as the outline of a new idea, a biography of the Prophet Muhammad.[43]

Brevoort wrote to announce that he and Ebenezer had printed copies of the completed *Columbus* manuscript to show to potential American publishers, and anticipated a quick sale, as well as an eager American audience. "Many persons of the highest literary standing among us . . . have expressed their satisfaction upon hearing that you were engaged on a subject which they think properly belongs to us," Brevoort wrote, "—so that you have every reason to expect a candid & friendly reception."[44]

Irving was feeling good, even a bit cocky, about his future prospects. "So ends the year 1827 tranquilly," he confided in his last journal entry for the year. "It has been a year of labor, but much more comfortable than most I have passed in Europe, and leaves me in a state of moderate hope as to the future—."[45] *Columbus* was on its way to the printers, and he was paid well for his efforts, something he couldn't resist crowing about to the patient Thomas Storrow. "You see how Columbus has turned out better than you anticipated as to profit," Irving boasted.

On February 8, 1828, *The Life and Voyages of Christopher*

Columbus was published in London in four thin octavo volumes, with a steep price tag of 2 guineas for the set, about $200 today. The critics, and Irving, were shocked by both the presentation and the price. Irving had earlier complained to Murray—in another of his unanswered letters—that there wasn't enough material to fill four volumes, so Murray had simply printed the book with a larger typeface and broader margins to make up the difference. To Irving's embarrassment, the large type made even more obvious the gross number of typographical errors in the work. He had given Aspinwall no explicit directions regarding proofreading, so the colonel had left such details to Murray's typesetter, who, when unable to decipher Irving's cramped handwriting, had simply guessed—and the book suffered for it.

The American edition was much cleaner, likely due to careful administration by Ebenezer and Brevoort. Ebenezer had initially approached Carey & Lea of Philadelphia, who had published an edition of Irving's *Traveller*, but the publisher had balked in a "cold & discouraging" manner, Brevoort reported. The New York firm of G. & C. Carvill, however, jumped at the opportunity, and published the book in a more fitting three volumes, at the price of $6.75 for the set, about $140 today.[46]

For the first time in his career, the name appearing on the title page was not a pseudonym but Irving's own. He was proud of *Columbus*. "If the work succeeds it will be of immense Service to me," he told Brevoort; "if it fails it will be, most probably, what many have anticipated, who suppose, from my having dealt so much in fiction, [that] it must be impossible for me to tell the truth with plausibility."[47]

If readers were skeptical of Geoffrey Crayon's ability "to tell the truth with plausibility," they had plenty of confidence in Washington Irving. *Columbus* was well received by readers, critics, and a new audience, serious historians—a literary hat trick. "This volume will add to the already well-deserved reputation of Mr. Irving," said the *Southern Review:* "Mr. Irving stands, as yet, unique in American literature. He is our only writer, whose successive publications had

added to his fame. . . . We rejoice to see him, a writer of acknowledged fancy and wit, setting an example of laborious investigation,
and careful study, than which nothing is more wanting in our literature."[48]

It was Irving's style—a blend of the sober, factually based
"philosophical history" so popular in his time and Geoffrey Crayon's
more colorful prose—that earned the most praise. Irving had created something new with *Columbus*—a widely accessible, highly
readable biography that was also factually correct, historically accurate, and fully documented. While many critics were uncertain how
to judge such a serious work from Irving—wasn't this the same
writer who had written a *mock* history of New York?—Irving
brought it all together with his usual elegance, which convinced his
critics he knew what he was doing. As his friend Alexander Everett
explained in the *North American Review*, "Such have been the good
taste and felicity of our author in the selection of his subject; such
his diligence, research, and care in giving the highest finish and perfection to the style; that he has been able to bring out a work, which
will rank with the very best histories of any age or nation."[49]

The best and most reassuring review, however, came not from
any literary critic but from Henry Brevoort, who assured Irving of
his "complete success" and confirmed that his countrymen were

> struck with the dignity of your style—the depth of your
> researches—your clear & unbroken narrative of events &
> above all with the romantic interest which you infused into
> every portion of the work—All seemed gratified that the
> discoverer of the new world should have found a biographer,
> worthy of his fame, in one of its sons. . . . I do hope that this
> universal concurrence of opinion as to the value of your
> labours amongst us, will at once banish from your mind
> every feeling of distrust as to the kindness & cordiality of
> your countrymen.[50]

For the first time in his career, Irving felt like a serious writer,
who could earn his living by his pen. Beginning with Oldstyle,

writing had really been the only job he ever had. Yet Irving had continued to believe writing was a pastime, not an occupation. He had viewed the success of *History of New York* and *Sketch Book* as evidence that he could write books that would please readers, even as the lukewarm response to *Bracebridge* and *Traveller* had convinced him that he should have a "real" job. Through it all, he considered himself a dabbler who wrote light, pleasing, easy-on-the-eye fiction—certainly not the kind who wrote dense, well-researched, and well-documented nonfiction.

With *Columbus*, he proved not only that he could be taken seriously as a writer, but that he could take writing seriously. For the seventeen months between March 1826 and August 1827, writing had been his full-time occupation. The final draft of *Columbus* stretched through 127 chapters in eighteen "books," running about 340,000 words—and that wasn't counting the numerous rewrites and notes Irving had scrawled since beginning the project. The late nights, the depression, the "out of order" days belonged not to Geoffrey Crayon but to Washington Irving—but so did the accolades, the praise, and the success.

With *Columbus* in print, Irving was ready to quit Madrid. He had been trying to leave the city for some time, but various circumstances—especially Peter's increasingly precarious health—had kept him rooted. By the end of February, however, Peter had decided to head to France to recover his strength, leaving Washington free to look for new quarters. On a sunny March 1 he sadly said good-bye to his ill brother—"It seemed on taking leave of him at Madrid, as if I had parted with half of myself," he said[51]—and climbed into a diligence bound for southern Spain.

On the evening of March 9 he caught his first glimpse of Granada beneath the Sierra Nevadas, with their snowy peaks burning red in the setting sun. The sight took his breath away. "It is a most picturesque and beautiful city, situated in one of the loveliest landscapes that I have ever seen." In the fifteenth century, at the height of its power as the capital of the Moorish kingdom, Granada's population had been more than half a million. Four centuries later, as Irving entered the city, it was a shadow of its former glory and had only a little over 20,000 inhabitants. Yet even in its depleted state, it met Irving's expectations. "Granada, *bellissima* Granada!" he enthused.[52]

Sitting on a hill above the city was its famous Alhambra, an ornate complex of Moorish buildings that included a citadel, palace, administrative quarters, and residences. Irving immediately approached Don Francisco de la Serna, the governor of the Alhambra, as well as to the archbishop of Granada, to request complete access. Celebrity had its advantages; open access was granted willingly.

With the help of a seventeen-year-old guide named Mateo Ximinez, Irving excitedly explored the darkened corridors of the palace, listening to Mateo's seemingly endless stories about the Alhambra. "The Alhambra differs in many respects from the picture that had been formed by my imagination, yet it equals my expectations," said Irving. "It is impossible to contemplate this delicious abode and not feel an admiration of the genius and poetical spirit of those who first devised this early paradise."[53]

As Mateo chattered, Irving scrambled about the palace looking for the portal that King Boabdil had allegedly sealed when he left the place for the last time, and visited the small chapel where the vanquished king had finally surrendered. It was a grand, magical place, and Irving thought he might write a book about it, though he feared his pen couldn't do the palace justice. "How unworthy is my scribbling of the place," he sighed.[54]

He filled his notebooks with descriptions and observations. It was writing for the joy of it, similar to his Scottish journals from nearly a decade before. His intent was simply to capture the moment in words: "6½ [P.M.]—Garden of the Generalife Sun going down—over the tower of the Vela—between the tower & the Cypress trees—bells ringing—guns firing salvo echoes off Mountains—birds singing—people on distant hills dancing Suavity of air—birds singing—beauty of vega—driver from Alhambra— Cypress trees of the Generalife—Silver crescent of the moon."[55]

With some regret, Irving left Granada to continue his tour of

Andalusia before finally settling in Seville in mid-April. He moved into a boardinghouse run by a woman with the unfortunate name of Mrs. Stalker, where he unpacked his Granada manuscript—then did very little writing. There were theaters to visit, dances to attend, bullfights to watch, and Seville was enchanting, especially in the spring. "As you pass by the houses you look into beautiful courts, with marble pillars and arcades; fountains and jets of water, surrounded by orange and citron trees," he noted mistily, "and all lighted up by lamps and lanthorns . . . so that you see groups of people seated among the trees and hear the sound of guitars."[56]

Murray pressed him for corrections and additions for a second edition of *Columbus*—all reasonable requests, but it galled Irving that Murray wasn't communicating with him directly, choosing instead to make Obadiah Rich his intermediary. He hinted to Aspinwall that if Murray didn't treat him more respectfully, he would look for another British publisher. "Mr. Murray has behaved so strangely towards me in the course of the publication of *Columbus* that I am at a loss how to consider him either as friend or a man of business," Irving griped, "and shall have to make some inquiries and obtain some explanations before I enter upon further dealings with him."[57]

By early May Irving was constantly at work on Granada, as well as on the corrections to *Columbus*. For the latter, he needed access to the Archives of the Indies, with its enormous repository of books on North and South America, but he learned that only the express written permission of the king would open those doors to him. Undeterred, Irving asked Everett to secure such a letter for him.

The summer heat was oppressive, especially in his stuffy rooms in Mrs. Stalker's boardinghouse, so on July 1 Irving moved into a cooler summer cottage with John Nalder Hall, a consumptive young Englishman. The cottage, dubbed Casa Cera, was about half a league from Seville and an ideal place to work because of the quiet. "The mornings and evenings are cool for the prevalence of the sea breezes, and the nights are delicious," Irving wrote.[58]

Encouraging news arrived from Ebenezer that he and Brevoort had negotiated an agreement with American publishers Carey & Lea—now officially Carey, Lea & Carey—that would provide Irving with a regular income of $600 annually for the next seven years in exchange for exclusive American rights to his first four books. A grateful Irving passed most of these profits on to Ebenezer, who was still recovering from the Welles & Williams crash of 1825. With the exception of his continued holdings in the Bolivian mines, Washington's finances were, perhaps for the first time, relatively secure. He assured Peter that revenues from *Columbus* and his upcoming book on Granada would guarantee that "neither of us have any further perplexity or trouble on this head."[59]

Irving made a side trip to Palos to see where Columbus had departed for the New World, a nugget of information he incorporated into the revised edition. In mid-August Everett, ever the miracle worker, forwarded to Irving a letter from the king granting him permission to explore the Archives of the Indies for new materials on Columbus—a rare honor for any historian, especially one who wasn't Spanish. Irving was grateful to Everett, though disappointed to find little in the archives that he hadn't already seen among Navarette's papers.

On August 31 he mailed Aspinwall the first part of his Granada book, which he called *A Chronicle of the Conquest of Granada,* and asked the colonel to see if Murray would be willing to pay 2,000 guineas for the complete manuscript. If not, Aspinwall could sell it elsewhere. "I am so thoroughly dissatisfied with him [Murray] on account of the manner in which he has acted while publishing Columbus," Irving groused, "—never answering my letters nor giving me any information concerning the work, nor in short acting towards me either as a friend or a man of business."[60] As he had with Brevoort, Irving attributed silence to displeasure or disenchantment. In reality, it was neither. Murray was simply overworked—but Irving was more than ready to have his feelings hurt.

In early September Irving and the sickly Hall moved out of Casa Cera and into a country house in Cadiz with a fine view of the

water. "Here I live quite out of the world," Irving wrote, "my principal walk is on the terraced roof of the house, I rarely receive a visit,
or pay one, but amuse myself by reading and scribbling."[61] He continued polishing *Granada* and dabbled at pieces on Ponce de Leon
and Balboa. Hall's health continued to deteriorate—he would die
two months later—and Irving did his best to lift the young man's
spirits by chatting with him in the evenings, sometimes reading
aloud passages of *Granada*.

At the beginning of October Irving received—at last!—several
long-overdue letters from Murray. In flattering tones he knew would
resonate with Irving, the savvy Murray informed his author that
the first edition of *Columbus* had nearly sold out and that he would
go back to press with the second edition shortly. The ingratiation
had its desired effect. "I have felt hurt and offended at times by
your neglect of writing to me," Irving told Murray, "but you ultimately wrote in a manner to shew that whatever disadvantageous &
discouraging constructions I may have put upon your silence have
been incorrect." Murray's letter was "a very gratifying one," Irving thought. "The sale [of *Columbus*] continues excellent and
steady, and he appears to be very well satisfied." Murray was so satisfied, in fact, that he tried to lure Irving to London to edit a new
monthly magazine, dangling an annual salary of £1,000, plus 100
guineas for any articles he might want to write for the *Quarterly
Review*.[62]

Irving surely cocked an eyebrow at this offer. "The salary and
other offers for casual writing would ensure me at least seven thousand dollars a year," he told Ebenezer. But Irving refused. He wanted
to go home. "I cannot," he told Murray, "undertake any thing that
should oblige me to reside out of my native country; to which,
though I so long remain absent from it, I have a constant desire to
return." It was an odd excuse; while Irving had lived abroad for thirteen years, his residence had been, for the most part, by choice. Perhaps the thought of being obligated by a permanent job to remain
in Europe was too daunting. Regardless, it was as good an excuse as
any to keep out of the dreaded editor's chair.[63]

As for the offer to write for the *Review*, its snotty attitude toward all things American left him cold. *"Between ourselves,"* he whispered to Aspinwall, "were this offered for any other work it would be tempting in the extreme, but I cannot bring myself to write for a work that has been so hostile to my country."[64]

At about the same time as these discussions, Aspinwall delivered the complete *Granada* manuscript to Murray. Again, the publisher took his time to consider his options. He was more interested in publishing an inexpensive abridged, duodecimo edition of *Columbus*, which might prove even more profitable than the pricey four-volume, octavo-sized first edition. Irving admitted such an idea had merit, provided the abridgment were done carefully—but he wasn't about to do it himself. "If it could be done by any judicious hand, retaining all the important and popular points of the work, I should have no objection to look over and touch up the abridgment and sanction it with my name."[65]

In November Peter informed him that an unnamed publisher was planning to release an abridged edition of *Columbus* in the United States. Irving was incensed. "I cannot endure the idea that a paltry poacher should carry off the fruits of my labors," he fumed. On November 19 he began his own abridgment, and completed it in a remarkable nineteen days. "Hard work," he said to Peter, "but I think it will be all the better for being written off at a heat." To "drive the pirate ashore," speed was more important than profit. Irving allowed Murray to have the abridged manuscript for free, and asked Ebenezer to publish it in America immediately.[66]

Ebenezer and Brevoort did a masterful job of not only steering the project quickly through production, but also negotiating its sale. Washington had asked that Carey, Lea & Carey—who had exclusive American rights to his first four books—have the option to the abridgment. Ebenezer and Brevoort, however, believed this was unfair to the Carvills, who had published the first edition of *Columbus*. Making it clear to the Carvills that he was more than prepared to send both works to a rival publisher, Ebenezer asked for a hefty $6,000 for the second edition and abridgment—"a price,"

Brevoort admitted, "which we did not believe they would give." But the Carvills agreed, and a surprised Brevoort encouraged Irving to submit all future works on a nonexclusive basis, as "competition will always increase the price."[67] With his British and American contracts combined, Irving earned about $23,000 from both editions of *Columbus* and its abridgment—close to half a million dollars today—making it one of the most profitable books he ever wrote.

The money rolled in. In late December Aspinwall informed Irving that Murray had finally agreed to purchase *A Chronicle of the Conquest of Granada* for the 2,000 guineas—about $200,000 today—Irving had demanded. Irving did just as well with the American edition, which Carey, Lea & Carey acquired for $4,750—about $100,000 today—payable in regular installments over five years.

Money always brought out Irving's forgiving nature. "Murray has a gentlemanlike mode of publishing and of transacting his business that makes it highly satisfactory to bring out a work under his auspices," he gushed forgivingly to Aspinwall. "He has, also, very excellent points in his character . . . which atone for those faults in the conduct of his affairs which occasionally give annoyance."[68]

It had been a productive year for Irving, with *Columbus* published, *Granada* on its way, a second edition and abridged *Columbus* in the works, and enough notes on the Alhambra and other Spanish explorers for two more books. "I look forward without any very sanguine anticipations," Irving confessed in his journal on December 31, 1828, "but without the gloom that has sometimes oppressed me. The only future event from which I promise myself any extraordinary gratification is the return to my native country, which, I trust, will now soon take place."[69]

The year 1829 began with a pleasant surprise. For his work on *The Life and Voyages of Christopher Columbus*, Irving was unanimously elected as a member of Spain's Real Academia de la Historia. Membership in the academy was quite an honor—very few non-Spaniards had ever been elected—and Irving, who was usually embarrassed by such scholarly laurels, wrote a magnanimous letter of thanks, in Spanish, to Diego Clemencín, secretary of the academy. "I hope you will be good enough to make known to that illustrious body the great debt of gratitude that I feel toward it, and assure it that I shall at all times gladly dedicate my scant talent and learning to its prosperity and distinction."[70]

Despite his initial New Year's enthusiasm, Irving was tired and "out of order" for much of January. He dabbled at a new story, "The Legend of the Enchanted Soldier," but pronounced the effort "lame." "I have done little or nothing," he sulked to Peter in February. He had so overworked himself preparing the abridgment of *Columbus*, he said, that his "cutaneous complaint" had flared again. Any writing could only be done with "great difficulty."[71]

News of Andrew Jackson's victory over John Quincy Adams in the 1828 presidential election reached Spain in early 1829. Irving was pleased Jackson had secured a solid majority, but he diplomatically informed the Adams-appointed Everett that he admired Adams, too. "I am loth to see a man superseded who has filled his station worthily," he told Everett, though he defended Jackson as likely to be a "sagacious, independent, and high-spirited" president. "I believe that a person like yourself, who has filled his office faithfully, ably, and respectably, will never be molested," he reassured Everett.[72] He was wrong.

Talking American politics only made Irving more homesick, as did attending a dinner in honor of George Washington's birthday with the British and American delegations. "I have a craving desire to return to America," he told Peter. "It incessantly haunts my mind and occupies all my dreams."[73] Such thoughts were making it difficult to keep writing. He believed he had completed his first draft of his book on Spanish explorers, *Voyages and Discoveries of the Companions of Columbus*, but he still wanted a peek at Navarette's upcoming *Coleccion* installment. Navarette made it clear to Irving that the book had been commissioned by the king himself, so releasing it to anyone but the king first would be an act of disloyalty—a point Irving grudgingly conceded.

Irving was less gracious, however, when it came to Murray,

who had expressed concerns about the profitability of *Granada*. Murray's "croaking," Irving told Aspinwall, "knocked my pen out of my hands for a day, but I resumed it and pursued my plans." He had had it with Murray's lack of faith.[74]

On April 20 Carey, Lea & Carey published *A Chronicle of the Conquest of Granada* in New York. This time, the American edition preceded the appearance of its British counterpart by about a month. Murray had secured the copyright on March 5, but held back publication until the British Parliament completed its debate on "the Catholic question," an act to overturn laws discriminating against Roman Catholics. Until the debates concluded, the public could "read, talk, and think of nothing else."[75] Murray's instincts were unerring when it came to gauging the timing of publication; however, he had made another critical decision regarding *Granada* that backfired badly.

Unlike *Columbus*, Irving never intended for *Granada* to be a straightforward history. "It is founded on facts diligently gathered . . . out of the old Spanish Chronicles, which I have endeavored to work up into an entertaining and popular form, without sacrificing the intrinsic truth of history," Irving had explained during the work's early stages.[76] If *Columbus* was historical romance, Irving said, then *Granada* was romantic history—as such, he didn't want readers to believe he was trying to pass it off as entirely factual. Therefore, Irving argued, he wished to publish under a pseudonym, and asked that the work be credited to "Fray Antonio Agapida." Murray hadn't agreed with that argument, or to the pseudonym. In his view, the best way to guarantee book sales and to recover the significant amount of money he had invested in *Granada* was to put Washington Irving's name on the title page. And so he had.

Irving was furious. Murray's change was "an unwarrantable liberty," he fumed, "and makes me gravely, in my own name, tell many round untruths. . . . Literary mystifications are excusable when given anonymously or under feigned names, but are impudent deceptions when sanctioned by an author's real name."[77] He angrily lectured his publisher:

By inserting my name in the title page as the avowed author, you make me personally responsible for the verity of the fact and the soundness of the opinions of what was intended to be given as a romantic chronicle. I presume you have done this to avail yourself of whatever attraction my name might have in drawing immediate attention to the work, but this might have been effected in some other way, without meddling with the work itself, which ought never to be touched without the knowledge and consent of the author—I am sorry to make these complaints, but these matters displease and annoy me.

That out of the way, he reproached Murray for his lack of faith in the profitability of his writings, using angry words that Murray, quite literally, threw back in his face years later:

I have been annoyed too by your forebodings of ill success to this work . . . remember too that you lost heart about the Success of Columbus . . . and yet you see it continues to do well—I trust that you will be equally disappointed in your prognostications about the success of the Conquest of Granada, and that it will not eventually prove disadvantageous either to your purse or my reputation. At any rate, I should like hereafter to make our arrangement in such manner that you may be relieved from these apprehensions of loss and from the necessity of recurring to any management of the press to aid the publication of a work of mine.[78]

Irving's huff met with stony silence.

While Irving hoped the book would resonate not only with "mere readers for amusement," but "among the literary," he had probably done his job too well. The literati embraced it—the poet William Cullen Bryant hailed it as "one of the most delightful of his works"—but casual readers were uncertain what to make of it. For all his fussing about the pseudonym, Irving had confused his audience, who were unsure where the history ended and the romance began. The *Edinburgh Literary Journal* summed up the confusion best: "We were unable to make out whether we were to expect a piece of fiction, a history, or a mixture of both."[79]

On May 1 Irving left for Granada. "I mean to indulge myself with a luxurious life among the groves and fountains of the Alhambra," he told Peter. It would also be an opportunity to see the palace and the gardens in their summer colors, "in the most splendid season," Irving sighed, "with moonlight nights."[80] On his arrival, Irving's old acquaintance, Alhambra governor Don Francisco de la Serna, offered Irving his own apartments in the Alhambra during his stay in the city. Irving didn't need to be asked twice. He moved into the governor's elegant but sparsely furnished rooms, with unlimited access to the palace and grounds. The governor also promised Irving full access to the scattered remains of the Moorish archives he had collected, a prize Irving thought he might use for *Companions of Columbus*.

In the quiet of the governor's rooms, Irving tinkered with the manuscripts he had on hand, "so as to present some other work to the public before long," he told Brevoort. The unfinished *Companions of Columbus* was in his trunks, as was the groundwork for a biography of Muhammad. Yet those seemed like too much work. The longer Irving stayed in the palace, the more he was convinced his experiences there would make an entertaining book. "Nothing could be more favorable for study and literary occupation than my present abode," he told Peter. "I am determined to linger here until I get some writings under way connected with the place."[81]

To Irving's delight, Mateo Ximinez, his "poor devil historian of the ruins," continued to regale him with more tales. Irving filled his journals with detailed notes. "I take my breakfast in the Saloon of the Ambassadors in the Court of the lions," he told one correspondent, "and in the evening when I throw by my pen I wander about the old palace until quite late, with nothing but bats and owls to keep me company."[82]

In early June Irving abandoned the governor's chambers for the more remote and more beautiful apartments that King Philip V had built for his wife, Elizabeth of Farnese. He ventured to the city only to visit the duke of Gor, "an acquaintance exactly to my taste," Irving said, who shared his enthusiasm for Spanish history. The duke left his sprawling palace home at Irving's disposal, and granted him permission to visit the exclusive Jesuit library at the university, where Irving sometimes spent all day among old books and manuscripts.[83]

For the first time in ages, Irving was content. He was delighted with his surroundings—"It almost seems to me a dream, that I should be lording it in the deserted palace of the unfortunate Boabdil el chico," he said—but he was certain he was only several months from at last returning home. "My dear Brevoort," he wrote in late May, "the happiest day of my life will be when I once more find myself among you all. . . . My dearest affections are entirely centered in my country."[84]

If he was brooding at all, it was about the fate of *Granada.* While the book had been published on May 23, Irving had not heard of its status by late June, and believed Murray was still delaying its publication. "He has been playing fast and loose in such a manner with this work," he griped to Aspinwall.[85]

Another source of annoyance were the stubbornly unproductive Bolivian mines, which had at last frustrated him to his breaking point. "I wish them to be forfeited," he told Aspinwall.[86] Dumping his shares cost him most of the profits from the first British edition of *Columbus*, but he was finally free of the financial albatross that had siphoned away his money since 1825.

But those concerns were a continent away. As the Granada evenings turned warmer with the advancing summer, Irving grew more content with his solitude. The gardens brimmed with strawberries and apricots, and the sun made the courtyard pools so hot during the day that he could take warm baths in them by the evening. "One really lives here in a species of enchantment," he told Peter with satisfaction.

The enchantment came to an end in July. Just as his Spanish adventure had begun with an appeal from one American embassy, so it would end with a call from another, as the newly elected Jackson administration reorganized its diplomatic corps. In Madrid

Everett was replaced by former Vermont governor Cornelius Van Ness. Meanwhile, Senator Louis McLane of Delaware was hustling to London, to take the post of American minister to the Court of St. James's.

The British post was a critical one; McLane was coming to London to assure the English that Andrew Jackson was no John Quincy Adams, and that the issues that had bogged down the prior administration—like trade with the British West Indies—would be open for negotiation with the new government. McLane needed a good secretary, one who could not only write well but was familiar with London, could socialize easily, and could maneuver effectively among British government officials and nobility. Secretary of State Martin Van Buren believed he had an ideal candidate.

"Your brother the Judge [John Treat] received a very polite letter from Mr. Secretary Van Buren," Brevoort informed Irving on July 18, "in which he states it to be the intention of the government to offer you the appointment of Secretary of Legation in London, and is desirous of ascertaining whether you would accept the office."[87] Brevoort, John Treat, and Ebenezer had already discussed the offer, and their advice was unanimous: "We hope you will agree with us that it is not a thing to be rejected, especially as it is offered without any solicitations on your part. . . . It is certainly an honorable mark of confidence in you by the government, and they can have no possible design beyond that of manifesting to the world the high regard entertained by your Country for your character."[88]

Paulding, still serving as a naval agent in New York, had also pushed for Irving's appointment, and when Van Buren checked with John Treat to see if Washington was really interested in the post, John Treat said yes. When President Jackson at last extended the offer, Irving could hardly refuse. The decision had already been made for him.

"I have a thorough indifference to all official honors," Washington told Peter, who probably knew better, "yet having no reasons of stronger support for declining, I am disposed to accord with what appears to be the wishes of my friends." Washington saw the offer "as emanating from my country, and a proof of the good will of my countrymen," he told Ebenezer, "and in this light it is most glittering and gratifying to me." He accepted the position, on one condition. "Should I find the office of Secretary of Legation irksome in any respect, or detrimental to my literary plans, I will immediately throw it up, being fortunately independent of it, both as to circumstances and as to ambition." Clearly, he hoped it would not be a full-time job.[89]

Four days after receiving notice of his nomination, Irving notified Minister McLane of his acceptance, and promised to meet the new ambassador in London as quickly as he could. "It gives me great satisfaction, sir," he wrote tactfully, "to be associated in office with one of whom public report and the private communications of my friends speak in the highest terms of eulogy."[90]

Washington Irving was officially an employee of the United States Department of State. His friends and family were pleased. For the most part, Irving was too—but away from the eyes of his immediate circle, he qualified his enthusiasm for the new position. "I only regret," he wrote, "that I had not been left entirely alone, and to dream away life in my own way."[91]

11

Politician

1829–1832

What a Stirring moment it is to live in. . . . It seems to me as if life were breaking out anew with me, or that I were entering upon quite a new and almost unknown career of existence.

—Washington Irving to Henry Brevoort, March 1, 1831

IRVING'S FAMILY AND FRIENDS were thrilled with his decision to accept the post to the Court of St. James's. "Everybody here thinks you ought to have been the Minister," Brevoort told Irving half-jokingly, but Irving was quick to dismiss such suggestions. "Whatever ambition I possess is entirely literary," he assured his supporters. "If the world thinks I ought to be a minister, so much the better; the world honors me, but I do not degrade myself. . . . It is better that half a dozen should say why is he seated so low down, than any one should casually say what right has he to be at the top."[1]

By late September 1829, Irving was in London. He and his new boss, Minister Louis McLane, set to work putting their new offices in order, sorting through the papers of the prior administration, and reviewing their diplomatic instructions from President Jackson. The new foreign policy of the American government—at least as it related to England—was as straightforward as President Andrew Jackson himself: "To ask nothing that is not clearly right," Jackson told Congress, "and to submit to nothing that is wrong."[2]

While Jackson's predecessor, John Quincy Adams, believed foreign policy wasn't quite that simple, Jackson maintained that Adams had bungled his relations with the British by making things far too political and complicated. That was especially true, he thought, of the negotiations regarding trade with the British West Indies, which had been closed to the United States since as far back as the Revolutionary War. In retaliation, the United States had imposed trade restrictions on British ships and ports, and for decades the two countries had engaged in dueling duties, fees, and regulations.

In fairness, Adams *had* come close to resolving the issue, playing competing trade interests in Britain and Canada against each other, but without success. Then, in July 1825 Parliament approved legislation lifting many of its restrictions on American ships involved in West Indies trade, on the condition that the Americans remove *their* restrictions on British ships. Congress scuffled over the issue, wary of handing Adams a victory in the matter—there were still sore feelings over the alleged "corrupt bargain" that had elevated Adams to the presidency without a clear majority of electoral votes—and refused the offer. Since then, the West Indies had remained off limits to American ships.

The dispute was a perpetual sore spot with the growing and increasingly powerful merchant class. President Jackson confidently assured Americans that the problem was nothing a little straight talk couldn't solve, but first he had to smooth ruffled English feathers. Hence, his directions to McLane—which had come largely from Secretary of State Martin Van Buren—were to first ingratiate himself with the English, and then get them back to the negotiating table.[3]

Jackson and Van Buren had an ideal team in Washington Irving and Louis McLane. Only three years younger than Irving, the Delaware-born McLane was, like Irving, an attorney and veteran of the War of 1812. He had served in the U.S. Congress continuously since 1817, sitting first as Delaware's lone congressman, then as a senator from March 1827 until his appointment as minister.

McLane's peers found him "correct, conciliating, and spirited," "someone who would give no insult, and he would receive none"— very much in line with Jackson's approach to governing. Irving was impressed. "I am perfectly delighted with him," he told Brevoort, "and doubt not that we shall live most happily together."[4]

Not quite together. Irving and McLane took up facing houses on Chandos Street in Cavendish Square. While McLane set up quarters at No. 9, Irving remained easily available to the minister across the street at No. 3, where he retreated to work or write. Unfortunately, there was very little time for writing.

McLane had deftly assigned most of the busywork that normally fell to the secretary of the legation—the "scribe work," Irving called it[5]—to a younger gentleman, and utilized the sociable Irving as an aide-de-camp. As they circulated in court, McLane and Irving began gently opening up diplomatic channels, casually informing Foreign Secretary Lord Aberdeen of their government's willingness to negotiate on the West Indies issue.

Most of the time, however, Irving's duties involved day-to-day maintenance of the legation, providing sailors with temporary pocket money until their funds arrived, processing passports, and sorting through the various parcels of letters and gifts the embassy received regularly—all for a paltry $2,000 annual salary. This was clearly not the part-time job he had anticipated when he left Spain, but he promised friends he would remain at his post for at least a year.

Now that Irving was in London, Murray could no longer ignore him or refuse to answer his letters. Here Irving could conduct any business with the publisher personally, rather than through Aspinwall. Despite their recent tiff over Granada, Murray—who knew a thing or two about diplomacy—graciously invited Irving to dinner, along with Newton, Leslie, Moore, Rogers, and Lockhart. On October 5, 1829, Irving presented himself on the doorstep of 50 Albemarle Street and was greeted by Murray like an old friend.

The dinner party that evening was quieter than other parties Irving had attended in Murray's drawing room, but that was understandable; they were all older now. Murray was fifty-one years old, with a son, John Murray III, old enough to join the family business. But it was the forty-six-year-old Irving who had changed the most since their first meeting in 1817. He was now one of Murray's senior statesmen, and he looked it.

He was heavier—he had been struggling with his weight since Madrid—and his new frock coat compensated for his broadening girth. His hair was streaked with gray and strategically brushed to cover a thin spot on the top of his head. His eyes, while still as piercing as ever, now peered at Murray from under slightly droopy eyelids that had a tendency to close slowly when dinner conversation hit a lull—a habit that caused Moore and Murray much hilarity. Irving's portrait hung alongside those of Thomas Moore and Walter Scott in Murray's drawing room.[6] Despite their differences, they had accomplished much together.

If Murray was known across the continent as the "Emperor of the West [End],"[7] then Irving was his Pope of Prose. Irving's influence was perceived to be so strong and far-reaching that he was plagued by constant appeals from aspiring and established writers for his assistance. Mary Shelley's seventy-one-year-old father, William Godwin, approached him for help in getting his novel *Cloudesley* published in the United States, while Thomas Moore sought his guidance in finding an American publisher for his *Life of Byron*, which Murray was scheduled to release in January 1830.

The irony was that Irving couldn't persuade his own publisher to issue a third edition of *Columbus*. "I am continually applied to by writers to help their works into the press," Irving told Brevoort. "There is no person less able to do so than I. My only acquaintance among the publishers is Murray; who is the most difficult being on earth to please—."[8]

Nevertheless, Irving sent Godwin's and Moore's manuscripts to Ebenezer for his brother to peddle in New York. While he found no takers for Godwin's project—American publishers fretted that the market was "crowded to suffocation" with novels—he had better luck with Moore's book on Byron. "Not merely one of the most fascinating pieces of biography extant," Irving gushed, "but one of the most splendid documents on the History of the human mind and the human heart." Capitalizing on the lesson he and Brevoort had learned from the sale of *Columbus*, Ebenezer managed to engage two publishers in a bidding war, finally accepting an offer of $1,500 from Harper's.[9]

In late 1829 Irving had an astonishing $37,400—almost $800,000 today—stashed away in New York banks, where Ebenezer and John Treat kept a watchful eye on his accounts, and doled out money in small amounts. John Treat was firm as he reminded Washington why such strict oversight was necessary: "Your investment in Bolivar mines and in steamboats in France, had given me uneasiness on your account, and I was satisfied that if the funds which had been accumulated for you in this country were suffered to remain here that they would be in the hands of those who would keep them secured for you, and enable you to reap a permanent benefit from them." When it appeared Washington was too careless with his money—such as when he asked his brothers for $2,000 to spend on wedding gifts—Ebenezer was quick to wag a disapproving finger. "You should first determine what is necessary for the support of yourself and Peter," he told Washington, "and put that money securely by, before you undertake to give way to your generous feelings." Washington wilted under such fraternal pressure, asking that his brothers set aside a certain amount of his profits to invest in stocks to provide a regular income for Peter. For the first time, Irving's money was as secure as his literary reputation.[10]

Irving's literary reputation was valuable to McLane, and he kept the writer at his side as they plunged deeper into diplomatic waters. It was a shrewd decision; ministers, government officials, and nobility all opened their doors to McLane and his American celebrity sidekick. "I have received repeated expressions of kindness and good will from various officers of the government," said a pleasantly surprised Irving, "who have taken occasion to express their satisfaction at my having been appointed to the legation."[11]

The two had their work cut out for them. The English government was still smarting over its treatment at the hands of John Quincy Adams, and there were hard feelings to overcome. "It was necessary first to remove certain jealousies and prejudices," Irving reported, "to inspire a confidence in the character and intentions of our present administration and in the frank and conciliatory nature of our present mission." It was delicate work, but Irving felt their perseverance would result in a breakthrough. "Ministers have been induced to enter freshly and fully into discussions of topics which for some time past they had treated as no longer matters of negotiation," he noted.[12]

Actually, the British had returned to the negotiating table largely in response to a proposal McLane and Irving had crafted together; namely, that the American government use the Parliamentary Act of 1825—which called for a mutual easing of restrictions on trade—as its starting point for discussions. Jackson concurred, and McLane and Irving conceded to their English counterparts that the United States had made a mistake in not accepting Parliament's 1825 offer. They were willing to do so now. As an act of good faith, McLane told the British he would ask Congress for legislation removing American restrictions on British ships coming from the West Indies. "This proposition," Irving reported, "so worthy of the administration of a Great people, evidently surprized the cabinet; and forced from them an acknowledgement of its frankness and magnanimity."[13]

Irving believed that the British government would accept the offer he and McLane had laid on the table, but it took some time. On the American side, Jackson, Vice President John Calhoun, and Van Buren needed to persuade Congress to introduce the legislation McLane had promised. As for the British, "they avow that there are circumstances, which they cannot explain, operating to render it inexpedient at this moment to comply with our propositions," Irving reported, "though they acknowledge that they must ultimately do so, and that the difficulties and embarrassments of an arrangement are every day encreasing."[14]

The British foot-dragging was due to two factors. First, British traders in Canada—who could trade with the West Indies, and easily move goods across the U.S.-Canada border—pressured their government to maintain the status quo. Second, negotiations had stalled with the encroaching winter; more and more members of Parliament, the court, and the ministry had retreated to their estates in the country. While Geoffrey Crayon, Gentleman, had sighed admiringly over such a quaint British custom, Washington Irving, Diplomat, was irritated: "The very season of the year has been unpropitious to the prompt dispatch of diplomatic business, for it is the great season of field sports, when every English gentleman who has an estate in the country or has access to that of a friend, makes a point of absenting himself as much as possible from town. . . . The frequent absences of Cabinet Ministers on excursions of the kind have repeatedly delayed interviews and interrupted & protracted the whole course of negotiation."[15]

Irving and McLane would have to wait for spring. That was fine with Irving; at last, he had some time for himself, and sprinted to Birmingham to visit the Van Warts for a few days. Returning to London in early December, he socialized with Newton and Leslie, as well as with another young artist, a protégé of Allston's, who had presented Irving with a letter of introduction from Brevoort. "I beg to make you acquainted with the bearer, Mr. S[amuel] F. B. Morse," it read. "A gentleman for whom I entertain very cordial feelings of regards,—He is, as you probably know, one of our best painters."[16] Or, at least he was at the moment; Morse's first working prototype of the telegraph was still several years away.

There was also, at last, time to write. Rather than return to the manuscripts he had stashed away in his trunks, Irving mulled over several new ideas. Briefly, he considered writing a history of the United States, but shelved that in favor of another project he thought would be more popular—and more profitable. "I mean a Life of [George] Washington," he told Peter. "I shall take my own time to execute it, and will spare no pains. It must be my great and crowning labor."[17] Gone were the misgivings he had expressed to

Constable in 1825 when the publisher had suggested he tackle a life of the first president. With *Columbus*, he had proven to himself that he could research and write a major, important biography.

Starting such a project, however, was a challenge—and Irving was loath for literature to be such hard work. "My idea is not to *drudge* at literary labor, but to use it as an agreeable employment," he told Peter. "We have now sufficient funds to ensure us a decent support, should we choose to retire upon them. We may therefore indulge in the passing pleasure of life, and mingle amusement with our labors."[18] It was the old pattern: when Irving had money, his motivation to write disappeared.

There was the day-to-day maintenance of the legation to oversee, as well as countless social obligations. Thomas Moore had moved back to the city, and was always ready to lead Irving by the arm from one drawing room to another. Irving dined with Samuel Rogers, the two chatting easily as literary equals, then swept into Obadiah Rich's antiquarian bookstore in Red Lion Square to look for yet another obscure volume of Spanish literature. In the midst of it all, he changed residences, moving to 8 Argyll Street, which was halfway between McLane and Murray. Irving's social calendar was as frantic as it had ever been. "I am so hurried by fifty thousand petty concerns which overwhelm a man in this great wilderness," he said.[19]

A request from the Royal Literary Fund to sit as a member of its board was politely rejected, but Irving was less successful in refusing laurels from two other admiring organizations. On April 3, 1830, his forty-seventh birthday, he learned that the Royal Society of Literature, citing his work on *Columbus* and *Granada*, had chosen to award him one of its Gold Medals for "Literary works of eminent merit, or of important Literary Discoveries." Two months later he received notice of another honor, this time from the Reverend Arthur Matthews at Oxford University, who informed him that the university would be conferring on him an honorary Doctor of Civil Law, and wouldn't take no for an answer. "Overruling the ultra-modesty of your scruples," Matthews wrote, "I have not hesitated to *commit* you with the academical authorities of Oxford." The ceremony was postponed until the following year—at which point Irving told Peter he hoped the university would forget about it— but in 1831 he received an honorary Doctor of Civil Law from Oxford, to the delight of its graduating students, who hooted "Diedrich Knickerbocker!" and "Geoffrey Crayon!" as the degree was conferred. Irving was touched by the spectacle, but could only shake his head at the irony of having such a distinguished legal degree conferred on one of New York's most uninterested attorneys. Later in life, he asked that the degree be removed from his official biography, saying it was "a learned dignity urged upon me very much 'against the stomach of my sense,' and to which I have never laid claim."[20]

In May 1830 a lengthy anonymous review of *Granada* appeared in the *Quarterly Review,* which forcefully defended the use of Irving's Fray Antonio Agapida pseudonym as a literary device that successfully allowed him to color real-life events with a tinge of romance.[21] The review had been written by Irving at Murray's request, an olive branch the publisher extended as a mea culpa for altering the title page of *Granada.* It was a cathartic bit of writing, but it was not the last Irving would hear of *Granada* and the Agapida affair.

Spring saw the ministry back at work. McLane's proposition was still pending, and President Jackson aggressively pressed Congress to pass the necessary legislation. On May 29 Congress did just that, approving a bill to remove restrictions on British ships, provided the British did the same for American ships. With the strength of the congressional action behind them, McLane and Irving believed they might finally seal the deal.

It was far from done. In April, as Jackson asked Van Buren to prepare a tough response in the event the English didn't accept the American offer, McLane and Irving pulled aside Lord Aberdeen, the British foreign secretary, and argued that the pending deal represented more than just agreement on the West Indies issue. Opening up fair trade between their two governments, they explained, would mark a new beginning in U.S.–U.K. relations, which had been rocky since America's independence. Aberdeen needed time to work it out with his government. He promised McLane that he would do his best.

It was exhausting work. For the last several months, Irving—who realized his own hopes of returning home had been stymied by his stint with the legation—had been trying to convince other friends to join him in London. His persuasive efforts were focused largely on Gouverneur Kemble, who, like Irving, was still a bachelor, with "neither wife nor child to anchor you to home." At last there was a letter from his friend in New York informing him that he would be moving to Europe for "two[,] three or four years, unless I find things there very different from what I am prepared to expect." With great anticipation, Irving read on: "I am tired with the sameness of this nutshell circle of existence, & unless I break from it now, I shall be doomed to walk in it to the end of my days. I cannot tell how long after our arrival, it may be in my power to have the gratification of taking you and your brother by the hand." The name signed at the bottom of this agreeable and most unexpected letter was not Gouverneur Kemble. It was Henry Brevoort![22]

"I look forward with the greatest delight to the prospect of our once more meeting," Irving wrote Brevoort excitedly. He was too busy with diplomatic work to greet Brevoort and his family when they landed at Le Havre on June 8, he explained, but would make every effort to connect with him as quickly as possible. To the frustration of both Irving and Brevoort, it was some time before they saw each other in Paris.

At the end of May an interesting invitation arrived from Mary Shelley for Irving to spend an evening with her and her father. Thomas Moore had tried without success to bring the two together for months, "but he [Irving] always put it off," Moore told Mrs. Shelley, "with some excuse or other."[23] This time Irving accepted.

What the two discussed that evening remains a mystery. Perhaps Irving finally told Mrs. Shelley he was not romantically disposed toward her. Or perhaps she, seeing him grown somewhat stout and balding, decided she was no longer interested in him. Or maybe they simply had a nice dinner. Whatever the topic of discussion, it was the last time they saw each other.

McLane and Irving had yet to hear from Aberdeen, but things suddenly tilted their way on June 26, when King George IV—who was not predisposed to resolve the West Indies issue—died at age sixty-seven. William Henry, the Duke of Clarence and third son of George II, ascended to the throne as King William IV. Unlike the extravagant, unpredictable George, William was levelheaded and unassuming, known—at least at the beginning of his reign—for easily moving among the people. Irving liked him immediately. "He is determined that it shall be merry old England once more," Irving said, and he and McLane were quick to ingratiate themselves with the new monarch, chumming up to the king so amiably at a royal dinner "that some of the *corps diplomatique* showed symptoms of jealousy." A deal, however, was still up in the air.[24]

Irving had other negotiations to worry about. He wrote to Murray in early July to ask him to make a formal offer for the unfinished *Companions of Columbus*. "I could furnish copy to the printers immediately," he lied, "but every day that I withhold it makes the work better."[25] Murray's answer apparently left much to be desired. "The terms you mention," Irving sniped at his publisher, "are much below what I had expected." However, he continued, "should you be disposed to give five hundred guineas for my volume of voyages, we may settle the matter at once."[26] Murray accepted Irving's counteroffer the same afternoon.

Satisfied, Irving left for a three-week stay in Paris, where he was reunited with Henry Brevoort. It is impossible to know their feelings upon seeing each other for the first time in fifteen years; each left the details of their reunion unrecorded in letters or journals, or any such recollections are missing. The thirty-something young men of 1815 were now both in their late forties, and Brevoort bragged rakishly that he had aged better than Irving—"I do believe I might pass myself off *abroad*, for a fresh bachelor of 35."[27]

Irving was back in London at the end of August, completing

Companions for Murray, and huddling with McLane on Chandos Street. Negotiations were moving rapidly. There was a last-minute tussle over details, but McLane recognized that limited trade was better than no trade at all.[28] They reached a deal.

"I have the satisfaction to inform you that I have succeeded in my negotiations for the colonial trade!" McLane wrote to Senator Levi Woodbury. "This government consents to restore to us the direct trade with her colonies upon the terms of my proposition."[29] McLane was a skilled negotiator, but he enjoyed a number of lucky breaks. The new king, William IV, was more willing to negotiate an agreement. McLane also had a more receptive foreign secretary in Lord Aberdeen, as opposed to George Canning, who had given President Adams such headaches. But McLane and Irving could rightly be proud of their roles in negotiating a critical issue that had impeded relations between the two countries for six decades.

His primary mission accomplished, McLane vacationed in Paris, leaving Irving as chargé d'affairs for the next two months. Upon the minister's return in October, Irving dashed to Birmingham for ten days to work in earnest on his book on the Alhambra. For most of the autumn, he made massive revisions to *Companions of Columbus* even as the typeset pages rolled off Murray's presses. Murray seemed pleased with what he had seen so far; his good mood was probably due in part to the success of the abridged edition of *Life and Voyages of Christopher Columbus*, which was selling briskly.

Voyages and Discoveries of the Companions of Columbus was published on December 30, 1830. Irving accepted his 500 guineas, and happily handed it over to Peter. Ebenezer had negotiated a generous agreement for the American edition with Carey, Lea & Carey, securing $1,500 for a print run of 3,000 copies to be sold within three years. *Companions* sold respectably in both England and the United States, though nowhere near the stellar numbers of the *Columbus* abridgment, which had sold well over 10,000 copies in the United States. Like *Granada*, *Companions* fared better with critics than readers. British reviewers appreciated the work and research that had gone into the volume, and as always, Irving's way with narrative impressed the most. American reviewers were equally as flattering, and believed Irving had cemented his literary reputation. According to the *American Quarterly*, Irving could "take his stand among those writers who have done more than amuse the fancy, or even gratify the heart. He is to be classed with historians of great events."[30]

With *Companions* in print, Irving retired briefly to Birmingham to relax and sort through his other manuscripts. To his annoyance, he was in no mood to write. "I have been visited by one of the most inveterate fits of mental inertness that I have ever experienced," he told Peter. He returned instead to his official duties in London, which were becoming increasingly hectic as well as banal. "As long as I remain in London I shall be worth nothing either to my friends or to myself," he told Brevoort peevishly, "& this I foresaw & foretold when I was advised to come here."[31]

That same spring, a firestorm of petty politics and personalities brought about major changes in Andrew Jackson's Cabinet. When the dust settled, McLane was recalled to the United States to assume the post of secretary of the treasury, and Martin Van Buren was on his way to London, where he awaited confirmation as the new American minister to the Court of St. James's. Until Van Buren arrived, however, Irving was the de facto American minister, "though it is expressly stated that I remain on *secretary's pay*," he complained to Peter.[32]

Irving grumbled about the salary, but he took the job seriously. To his surprise, he was good at it. A keen observer and people-watcher, Irving had better political instincts than he gave himself credit for. He wrote new secretary of state Edward Livingston chatty yet informative dispatches, and expertly managed the more mundane, day-to-day services of the embassy.

Monitoring his friend from Paris, Brevoort couldn't resist indulging in some good-natured ribbing. "So you are now left sole guardian of our nation's honor and welfare *near* his gracious Majesty's Court of St. James!" Still, he was sympathetic; he knew

Washington Irving
by John Vanderlyn, 1805
During his first visit to Europe in
1805, the twenty-two-year-old Irving
paid Vanderlyn for this pencil
drawing, the first known likeness of
the aspiring writer. The hairstyle,
it was later admitted, was
"a peculiarity."
Courtesy Historic Hudson Valley,
Tarrytown, N.Y.

Washington Irving
by Gilbert Stuart Newton,
1830
At age forty-seven, Irving
had written four international
best sellers, including a
comprehensive biography of
Christopher Columbus, and
was serving with Minister
Louis McLane in the
American legation in
London. Irving thought this
portrait was "the most
accurate likeness that has
ever been taken of me."
Courtesy Historic Hudson Valley,
Tarrytown, N.Y.

Top: *Washington Irving by Felix O. C. Darley, 1848*
Darley captured a candid Irving, just returned from Madrid after his tenure as minister
to Spain, lounging on the lawns of Sunnyside. That same summer, Irving was made an
executor of the will of John Jacob Astor. Courtesy Historic Hudson Valley, Tarrytown, N.Y.

Above Left: *Washington Irving by Charles Martin, 1851*
Pronounced the "patriarch of American letters" by *Harper's New Monthly*, the sixty-
eight-year-old Irving was sketched by Martin at Sunnyside in December 1851.
While Irving claimed "great repugnance to having a daguerreotype taken," he
declared this idealized portrait "excellent." Courtesy Library of Congress.

Above Right: *Washington Irving by Mathew Brady, 1850s*
Retired from public life, Irving still actively maintained reams of correspondence and
was well into his seventies when he completed his five-volume *Life of George Washington*.
Courtesy Library of Congress.

Washington Allston
The gifted and charismatic artist nearly convinced the young Irving to become a painter in Rome. "There was something, to me, inexpressibly engaging in the appearance and manner of Allston," Irving remembered. "I do not think I have ever been more completely captivated on a first acquaintance."
Courtesy Library of Congress.

Matilda Hoffman
A miniature portrait of Irving's doomed, consumptive seventeen-year-old fiancée. Irving's finest burlesque, *A History of New York*, was written in the months following her death in 1809.
Courtesy Historic Hudson Valley, Tarrytown, N.Y.

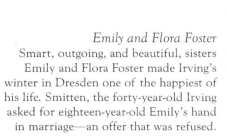

Emily and Flora Foster
Smart, outgoing, and beautiful, sisters Emily and Flora Foster made Irving's winter in Dresden one of the happiest of his life. Smitten, the forty-year-old Irving asked for eighteen-year-old Emily's hand in marriage—an offer that was refused.

Charles Leslie, self-portrait
Leslie was in the tight circle of artistic
young men surrounding Irving as he
completed *The Sketch Book* in London in
1819. The painter regularly encouraged
Irving as he dallied over incomplete
manuscripts like *Bracebridge Hall*.
Courtesy Historic Hudson Valley,
Tarrytown, N.Y.

James Kirke Paulding
Paulding served as Irving's primary collaborator
on *Salmagundi* and, with Henry Brevoort,
helped craft the newspaper hoax that launched
A History of New York. Courtesy U.S. Navy Art
Collection.

Gouverneur Kemble
A lifelong friend and fellow bachelor,
Kemble was a founding member of the
fun-loving "Lads of Kilkenny." His
family mansion, which Irving dubbed
"Cockloft Hall," served as
headquarters for the group.

Walter Scott
Irving's idol and literary father, Sir Walter Scott was an early admirer of *A History of New York* and pronounced *The Sketch Book* "positively beautiful." Scott actively promoted *The Sketch Book* and referred Irving to his own publisher, John Murray II. Courtesy Library of Congress.

John Murray II
Irving's patient and long-suffering English publisher, presided over an enviable stable of talent that included Walter Scott, Lord Byron, and Jane Austen. He and Irving feuded regularly over terms and profits, but maintained a grudging mutual admiration for thirty years. Courtesy National Portrait Gallery, London.

Martin Van Buren
Fellow New Yorker Martin Van Buren met Irving in the American legation in London in the fall of 1831. Learning that Van Buren's nomination as minister had been rejected by the U.S. Senate, Irving predicted the move would propel Van Buren to the presidency. Despite evolving political views and a brief falling-out, the two remained friends.
Courtesy Library of Congress.

Louis McLane
The American minister was Irving's boss in the legation at the Court of St. James, and deftly leveraged Irving's charm and literary reputation to broker an agreement on the West Indies trade dispute. A decade later, the two negotiated the boundary of the Oregon Territory on behalf of the American government.
Courtesy U.S. Department of the Treasury.

Ebenezer Irving
Older brother Ebenezer was a steadying influence on Washington, negotiated his literary contracts, and helped secure his American copyrights. Ebenezer's daughters served as Sunnyside's official hostesses.
Courtesy Historic Hudson Valley, Tarrytown, N.Y.

Sarah Irving Van Wart
Sarah was Washington's favorite sister. He came to regard the house she shared with her husband, Henry Van Wart, in Birmingham, England, as his second home and penned the first draft of "Rip Van Winkle" there.
Courtesy Historic Hudson Valley, Tarrytown, N.Y.

Above: *Sunnyside, Currier & Ives print*
Irving's picturesque residence in Tarrytown, New York, attracted tourists from all walks
of life and was a popular subject for magazine illustrations, sheet music
covers, and even postcards. Courtesy Library of Congress.

Below: *Sunnyside today*
Irving's beloved riverside home, as it appears today, still welcoming guests.
Courtesy Historic Hudson Valley, Tarrytown, N.Y.

Irving wanted to return to his manuscripts. "I imagine you are not ambitious of being burdened with these mighty responsibilities & that you look forward impatiently for the time when you will be released from diplomatic bondage."[33]

His position as chargé d'affairs didn't just consume all Irving's spare time; it also devoured all his spare money. As the primary representative of the American government, he was expected to hire carriages and servants for ceremonies, levees, and dinners—all at his own expense. Submitting the embassy's statement of accounts to the U.S. Department of Treasury in July, he made clear to the auditor that performing the duties of a chargé d'affairs on a secretary's salary was an inexcusable hardship. "Neither my taste and inclination, nor my general ideas of becoming economy," he lectured, "will permit me to incur any unnecessary expenditures in this, or in any other particular."[34] He expected to be reimbursed.

By the end of the summer Irving had had enough. His duties with the legation had clearly become more than he had bargained for. He had practically no time to write, and the out-of-pocket expenses, especially those he had shouldered for the king's coronation ceremonies in early September, were slowly eating away at his literary profits. He had made up his mind that he was going to resign. Van Buren couldn't arrive fast enough. "I shall then turn my attention to my own private affairs," Irving told McLane, "and make preparations for my return to the United States."[35]

Van Buren arrived in London on September 13. Irving accompanied the new minister to present his credentials to Lord Palmerston on September 19, and to the king on September 21. Now all that remained for Van Buren to officially assume his duties was his confirmation by the United States Senate, which would return to session on December 5.

Irving took to Van Buren immediately. "I . . . do not wonder you should all be so fond of him," Irving told McLane. "His manners are most amiable and ingratiating, and I have no doubt he will become a favorite at this court, and will continue those amicable relations you have so advantageously established." Despite his feelings for Van Buren, Irving submitted his resignation to Secretary of State Livingston. His decision, he told the secretary, had nothing to do with politics or personalities; he simply wanted to get back to writing. "I was anxious for an enterval of entire leisure, requisite to arrange my affairs for a return to my native country. I pray you Sir to communicate these things to the President, and to assure him of my continued sense of the confidence with which he originally honoured me."[36]

Following his resignation from the legation, Irving moved out of Argyll Street and in with Van Buren at 7 Stratford Place, where the two New Yorkers—who were only four months apart in age—developed a genuinely warm rapport. Apart from his personal fondness for Irving, Van Buren quickly recognized what a loss Irving's resignation was for the legation. "An intimate acquaintance with him [Irving] has satisfied me that I was mistaken in supposing that his literary occupation had given his mind a turn unfavourable to practical business pursuits," Van Buren confided to President Jackson. "So far from it, I have been both disappointed, and pleased, to find in him, not only great capacity, but an active and untiring disposition for the prompt, and successful charge of business."[37]

Putting his affairs in order for his return to the United States would take Irving some time, and he still hoped to sell his life of Muhammad or his collection of Alhambra stories—or both—to Murray before he left. There was also a critical bit of personal business to attend to. In late September Irving had accepted an invitation from John Lockhart to dine with him at home. Lockhart's wife, Sophia, was there, as was her sister Anne.

So was Sophia and Anne's father, Sir Walter Scott.

At sixty years old, Walter Scott was a crippled, withered husk. He had suffered a stroke—his second—at the beginning of 1831. His remaining good leg had been hobbled by rheumatism, and he barely shuffled along by leaning on a heavy stick. But his mind was sharp, and his physical deterioration depressed him badly. "I have sufferd terribly," Scott confessed in his journal. "I often wish I could lie down and sleep without waking." His wife had died in 1826, leaving him alone in cavernous Abbotsford, where he still worked, even after his stroke, on his latest *Waverly* novel. Concerned for both his mental and physical health, Scott's family had arranged for him to make a tour of Italy. On his way, Scott had insisted on stopping in London, and Lockhart emphasized to Irving that Scott had expressly asked that Irving be invited to dinner.[38]

On the evening of September 28 Washington Irving sat at Lockhart's table beside a creaky Sir Walter Scott. It had been a long time since that memorable August of 1817, when Irving and Scott had shared their first dinner together at Abbotsford. Back then, Irving had been the young, aspiring writer, and Scott the older, famous, established author. Now Irving's own literary fame rivaled, and in some places exceeded, Scott's own. But this never changed Irving's feelings for the man. Scott was his literary father, the savior who had rescued *The Sketch Book* from a failed publisher, and Irving's devotion to the Scotsman remained complete.

During dinner, Scott could barely speak—and when he did, the stroke had so slurred his Scottish burr that he was difficult to understand. It was frustrating for Scott, and wrenching for Irving to watch. "How different from the time I last dined with him," Irving said later, "when Scott was the life of the company, all hanging on his lips; every body making way for his anecdote or story." As dinner wound down, Lockhart motioned for Irving to offer Scott his arm. Scott took it, hauled himself to his feet, and leaned heavily on his literary protégé. "Ah, the times are changed, my good fellow, since we went over the Eildon hills together," he told Irving. "It is all nonsense to tell a man that his mind is not affected, when his body is in this state." The two men stood arm-in-arm for a while, in quiet conversation. As Irving descended the steps of Lockhart's home into the London chill that evening, he was in a contemplative mood, perhaps understanding that he would never see Scott again. Sir Walter Scott died at Abbotsford the following September, a little more than a month after his sixty-first birthday.[39]

The afternoon following the dinner, Irving called on Murray

to discuss his projects. Neither was close to finished; Irving had only the first twenty-one of a proposed seventy chapters of Muhammad sketched out, and the Alhambra was just a hodgepodge of short essays. In a colossal bluff, Irving assured his publisher that he was very close to completing Muhammad, and offered it to Murray for what Irving considered an economical 500 guineas. As for Alhambra—a "Spanish *Sketch Book*," Irving called it, hoping those last two words resonated with Murray—he promised that the book would be ready within the year, and that Murray could have it for 1,000 guineas.

Irving believed Murray was deliberately and unfairly stingy with him, but the truth was that Murray was still wrestling with financial troubles. Even his usually steady *Quarterly Review* was losing money, and while Lockhart had recommended that Murray reduce costs on the magazine by lowering salaries, Murray had refused to do so. Instead, he chose projects carefully and limited the number of new titles he acquired each year. Despite Irving's literary reputation, Murray could no longer afford to contract works he hadn't read. He asked to see Irving's manuscripts first.

If Irving believed his bluff had been called, he never blinked. He promised to send the completed chapters of Muhammad, and told his publisher, "I'll be anxious to get this matter settled." Murray responded noncommittally, "Yes, I'll write you."[40]

Murray likely believed he had only bought himself some time to review Irving's manuscripts, but Irving somehow believed that the Prince of Booksellers had committed to purchasing both his books. That evening, as Irving prepared to leave for Castle Van Tromp, he lost no time in notifying Aspinwall that he needed him to finalize the paperwork with Murray.

Writing to Aspinwall from Birmingham five days later, Irving forwarded the draft chapters of his life of Muhammad—or *Mahomet*, as Irving preferred to spell it—for Aspinwall to take to Murray. "Attend to this as soon as possible," Irving told the colonel, "as I wish no time to be lost in getting the works through the press."[41] That same afternoon, he sent a similar note to Murray:

I had not time to make a written agreement for the works about which we bargained. I have therefore requested my friend & agent Col Aspinwall to call upon you and arrange in my name the terms of payment, and reduce the whole to writing. In our conversation you will recollect it was agreed that I should receive 500 Gs. For the Legendary life of Mahomet, and 100 Gs. For the Miscellaneous Volume [*Alhambra*]. . . . I will thank you to have the work [*Mahomet*] put to press as soon as possible. . . . I will commence sending MS: of the Miscellaneous volume shortly, so that both works may be out before Christmas.[42]

Expecting a formal agreement—and down payment—in his hands shortly, Washington left for Sheffield, about ninety miles north of Birmingham, to stay with his nephew Irving Van Wart for a week. Within a few days, however, Washington fired off another missive to Aspinwall: "I am anxious to have the arrangement made and the works sent to press immediately, and printed *rapidly* so as to have them in type by the end of the next month, that I may be *free*."[43] Murray's response to these presumptuous overtures was typical: complete silence. He didn't respond until he was ready. Until he finished reading *Mahomet*, he had nothing to say.

Murray's silence sorely tested Irving's patience. "I would wish to have the works published by some other person or in some other manner, if he cannot accommodate me by prompt attention to them," he griped to Aspinwall on October 18.[44] Murray's continued silence sorely tested Irving's patience. He ranted to Aspinwall:

I am excessively annoyed by these delays concerning the publication of my works. I want to have them bolted through the press *immediately*, that I may not be tied down in England. . . . The fact is Mr. Murray's irregular mode of conducting business has always been an annoyance to me, and of late he has been wanting in consideration and punctuality in money matters. . . . I am not in a very favorable mood therefore to put up with any more of his delays and negligences, and would be quite willing to deal with some other bookseller who is a mere man of business.[45]

Irving enclosed a letter for his agent to deliver to Murray. "I think [it] will rouse him," he wrote, "if he is really desirous of having the works."[46]

The letter was all bluff and swagger, a performance intended to intimidate rather than persuade. Irving reminded Murray that he had two works "ready for the press"—an overstatement if not outright lie—and scolded his publisher for the delays in finalizing their prior agreement. If Murray wasn't interested, Irving would go elsewhere:

> As this delay is excessively annoying to me and impedes all my plans and movements, and as it is very probable that you may not be desirous of publishing at this moment, I am perfectly willing that what has passed between us on the subject should be considered as null and void, and in such case will thank you to return to Col Aspinwall the MS: already left with you. . . . As to the other work [Alhambra], I do not think there is any likelihood of your being able to get it out as early as I wish—I trust, therefore, you will not take it amiss if I seek some other person or mode to publish it.[47]

Irving had overplayed his hand. Murray would be neither lectured nor intimidated. On October 25 the publisher fired back:

> My reply was "Yes, I'll write to you," and the cause of my not having done so earlier, is one for which I am sure you will make allowances. You told me upon our former negociations, and you repeated it recently, that you would not suffer me to be a loser by any of your Works; and the state of matters in this respect, I am exceedingly unwilling because it is contrary to my nature to submit to you, and in doing so at length, you will I am sure do me the justice to believe that I have no other expectation than those which are founded

upon your own good feelings. The publication of Columbus cost me. Paper—Print—Advertising—Author £5,700 and it has produced but £4,700—Grenada cost £3,073 and its sale has produced but £1,830, making my gross loss of £2,250.—I have thought it better to communicate with yourself direct, than through the medium of Mr. Aspin-wall.—

Let me have time to read the two new MSS—and then we shall not differ I think about terms.[48]

As his coup de grâce, Murray enclosed a copy of Irving's May 9, 1829, letter, throwing back in his face words Irving had written in anger more than two years before: "At any rate [Irving had written], I should like hereafter to make our arrangements in such a manner that you may be relieved from these apprehensions of loss, and for the necessity of recurring to any management of the press to aid the publication of a work of mine."[49] With the stroke of a pen, Murray had downgraded Irving from the House of Murray's most valuable author to an economic liability.

On October 29 a fuming Irving wrote Murray a lengthy response. In Irving's view, Murray was trying to renege on a verbal agreement. "Nothing apparently remained to be settled but the dates of payment," he explained. "By your letter of the 25th, however I find you do not consider any arrangement existing between us. You now say, 'Let me have time to read the new MS & then we shall not differ I think about the terms.' No stipulation of this kind was even hinted at when we made our bargain."[50]

As for Murray's argument that Irving was a financial drain, Irving had none of it: "I do not know whether you intend the State-ment you give of loss on two of my works as your reason for departing from the present arrangement—but on that point I will observe that Columbus and the conquest of Granada are copy right works, the sales of which cannot be considered as at an end; espe-cially as they are on historical subjects, which, though they may not have the immediate sale of works of fiction, are more permanent in their circulation." Irving was confident Murray would recoup his investment. "If you would give me and my works a fair chance," he scolded his publisher, "I have no doubt you would find both of us to work well in the long run, but you must not always expect to clear the price of a farm by the first years crop." He would take *Mahomet* elsewhere, he told Murray. But if he wanted *The Alhambra*, it was still available.[51]

If the two had cared to sit down and discuss rather than fight, they might have come to the mutual conclusion that the root of their problems lay with the shaky state of the current publishing market (Irving privately admitted as much to Peter). Irving was hardly the financial albatross that Murray said he was, but, given both Irving's recent track record and the condition of the market, Murray *was* justified in asking to see a complete manuscript before making an offer, rather than relying on first drafts and vapor trail promises. Neither publisher nor author was in a reasonable frame of mind. Irving pulled *Mahomet* off the table, and Murray rejected *The Alhambra*. Stalemate.

Irving was in a foul mood. Despite a side trip to Byron's home at Newstead Abbey in late October, during which time the home's curator, Colonel Wildman, invited him to return for a prolonged stay, Irving returned to London in early November under a storm cloud. At his desk on Stratford Place, he took out his *Alhambra* manuscript, intending to work, but merely stared at the pages. He was too angry. "The restlessness and uncertainty in which I have been kept," he growled to Peter, "have disordered my mind and feelings too much for imaginative writing."[52] He wanted to go home.

There was still Van Buren for company, now joined by his son John, a witty, personable, and good-looking twenty-two-year-old. Van Buren's formal nomination as minister had been forwarded to the U.S. Senate on December 7, but as of mid-December there was no indication of when he might be confirmed. With London quiet, Irving and the Van Burens set out on a rambling winter tour of central England, winding their way first through Oxford, then spending several days at Stratford-upon-Avon, where the three travelers stayed in the same Red Horse Inn Irving had visited more than a decade before, and written of in *The Sketch Book*. In this little corner of Stratford, at least, Washington Irving—rather, Geoffrey Crayon—was nearly as popular as William Shakespeare. His portrait hung in the room he had occupied in the inn, and the landlady delighted in showing him a poker she had locked away in her archives on which she had engraved "Geoffrey Crayon's Sceptre."[53] Irving was amused, and the Van Burens were impressed.

In January 1832 Irving made an extended trip to Nottingham for a stay at Lord Byron's estate, Newstead Abbey. Byron's home was a mixture of convent and mansion—an "irregular grey pile, of motley architecture," Irving called it.[54] He stayed in Byron's own bedroom, adjacent to the ruins of the abbey's old chapel and called "The Rook Cell" because of the enormous number of crows that lived in the nearby chapel grove. Here Irving slept in Byron's bed, lounged on Byron's sofa . . . and sulked about John Murray.

"I wish you to execute a commission of me, with Mr. Murray," Irving wrote to Leslie on January 9, 1832. This assignment, however, had nothing to do with any of his projects. It involved a manuscript Irving had forwarded to Murray from his old friend James Renwick, who was looking for an English publisher for his book *The Elements of Mechanics*. Not surprisingly, Irving had yet to hear back from Murray. "This conduct is so contrary to all laws of courtesy as well as rules of business," Irving spluttered to Leslie, "that it is difficult to treat it with proper temper." Running vertically down the left margin, Irving had written, as an angry afterthought, "In case he [Murray] should refer to the past—I do not wish you to say anything on the subject to him: neither am I desirous of renewing my literary connexion with him—*I am tired of him*."[55]

He was so upset, he found it difficult to work. He cobbled together some rough notes, stories, and sketches about the abbey and its surroundings—enough "for a very popular little volume," he thought—and poked halfheartedly at *The Alhambra*. "It has only been within a very few days that I have been able to touch my papers, and that very unsatisfactorily," he wrote to Peter in late January. "I am annoyed & provoked with myself but it is of no use—these moods will have their way."[56]

Worse, he received a letter from the American poet William Cullen Bryant, asking if he would approach Murray about publishing an English edition of Bryant's latest book of poetry. Bryant wasn't picky about payment—"I had rather that he should take it for nothing," he wrote, "than that it should not be published by a respectable bookseller."[57] Given Irving's strained relationship with Murray, it was an unfortunate bit of bad timing.

Irving promised Bryant to do what he could, but warned the poet, "The book trade is at a present in a miserably depressed state in England and the publishers have become shy and parsimonious." As for Murray, "[he] has disappointed me grievously in respect to other American works entrusted to him and . . . has acted so irregularly, in recent transactions with myself, as to impede my own literary arrangement and oblige me to look round for some other publisher."[58]

Irving wrote to Renwick with a response from Murray—relayed through his son, John Murray III—regarding the fate of *The Elements of Mechanics*. "All business & especially that of bookselling is suffering such stagnation at this moment," John Murray III wrote, "that my father has been compelled to decline almost every *new* undertaking which has been proposed to him." That was typical, Irving told Renwick. "He [Murray] was never a good man of business and of late seems to have become completely irregular." As if on cue, several days later, the younger Murray sent another note to Irving, this time rejecting Bryant's book of poetry. It was the final straw. "I have broke with Murray," Irving said on February 6.[59]

Irving took Bryant's book to John Andrews, "a fashionable bookseller," who agreed to publish it, provided Irving edit it and write an introduction. Irving groaned; such arrangements were becoming more and more typical. He agreed, writing a laudatory "dedicatory letter" for the volume's opening pages, and editing the book so quickly that a printed volume was delivered to Bryant on

March 6. It had been relatively easy work, but one editorial emendation came back to haunt Irving years later. In the first stanza of Bryant's poem "Song of Marion's Men," commemorating the Revolutionary War hero Francis "Swamp Fox" Marion, Bryant had written the opening lines:

> Our band is few but true and tried,
> Our leader frank and bold;
> And the British soldier trembles
> When Marion's name is told—

Publisher Andrews, however, was uncomfortable with Bryant's portrayal of the British as trembling. Such a sentiment, Irving explained to Bryant, "might startle the pride of John Bull on your first introduction to him,"[60] and Andrews therefore asked Irving to modify the stanza to remove the offensive verb. Given the context of the poem, it was a silly change—the entire poem is a celebration of the kind of American pluck that won the American Revolution—but Irving, without checking with Bryant first, agreed to rewrite the offending lines as

> And the foeman trembles in his camp
> When Marion's name is told.—

Luckily Bryant approved the change—indeed, was pleased with his British literary debut—but the edit caused headaches for Irving in 1837, when critics accused him of mutilating Bryant's work in order to ingratiate himself with the British.

Returning to his own literary efforts, Irving sent a packet to Ebenezer in late winter containing the first part of *The Alhambra*. While it was assumed Lea & Carey would publish the book in the United States, Irving still hadn't lined up a British publisher. Without Murray, Irving confessed to one correspondent, "I hardly know whom to turn to—Some [publishers] are disabled and all are disheartened."[61] He asked Aspinwall to find a suitable British home for the work.

In late February, as Irving and Van Buren sat over breakfast on Stratford Place, Van Buren finally received news regarding his official confirmation as minister. In a partisan squabble, the Senate had rejected his nomination. "It will kill him," several of his opponents snickered, "kill him dead."[62]

Counseling a dejected Van Buren in London, however, Washington Irving thought otherwise. While Van Buren's rejection had taken them both by surprise, Irving rightly believed Van Buren had become a political martyr. "I cannot but think the sympathy awakened by this most vindictive and unmerited outrage offered to him, will be sufficiently strong and permanent to ensure him a signal triumph," he told McLane.[63] Now in diplomatic limbo, Van Buren asked Irving whether he should continue to attend official events. Irving was emphatic—and remarkably prescient—in his counsel:

> I advised him to take the field and show himself superior to the blow leveled at him. He accordingly appeared at all the court ceremonials, and to the credit of John Bull, was universally received with the most marked attention. Every one seemed to understand and sympathize in his case; and he has ever since been treated with more respect and attention than before. . . . This I consider an earnest of the effect that will be produced by the same cause in the United States. I should not be surprised if this vote of the Senate goes far towards ultimately elevating him to the presidential chair.[64]

Sympathetic letters poured into Stratford Place, some insisting that Van Buren return "sword in hand" to fight for his nomination in the Senate, while others counseled him to stay away. "We had long talks on the subject," Irving confided to Peter. "The result was, that he determined to remain here a few weeks . . . by which time the public sentiment will have had time to express itself fully and sincerely, without any personal agitation on his part."[65] Van Buren returned to America, but not before a tour of Europe.

Irving was ready to go home, too. *The Alhambra* was scheduled for publication in America by early May, and Aspinwall had found him an English publisher. Henry Colburn, who had been courting Irving as far back as *Bracebridge Hall*, at last landed the coveted author. He offered Irving the 1,000 guineas he wanted, provided he finish the book by the beginning of April. That was all Irving needed to hear; his completed manuscript was delivered to Colburn on March 28.

Irving was exhausted. Completing *Alhambra* had been exceedingly difficult. He was burned out on politics, sick of John Murray and his depressed publishing market, and tired of England. It was time to say good-bye.

On April 1 Irving bid farewell to Van Buren. "The more I see of Mr. V.B., the more I feel confirmed in a strong personal regard for him," he told Peter. "He is one of the gentlest and most amiable men I have ever met with; with an affectionate disposition that attaches itself to those around him, and wins their kindness in return."[66] Following his tour of Europe, Van Buren returned home on July 5. In his absence, he won the Democratic nomination for vice president for the 1832 election.

On April 11, 1832, after bidding Peter a heartfelt and painful farewell in France, Washington Irving boarded the ship *Havre*, bound for New York. After seventeen years away, the most famous man in America was finally coming home.

12

Frontiersman

1832–1834

The period that has passed since my arrival in this country has been one of the greatest and mostly delightful excitement I have ever experienced. . . . Wherever I go, too, I am received with a cordiality, I may say an affection, that keeps my heart full and running over.

—Washington Irving to Peter Irving, April 1, 1833

*L*ATE IN THE AFTERNOON of May 21, 1832, James Webb, editor of the *New York Courier and Enquirer*, received word from one of his numerous "news collectors"—the nineteenth-century equivalent of paparazzi—that there was a ship anchored just off Sandy Hook, New Jersey, unable to enter New York Harbor because of an unforgiving headwind. The ship was the *Havre*, and among its passengers was Washington Irving.

The wily Webb immediately dispatched one of his "news-boats," the schooner *Eclipse*, to sail out to the *Havre* to fetch America's best-known writer and celebrity.[1] While Irving was slightly embarrassed at being singled out for such star treatment, he nevertheless boarded Webb's schooner. He was eager to get home.

As the *Eclipse* sailed back to port, Irving saw that the city he had left in 1815 had changed markedly in his absence.

I was astonished to see its once wild features brightening with populous villages and noble piles, and a seeming city, extending itself over heights I had left covered with green forests. . . . I beheld a glorious sunshine lighting up the spires and domes, some familiar to memory, others new and unknown. . . . I have gazed with admiration upon many a fair city and stately harbor, but my admiration was cold and ineffectual, for I was a stranger. . . . Here, however, my heart throbbed with pride and joy as I admired—I had a birthright in the brilliant scene before me.[2]

Irving was thrilled to be back, but the feelings of dread that had plagued him for nearly as long as he had been famous—the fear that his countrymen, convinced he had forsaken them for all things English, would give him the cold shoulder—gripped him. The negative, wailing reviews—smugly clipped and mailed to him by his anonymous stalker—still swam before him. He had made "dextrous compliments to English prejudices," critics said, or had written too much "*of* and *for* England, rather than his own country." "By degrees I was led to doubt the entire sentiment of my countrymen towards me," Irving fretted. He was all but convinced that he would be booed or egged in the streets.[3]

To no one's surprise but his, quite the opposite was true. An aging Ebenezer, with a houseful of daughters on Bridge Street, wrapped his arms around his brother and welcomed him into his home. James Renwick, now one of the most esteemed civil engineers in the country, paid his respects, as did the steady James K. Paulding, mourning the recent loss of a child, but otherwise his cheerful self. Former mayor Philip Hone spent several days with Irving, guiding him through the booming city which, in 1832, was contained largely below Houston Street. Hone, who hadn't seen Irving since London in 1821, thought he looked "exceedingly well," if a bit stout, and rightly believed Irving was "delighted in being once more in his native city."[4] As Irving told Peter:

I have been absolutely overwhelmed with the welcome and felicitations of my friends. It seems as if all the *old standers* of the city had called on me; and I am continually in the midst of old associates who, thank God, have borne the wear and tear of seventeen years surprisingly. . . . This, with the increased beauty, and multiplied conveniences and delights of the city, has rendered my return home wonderfully exciting. I have been in a tumult of enjoyment ever since my arrival; am pleased with everything and everybody, and as happy as mortal being can be.[5]

It was fitting that he had been brought ashore by a newsboat, for Washington Irving was all that New York could talk about. "His celebrity has been of a nature so unalloyed and universal," gushed the *New-York Mirror,* "that the appearance of the *man* among us is almost like the coming to life of some of those departed poets and authors whose works enrich our libraries, and whose names are cherished as something sacred and apart from those of the living." While less effusive in his rhetoric, Hone had to agree. "The return of Geoffrey Crayon has made old times and the associations of early life the leading topics of conversation amongst his friends."[6]

New Yorkers were proud that America's best-known writer was a native son. Irving's New York writings, like *Salmagundi* and *A History of New York*, were suddenly topics of conversation again. His portrait was printed—suitable for framing!—and biographical essays appeared in newspapers and literary magazines. Invitations to lavish celebratory dinners in his honor came in from Baltimore, Philadelphia, and elsewhere.[7] Irving, embarrassed by the fuss, refused all but one.

"A number of your townsmen," began this particular invitation, "impatient to evince to you their feelings of gratification at your return among them, to express the interest they have felt in your career in every period of its encreasing brilliancy, and pay a just tribute to your private worth . . . beg that you will appoint some day when you will honor them with your company at a public dinner." The first signature at the bottom belonged to his old friend James Renwick, followed by those of more than forty of New York's most distinguished gentlemen, including Judge Hoffman's son, Charles

Fenno Hoffman, Philip Hone, several Ogdens and Livingstons, and a Stuyvesant.

Irving was both flattered and flustered by the invitation. It was one he could hardly refuse—this was, after all, the hometown crowd. "No sooner does a citizen signalize himself in a conspicuous manner in the service of his country," Irving's Mustapha had mused in *Salmagundi* twenty-five years before, "than all the gourmandizers assemble and discharge the national debt of gratitude—by giving him a dinner." That still held true, but even as Irving penned his acceptance, butterflies fluttered in his stomach. Etiquette required him to make a speech. Chatting in a parlor or over newspapers was one thing; standing before a crowd was another. "I look forward to it [the dinner] with awe," Irving told Peter, "and shall be heartily glad when it is over."[8]

On the evening of May 30, nearly three hundred elegantly dressed gentlemen filed into the fashionable City Hotel, which John Jacob Astor had built on prime Broadway real estate. They chatted casually until 6:00 P.M., when the doors at the end of the hall opened. The room fell into a momentary hush, then erupted into wild applause and whoops as the president for the evening's event, New York chancellor James Kent, strode into the room arm-in-arm with Washington Irving. Thirty years prior, Kent had listened to the nineteen-year-old Irving hack and wheeze in the rooms next to him at Ballston Springs and had predicted an early demise. Now he escorted that same gentleman to the center table, beside a beaming Paulding.

Various toasts were made that evening—to Walter Scott, Peter Irving, the first settlers of New Amsterdam, James Fenimore Cooper, George Washington, and others. There were lengthy speeches describing Irving's life and career, lauding his place in literature, and subtly hinting that the evening's honoree should write more about American themes. But it was Irving everyone had come to hear. As Kent concluded his introductory toast, Irving slowly rose to his feet. The audience roared its approval.

Irving, paralyzed with stage fright, began to speak in a halting, almost inaudible whisper. He apologized to the crowd. The room rang with encouraging applause, and Irving began anew, this time with more poise. "Mr. President and gentlemen," he said, "I find myself, after a long absence of seventeen years, surrounded by the friends of my youth. . . . The manner in which I have been received . . . has rendered this the proudest, the happiest moment of my life."

He looked appreciatively around the room. Besides Paulding, there was his brother John Treat Irving, now a successful and well-respected judge; Gilbert Stuart Newton, his constant companion in London; and sixty-six-year-old and still-sturdy Judge Hoffman. The only person missing was Henry Brevoort—yet he *was* there, in the faces of every mutual friend in the room. "I fancied myself seated at the table," Brevoort later told Irving warmly, "mingling with our loyal friends & townsmen in cheering & greeting your long expected return."[9]

Irving was among friends. Perhaps emboldened by the supportive atmosphere in the room, he—who normally guarded his public image very closely—let the mask fall, if only for a moment:

> I have been led, at times, to doubt my standing in the affections of my countrymen. Rumors and suggestions had reached me that absence has impaired their kind feelings—that they considered me alienated in heart from my country. Gentlemen, I was too proud to vindicate myself from such a charge; nor should I have alluded to it at this time, if the warm and affectionate reception I have met with on all sides since my landing . . . had not proved that my misgivings were groundless.

It was a sensitive subject for Irving, but he had made a clean breast of things. On his part, all doubts about his countrymen's affections were gone. The crowd murmured its approval—but to anyone in the room who still questioned his patriotism, Irving offered a defiant response: "I am asked how long I mean to remain here? They know but little of my heart or my feelings who can ask me this question. I answer, '*as long as I live.*'" At this, "the roof," reported the *Mirror,* "now rung with bravos; handkerchiefs were waved on every side, 'three cheers' again and again." Irving raised his glass in a toast. "Our City!" he proclaimed. "May God continue to prosper it!"[10]

The applause was thunderous; Irving was relieved. He had made the dreaded speech, and done a good job of it. "Washington was a little nervous at the prospect of a *speech,*" Newton recalled later; "but the real feeling of the moment burst forth, and he not only got on well, but with real eloquence." Reading Irving's comments in the newspapers in Paris, a sympathetic Brevoort likely smiled. "I doubted whether your nerves would carry you through a public speech," Brevoort hooted at him, "but go to, you are an orator, & now may aspire to the dignity of bourgomaster in Gotham!"[11]

His friends' accolades aside, Irving hoped that he had left himself some wiggle room in his jingoistic vow to remain in the country. "It was from my lips before I was aware of its unqualified extent," he confessed somewhat embarrassed to Peter. "It is absolutely my intention to make our country my home for the residue of my days . . . but I shall certainly pay my friends in France, and relations in England, a visit."[12]

At the moment, there was more than enough to entertain him in New York. The city had crept northward up the island—Henry Brevoort's elderly father at Fifth Avenue and Tenth Street was grouchily complaining about the "encroachment of the city on his domains"—with plenty of hotels, taverns, and coffeehouses where Irving could read the papers or chat with friends. The Battery, grown into a lush park, offered shady walks and a scenic vista from which to watch ships entering the city harbors. Gas lamps, introduced in 1823, lit the streets at night. There was a new Masonic Hall on Pearl Street and several recently opened theaters and dance halls. Broadway was more fashionable than ever, still crammed with well-dressed couples, though gentlemen now wore trousers instead of knee breeches. The population had exploded from the 80,000 of 1815 to nearly half a million. It was overwhelming. "If I had anything to deplore," Irving reflected later, "it was the improvement of my home. It had outgrown my recollection from its very prosperity, and strangers had crowded into it from every clime, to participate in its overflowing abundance."[13]

New York was interesting, but Irving had business to attend to elsewhere. In early June he traveled to Washington, D.C.—the "splendid steamboats" and railroads now shuttled him from New York to the capital city in two quick days[14]—to pester the U.S. Department of Treasury about the money he believed he was still owed for his expenses as chargé d'affairs.

For two weeks Irving dallied in the capital, staying in the home of his former boss, Louis McLane, who was serving in Jackson's reorganized Cabinet as secretary of the treasury, and "in better tone of spirits," Irving thought, "than he was at London." He called on Senator Henry Clay, who Irving still liked and admired despite Clay's opposition to Martin Van Buren, and had a friendly meeting at the White House with President Jackson, who was more impressive in person than Irving expected. "I suspect he is as *knowing,* as I believe he is *honest,*" Irving wrote admiringly. Jackson, who was a full-blown Irving fan from his correspondence and conversations with Van Buren, chatted casually with the writer about his time in London and hinted at future political appointments. Irving diplomatically waved off such suggestions. "I let him know emphatically that I wished for nothing more," he told Peter, "that my whole desire was to live among my countrymen, and to follow my usual pursuits. In fact, I am persuaded that my true course is to be master of myself and of my time."[15]

In the meantime, his latest book, *The Alhambra,* was in bookstalls in New York and Philadelphia, only a month after its publication in London. Like Walter Scott, who couldn't seem to give up writing as the pseudonymous "Author of Waverly" even after being identified, Irving could never resist the urge to appear in his Geoffrey Crayon guise. *The Alhambra* was published in London under Crayon's name, and attributed in the United States to "The Author of The Sketch Book." At this point, readers no longer cared if

Irving wrote as Geoffrey Crayon, Diedrich Knickerbocker, or Fray Antonio Agapida. If it was by Washington Irving, they bought it. This time, it was worth their money. His last two works, *Granada* and *Companions of Columbus,* had resonated with critics but had been regarded with indifference by readers. With *The Alhambra,* Irving returned to what he did best: short, descriptive, elegant essays.

A colorful fusion of legend and travelogue, *The Alhambra* was and still is the most accessible of Irving's Spanish-themed books. Irving had initially pitched it as a Spanish *Sketch Book,* and that description was still apt; most reviews compared *The Alhambra* favorably with *The Sketch Book.* Readers who had waded patiently through Irving's history books applauded this return to lighter fare, and with good reason. Unlike the sometimes forced sentimentality of *Bracebridge Hall,* Irving's affection for the Alhambra, its people, and its history was genuine, and it shone through in his writing. In one of the most perceptive reviews of the work, the *New-York Mirror* observed, "His people move, look, and walk, with an individuality and a force only to be produced by the hand of a master. We are *there* actually, while reading the Alhambra. We see the summit of the Sierra Nivada [*sic*]; we hear the rills and fountains playing through the palace; we see the moon, pouring her floods of light into every court and hall and ruined decorations."[16]

If American critics viewed *The Alhambra* through the rose-colored glasses of Irving's triumphant return to the United States, as some claimed, then the British must have been equally taken by Irving's prior residence among them, for the reviews were just as good in England. "Were a lecture to be given on the structure of true poetical prose," declared the *Westminster Review,* "nowhere would it be possible to find more luculent examples" than in *The Alhambra.* Irving's friend Thomas Moore declared that Irving had "added clarity" to the English language.[17]

Returning to New York from D.C. in late June, Irving spotted an old friend, the actor Tom Cooper, at the upscale Mansion House Hotel in Philadelphia. Cooper invited him to spend the afternoon at his home in Bristol, where he lived with his wife of twenty years, the former Mary Fairlie. To Irving's delight, the Fascinating Fairlie with whom he had flirted twenty-five years before had lost none of her charm. "She was pale, and thinner than I had expected to find her," Irving told Peter, "yet still retaining much of her former self. I passed a very agreeable and interesting day there."[18] It was well that he did; Mary died eight months later.

New York's sweltering July humidity convinced Irving it was time to head upriver toward the shadier climes of the Catskills. He didn't travel alone, however. On board the *Havre*, Irving had made the acquaintance of Charles Latrobe, a thirty-one-year-old English dilettante, and a young Swiss entrusted to Latrobe's care, twenty-year-old Count Albert-Alexandre de Pourtales. At the time, the two gentlemen had excitedly expressed a desire to tour America, and Irving now invited them to join him and Paulding on a trip to West Point and the Catskills.

Boarding a steamboat in New York Harbor, the group arrived at West Point "in about *four hours!*"[19] an impressed Washington reported to Peter. Disembarking at West Point, they were met by a gigantic barge belonging to Irving and Paulding's fellow Lad of Kilkenny, Gouverneur Kemble, who could afford such luxuries. Following the War of 1812, Kemble had founded the West Point Foundry Association, chartered by President Madison to produce cannons, rifles, and other artillery for the U.S. government—and had made a fortune. While Kemble was not as wealthy as Henry Brevoort, his still-considerable income was perhaps somewhat more stable, based as it was almost entirely on government defense contracts.

Kemble's barge ferried the group to his riverside home, hidden among the trees in a deep cove near Cold Spring Harbor. One of Irving's few close friends who remained unmarried, Kemble had a snug retreat that Irving thought the ideal bachelor's paradise. It was Cockloft Hall all over again.

After several days, the group traveled upriver into the Catskills. This was Irving's setting for "Rip Van Winkle," only now it was Irving who rubbed his eyes in awe after a twenty-year absence.

Where there had been only trees and brush, now stood an enormous luxury hotel on the edge of a precipice. Irving was too excited about the view from his hotel window to complain about this commercial encroachment into the very mountains he had made famous.

Upon his return to New York two days later, Irving found the city a virtual ghost town. A cholera scare had sent many New Yorkers fleeing for healthier climates. Irving, who was normally inclined toward hypochondria, scoffed at the "exaggerated alarm" of his fellow Gothamites. Still, it was serious; by mid-August 2,565 New Yorkers were dead. Despite his bluster, Irving left for Boston, and spent four days touring the town with Newton, who was preparing to marry a local girl later that month. As Irving bid farewell to Newton that summer, he could hardly have imagined it was the last time he would see the young painter. Newton returned to London in October 1832. Three years later, suffering from severe mental illness, he died in a Chelsea asylum at the age of forty.

With the cholera epidemic still raging, Washington and Ebenezer retreated up the Hudson. The two settled in a Tarrytown cottage where their sister Catharine had corralled other family members, including her only surviving daughter, Sarah Sanders Paris—a smart and charming girl of nineteen, who soon became Washington's favorite niece.

During one of his afternoon strolls, Irving wandered down to the home of his nephew Oscar Irving, William's third son, who lived just within eyesight of the Hudson River. A small parcel of land that lay between Oscar's property and the Hudson caught Washington's attention. It was the old Van Tassell property, which had a run-down farmhouse that had originally been used as a tenant house for Philipsburg Manor just up the river.

Since his visit to Kemble's cottage at Cold Spring Harbor, Irving had considered building a home of his own. After living most of his adult life as a guest in someone else's house, he was determined to have one of his own, worthy of his fame and large enough to accommodate a regular stream of family and visitors. The house on the Van Tassell property was small and poorly maintained, but the entire property was attractive. It was also for sale.

Mulling it over, Irving set off on what he thought would be just another quick tour of western New York. After a chance encounter with Latrobe and Pourtales, the three traveled together across Lake Erie to Ashtabula, Ohio, on board the steamboat *Niagara*. Irving struck up a conversation with Henry Ellsworth, the lead member of President Jackson's Indian Commission, appointed to survey the territories set aside for tribal relocation under the terms of the inauspicious Indian Removal Act of 1830. As part of his official duties, Ellsworth was headed to Cincinnati and to Fort Gibson in Arkansas, where he would rendezvous with the rest of his team. Ellsworth invited Irving along. "The offer," Washington told Peter, "was too tempting to be resisted: I should have an opportunity of seeing the remnants of those great Indian tribes, which are now about to disappear as independent nations, or to be amalgamated under some new form of government. I should see those fine countries of the 'far west' while still in a state of pristine wildness, and behold herds of buffaloes scouring their native prairies, before they are driven beyond the reach of a civilized tourist."[20]

There was more to it than romantic wanderlust. Now that he was back in the United States, Irving was determined to write an American work, a defiant answer to those critics who complained that he had squandered his talents on English and Spanish themes. His series of bitter American essays had been cast by his own hand into a Spanish fireplace. Since that purging, his journals had remained free of any notes on American themes. As always, he needed inspiration to write—and the best place to find such inspiration, he decided, was out on the prairies with Ellsworth.

Five days later Ellsworth and Irving arrived at Cincinnati, in company with Latrobe and Pourtales, who had abandoned their plans to travel to Canada in favor of the American plains. Irving's reputation had preceded him in Cincinnati; while he was attending a performance at the Columbus Street Theater on his first evening in town, the theater manager stepped onstage during the intermission and announced excitedly that Washington Irving was in the house! "You may conceive how I felt on finding all eyes thus suddenly turned upon me," an embarrassed Irving reported to his sister. "I have . . . induced my companions to hasten our departure, that I may escape from all further importunities of the kind."[21]

They were off the next morning, chugging down the Ohio River in a steamboat. For ten days Irving coursed toward St. Louis, scanning the shore for the ragged huts occupied by slaves who worked the nearby Kentucky plantations. He was never an outspoken abolitionist—such a hot topic inevitably led to the kinds of arguments in which he was loath to engage—yet his natural tendency was to side with the oppressed. One afternoon, as he and Ellsworth gathered firewood during a stop in Wabash, Irving struck up a conversation with a slave woman, and asked her about her children. "As the tears started in her eyes," Irving recorded in his journal, "she got up [and] crossed the hut—'I am not allowed to live with them—they are up at the plantation.'"[22] Such wrenching true stories turned his stomach, yet Washington Irving was no James Fenimore Cooper; he never risked his reputation espousing controversial political views. His opinions remained his own.

The group arrived in St. Louis in mid-September. The town was a small but lively trading post, with a population of only 6,600. While it had only been chartered for ten years, its residents had been remarkably industrious and Irving was impressed, both with its people and its productivity. "St. Louis promises to become a very important place," he predicted.[23]

While there, Irving wasted no time calling upon a gentleman who was nearly as famous as he: William Clark—"The Governor," locals still called him—who had explored the American West with Meriwether Lewis in 1803. Still active at sixty-two, with gray-red hair down to his shoulders, Clark looked every inch his rugged reputation. Irving found him good company, and as the two dined on fried chicken and bison, Clark entertained Irving with stories about Indians and life on the frontier.

As superintendent of Indian affairs—a title he held until he died in 1838—Clark had been involved in the recent settlement of the Black Hawk War. A war in name only, it had been an uprising, led by the Sauk chief Black Hawk, of five hundred Indians and their families in protest of treaty violations. The protesters had been beaten back, then slaughtered, by an army of 3,000 militia. Black Hawk surrendered to the authorities on August 27, just two weeks prior. Clark had helped negotiate the new treaty with Black Hawk and his supporters, and the chief was now held prisoner in the nearby Jefferson Barracks.

Awestruck, Irving was determined to visit this noble captive chief. What he saw was disappointing. Black Hawk, Irving reported to his sister in incredulous tones, "is an old man upwards of Seventy: emaciated & enfeebled by the sufferings he has experienced and by a touch of cholera." He had a hard time believing this was the man who had committed the atrocities attributed to him in the newspapers. "I find it extremely difficult, even when so near the seat of action, to get at the right story of these feuds between the White & the red man," Irving said, "and my sympathies go strongly with the latter."[24]

On September 15 the group set out from St. Louis on horseback, heading west for Independence, Missouri, on the state's western border. Once again, Irving's fame sped ahead of him. When they arrived in Columbia several days later, the local paper was already promoting his tour, declaring that Irving was out to "acquire a valuable fund of materials in his progress, for interesting works or Sketches, which, ere long, we may have the gratification of perusing." It was a journalistic hunch, but it was a good one; Irving *was* writing again, scribbling in his journals early in the morning or just before going to bed.

Irving loved riding on horseback; his health had never been better, and he was delighted with what he had seen of the West so far. "The Magnificence of these western forests is quite beyond my anticipations," he reported happily to Catharine. It was mostly open prairie, but he wasn't bothered a bit; he thought sleeping in a tent under the stars was "a very sweet and healthy kind of repose."

The sophisticate who had slept in Byron's bed at Newstead Abbey and in the governor's apartments of the Alhambra was a Boy Scout at heart. "Camp—Fire—meat roasted on sticks—," Irving wrote with excitement in his journal. "Savory—our salon of trees lighted up by fire—sky & stars in the centre . . . we sit on bearskins & the meat put on spits before us—cut it off with knife & eat—coffee . . . Stretch a tent on cords. Spread our mats and sleep."[25]

For ten days the party wound its way down the western Missouri border, "over wide monotonous prairies," angling toward Fort Gibson in what is now eastern Oklahoma. Irving scouted for prairie hens, hunted wolves, and traded with the Osage Indians. As he sat in his tent in the evenings, he jotted down various stories he had gleaned from the wandering Indians. He was particularly fascinated by the burial customs of the Osage. "A chief lately deceased was buried sitting up under a mound," he recorded one evening. Another night, he wrote of a little girl buried with her toys and pet horse—just the sort of weepy tale that resonated with Geoffrey Crayon.[26]

Arriving at Fort Gibson on October 8, Ellsworth learned to his annoyance that the other members of his commission hadn't arrived. Having made it this far, he was determined to continue to survey, mark the land, and resolve any disputes with the Indians. There were bound to be problems with the surrounding tribes— apart from resentment, the forced relocation was also going to shove relatively peaceful, agrarian tribes up against more warlike hunting groups, causing conflict—so Ellsworth needed an armed escort.

Fortunately, a group of more than a hundred rangers, under the command of Captain Jesse Bean, had left the fort only two days earlier, in search of Pawnees with whom they hoped to discuss a possible treaty. Ellsworth was determined to catch them, and dispatched a small group of Creek Indians to ride ahead to inform Bean's men that they were on their way. Deputizing Irving as his secretary for the tour—for which Irving received a saddle, bridle, blanket, bearskin, and India mat, but no pay—Ellsworth and company left the fort in early October, following the Arkansas River northwest toward present-day Tulsa.

Irving, Ellsworth, Latrobe, and Pourtales had been traveling together now for more than two months. While tempers flared from time to time, for the most part there was good chemistry among the group. Irving was genuinely fond of the Yale-educated Ellsworth, calling him "a very gentlemanly and amiable person."[27] A former president of the Aetna Insurance Company of Hartford, Connecticut, the thirty-nine-year-old Ellsworth still looked more insurance agent than frontiersman; yet Irving found him a rugged enough traveler—Ellsworth could jerk venison and brew prairie tea from goldenrod—and an excellent companion.

He was intrigued by Latrobe, whom he regarded as a kindred spirit. Irving described the gentleman, the nephew of the architect Charles Latrobe, as "a citizen of the world, easily adapting himself to any change." A sometime botanist, geologist, musician, and butterfly collector, Latrobe was "a man of a thousand occupations." While living in Switzerland in the mid-1820s, he had met the Pourtales family, and had been appointed guardian to the young count for his trip abroad. While Irving thought Latrobe and Pourtales were "most agreeable traveling companions," he sometimes found the latter exhausting. Twenty-one-year-old Pourtales was more interested in pursuing young Indian women than he was in hunting prairie hens, and Ellsworth sighed somewhat derisively that he was certain the young count's parents had sent him to America "to sow his wild oats in a foreign country . . . [which] I am sure will be done, unless his wild store is beyond measurement."[28]

Their group—"the Irving party," they were called, to Ellsworth's irritation—finally caught up with Captain Bean's rangers on the morning of October 13. Later that day, Irving participated in his first "bee hunt," learning how to smoke honeybees from a tree, and then extract the honeycomb and its stores of sweet honey. These rangers reminded Irving of Robin Hood's merry men, and he jotted down their casual, playful talk in his journals, rising each morning to the sound of their bugles, and dining each evening on the venison and turkey that fell before the sharpshooters. It was a "delightful mode of life," he wrote in his notebook happily: "Exercise on horseback all the fore part of the day diversified by hunting incidents— then about 3 oclock encamping in some beautiful place & with full appetite for repose, lying on the grass under green trees in genial weather with a blue cloudless sky—Then so sweet sleeping at night in the open air & when awake seeing the moon & stars through the tree tops—Such zest for the hardy, simple but savory meals the product of the chase."[29]

Approaching Stillwater, they turned south into the territory of the Pawnees, "the terror of that frontier," Irving wrote with a shudder. His fear soon gave way to excited anticipation. This was buffalo country, Irving noted, and "the expectation of falling in with buffalo in the course of the day roused every one's spirits."[30]

In late October, as the troop curved just east of present-day Norman, Oklahoma, Irving and Pourtales spied two buffalos in a tree-lined ravine. Sneaking up on horseback, Pourtales fired a double-barreled shotgun and missed, sending the animals off in different directions. Irving and the count separated, each in hot pursuit of a buffalo. Armed with two brass-barreled pistols, Irving rode at a full gallop alongside the terrified animal, fired twice . . . and missed both shots. His prey scrambled down a ravine and out of sight. Dejected, Irving circled back toward Pourtales—and stumbled upon an entire herd. This time, Irving didn't miss; "a fortunate shot brought it down on the spot," he reported modestly, and the bull fell in a heap at his feet, mortally wounded.

Dismounting, Irving stood beside the enormous beast, preparing to dispatch it with a final bullet . . . and suddenly regretted ever shooting it in the first place.

> Now that the excitement was over, I could not but look with commiseration upon the poor animal that lay struggling and bleeding at my feet. His very size and importance, which had before inspired me with eagerness, now increased my compunction. It seemed as if I had inflicted pain in proportion to

the bulk of my victim, and as if there were a hundred fold greater waste of life than there would have been in the destruction of an animal of inferior size. . . . To inflict a wound thus in cool blood, I found a totally different thing from firing in the heat of the chase.[31]

Grimly, he shot the animal behind its shoulder. An impressed ranger caught up with Irving, and helped him carve out the buffalo's tongue as a trophy. Irving accepted the prize, but he was through being a sportsman. "I am determined," he told Peter later, "to rest my renown as a hunter, upon that exploit, and never to descend to smaller game."[32]

By the beginning of November, thunderstorms hampered the party's progress. Supplies were running low—Irving complained that he had to drink his coffee without sugar—and wet wood made it impossible to start campfires. As they crossed the marshy, thorny Cross Timbers region, Irving's horse went lame. He had developed a rash, and grumbled about eating skunk. It was also getting colder; he recorded in his journal that the cup of water he left by his bed had frozen overnight.[33]

The company finally slogged its way out of the muddy plains and back into Fort Gibson on the morning of November 9. Irving had had enough of life as a frontiersman; his journals were crammed with more than enough notes for a book, and he wanted to return to New York to begin writing. Two days later, he bid his fellow travelers good-bye, and without a backward glance climbed aboard the steamboat *Little Rock.* As he floated upriver and eyed the elegant plantation houses that dotted either side of the Mississippi River, he made up his mind to purchase the Van Tassell property near Tarrytown. "I am more & more in the notion of having that little cottage below [Oscar Irving's] house," he wrote Catharine, "and wish to tell him to endeavor to get it for me."[34]

When he passed through South Carolina that winter, Irving stopped to spend a day with his old friend William Campbell Preston, whom he hadn't seen since their trip to Scotland in 1817. Since leaving Edinburgh in 1819, Preston had established a successful law practice, and in 1828, at age thirty-four, had been elected to the South Carolina State Legislature, where he was one of the state's most active and outspoken defenders of slavery. A charismatic speaker, Preston and South Carolina governor James Hamilton were presently campaigning for the rights of states to nullify objectionable federal laws. It was one of the first major rifts between the states and the federal government, a stutter step toward the outbreak of the Civil War thirty years later.

The trouble had actually started in 1828, with the passage of a protective federal tariff—the "Tariff of Abominations," South Carolinians called it—that promoted northern trade at the expense of southern markets. President Jackson, inheriting the problem from John Quincy Adams, attempted a modified tariff, but the South still smarted from a policy they considered pro-northern. Vice President John Calhoun, himself a South Carolinian, had proclaimed that states had every right to declare federal laws inoperative within their boundaries when such laws violated their interests or sovereignty.[35] Following Calhoun's lead, Hamilton and Preston issued an Ordinance of Nullification, declaring the tariffs of 1828 and 1832 null and void in South Carolina.

Listening to Preston and Hamilton congratulate each other over dinner on the passage of their defiant ordinance, Irving understood that there was something inherently dangerous in South Carolina's position. "It is really lamentable to see so fine a set of gallant fellows, as the leading Nullifiers are, so sadly in the wrong," he told Peter. "I grieve to see so many elements of national prejudice, hostility, and selfishness, stirring and fermenting, with activity and acrimony." As Irving bid Preston and the governor good-bye, Hamilton shook his hand warmly and invited Irving to visit again. "Oh yes!" came Irving's tightlipped reply. "I'll come with the *first troops*."[36]

On December 10, Jackson issued a proclamation declaring nullification laws "incompatible with the existence of the Union . . . and destructive of the great object for which it was formed." South

Carolina, he warned, was on the brink of treason.[37] Jackson had drawn the line in the sand. The Nullification Crisis was under way.

When Irving arrived in Washington, D.C., in December, he sensed that something exciting, and important, was happening. "Washington is an interesting place to see public characters," he told Peter, "and this is an interesting crisis." His plans to remain in the nation's capital for "but a few days" stretched into three months.[38]

Thanks to his friendships with McLane and Van Buren—who had just been elected vice president of the United States ("Did I not prognosticate how it would be?" Irving ragged Van Buren)—Irving had an insider's view of the debate, lingering over long dinners each evening at the McLanes' to catch up on the latest gossip from the president's Cabinet. He was spending so much time at the McLanes' that a rumor made its way around the city that he was planning to marry McLane's daughter Rebecca—a charge Irving found hilarious. "I had thought that such an ancient gentleman as myself might play the part of uncle to a young belle, without being suspected of being her beau," an amused Irving told fellow bachelor Gouverneur Kemble. "Some men cannot look over a hedge without being charged with an intention to steal a horse."[39]

As Calhoun and Daniel Webster thundered at each other on the floor of the U.S. Senate, President Jackson huddled privately behind the scenes with McLane and House Ways and Means chairman Gulian Verplanck—another old New York friend of Irving's—on a reduced tariff bill. At the same time, the president forwarded his "Force Bill" to the Congress (the *War* Bill, nullifiers said derisively), warning South Carolina that it was the duty of the chief executive to enforce the laws of the nation—by force, if need be. As Jackson swaggered, critics in Congress howled, and Irving spent weeks seated in the gallery of the Capitol watching the "outbreaking," as he called it.

While Irving found plenty of time to watch the debates at the Capitol, visit with President Jackson, or dine with McLane or Van Buren, there was one thing that *wasn't* getting done. "I have been trying since my arrival in Washington, to resume my pen, and get into a career of literary occupation," he told Catharine, "but find it almost in vain. My mind is too discomposed and my attention distracted by too many objects & concerns, and I fear it will be Some time before I again get into those moods and employments most congenial to my taste—."[40]

By late February, Calhoun and Webster were regularly packing the Senate galleries as they brought debate on the Force Bill to a close. At 10:00 P.M. on February 20, the Senate moved to a final vote. Angry nullifiers stalked out in protest, allowing the bill to sail through the Senate by a vote of 32 to 1. This was the kind of political drama Irving relished. While politicking and campaigning were still repugnant to him, he was fascinated by the debates and horse trading that went with the legislative process. "I think my close attendance on the legislative halls," he told Peter later, "has given me an acquaintance with the nature and operation of our institutions, and the character and concerns of the various parts of the Union, that I could not have learned from books for years."[41]

Irving was politically savvy enough to recognize that the debate over nullification was more than just an intellectual exercise on states' rights. It went to the very heart of the structure and intent of the Constitution, and Irving wasn't certain the document could withstand the assault. As Clay and Calhoun worked on a compromise tariff bill, Irving speculated to Peter on the disastrous effect a botched agreement could have on the country. "I hope such a bill may be devised and carried as will satisfy the moderate part of the nullifiers," he wrote, "but I confess I see so many elements of sectional prejudice, hostility, and selfishness stirring and increasing in activity and acrimony in this country, that I begin to doubt strongly of the long existence of the general union."[42]

By the beginning of March, Clay and Calhoun had their compromise, proposing a gradual lowering of tariffs in exchange for South Carolina's withdrawal of its nullification ordinance. With some deft political maneuvering, both the compromise and the Force Bill were passed by Congress, and Jackson signed both bills on

March 2, two days before he and Van Buren were inaugurated. (South Carolina would have the last laugh, declaring Jackson's Force Bill null and void, before repealing their Ordinance of Nullification under the terms of the tariff agreement.) "Nullification is dead," Jackson said, but "the next pretext will be the negro, or slavery question."[43] For now, the Union held.

The drama over, Irving headed back toward New York, stopping first in Baltimore for three weeks to call on a new acquaintance, John Pendleton Kennedy. A disinterested lawyer, part-time politician, and aspiring novelist, Kennedy was something of an Irving wannabe. Kennedy's first novel, *Swallow Barn*, written under the pseudonym "Mark Littleton," was essentially *Bracebridge Hall* set in the American South. Kennedy's book had its fans; in fact, Irving counted himself as one of them, and had written the Marylander an appreciative letter. Kennedy became one of Irving's most trusted advisers—he served a similar advisory role to an up-and-coming young Baltimore writer named Edgar Allan Poe—and Kennedy and his wife would be regular visitors at Sunnyside. At the moment, however, Kennedy was merely another in Irving's growing circle of literary friends and admirers.

By April 3, 1833—his fiftieth birthday—Irving was in New York, home after an absence of nearly seven months. During that time, the letters, honors, and invitations had continued to pile up in Ebenezer's parlor. Sifting through the mail, Irving learned to his amusement that he had been awarded an honorary Doctor of Laws degree by Harvard—yet another honorific for New York's worst attorney. "To merit such rewards from my country is the dearest object of my ambition," he wrote to Harvard president Josiah Quincy, with just a trace of a smile, "but, conscious as I am of my imperfections, I cannot but feel that my Countrymen are continually overpaying me."[44]

In fact, his countrymen couldn't get enough of him. While he remained wary of official public displays, Irving was always happy to accept private invitations from friends, admirers, politicians, actors, and anyone else who wouldn't ask him to make a speech. Consequently, his first weeks back in New York were a blur—and Irving loved it. "The period that has passed since my arrival . . . has been one of the greatest and mostly delightful excitement I have ever experienced," he told Peter. "Wherever I go, too, I am received with a cordiality, I may say an affection, that keeps my heart full and running over."[45]

Irving clearly owned American hearts; all they wanted in return was a new book. In this, however, Irving was bound to disappoint; he was being pulled in too many directions to settle into the quiet he needed to successfully wield his pen. "Time and mind are cut up with me like chopped hay," he told Peter, "and I am good for nothing, and shall be good for nothing for some time to come, so much am I harassed by the claims of society."[46] Writing was very much on his mind, so Irving responded as he usually did when the threat of work loomed before him: he went on vacation. For two weeks in September, he and Martin and John Van Buren traveled in an open carriage from Albany, New York, to Communipaw, New Jersey, a reprise of the tour of central England the three had taken together in 1831.

Irving was delighted with the early leg of the trip, when they toured Kinderhook, Van Buren's hometown and the place where Irving had spent some of the bleakest, yet most productive moments of his life. Here Irving visited with Brom Van Alstyne, the inspiration for the character of Brom Bones who had terrorized poor Ichabod Crane, and the original Ichabod Crane himself, his old friend Jesse Merwin. Perhaps the vice president cocked a curious eyebrow as they passed the Van Ness manor where Irving had written most of *A History of New York* in 1808; in 1839, Van Buren purchased the old Van Ness home and lived there until his death in 1862.

During their tour, Irving and the vice president talked casually of politics and of Jackson's still-shaky Cabinet. There was discontent in the president's new Cabinet over issues relating to the Second Bank of the United States. Jackson was against it; others in his Cabinet—most notably Louis McLane—were for it. The president respected McLane's disagreement, but McLane didn't know when to stop pushing Jackson on the issue. Consequently, McLane was transferred from his post as treasury secretary to the office of secretary of state. McLane and the president feuded anew, this time over France's failure to comply with the terms of an 1832 treaty. There was speculation that McLane was quitting, so in late September, Irving set out for Washington, D.C., to gauge his friend's mood and, if necessary, talk him out of resigning.

He found McLane in surprisingly good spirits and determined to remain at his post, despite his friction with the president. There was another surprise in D.C.: suddenly, Irving was motivated to write. As he hunched over the desk in his Capitol Hill apartment, even he admitted "it is an odd place and time for a man to amuse himself with literary avocations, but it shows how little I am of a politician."[47]

There was more to it than this. As usual, nothing sparked life into Irving's pen faster than the threat of looming financial hardship. This time, a number of his investments—made under the guidance of business managers Ebenezer and John Treat—were doing poorly. Washington reassured Peter that any financial losses could be recovered by profits from his existing copyrights; however, under the terms of the agreement Brevoort and Ebenezer had negotiated in 1828, Carey & Lea still owned a limited copyright to Irving's first four books until 1835. Until then, Irving would either have to make do with his existing funds, or write a new book. There was really no choice. Irving still wanted to buy the Van Tassell property, and he wanted to build a new house. To do that, he needed money. The pen scratched away. "I am, as you know, dammed up by the necessity (or fancied necessity) of producing a work upon American subjects before I can give vent to the other materials that have been accumulating upon me,"[48] he told Peter— and he was right. American readers had had enough of elegant musings on England and Spain; they expected a book on American themes.

Irving settled back into Ebenezer's home on Bridge Street to spend the winter "in a course of regular literary occupation" in the relative quiet of his brother's parlor. Even as he began writing in earnest and attempted to refuse most invitations, there were still distractions: a new opera house had opened nearby. Unlike Paris, where the street noise had been an annoyance, Irving found the whoops and clattering from the crowds on Broadway oddly reassuring. "The city overflows with strangers, more than any city of the same size in the world," he told Peter. "The theater is constantly crowded, and is a perfect gold mine."[49] Despite his best efforts, his writing slowed to a trickle in the early months of 1834.

Instead, Irving dawdled with Van Buren, continuing their conversations about the fate of Louis McLane, still unhappy in Jackson's Cabinet. The vice president assured Irving that McLane would remain at his post, although privately Van Buren wasn't trying very hard to persuade McLane to stay. He had a hard-line Jacksonian and longtime ally, Georgia senator John Forsyth, standing ready to assume McLane's position. McLane finally submitted his resignation in June—and unbeknownst to Irving, Van Buren had practically pushed McLane out the door.

Irving's work on his American book continued through the summer, even as he split his time between obligations to family and friends. He was generally pleased with his progress, though he fretted that he would be unable to meet his fans' inflated expectations. He hoped the book would be worth their wait.

As Irving closed in on the last chapters, another American project suddenly fell into his lap. For years, friends and admirers had regularly approached him with book ideas. His brothers urged him to write a novel. Constable suggested a biography of George Washington. Henry Brevoort recommended an extended biography of Hernán Cortés. The suggestion of this particular admirer, however, could not be ignored.

"John Jacob Astor is extremely desirous of having a work written on the subject of his settlement of Astoria,"[50] Washington wrote to Pierre M. Irving in September. The millionaire Astor had amassed his fortune largely in the fur trade, establishing companies across the American frontier, including one at Fort Astoria, on the Columbia River in the Pacific Northwest. Now retired from the fur trade, Astor thought an account of his company's exploits in the West was one worth telling. Who better to tell the story of the richest man in the United States than the nation's most famous writer?

Irving was a longtime friend of Astor, but shrewdly recognized that Astor's purpose in asking for the history was motivated by ego, not enlightenment. The millionaire wanted "something that might take with the reading world," Washington told Pierre, "and secure to him the reputation of having originated the enterprise and founded the colony that are likely to have such important results in the history of commerce and colonization." Further, he explained, Astor was now in "want of occupation and amusement, and thinks he may find something of both in the progress of this work."[51]

Curiously, Irving decided to play hard to get. Astor left his journals, letters, articles, and other documents entirely at Irving's disposal, and was willing to pay "liberally" for the project. Irving needed the money for his house and property, but he demurred, telling Astor he was too busy to do it himself. There was another, more driving consideration: despite his desire to appear in print again and the obvious financial attractiveness of the offer, he was simply too lazy to sort through Astor's voluminous piles of letters and documents. He had done that for his *Columbus* biography, and it had nearly wrecked him. At fifty-one years old, he wasn't willing to commit another year of his life to a densely researched biography.

Instead, he proposed to Astor that he hire Pierre as a literary researcher and assistant, to sort through the materials and put together a rough, notated outline, on which Washington would then put the "finishing hand." Despite his display of reluctance, Washington wanted the easy money this project promised. After a quick discussion with Astor, he told Pierre the millionaire was willing to pay the young man "whatever might be deemed proper for your services."[52]

Pierre agreed to do it for $2,000, on condition that the research require no more than a year of his time and that he receive no share of the profits of the book. Relieved, Washington convinced Astor to up Pierre's commission to $3,000—about $75,000 today. Astor not only agreed, but insisted Pierre live with him in his winter residence in New York while the young man worked.

Washington already had a strong sense of the book's overall feel and structure. "My present idea is to call the work by the general name of *Astoria*—," he told Pierre, ". . . under this head to give not merely a history of the great colonial and commercial enterprise, and of the fortunes of his colony, but a body of information concerning the whole region beyond the Rocky Mountains. . . . I think, in this way, a rich and varied work may be formed, both entertaining and instructive."[53] In other words, he hoped to do for Astor precisely what he had done for Columbus—write a factually accurate biography that would also be accessible to casual readers.

It was all too much for another famous American. "He is to be Astor's biographer!" sputtered James Fenimore Cooper. "Columbus and John Jacob Astor! I dare say Irving will make the last the greatest man!"[54]

13

Sunnyside

1834–1842

He who has to fag his pen for a livelihood, has very little inclination to take it up when he is not driven thereto by sheer necessity.

—Washington Irving to Sarah Van Wart, December 1840

IN NOVEMBER 1834, as Pierre Irving began his research for *Astoria* in Astor's Hell Gate home, Washington completed his manuscript of *A Tour on the Prairies*, his first book since *A History of New York* to be entirely conceived and written in the United States. Despite his best efforts to manage the hype, expectations were running high. "I feel reluctant to let it go before the public," he confessed to Peter. "So much has been said in the papers about my tour to the West, and the work I was preparing on the subject, that I dread the expectations formed, especially as what I have written is extremely simple, and by no means striking in its details."[1]

Since his return to America more than two years before, friends, fans, and readers had constantly reassured him that they still held him in high regard and never doubted his patriotism—just the sort of stroking his fragile ego needed. Still, Irving had his share of critics and skeptics—like James Fenimore Cooper, critical of America yet fervently protective of it, who sneered that Irving's patriotism was a ruse. As far as Cooper was concerned, Irving had turned his back on his merchant-class roots and ingratiated himself with the English upper crust. Worse, Cooper believed Irving had flattered his way around society, hobnobbing with artists, politicians, and millionaires—the snooty American aristocracy that Cooper so loathed. According to such cynics, Irving had frittered away the goodwill of his American readers by catering to sycophants and wannabes. In their view, if he wanted to win back the affections of Americans, he had much work to do.

Irving withered at the thought of such criticism, and worried whether *Prairies* could stand on its own merits. For the next several weeks, the finished manuscript sat untouched as he mulled over the best way to ensure a positive reception. By early January he had what he thought was a surefire solution: he would publish *A Tour on the Prairies* as part of a multivolume collection under his Geoffrey Crayon pseudonym. The device was probably unnecessary, but the security of Geoffrey Crayon's name steeled his nerves enough to let the manuscript go.

In February 1835 he mailed Aspinwall the proofs for *A Tour on the Prairies*, volume one of a collection Irving was calling *The Crayon Miscellany*. His asking price for the first volume was 500 guineas—about $3,000—but Irving was prepared to take less, advising Aspinwall to simply "make such bargain as you can" with any publisher that would publish it as quickly as possible. In early April Aspinwall informed an increasingly nervous Irving that he had landed a reputable British publisher for *The Crayon Miscellany*: John Murray.[2]

Despite the scuffle over *The Alhambra* and *Mahomet* that had put Irving and Murray at odds in 1831, Aspinwall had rightly gauged that 1835 was a good time to reconcile with the Prince of Booksellers. Murray's fortunes had improved, and he was receptive to renewing his relationship with the writer who, regardless of his mood swings and ego, was still one of the most successful he had published. But Murray had learned to pay lower prices for copyrights, and wasn't about to permit even a proven writer like Irving to determine his own advance. He refused Irving's 500-guinea asking price for *A Tour on the Prairies*, but agreed to pay £400 up front.

It was a reality check, but Irving was delighted with the arrangement. "I am glad to be once more in dealings with Murray," he told Peter, "The price is not so high as I used to get, but there has been a great change in the bookselling trade of late years."[3] Murray had made his point, but Irving had, too; they needed each other. The hard feelings were gone, and Irving even allowed the first volume of *Miscellany* to go to press in London with minimal input or meddling.

That wasn't the case for the U.S. edition. Nervous about his American reappearance, Irving continued tinkering with his manuscript until the last minute, inserting an introduction in which he discussed his seventeen-year stay in Europe, his decision to write a book on an American subject, and the still-touchy issue of his allegiance to his country: "I make no boast of my patriotism. I can only say, that, as far as it goes, it is no blind attachment. . . . I have seen what is brightest and best in foreign lands, and have found, in every nation, enough to love and honour; yet, with all these recollections living in my imagination and kindling in my heart, I look round with delightful exultation upon my native land, and feel that, after all my ramblings about the world, I can be happiest at home."[4] They were sincere words. But the fact that they were missing from the British edition only fueled speculation that Irving was pandering to audiences on both sides of the Atlantic.

A Tour on the Prairies was published in the United States by Carey, Lea & Blanchard on April 11, a month after its London debut. It was Irving's long-awaited American book—and to many American readers, the wait was worth it.

"Irving on the prairies!" bubbled an effusive reviewer in *Western Monthly Magazine*. "Washington Irving among the honey-bees, the wild horses, and Osages of the frontier! . . . It is one of the best of the author's productions." In the pages of the *North American Review*, Edward Everett lauded Irving for at last addressing an American theme, and hailed the book as a "sentimental journey, a romantic excursion, in which nearly all the elements of several different kinds of writing are beautifully and gaily blended." The public's enthusiasm was reflected in strong sales, as demand drove the book into a second printing. By November it had sold more than 8,000 copies, netting Irving a generous $2,400. The reception in England was just as encouraging, and Leslie mailed Irving packets of approving reviews. "We hope," sighed one, "that this will not be the last of the Crayon Miscellanies."[5]

It wasn't. Six weeks later came the second volume in the collection, *Abbotsford and Newstead Abbey*, Irving's fond tribute to the homes of Walter Scott and Lord Byron. After receiving the manuscript from Aspinwall in March, Murray had given the pages to his favorite elbow critic, John Lockhart, for review and comment. Abbotsford, the home of Lockhart's father-in-law, was a topic close to Lockhart's heart, and Irving's manuscript—a loving recollection of his first meeting with Walter Scott in 1817—met with the critic's enthusiastic approval. He told Murray that he absolutely *had* to publish it. With this ringing endorsement, Murray offered Irving £600—an arrangement Irving regarded as "perfectly satisfactory."[6]

The second volume was well received by American readers and critics, who didn't seem to mind that Irving had returned to European topics. Edgar Allan Poe, now writing for the *Southern Literary Messenger*, thought this book even better than the first. "In *Abbotsford and Newstead Abbey*, the author of the *Sketch Book* is at home," enthused Poe. "By no one could this offering to the memories of Scott and Byron have been more appropriately made."[7]

Irving was relieved. In the eyes of readers, he was not only back, he was just as good, if not better, than before. And he was well compensated for it; by summer 1835, *The Crayon Miscellany* had netted him nearly $4,000—about $90,000 today—and that didn't even include his British advance. Further, Ebenezer had negotiated an agreement to extend Carey, Lea & Blanchard's exclusive publishing rights for another seven years for an annual payment of $1,150. There had been some niggling over the details, but Washington was relieved to know he had a regular source of income for at least the next seven years. "I am content," he told Peter in April, "and feel no further solicitude in money matters, excepting to acquire the means of benefiting others."[8]

Irving spent the spring cloistered in the city, shuttling between Ebenezer's Bridge Street home and Astor's Hell Gate manor, where Pierre continued to sort the seemingly endless piles of journals, letters, and clippings. By mid-May Washington began his initial draft of *Astoria*, using Pierre's dense jumble of information to cross-reference resources and track down any quotes, stories, or other details he needed.

It wasn't all work, however. Brevoort returned to New York in May, settling permanently on Fifth Avenue while he continued to amass a fortune in land speculation. Such investments were fashionable—the nineteenth-century equivalent of dot-com ventures—and Irving found himself caught up in the fever. Approached in early June with the offer of a significant share in a waterside parcel of land in Baltimore, he wrote to John P. Kennedy for the inside line on the investment. "I see you think me infected by the fever of speculation, and this present request may confirm you in the opinion," he explained almost apologetically. "I have no eagerness for wealth; but I have others dependent upon me for whom I have to provide."[9]

Such gentlemanly protestations aside, he did need the money. On June 7 Irving formally acquired the two-room stone farmhouse on the Van Tassell property for $1,800—and he had big plans for it. He was determined to make it a proper home, with comfort and space enough to tempt his family not only to visit, but to stay. Already he had engaged his neighbor, the painter George Harvey, to help him rebuild and renovate the place. "My idea is to make a little nookery somewhat in the Dutch style, quaint, but unpretending," Irving explained. "It will be of stone. The cost will not be much." That was wishful thinking, as he soon discovered.[10]

In mid-July Irving shipped Aspinwall the finished pages of *Legends of the Conquest of Spain*, the third volume of *The Crayon Miscellany*. He was no longer concerned about the particulars of Aspinwall's negotiations with Murray. "I leave the arrangement

entirely to you and wish every thing to be done to Mr Murrays satisfaction," he told his agent. "It really gives me great pleasure to be
again in business relations with him."[11]

He should have been concerned. Irving had cobbled *Legends*
together from the remains of several Spanish manuscripts he had
dredged from his trunks, and Murray's elbow critic thought the
effort was shabby. "I have looked over Irving's *very rough* proofs &
am sorry to say I think the whole affair feeble and vapid," Lockhart
told Murray in disgust. Murray purchased the book anyway, though
for a paltry £100, and had the last laugh, as public demand sent *Legends of the Conquest of Spain* into a second printing. In the United
States, Carey, Lea & Blanchard was confident readers would buy
the third installment from Crayon, paying Irving $1,500. It was
enough. "I look forward now with confidence, of being able to keep
up the series from time to time, with ease to myself, and with much
advantage in every respect," Irving said.[12]

If he hoped to get away with using the *Miscellany* as a repository for any vagrant manuscripts he might have lying around, critics
had none of it. While the third volume of the *Miscellany* sold, even
friendly critics were blasé in their assessment. "If any other person
than Irving had written the book," said Philip Hone, "the publishers would have sold fifty copies."[13] Such a lukewarm reception
ensured that the third volume of *The Crayon Miscellany* would also
be the last.

That was fine with Irving. He had exhausted the materials
lying fallow in his trunks, and had been paid well for it. He could
devote his attention to *Astoria*, and to his cottage, where George
Harvey and his crew were turning the simple stone farmhouse into
the "nookery" that had existed only in Irving's imagination. He
opted to stay with Astor in Hell Gate until the work was completed.
With its riverfront lawns and fragrant gardens, Astor's home was
conducive to Irving's creative temperament. "The consequence is,
that I have written more since I have been here than I have ever
done in the same space of time," he observed.[14]

It was at Hell Gate in early autumn that Irving met one of

Astor's colorful acquaintances from the fur trade, army captain Benjamin Louis Eulalie du Bonneville. A French-born West Pointer, Bonneville had taken leave from the army in 1832 to lead one of the first American expeditions to survey the western territories beyond the Rocky Mountains. When Bonneville hadn't returned in the prescribed amount of time, however, the army had presumed him dead and struck him from their records. Bonneville came to Astor seeking career advice, but it was Irving who took most of the explorer's time, pressing him for tales of his adventures. "There was something in the whole appearance of the captain that prepossessed me in his favor," he said.[15]

Irving returned to Tarrytown to oversee construction on his house. He put the spur to his masons to complete the exterior before the cold set in, but bogged Harvey down with minutiae that threatened further delays. Irving fussed about the best way to inscribe Harvey's name over the south door, and demanded to know how the windows would be glazed. He ordered one bedroom "finished in a different way from the others," and for a sloped inner bedroom wall to be covered with striped paper "to resemble the curtain of a tent." Old Dutch cottages, he told Harvey, had "crow steps" on their gabled ends, and so must his.

Irving knew his micromanagement was trying Harvey's patience—"I think I have given you explanations enough to perplex and confound you," he told his renovator good-naturedly—but this was to be his home for the rest of his life, and he was leaving no detail to chance. Even in its unfinished state, he was enormously proud of his cottage. "It is a tenement in which a man of very moderate means may live," he said, "and which yet may form an elegant little snuggery for a rich man."[16]

The modest little farmhouse had quickly swollen beyond Irving's initial intentions. "Like all meddlings with stone and mortar, the plan has extended as I built," he confessed to Peter.[17] It was also more expensive than he had anticipated.

Unfortunately, Irving's already strained finances were hobbled further in December, when fire swept through fifty acres of the southern tip of Manhattan, burning down hundreds of businesses. Ebenezer's was unscorched, but he, John Treat, and Washington had each lost thousands of dollars invested in insurance companies. "The fire," Washington told Peter glumly, "has singed almost everybody."[18]

But there was some good news: Peter would come home in the spring of 1836. Washington could barely contain his excitement, and promised his brother the cottage would be ready to receive him. "Here you shall have a room to yourself that shall be a *sanctum sanctorum* . . . you will have those at hand who love and honor you, and who will be ready to do anything that may contribute to your comfort."[19]

But winter weather hindered its completion. Frustrated and impatient, Irving returned in earnest to working on *Astoria*, filling gaps in his narrative by interviewing Astor, his employees, and colleagues. Irving was amazed at the ease with which Astor seemed to make money; the man seemed to have a predisposition for choosing successful projects. It was typical of Irving's luck that the one scheme in which Astor convinced him to invest—shares in land in Green Bay, Wisconsin—promptly went bust.[20] Astor bought Irving's shares back several years later, but at a loss to Irving of nearly $2,000.

Work on *Astoria* was interrupted in March by the reappearance at Hell Gate of Captain Bonneville, preparing to again make his way west. This time, it was Irving, not Astor, whom Bonneville had come to see. Over the winter, Bonneville had written a book about his adventures in the West, but had been unable to find a publisher. Spreading his maps, papers, and manuscript on a table, he asked Irving if they might be useful to him. "I glanced over the [papers]," Irving wrote later, "and observing there were materials on which I thought I could found a work that would be acceptable to the public, I purchased the [manuscript] of him"[21] for $1,000.

By late spring *Astoria* was nearly finished, and work was progressing at his increasingly expensive Tarrytown home. The cottage, he told Pierre, "reminds me of those fairy changelings called Killcrops, which eat and eat and are never the fatter." Until it was done, Peter—back in the United States after twenty-seven years abroad—was bunked in Ebenezer's home in New York City.

At last, in late September the cottage—the Roost, as Washington called it—was finished. Throughout the fall, he organized his study and prepared the upstairs bedrooms for Peter's arrival. Even with the help of several willing nieces, it was more work than he expected. "I have too many things to attend to in getting my little establishment under way," he told Kemble somewhat frantically.

In late October 1836 *Astoria* was published simultaneously in the United States and London. Carey, Lea & Blanchard paid Irving a generous $4,000, which was just the sort of windfall he needed to cover the cost overruns at the Roost. In London, however, a skeptical John Murray had politely rejected the book, believing British readers would have little interest in American aristocrats. Richard Bentley, Irving's copublisher on *The Alhambra*, had gambled £500 that Irving's name and a fascination with the American West would resonate with the English.

Bentley was right; *Astoria* received glowing reviews on both sides of the Atlantic. "A more finished and exquisite narrative we have never read," wrote the *Westminster Review*, "our critical labors have seldom brought us so much pleasure as that derived from the perusal of *Astoria*." The *American Quarterly Review* agreed. "The narrative of all these adventures should be perused in Mr. Irving's words, no pen is so fit as his to exhibit all its various phases." The most important critic of all, John Jacob Astor, was "greatly gratified."[22]

Irving scarcely noticed his reviews; he was already moving ahead with his book on Captain Bonneville. He continued to ride the wave of land speculation, signing on with Kemble to pursue schemes in Michigan, and with Pierre and Ebenezer on lands in Toledo, Ohio. He still had no luck; indeed, the Toledo venture would prove to be particularly disastrous, losing the Irvings $20,000.

At this point, his unbroken string of botched investments was almost funny. "I am so accustomed . . . to find *swans* turn out mere *geese*," Washington told Pierre, "that I have made up my mind not to be grieved."[23]

Such aplomb was typical. Home ownership was sitting well with Irving, and he was in high spirits. "Everything goes on cheerily in my little household, and I would not exchange the cottage for any chateau in Christendom," he beamed. Even a harsh winter snowstorm didn't dampen his mood, "as there shall be good sleighing," he told Pierre. Even better, he now had the company of Peter, who had arrived in December.[24]

In early January 1837 he reported to Pierre that he was "getting on briskly" with his Bonneville manuscript. He hoped the book would more than earn back the $1,000 he had paid for the captain's papers. A review of his finances convinced him that he was in no immediate danger of *"running aground,"* but if his investments didn't pan out, he would need to write regularly—and at the moment, he was fresh out of ideas.[25]

It was cold in Tarrytown that winter; the Tappan Zee had frozen to a sparkling sheet of ice. Peter was fine company, but Washington, as he had all his life, craved female companionship. Ebenezer's five daughters had returned to their father in New York at the beginning of the winter, but the niece he really missed was his sister Catharine's daughter, Sarah Sanders Paris, who had helped supervise construction of the cottage and laid out its grounds. "The house wants a head while you are gone," he told her in one of his many lengthy, chatty letters to her.[26]

In late January came sad news; Judge Hoffman had died at the age of seventy. Irving made the snowy trip to New York for the funeral. While in the city, he came across one of the most blistering attacks ever leveled against him, his patriotism, or his work.

In the *Plaindealer*, editor William Leggett snidely charged Irving with "mutilating books" in a blatant attempt to curry favor with English readers. Leggett questioned Irving's motives in writing a patriotic introduction for the American edition of A *Tour on the*

Prairies while conveniently eliminating it from the British version. "He has an undoubted right to do [so]," Leggett twitted haughtily, "whatever we may say of its spirit." What hurt more was the assertion Leggett made regarding Irving's decision to alter "objectionable" lines contained in the collection of William Cullen Bryant's poems that Irving had edited in 1832: "Our respect for Washington Irving underwent a sensible diminution when we perceived that, in supervising the republication of Bryant's Poems in London, he changed a passage in the piece called Marion's Men . . . in order to substitute something that might be more soothing to [English] ears."[27]

Irving was livid. "I have always made it a rule never to reply to attacks, to which I have of late years added another—never to read them," he had once told Alexander Everett.[28] But Leggett had gone too far. This was an attack on not only his work but his character and reputation. For the first time in his life, he put his pen to paper to refute one of his critics.

"Though I have generally abstained from noticing any attack upon myself in the public papers," Irving railed to Leggett, "the present is one which I cannot suffer to pass in silence." The change to the line in "Song of Marion's Men," he pointed out, had been made only at the request of Bryant's English publisher. "I doubt whether these objections would have occurred to me," he fumed, "had they not been thus set forth."

Regarding Leggett's claim that he had modified A *Tour on the Prairies* to cater to two different audiences, Irving responded, "Your inference is that these professions [of patriotism] are hollow . . . and that they are omitted in the London edition through fear of offending English readers. Were I indeed chargeable with such baseness, I should well merit the contempt you invoke upon my head." But "what had the British public to do with those home greetings[?]" he asked. "There was nothing in them at which the British reader could possibly take offence; the omitting of them, therefore, could not have argued 'timidity' but would merely have been a matter of good taste; for they would have been as much out of place . . . as would have been my greetings and salutations to my family circles, if repeated out of the window."[29]

Leggett backed down, and allowed Irving's word to be the last.

With that unpleasantness behind him, Irving returned to his cottage—"Wolfert's Roost," he now called it, a nod to Wolfert Acker, who had built the original two-room farmhouse—and continued his work on the Bonneville book. He was so preoccupied that he nearly forgot to write a letter of congratulations to Martin Van Buren, who had been elected president of the United States the previous November. Writing to Van Buren in February, Irving couldn't resist reminding his friend that he had predicted his rise all along. "I hope . . . to take a breakfast with you in commemoration of that memorable breakfast in London when you received news of your rejection, which I then considered the seal of your political advancement." He wished Van Buren well and offered some unsolicited advice: "There is but one true rule for your conduct: act according to the sound dictates of your head and the kind feelings of your heart, without thinking how your temporary popularity is to be affected by it, and *without caring about a re election.*"[30] It was wise counsel—and to Irving's later annoyance, Van Buren followed it.

As he closed in on the end of his manuscript, Irving was genuinely excited about his Bonneville book. "It is *all true,*" he gushed to Aspinwall. "It is full of adventure, description, and Stirring incident; with occasional passages of humor." It was also, he thought, worth a thousand guineas, and he directed Aspinwall—who didn't even have the complete manuscript—to start negotiations with publishers. As he forwarded the last batch of pages to Aspinwall in late March, however, he had significantly reined in his expectations. "I hope you will be able to get a tolerable price for the work, but with whatever you do get I shall feel satisfied, knowing that you always make the best bargain in your power."[31] As usual, Aspinwall delivered, nudging £900 from publisher Richard Bentley, nearly twice what Bentley had paid for *Astoria.*

The Adventures of Captain Bonneville was published in London in early May 1837. Six weeks later, after an irritating delay, Lea,

Carey & Blanchard published the book in the United States. Despite Bentley's best promotional efforts, *Bonneville* bombed in the United Kingdom. English readers were tired of Irving and his American subjects, a grim bit of irony given all he had done to convince critics he had never cultivated a British audience. British critics had a field day, taking their shots at Irving and all things American.

Irving's latest book, sniffed the *Literary Gazette*, was "more prolific of extraordinary heroism in females, than we were prepared to expect among these savages." The *Monthly Review*, while conceding that Irving still wrote with his typical "ease and grace of style," lamented that he had sunk to "book-making," and that the seams were showing. *Bonneville* had "the appearance of affectation" and "the aspect of feebleness."[32]

Perhaps the most condescending review came in the pages of *Blackwood's Edinburgh Magazine*, which bemoaned that Irving "now occupies himself with simpler tasks than the offspring of his own brains, and acts as accoucheur to the teeming memories of the half-smugglers and half-banditti who supply the Indians with brandy and the Europeans with beaver."[33]

American readers and reviewers were more forgiving. The *New York Review* hailed Irving as "a man of genius" for his ability to elevate "common subjects" to new heights.[34] Further testimony to his genius—or, perhaps, his shrewdness—was that he had convinced Lea, Carey & Blanchard to pay him $3,000. It wasn't *Astoria* money, but it was enough to recover his investment in Bonneville's materials.

The cottage continued to siphon away his remaining funds. At the end of March he drew on Aspinwall for £500—the entirety of his English profits on *Astoria*—to maintain and expand his property. By summer 1837 he had extended the boundaries of his farm from ten acres to fifteen, more than enough room for gardens and walking paths.

His house was quickly becoming a stopping place for friends and fans who trekked to Tarrytown to see the home of America's most famous writer—and Irving, ever mindful of his image, wanted to ensure his cottage was well-stocked and presentable. Despite the regular expense, he had no complaints; he loved his role as ruler of the Roost, and extended open invitations to friends to stay with him. "There will always be a bed for you, and a most hearty welcome," he told Gouverneur Kemble. To Van Buren he promised "more comfort and quietude of mind than I fear You will experience in the *White House*."[35]

Irving was in need of the company. In June an increasingly ill Peter left the cottage for Manhattan to be closer to the hospital, leaving Washington alone in Tarrytown. With *Bonneville* published, he had no literary projects to occupy his time. He read the papers, strolled the woods near his house, and tried to bolster the sagging spirits of Martin Van Buren, whose presidency was bogged down in the economic disaster that had followed on the heels of the Panic of 1837.

A weakened Second Bank of the United States and the rise of smaller state banks had sparked the land speculation craze in which Irving, Kemble, Pierre, and countless others had been so caught up. Smaller banks that were printing the money and issuing the credit that made such speculation possible actually had no specie—hard cash—on hand. When President Jackson's Specie Circular required all land purchases to be transacted with hard money, many banks were stuck with paper money they couldn't redeem. The resulting panic and crash was the nation's worst economic catastrophe until the Great Depression of the 1930s. Bank failures in New York alone totaled nearly $100 million. The disaster was due more to the policies of Andrew Jackson than to Van Buren's, yet the soured economy and the blame hung heavily around Van Buren's neck for the span of his presidency.[36] "Your situation is an arduous one," Irving told the president sympathetically, "but a good heart and a clear head will I trust carry you safe through any trial . . . *dare to be unpopular rather than to do wrong* and your career will eventually be one which history will perpetuate with applause."[37] Not that Irving would stop speculating. Through the autumn and winter of 1837, he and Kemble—now serving in Congress—persisted in their land investment schemes. As the economy continued its downward slide in early 1838, there were whispers in Democratic circles that Irving had abandoned Van Buren—a charge he strenuously denied. "What—cut a President! Turn my back upon a friend when at the height of power!" he sputtered to Kemble only half in jest. "What the plague does he take me for[?]—I always suspected he had no very high idea of my merit as a politician, but I never imagined he could think me capable of so gross a departure from the ways of the political world."[38]

In truth, Irving harbored doubts about politicians in general. Posturing and demagoguery, he thought, were making it impossible to have any meaningful political discourse or identify real solutions to the depressed economy. Irving was a political pragmatist; he believed extremists, no matter which side of the issues they were on, were bad for politics and for people: "I have no relish for puritans either in religion or politics, who are pushing for principles to an extreme, and overturning everything that stands in the way of their own zealous career. . . . I always distrust the soundness of political councils that are accompanied by acrimonious and disparaging attacks upon any great class of our fellow citizens."[39]

Whether because of his political convictions or in spite of them, some Tammany Hall Democrats thought Irving would be an ideal candidate to run for mayor of New York against incumbent Aaron Vail, a defiantly anti-Jacksonian Whig. In March a "full deputation" of delegates approached Irving in Tarrytown to convince him to accept the mayoral nomination. "Of course I declined," Irving said. "Nothing could induce me to undertake an office for which I feel myself so little fitted." Months later, he beat back similar demands to run for Congress. "I must run mad first," Irving said.[40]

There was a more serious offer to consider: in late April President Van Buren offered Irving a post in his Cabinet as secretary of the navy. "I believe you possess in an eminent degree those peculiar qualities which should distinguish the head of that Department," Van Buren wrote, "and the successful and efficient employment of which is so important to this branch of public services." The president had spoken with Paulding and Kemble, he said, and both had vigorously supported Irving's nomination.[41]

Unfortunately, neither of those gentlemen had checked with Irving first. He was flattered, but refused: "It is not so much the duties of the office that I fear, but I shrink from the harsh cares and turmoils of public and political life at Washington, and feel that I am too sensitive to endure the bitter personal hostility, and the slanders and misrepresentations of the press. . . . I really believe it would take but a short career of public life at Washington to render me mentally and physically a perfect wreck, and to hurry me prematurely into old age."[42]

His decision was likely influenced by a recent loss. On March 15 John Treat had died in New York at the age of fifty-eight. A longtime judge of the Court of Common Pleas, John had a reputation as a workaholic, and the Irving brothers had been worried about his health for some time. "He will keep on until he gets some stroke of ill health," Washington had fretted to Ebenezer in 1833.[43] The family was convinced overwork and stress had hastened John's demise, and with his brother's death still haunting him, Washington was worried a similarly high-profile, high-pressure job might wear him down. Van Buren was disappointed and slightly hurt by Irving's refusal, and offered the job to Paulding, who accepted.

Peter's deteriorating condition was also a concern, and while Washington remained in his cottage in Tarrytown—again attended by a bevy of nieces—he kept in close touch with Ebenezer in the city for updates on Peter's health. In late June Washington made the trip to New York to spend several days with Peter in what the family was certain were his last days. On the morning of June 27, Peter died.

Peter's death devastated Washington. More than anyone else, Peter had understood him best. It was Peter who had encouraged him in his first shaky, boyish excursions into print in the pages of the *Morning Chronicle*, and who had trudged through obscure reference books in the early stages of *A History of New York*. Together, they had suffered the embarrassment of bankruptcy in Liverpool, and celebrated Washington's first international success with *The Sketch Book*. Neither had married. Peter had been Washington's solace and support, and Washington had loved him without question, generously forgiving his faults and shouldering his significant financial burdens.

Washington sank into grief. The cottage, while brimming with family, seemed empty, and Irving begged Brevoort and Kemble for company. For months Irving simply sat; his own health worsened. To his frustration, even writing was difficult; everything seemed to remind him of Peter: "My literary pursuits have been so often carried on by his side & under his eye, I have been so accustomed to talk over every plan with him and, as it were, to think aloud when in his presence, that I cannot open a book, or take up a paper, or recall a past vein of thought without having him instantly before me, and finding myself completely overcome."[44]

It wasn't until late November that the clouds began to lift. The company of his niece Sarah helped, as did the pleasant autumn weather. By the beginning of December he had started on a new project, a history of Mexico, and was excited by its prospects. The upkeep of his cottage was becoming increasingly expensive, and with his land investments drying up, he hoped his new project would bring steady sales and income. "If I can only have another course of literary exertion, and the public will but continue to receive my writings favorably," he wrote, "I may be enabled to render all my pecuniary concerns smooth and easy, and to keep the dear little flock around me in a pleasant and happy home."[45]

Unfortunately, Irving wasn't the only writer at work on a Mexican history. So too was historian William Hickling Prescott. Alerted by Joseph Cogswell of the New York Society Library that Prescott had a similar project in the works, Irving was crushed. Graciously, he informed Prescott that he would relinquish the topic to him, and offered to provide any manuscripts or assistance needed to complete his book. Prescott was floored, but grateful, and wrote Irving a lengthy, deferential letter of thanks. "I cannot sufficiently express to you my sense of your courtesy," wrote Prescott, "which I can very well appreciate, as I know the mortification it would have occasioned me, if, contrary to my expectation, I had found you on the ground."[46]

Irving's disappointment was palpable in his reply to Prescott, yet his deference to the younger historian was sincere. Prescott's earlier writings, Irving told him, "gave me at once an assurance that you were the man to undertake this subject; your letter shews that I was not wrong in this conviction." Forfeiting the project had serious financial consequences. "I doubt whether Mr. Prescott was aware of the extent of the sacrifice I made," Washington later confessed to Pierre. "When I gave it up to him, I in a manner gave him up my bread, for I depended upon the profit of it to recruit my waning finances. I had no other subject at hand to supply its place."[47]

Then, like a serendipitous bolt from the blue, came Knickerbocker.

In February 1839 editor Lewis Gaylord Clark offered Irving an annual salary of $2,000 to contribute regularly to *Knickerbocker Magazine*. Irving groaned at the idea of returning to magazine work, with its monthly deadlines and space limitations. But he needed the income, and *Knickerbocker* offered relatively easy money. Unlike at the *Analectic*, he would have the luxury of leaving the editing to others. He accepted.

For his debut in the magazine, Irving slid into the comfort zone provided by his Crayon persona and playfully explained his decision to stand before readers in the pages of a magazine instead of in one of his books: "I am tired . . . of writing volumes . . . there is too much preparation, arrangement, and parade, in this set form of coming before the public. I am growing too indolent and unambitious for anything that requires labor or display. I have thought, therefore, of securing to myself a snug corner is some periodical work, where I might, as it were, loll at my ease in my elbow chair."[48]

For the first time, Irving placed his two most famous pseudonyms in the same room, staging an encounter between Geoffrey Crayon and Diedrich Knickerbocker at Wolfert's Roost. It was a clever and subtle way of reminding his readers—many of whom hadn't been born when Irving made his appearance as Knicker-bocker—of his first work. Irving was creating new histories and back stories for Knickerbocker, Crayon, and their contemporaries.

Readers were thrilled to have a regular dose of Irving, and Clark was roundly congratulated in the media for the coup he had scored in securing the celebrity author's services. "The content [in *Knickerbocker*, is excellent," the *New-York Mirror* hailed. "How can they be otherwise, when Geoffrey Crayon is among the contribu-tors?" Not everyone was so effusive. One colleague worried that Ir-ving was running out of gas. "Irving is writing away like fury, in the Knickerbocker," groaned Henry Wadsworth Longfellow, "—*he had better not;* old remnants—odds and ends,—about Sleepy Hollow, and Granada. What a pity."[49]

Such views, however, were in the minority. Irving's popularity and reputation soared. Readers requested his autograph, and his work appeared nationally in other magazines. Sailors on the Hud-son River gaped at Wolfert's Roost as they floated past, and Irving was pleased to welcome a number of eminent fans and guests to the cottage, including President Van Buren, who finally accepted Ir-ving's standing invitation to dinner in July 1839.[50]

As the nation's first and most famous author, Irving had aspir-ing writers seek his advice or approval. In October Edgar Allan Poe, behind flattering cover letters, provided Irving with published copies of two of his latest stories, "The Fall of the House of Usher" and "William Wilson," hoping for a good review. Irving's tastes in literature were decidedly old-school; he was unequipped to respond to Poe's dark genius. Perhaps out of deference to his friend, Poe's benefactor John P. Kennedy, Irving read both tales, and wrote Poe with his comments. Of the two stories, Irving preferred "William Wilson." "It is managed in a highly picturesque Style and the Sin-gular and Mysterious interest is well sustained throughout," he told Poe. "Usher" he thought might be improved "by relieving the style from some of the epithets."[51]

Not exactly a ringing endorsement, but it was enough for the shrewd Poe. "I am sure you will be pleased to hear that Washington Irving has addressed me 2 letters, abounding in high passages of compliment in regard to my Tales—passages which he desires me to make public—if I think benefit may be derived," Poe wrote to Joseph Snodgrass. "Irving's name will afford me a complete triumph over those little critics who would endeavor to put me down by raising hue and cry of *exaggeration* in style, of *Germanism* & such twaddle."[52]

Clearly Poe was not above exploiting Irving's reputation to further his own career. While he admired and envied Irving, he thought Irving's talents had always been undeservedly magnified. Publicly, however, Poe was careful to maintain a respectful attitude. A year earlier, he had turned down an offer from *American Museum* to write a slashing appraisal of Irving's work, but it had been tempting. "It is a theme upon which I would very much like to write, for there is a vast deal to be said upon it," Poe admitted privately. "Irving is much overrated, and a nice distinction might be drawn between his just and surreptitious and adventitious reputation— between what is due to the pioneer solely, and what to the writer."[53]

Though Poe believed otherwise, Irving was a staunch champion of America's maturing literature. Perhaps better than any other American writer, Irving understood from experience that literature was not only an art but a business. Ensuring that it prospered was a matter not merely of encouraging literary men and women to write but also of guaranteeing that their copyrights were protected. "If the copy right law remains in its present state," Irving told William Prescott, "our native literature will have to struggle with encreasing difficulties. No copy right to protect it in England and an influx of foreign and cheap literature to drown it at home." In an open letter in the January 1840 issue of *Knickerbocker,* he publicly endorsed legislation pending in the U.S. Congress, arguing for strong protection of American copyrights abroad. "For myself, my literary career, as an author, is drawing to a close, and cannot be much affected by any disposition of this question," he wrote, "but we have a young literature springing up and daily unfolding itself with wonderful energy and luxuriance, which . . . deserves all its fostering care." Unfortunately, the copyright legislation did not pass.[54]

In early 1840 Irving wrote an impassioned and highly confidential letter to Van Buren, pleading with the president to find a "respectable and reasonably profitable appointment" for Ebenezer, whose business was on the brink of collapse. The financial obligations of caring for Ebenezer and his five daughters, as well as other family members, were becoming more than Washington could sustain, and he confessed to Van Buren that a placement for Ebenezer would help reduce his own financial burden. "My own means . . . are hampered and locked up so as to produce me no income," he admitted to the president, "and I have had to depend upon the exercise of my pen, daily growing more and more precarious, to keep the wolf from the door." If he was unable to find Ebenezer a post, Washington said, "it will be a humiliation that will grind my spirit for the rest of my days."[55]

Irving's investments with Kemble continued to disappoint, and the updates he received from Kemble's agent in the field only confused him in their detail.[56] In April, in dire need of money, he renewed his contract with Clark at *Knickerbocker*, despite being tired of cranking out the miscellaneous letters, essays, and short stories. To his sister Sarah, he confessed that he was worried he might be writing himself out: "God grant me a little longer health and spirit to work, and good will on the part of the public to receive my poor productions, and I will try hard to get once more ahead. I think, as poor Scott said, I have yet a good deal of work in me, though as years gather on, it seems harder than formerly to bring it out."[57]

Between regular walks in the woods near his cottage and his obligations to *Knickerbocker*, Irving spent most of his summer and autumn trying to secure a placement for Ebenezer. Van Buren, however, appeared to have taken Washington's earlier advice to put principles ahead of popularity. By October it was obvious the president was not inclined to provide the requested appointment for

Ebenezer, no matter how much Washington prostrated himself on his brother's behalf.

That was it. Washington Irving was through with Martin Van Buren. Van Buren's conduct, he seethed, "betrayed heartlessness in friendship and low mindedness in politics. . . . Concluding him, therefore, unfit for his high station, I determined to abstain from voting for him."[58] To Irving, family was immeasurably more important than friendship, even when that friend happened to be president of the United States. He publicly threw his weight, and considerable clout, behind William Henry Harrison and his new Whig party in the 1840 election—one Van Buren lost.

The whole incident was distasteful to Irving, and it hadn't resolved any of his problems. He still had family to care for and a cottage to maintain, and the thought of having to continue writing for a living irritated him. He wanted an income independent of the "irksome fagging" of his pen. Worse, his favorite niece Sarah was engaged to marry Thomas Wentworth Storrow's son and would be moving to France. It was an ideal marriage that would unite Irving's family with that of one of his dearest friends, but the thought of losing Sarah, whom he had come to regard as a daughter, was "a bereavement." "How I shall do without her I cannot imagine," he told his sister. "Thus you see, though a bachelor, I am doomed to experience what parents feel, when their children are widely separated from them by marriage."[59]

To supplement his income, Irving published a biography of the Irish writer Oliver Goldsmith for Harper's Family Library series. Irving had taken on the project to pay the bills, and simply revised and expanded the short essay he had written for Galignani's 1825 collection of Goldsmith's work. "He who has to fag his pen for a livelihood has very little inclination to take it up when he is not driven thereto by sheer necessity," Irving said.[60]

He was also at work on a biography of Margaret Miller Davidson, a precocious poetess who had died of tuberculois in 1838 at the age of sixteen. Irving had been casually acquainted with the Davidson family for several years, and after Margaret's death, her mother bundled together various manuscripts and a rough biographical outline of her daughter's life, which she gave Irving in the hope he could shape it into a book. Irving, whose own life had been forever changed by the death of another consumptive young woman, agreed to be her biographer, on condition that any profits from the book reverted to her family. He worked quickly, and in February 1841 he sent the finished manuscript to Lea & Blanchard (now sans Carey), declaring it "deeply interesting and affecting."[61]

In March the short story "Don Juan: A Spectral Research" appeared in *Knickerbocker*. Irving had written thirty pieces in thirty-two months, and with this contribution, his stint at the magazine was over. "I find these monthly obligations to write extremely irksome," he said, but he would miss its regular pay. "I must cast about for some other mode of exercising my pen and making out the expenses of the year," he sighed. "Would that I could throw it by altogether, or at least only exercise it for my amusement."[62]

On March 31 Sarah Sanders Paris—now Sarah Storrow—left with her new husband for France. As Washington feared, her absence devastated him. "I cannot but feel the loss of her constant companionship as a great bereavement, and hardly know how I shall get reconciled to it." For months afterward, he didn't. "Every object," he wrote her sadly, "brings you to mind."[63]

His latest book, *Biography and Poetical Remains of the Late Margaret Miller Davidson*, appeared in June. "I think you will find her biography one of the most affecting things you have ever read," he wrote to his sister. With its sentimental subject and Irving's elegant, sympathetic treatment, it was no wonder the public devoured it. "Did you ever meet with any novel half so touching?" William Prescott asked one correspondent. "How fitting that her beautiful character should be embalmed in the delicate composition of Irving!" Such enthusiasm was welcome, but Irving credited the public's embrace to the subject matter, not his talent. "I do not attribute [its success] to any merit of mine," he wrote, "but to the extreme interest and pathos of the materials placed in my hands."[64]

With *Davidson* done, Irving was without a project. While he continued to draw a regular income from Lea & Blanchard for their exclusive rights to his work, most of his money was still tied up in shaky land speculation. He spurred his pen to write only letters now, exchanging correspondence with long-forgotten friends and sending gossipy missives to Sarah, whom he was encouraging to become a bluestocking. "Do not be careless about your intellectual powers as if not worth cultivating," he told her. "*Believe in yourself.*" In May he sent a warm letter to his old crony Joseph C. Cabell, whom William Irving Jr. had dismissed as a rogue in 1805, and who had since become a cofounder with Thomas Jefferson of the University of Virginia. The letter's most significant detail, however, was in the dateline at the top. Instead of "Wolfert's Roost," Irving had written "Sunnyside Cottage, near Tarrytown." Within two weeks, he simply wrote "Sunnyside."[65]

In his study, Irving regularly read European newspapers and periodicals, among them the weekly *Master Humphrey's Clock*, in which editor and lone contributor Charles Dickens was serializing his lengthy story *The Old Curiosity Shop*. Irving wrote the twenty-nine-year-old Dickens a complimentary letter, expressing his delight with Little Nell (whose unpleasant fate Dickens had yet to reveal) and his overall admiration for Dickens's writing.

Dickens was so flattered, he was nearly speechless. A lifelong reader and admirer of Irving, he had made his first excursion into print with the Irvingesque *Sketches by Boz*, a series of short stories published under a pseudonym. An appreciative letter from Irving was, in the Englishman's opinion, the master blessing the protégé. "There is no living writer, and there are very few among the dead, whose approbation I should feel so proud to earn," Dickens replied. He invited Irving to visit him in London, where the two could stroll the locations Irving had made famous, and described Irving's work in such detail that it was clear Boz was no mere casual fan. "Diedrich Knickerbocker I have worn to death in my pocket," Dickens exclaimed as he concluded his letter. "I have been so accustomed to associate you with my pleasantest and happiest thoughts, and with my leisure hours, that I rush at once into full confidence with you, and fall—as it were naturally, and by the very laws of gravity—into your open arms."[66]

Irving was so taken with Dickens that he did something out of the ordinary with literary correspondents: he wrote back. "In general I seek no acquaintances and keep up no correspondence," he told Dickens, "but towards you there was a strong impulse, which for some time I resisted, but which at length overpowered me." Irving praised Dickens's *Pickwick Papers*, but shrewdly detected that Dickens was already doing something more relevant in his work. "You have proved yourself equally the master of the dark and terrible of real life," Irving wrote. "Not the robbers, and tyrants and villains of high strained romance and feudal times and castellated scenes; but the dangerous and desperate villainy that lurks in the midst of the busy world and besets the every day haunts of society; and starts up the path of the plodding citizen, and among the brick walls of the metropolis."[67] It was an astute assessment of Dickens's work from the writer Poe had derisively tagged as an inoffensive, irrelevant *"quietist."*

Despite his earlier pronouncements about remaining in his native country for the rest of his life, Irving began to feel restless in his own backyard. Increasingly, he considered traveling to Europe—and with Dickens beckoning and Sarah living abroad, the pull was especially strong.

Obligations, however, kept him rooted at Sunnyside. By September he had the company of Ebenezer, who made the cottage his permanent residence after the collapse of his business. The financial yoke was firmly around Washington's neck now. "These cares and troubles bear hard upon the capability of a literary man," he fretted. His moods became erratic; his letters self-pitying one week, apologetic the next. But suddenly, he was writing again, dabbing at his long-forgotten biography of George Washington. The work was in no condition to show anyone, but "the manner in which I have executed it," Irving said, "satisfies me that I have 'good work in me yet.'"[68]

In late October came some good news. "Dickens is actually

coming to America," Irving informed his family, practically bouncing on his seat in anticipation. Dickens, too, was excited about the prospect of meeting Irving in person. "I look forward to shaking hands with you with an interest I cannot (and I would not if I could) describe," Dickens wrote elatedly.[69]

Dickens and his wife, Catherine, arrived in Boston on January 22, their first stop on a tour of the United States that would last until June. Irving met the Englishman in New York several days later and entertained him at Sunnyside. Irving's genuine fondness for Dickens was indisputable—he even agreed to preside over a February 18 dinner in Dickens's honor, an event at which Irving would be expected to make a speech.

Days in advance, Irving prepared lengthy remarks, which he slid reassuringly under his plate as the dinner began. As he rose to make his introductory remarks, the room broke out in applause. Flustered, he made his way through a few halting sentences, then stopped. After a number of feeble attempts, he merely raised his glass and shouted his toast—"Charles Dickens, the guest of the nation!"—then glumly sank into his seat. The pages of the speech sat untouched under his plate. "There," Irving muttered to the guests around him. "There, I *told* you I should break down, and I've done it."[70]

It didn't matter; the crowd loved it, and loudly cheered both writers. Cornelius Felton, later president of Harvard University, sat by Irving that night, and remembered the moment vividly. "It was delightful to witness the cordial intercourse of the young man, in the flush and glory of his fervent genius, and his elder compeer, then in the assured possession of immortal renown."[71]

Where Irving had been awkward, Dickens was dynamic. Laying a hand on Irving's shoulder, he rose and said warmly:

> I came to this city eager to see him, and here he sits! I need not tell you how happy and delighted I am to see him here tonight in this capacity. Washington Irving! . . . When, not long ago, I visited Shakespeare's birthplace, and went

beneath the roof where he first saw light, whose name but *his* was pointed out to me on the wall? Washington Irving— Diedrich Knickerbocker—Geoffrey Crayon—why, where can you go that they have not been there before? . . . who has associated himself most closely with the Italian peasantry and the bandits of the Pyrenees? . . . who embarked with Columbus upon his gallant ship, traversed with him the dark and mighty ocean, leaped upon the land and planted there the flag of Spain, but this same man, now sitting by my side? . . . And what pen but his has made Rip Van Winkle, playing at ninepins on that thundering afternoon, as much a part and parcel of the Catskill Mountains as any tree or crag that they can boast?[72]

The room erupted in thunderous applause.

A few weeks later, the two men prepared to leave New York for Washington, D.C., together: Dickens to continue his American tour, and Irving to do some research at Mount Vernon for his George Washington biography. But Irving had another bit of official business to attend to as well.

"I have been astounded, this morning," Washington had written to Ebenezer on February 10, "by the intelligence of my having been nominated to the Senate as Minister to Spain. The nomination, I presume, will be confirmed. Nothing was ever more unexpected. It was perfectly unsolicited."[73]

It may have been unsolicited, but Irving's vocal break with Van Buren and support for the opposing Whig party likely had something to do with the nomination. Irving's friend Daniel Webster, now secretary of state, had recommended him to President John Tyler—who had assumed the presidency following the death of William Henry Harrison—and the president had submitted Irving's name to the Senate on February 8. "Ah, this is a nomination everybody will concur in!" Henry Clay is rumored to have said. "If the President would send us such names as this, we should never have any difficulty."[74] Irving's nomination sailed through the Senate on February 10.

"I have determined to accept," Washington told Ebenezer. "Indeed, under all the circumstances of the case, I could not do otherwise." He also admitted that the minister's salary of $9,000 had made the offer particularly attractive. On February 18 Irving sent his formal acceptance to Webster and the Senate.

As he journeyed to Washington, D.C., where he would meet with President Tyler and receive further instructions, Irving's emotions were mixed. "The only drawback upon all this is the hard trial of tearing myself away from dear little Sunnyside," he wrote to Ebenezer. The next day he gave his brother the keys to his cottage. "I now abandon the care of the place entirely to you."[75]

Washington Irving was going back to Spain.

14

Minister

1842–1846

It is comforting to think . . . that I have "Uncle Sam" to take care of me, and I hope the good old gentleman will not "let go of my hand" until I am once more able to take care of myself; if that will ever be.

—Washington Irving to Sarah Storrow, November 5, 1842

WASHINGTON IRVING'S OFFICIAL NEW TITLE was an imposing mouthful: Envoy Extraordinary and Minister Plenipotentiary to the Court of Spain. One of America's first formal diplomatic posts, it was the same position that had been occupied by Arthur Lee, Benjamin Franklin, and John Jay as they worked to cultivate Spanish goodwill during the American Revolution. More attracted to the job's salary than its status, Irving looked forward to his time in Spain as more of a paid vacation than a full-time government job. "I shall apply myself steadily and vigorously to my pen, which I shall be able to do at Madrid, where there are few things to distract one's attention," he told Ebenezer, "and in a little while I shall amass a new literary capital."[1]

Before his departure, there were formalities to attend to in Washington, D.C., where Irving reviewed his instructions with Webster and dined with President Tyler. Irving's appointment was hailed enthusiastically by politicians and the public alike, and his presence electrified the city. He was mobbed by fans at a presidential reception and spent more than an hour during an evening walk "penned up against the wall," he wrote, "shaking hands with man, woman, and child from all parts of the Union, who took a notion to *lionize* me."[2]

There was also the matter of choosing a good secretary for the legation, a position Irving knew well from his service at McLane's side. Irving's top pick, Joseph Cogswell, was wooed away at the last minute by John Jacob Astor to assist in building and establishing Astor's newest pet project, the New York Public Library. Irving was embarrassed, as Cogswell's appointment had already been approved by the Senate, but he then recommended Alexander Hamilton Jr., the twenty-six-year-old grandson of George Washington's treasury secretary. It was a controversial choice, given Hamilton's Federalist roots, but Irving pled the young man's case in letters to Webster, Attorney General Hugh Legaré, and the president himself, finally telling Tyler to consider the nomination "as a *great personal favor to myself.*"[3] Hamilton was approved, and departed for Madrid later that spring with another young attaché Irving had picked for the legation, Henry Brevoort's twenty-four-year-old son, Carson.

Irving also had his business affairs, such as they were, to put in order. He left his power of attorney to Pierre, authorizing him to continue to work with Kemble on their land speculations. He also gave his nieces access to his funds, providing each with a yearly allowance of $100, in addition to their continued residence at Sunnyside. However, his most important assets—his writings—were in flux, and required a personal discussion with Lea & Blanchard in Philadelphia. His seven-year exclusive agreement with the publisher was set to expire in mid-1842, and Irving, anxious to have this regular source of income, was determined to negotiate and sign an agreement before he left for Spain.

Irving's first offer—$3,000 annually for exclusive rights to an author's revised edition, plus any new works—was firmly but politely refused by Lea & Blanchard. That was more than twice their current annual payment of $1,150. Citing a "distressed" market, the publishers made a counteroffer of $2,000 for two years of exclusive rights, or $5,000 if Irving wanted to throw in the unfinished *Mahomet* and any other new books he might complete. That offer frustrated Irving. "I am sorry to say your answer to my proposition does not by any means meet my views," he wrote. He asked Ebenezer to continue negotiations on his behalf.[4]

All that remained were the dreaded good-byes. Irving had wept during his farewell to Dickens in Washington, D.C., and had refused an invitation from fifty distinguished New Yorkers for a public dinner in his honor the night before he left for Spain. On the morning of his April 10 departure, he stood on his sister Catharine's doorstep, but the words caught in his throat; he couldn't even raise the knocker. "I reflected that a parting scene would only be agitating to us both," he said. He boarded the ship *Independence* without saying good-bye.[5]

On April 30, after twenty days at sea, Irving landed at Bristol, where he boarded a train to London. His hopes for visiting his sister in Birmingham were delayed by the eager American minister to the Court of St. James's, Edward Everett, brother of Irving's old friend Alexander Hill Everett, who wanted to present his famous fellow minister to Queen Victoria at her May 4 levee. Irving obliged grudgingly; he was already homesick—"looking back," he said, "with an eye of regret to the unpretending quiet of dear little Sunnyside." But he did want to meet the twenty-three-year-old queen, only five years into what would be a sixty-year reign. He was disappointed. "She is certainly quite low in stature, but well formed and well rounded," he wrote. "Her countenance, though not decidedly handsome is agreeable and intelligent." He also noted that her mouth tended to hang open.[6]

Despite "the bustle and agitation of public life," Irving was well received at court, and he gladhanded easily with the diplomatic and royal crowd. He was pleased to see two old acquaintances, Sir Robert Peel—now prime minister—and the foreign secretary, Lord Aberdeen, with whom he and McLane had negotiated in 1831. The three chatted casually of the ongoing dispute between their countries over the northeastern border between

Maine and New Brunswick, which was nearing resolution with the Webster-Ashburton Treaty.[7]

Official obligations completed, Irving made the short train trip to Birmingham. He and Sarah Van Wart, whom he hadn't seen in ten years, "*clasped* in each others arms without speaking," their eyes welling with tears. There had been a similarly emotional meeting several days earlier in London, when Irving had knocked on the door of 50 Albemarle Street. John Murray III, the publisher's thirty-four-year-old son, had escorted Irving into the familiar drawing room where he was reunited with the Prince of Booksellers, bent and crippled with rheumatism and leaning on his butler for support, but still as sharp-eyed and wry as ever. Irving choked back tears, barely able to speak, and was rescued by a sympathetic Mrs. Murray, who swooped in and eased them into conversation. It was their first face-to-face meeting since their estrangement; it was also the last. John Murray II died the following June, aged sixty-five.[8]

After two days in Birmingham, Irving returned to London for a stay at Westminster Abbey as the guest of the Foreign Office. Walking to his room each evening, he strolled through the vaulted passages and long arcades of the cloisters he had written of in *The Sketch Book* a lifetime before. The coincidence was not lost on him. "Am I always to have my dreams turned into realities?" he wrote.[9]

He hoped to enjoy the solitude, but there were too many obligations. He attended the queen's grand ball, considered *the* social event of the year, where he noted that the only person who didn't seem to be having any fun was the young queen, who was constantly pushing her crown up off her forehead.[10]

Irving left for France on May 21, taking with him Hector Ames, a young man he had hired as part of his legation staff and whose sister had married Washington's nephew Irving Van Wart in 1839. He wasn't quite family, but he was close enough.

At Le Havre and Rouen, Irving was overcome with emotion; these were the familiar places he and Peter had strolled, and Washington broke down as he walked through a church garden Peter had frequented. "My dear, dear Brother," he wrote sadly, "as I write the tears are gushing from my eyes."[11] Happier times and new memories awaited him in Paris, where his niece Sarah Storrow and her newborn daughter were ready to receive him.

Once there, the American minister to France, Lewis Cass, enthusiastically took Irving by the hand and steered him through diplomatic circles, proudly presenting him to King Louis-Philippe, whose coronation Irving had witnessed twelve years earlier. The flamboyant young chevalier of 1830 was now a slightly hunched middle-aged man, dressed in simple black clothes and pantaloons, and under constant surveillance after attempts on his life. The ministers and the king spoke mostly of the United States and its relations with Canada, Texas, and Mexico—a discussion that made Irving only more homesick.

Chatting with royalty and dining at fancy diplomatic dinners no longer excited Irving. As he sat at an elegant dinner in one of Paris's fanciest hotels, he could barely stifle a yawn. It was a scene, said Irving, "that would have enchanted me in my greener years of inexperience and romance," but now, "I have grown too wise to be duped by such delusions. . . . It is wonderful how much more difficult it is to astonish or amuse me then when I was last in Europe. It is possible I may have gathered wisdom under the philosophic shades of Sleepy Hollow . . . amidst all the splendors of London and Paris, I find my imagination refuses to take fire, and my heart still yearns after dear little Sunnyside."[12]

Irving arrived in Madrid on July 25 after four hot days of travel. He had arranged to move into the same rooms in the hotel of the duke of San Lorenzo that were being vacated by the previous American minister, Aaron Vail. Irving assumed the lease, purchased all of Vail's furniture, and retained all of Vail's domestic staff. The house was farther from the public walks than Irving preferred, but it was big—"a wilderness of nooks and corners, and dark corners and crinkum crankums, such as abound in old Spanish houses"[13]—and he liked it. It also provided good company, as the other half of the hotel was occupied by the Brazilian resident minister Cavalcanti de

Albuquerque and his American wife, whom Irving quickly grew to adore.

"I look forward to experiencing great satisfaction from the society of the young gentlemen who form my diplomatic household," Irving predicted to his sister. "It really appears to me that I could not have been better off for companions in their relative positions." Irving had known Hamilton for some time—the young man had lived with his parents in Tarrytown, near Sunnyside—and he was pleasantly impressed with Hamilton's drive and ability, calling him "full of life, activity, and intelligence; with great self possession and an excellent address."[14] Well-spoken and good-looking, Hamilton was the ideal right-hand man for Irving's Spanish adventure, filling the same role Irving had played for Louis McLane.

As for Carson Brevoort, Irving was pleased to have him nearby for more than diplomatic reasons. "My heart warms toward him. He seems like a new link in our old friendship," Irving told Henry Brevoort tenderly, "which commenced when we were both his age or even younger, and which I have always felt as something almost fraternal." The final member of his staff, Hector Ames, was "amiable" and "intelligent" but almost frustratingly quiet. "[He] sits in his corner of the carriage and says nothing," Irving shrugged.[15]

As his young charges put the makeshift embassy in order, Irving went to pay his respects to Count Almodóvar, the Spanish minister of foreign affairs. Irving needed an appointment to formally present his credentials to the Spanish government, but he also required some off-the-record advice on how and to whom his official papers should be proffered. It was a touchy issue, reflective of the tumultuous state of Spanish affairs.

In 1842 twelve-year-old Queen Isabella II was queen in name only. She could not formally assume the throne until she turned fourteen, her "age of majority." For the last nine years, the Spanish had clashed bitterly over whether Isabella had a right to rule in the first place. The conflict began in 1833, when the dying King Ferdinand VII, still without a male heir, had issued the Pragmatic Sanction, overturning the Salic law of 1713 that excluded women from the Spanish throne. That had cleared the way for his daughter Isabella, but had infuriated his brother, Don Carlos, who asserted his own right to the throne. For the next seven years, he and his Carlist supporters tried to take it by force.

In the meantime, Isabella's mother, Maria Christina, had been appointed queen regent, ruling Spain on her daughter's behalf—a brief reign that ended ignominiously. Egged on in her opposition to constitutional reforms by her uncle, King Louis-Philippe of France—who had his own plans for the Spanish throne—Maria Christina lost popular support. Fortunately, Isabella had a more devoted follower and defender in the dynamic general Espartero, who engineered the defeat of the Carlists in 1840, and drove Don Carlos out of the country. With the dust of war barely settled, Espartero and the queen regent clashed over politics, and the increasingly unpopular Maria Christina abdicated her regency, abandoned her children, and hurried to exile in France.

A mother deserting her children was bad enough, but the worst was yet to come. In October 1841 angry supporters of the exiled Maria Christina stormed the palace in an attempt to kidnap Isabella and her sisters. A gunfight erupted, but the girls remained safely barricaded in their bedroom with their governess. Espartero dealt harshly with the ringleaders of the attempted kidnapping, and Maria Christina, though declaring she had neither known of nor assented to the plan, remained with her uncle in Paris, stoking further unrest between Spain and France. It was perfectly suited to Irving's sense of the dramatic, and his heart went out to poor abandoned Isabella and her sisters. "Great heavens how much their mother has to answer for!" he wrote to Catharine. "How unworthily she has proved herself of her great trusts!"[16]

"Spain now enjoys a breathing spell," Irving concluded, "and I hope may be enabled to regulate her internal affairs and recover from the exhausting effects of her civil wars." But the drama had created a diplomatic dilemma for Irving and his fellow ministers—namely, when presenting their credentials, who should they consider the official representative of the Spanish government: Isabella, the queen who was not yet of age, or Espartero, the acting regent? Irving's orders from Webster were explicit; he was to present them to the queen. Yet Webster had also advised Irving to "regulate [his] conduct by circumstances." The new French minister, who had insisted on ignoring the regent and going directly to the queen, was rebuked by the Spanish government. The minister left Madrid in an angry huff, threatening to remove the French seal from the doors of the embassy in protest.[17]

Irving consulted with Almodóvar, and on August 1 Irving and Albuquerque—both dressed in full diplomatic uniform—presented themselves at the palace of Buena Vista, home of the regent, credentials in hand. Albuquerque, skeptical of the legitimacy of the regent, yet worried about offending, waited to see what the American minister would do. Irving had no doubt on how to proceed; in his mind, Espartero was the constitutional ruler of the country until the queen came of age. "I do but echo the sentiments of the President," Irving said to Espartero in Spanish, "in accompanying it with assurances of the high respect and regard of my Government, for the Sovereign of this Country; for its political institutions and for its People." With a bow, he laid his credentials in the regent's hands. Irving's words had the desired effect. Impressed, Espartero accepted the papers and welcomed Irving graciously. Following Irving's lead, Albuquerque and other ministers presented their credentials to the regent first.[18]

Escorted by Almodóvar, Irving and Albuquerque were then driven to the royal palace for a conference with the queen. They ascended the grand staircase, still scarred from the assault on the queen's bedroom ten months before—"What must have been the feelings of those poor children on listening from their apartment to the horrid tumult?" Irving shuddered—and waited in the salon until, at last, Isabella stepped into the room. Irving, who had promised to give his nieces detailed descriptions of royalty, sized up the queen carefully: "She is nearly twelve years of age & is sufficiently well grown for her years. She has a somewhat fair complexion; quite pale, with bluish or light grey eyes; a grave demeanor but a graceful deportment. I could not but regard her with deep interest, knowing what important interests depended upon the life of this fragile little being, and to what a stormy and precarious carreer she might be destined." Dressed in black and mourning the recent death of a cousin, Isabella looked to Irving like one of the ghosts he had written of in *Knickerbocker*, "gliding noiselessly like a shadow through the silent and twilight apartments of that great edifice, and looking so pale and almost melancholy!" The queen received him courteously. After a brief audience, Irving bowed and took his leave. He breathed a sigh of relief; it was over. His pragmatic approach had won the approval of both regent and queen, and had put the United States in a favorable light. "I feel installed in my official station and begin to realize that I am actually a Minister," he wrote.[19]

To his surprise, things were so slow during his first weeks in office that Irving was convinced he had landed an ideal post, with good pay, few responsibilities, and plenty of time for writing. "I shall go on with other literary matters that I have in hand, and trust that my present residence in Spain, like my former one, will be highly favorable for the exercise of the pen," he told Catharine.[20] His diplomatic duties consisted mainly of socializing with the Albuquerques, conversing with Espartero's dark-eyed wife—"affable, graceful and engaging," he observed appreciatively—and chumming up to the genial, though somewhat bumbling, Sir Arthur Aston, the British minister.

As he moved within diplomatic circles, Irving was surprised by how many were familiar with his books. "I must say, from every person with whom I have had any intercourse since my arrival I have experienced the most marked respect and cordial good will," he wrote. "All claim me an acquaintance from my writings, and all welcome me as a 'friend of Spain.'"[21] *The Alhambra* was a particular favorite. "I find that little work continually acting as a passport for me to the good graces of the Spaniards," he noted.[22]

Irving received news regularly from Sunnyside, where Catharine had taken over from Ebenezer as head of the household. Washington and his niece Sarah Storrow also began a weekly correspondence. It was hard work for the new wife and mother, who frequently apologized for writing what she was certain were boring letters. "Your letters could not be too frequent for me, nor their contents trivial," Irving assured Sarah. Every Thursday, he looked for a letter from her and sulked if one failed to arrive.

In late summer came word from Ebenezer that attempts to negotiate a continued publishing agreement with Lea & Blanchard had failed. With no American publisher to keep the presses cranking, Irving was in danger of going out of print. He found the prospect depressing. "Everything behind me seems to have turned to chaff and stubble," he confessed to Ebenezer, "and if I desire any further progress from literature, it must be by the further exercise of my pen." Of more immediate concern was the loss of the annual salary the prior agreement had generated. "I find my home resources are drying up in various quarters," he wrote Pierre in a mild panic, and urged his nephew to stabilize his investments. He promised Pierre that as soon as his books arrived in Madrid he would continue work on his biography of George Washington.[23]

In early September Irving and his boys vacated Vail's apartments in favor of the house of the marquis de Mos on Calle Victor Hugo. Leaving the company of Mrs. Albuquerque was perhaps the most difficult part of the move, but Irving wanted to be closer to the public walks and the other legations. The house was enormous—"I have such a range of *salons* that it gives me quite an appetite to walk from my study to the dining room," he joked[24]—but his own octagon-shaped room was cozier than the one in Vail's house, with high windows mounted in a cupola to let in light, and a connected study overlooking a run-down garden.

Despite assurances from Pierre that his finances were improving, Irving fretted about money. The stress made writing difficult, which put him in an irritable mood. An invitation from Sarah Storrow to visit her in Paris was brusquely dismissed. "I require, to get my mind in order, to have it undisturbed by any project of change of place; and to keep it in order, that I should remain on my working ground." But his pen remained stationary, and he was plagued by the fear that he might never write again. "On my contemplated literary campaign depends much of the ease and comfort of my after life," he moaned.[25]

To distract himself, he planned his first diplomatic dinner, which he hoped to host in his new quarters in late September. It would be a small gathering of ten—"a number which, if I can help it, I will never exceed," he declared—but as his first official function as a host, Irving was determined to make a good impression, even as he tried to keep costs down. His experience as the de facto minister in the English legation twelve years prior had taught him that out-of-pocket expenses were unlikely to be reimbursed by the U.S. Department of State, and this time he was determined to keep his own expenses to a minimum. His dinners would be tasteful, but modest. Hamilton set an elegant round table using the silver, candelabras, and good china Thomas Storrow had selected for him in Paris; Irving barked orders at the cook; and painters and masons scrambled to touch up the place at the last minute. To Irving's enormous relief, the evening was a success. "Dinners like this, social, tasteful, yet unpretending I can afford to give with tolerable frequency," he wrote with satisfaction.[26]

Back in Washington, D.C., however, it looked as if Irving had dropped off the map. He had sent Webster three dispatches and one private letter in August, but by his dinner party on September 30 he hadn't written to the secretary of state in more than a month. Webster was understandably curious and had asked one of Irving's nieces about him. Irving prickled when he learned of the inquiry, worried that Webster thought his silence meant he was slacking—which wasn't far from the truth. In a letter to his niece, he responded to the question: "As yet my mission has called for but little exertion of diplomatic skill, there being no questions of moment between the governments, and I not being disposed to make much smoke where there is but little fuel. If any question of difficulty or delicacy should arise, however, I will task my abilities, such as they are, to the utmost, to prevent Mr Webster from finding his confidence misplaced."[27] It didn't take long before Irving proved Webster's confidence in him to be warranted. Within a week, he was writing the secretary a carefully worded dispatch on official issues. Over the next three months, he wrote ten more.

The benevolent ruler of Sunnyside was an indulgent patriarch to his diplomatic family of Hamilton, Brevoort, and Ames. When the boys requested extended leave in October for a five-week trip through the Andalusia region, Irving willingly assented—then spent the next month in "solitary dignity," pacing the empty house like a nervous parent. He had both the quiet and the time he needed to write, but preferred the opera instead.

"I had hoped before this to have become completely launched in my literary tasks," he admitted to his niece in early November, "but some how or other I have not yet been able to enter into them with spirit. . . . It is comforting to think, therefore, that I have 'Uncle Sam' to take care of me, and I hope the good old gentleman will not 'let go of my hand' until I am once more able to take care of myself; if that will ever be." Until the creative spark returned, Irving considered the possibility of issuing an author's revised edition of his complete works, and asked Ebenezer to send copies of all his books. His time for such a project, however, was about to run out; Uncle Sam had need of him.[28]

"For two weeks past," Irving wrote in mid-November, "I have been very much at home, fagging at diplomatic business, having to make researches and treat about subjects quite foreign to my usual range of inquiry." In lengthy dispatches to Webster, he discussed Spain's growing political unrest, addressed rumors regarding the young queen's marriage, and analyzed the latest gossip about Espartero's true ambitions. Irving was that rarest of creatures, a diplomat with a best seller, and his official communications sparkled with thoughtful asides, literary references, and colorful descriptions of Spain's dramatis personae. It was little wonder that Webster immediately put aside all other official correspondence to read the latest diplomatic musings from his minister in Spain.[29]

"The minority of the Queen is made a fruitful Source of political agitation," Irving reported. At issue was the rising tension between Spanish liberals, who were pushing Espartero to adhere to a constitutional amendment preventing Isabella from assuming the throne until she was eighteen, and the Absolutists, who wanted Isabella to assume the throne as quickly as possible. The Absolutists were convinced Espartero wished to delay Isabella's ascendance to extend his own reign as regent and seize control of the government. Irving argued to Webster that Espartero was not that ambitious. "Prone to sink into apathy on ordinary occasions, to let things take their course; and to appear less in intellect than those about him," was Irving's frank assessment of the regent. If Espartero were riled into action, however, Irving assured Webster that it would take merely "the warning voice of the wary Statesman, to keep him from trampling involuntarily over the boundaries of the constitution."[30]

The marriage of the queen, Irving noted, was the country's other "political perplexity." It was rumored that King Louis-Philippe was maneuvering for one of his sons to marry Isabella, while others were arguing for the duke of Seville, or Queen Victoria's cousin Prince Leopold. The queen's mother had other plans, promoting her sister Louisa Carlota's son, the twenty-year-old homosexual duke of Cadiz. "All this would be mere diplomatic gossip, of little interest," Irving concluded thoughtfully, "did not every thing connected with the minority and marriage of the young queen bear upon the vital politics of the nation and affect the future destinies of Spain."[31]

The dramatic affairs of the court Irving could write of with excitement and elegance; economics, however, were another matter. "The statistics of trade about which I have had to occupy myself, are new to me," he groused to Pierre, "and require close attention for a time to master them." He found the topic boring and somewhat irritating. It was too much like going over the business ledgers in Liverpool, though he bragged to Sarah that he felt like "a school boy who has mastered a difficult lesson."[32]

There were times, too, when Irving grew frustrated with the lack of clear instructions from Washington, D.C. His annoyance wasn't so much with Webster, but with the political climate in the

United States, which seemed to encourage the regular rotation of Cabinet officers and government appointees. The lack of stability in the Cabinet and in the State Department, Irving said peevishly, made it difficult for him and his fellow ministers to do their jobs. "To carry on a negotiation with such transient functionaries is like bargaining at the window of a rail road car," he wrote. "Before you can get a reply to a proposition the other party is out of sight."[33] Webster resigned from Tyler's Cabinet six months later.

And there were literary disputes that required his attention. That fall, he was under attack from two different American journals. The first assault, in *Graham's Magazine*, smeared Walter Scott for "puffing" his own writings by inserting favorable notices of his own work in magazines, then splattered Irving by asserting that "Washington Irving has done the same thing, in writing laudatory notices of his own works for the review and like Scott, received pay for whitewashing himself."[34]

The review in question was the one Irving had written in 1830, at Murray's request, to clear the air about the Agapida fiasco in *The Conquest of Granada*. "I never made a secret of my having written that review," Washington told Pierre, and insisted that the article in question was written to be "*illustrative*, not *laudatory* of the work." Pierre was so upset by the attack in *Graham's* that he wrote the editor a blistering note, demanding an apology. The magazine retracted the article in its December issue, and Washington joked that he was relieved the matter had been resolved by Pierre's righteous indignation instead of his own, "so I retained the smoothness of my temper without a wrinkle."[35]

A more serious allegation, however, came from the pages of the *Southern Literary Journal,* in which critic Severn Wallis accused Irving of plagiarizing Navarette in *The Life and Voyages of Christopher Columbus*. It was a malicious charge, with no real merit, and Washington complained bitterly to Pierre of the unfairness of Wallis's claims. Washington had footnoted Navarette liberally in his work, and had publicly acknowledged his debt to the historian. Beyond that, Washington wasn't sure what more he could do. "What I am as an author," he told Pierre, "the world at large must judge. You know what I am as a man, and know, when I give you my word, it is to be depended upon."[36] Washington had no stomach for jumping into such a skirmish; fortunately, his old editor Lewis Clark leapt to his defense in the pages of *Knickerbocker*.

Hurt, though not surprised, by the attacks, Washington blamed the media's need to generate controversy to sell newspapers. "I have been so long before the public that the only way to make anything new out of me is to *cut me up*," he told Pierre with a sigh. Still, he recognized that the scuffle was mostly bluster, and joked to Pierre's wife that he could always argue that critics had him confused with someone else. "I begin to think I'll give out that I am not the Washington Irving that wrote that farrago of literature they are occasionally cutting up," he wrote, "and that I have never followed any line of life but diplomacy, nor written anything but despatches."[37] The literary crisis passed.

His boys returned to Madrid in mid-November, sunburned, healthy, and only slightly disappointed they hadn't been harassed by robbers.[38] He was glad to have them back. Only days later, Irving stood in a long line at the palace with Hamilton, Ames, and the rest of the diplomatic corps, ready for an audience with the queen on St. Isabella's Day. Protocol required that ministers line up according to the length of their service, and after only four months in Madrid, Irving was already third in line, behind the ministers of England and Portugal.

Irving was fascinated by the young queen and appreciated that, despite her constitutional responsibilities, she was still a child. Watching her trying to remember the appropriate responses as she received the long line of somber ambassadors and ministers, Irving could only feel sorry for her. "I had been so interested in contemplating the little sovreign that I had absolutely forgotten to arrange any thing to say," he recalled, "and when she stood before me I was, as usually with me on public occasions, at a loss." He fumbled for words, then turned his sputtering to his advantage. "I expressed my regret that my ignorance of the Spanish language rendered it so difficult for me to address her as I could wish," he told his niece later. The queen smiled, shook her fan coquettishly, and Irving backed out of the room with a relieved bow. He had made an impression.[39]

That winter, the Catalonian region erupted in violence. The dispute was financial—"wherever money is to be made there is a Catalan," Irving remarked—but it was enough to make the leadership in Madrid nervous, and Espartero and his troops marched to Barcelona to restore order. With a constant hail of mortar fire, they pummeled the city into submission, destroying more than four hundred buildings. Even as martial law prevailed in subjugated Barcelona, things were strangely calm in Madrid, where a loyal national guard kept the peace. As he and his boys sipped tea and played backgammon by the fire in their pink-walled salon, Irving dictated long accounts of the action, which Hamilton transcribed as fast as he could into dispatches for Webster.

Irving enjoyed the drama, but his diplomatic duties and their corresponding social obligations were starting to weigh on him. He could sympathize with the queen, who, as she attended yet another royal event, yawned behind her fan as the evening wore on. His official duties left him scant time to write and sapped him of energy. "I have been a little fagged of late by close study of some diplomatic questions, and the preparation of papers and letters for this government and the government at home, and I went to bed rather nervous," he told Sarah Storrow. He was also having nightmares again, something that hadn't happened since the early 1820s, when he had nearly collapsed under the strain of completing *Tales of a Traveller*.[40]

His frazzled nerves didn't escape the notice of his sister Catharine, who expressed concern about him shouldering their family's financial burdens. Irving realized then he had complained too much. "She ought to know that it is this which spurs me on to cheerful activity of mind and body and gives an interest to existence," he said. For all his carping about money and his anxiety over his stalled pen, Irving was proud to support his family:

Had I only myself to take care of I should become as inert, querulous and good for nothing as other old bachelors who only live for themselves, and should soon become weary of life, as indeed I have been now and then, when every thing went smooth with me and I had only to think of my own enjoyment: but I have never felt such real interest in existence, as desirous to live on, as of late years, since my life has become important to others: and I have never felt in such good humor with myself as since I have began to consider myself a "*pere de famille*."[41]

Seeing those words on paper was a release; Irving suddenly began writing again, working with obsessive regularity through Christmas and the new year. Nor did he neglect his official duties—and there was plenty for him to report. Espartero had returned from Barcelona, and his reception in Madrid, Irving wrote glumly, was "rather cold." Irving blamed the media for the public's poor perception of the regent, arguing that the newspapers had used the bombardment of Barcelona to paint Espartero as a bloodthirsty despot. But Irving entertained some doubt. "I am a novice in these scenes of political intrigue and may ultimately discover Espartero not to be the well meaning man that at present I think him," he admitted. "As long as he stands faithfully by the throne of the little queen, who has my strongest sympathies," he concluded, "I shall wish him well."[42]

Irving's pen scratched away, writing his life of George Washington, lengthy dispatches to Webster, and even longer letters to Sarah Storrow. It was a pace that would have worn down even a younger man; Irving's health began to fail. What started as a slight cold gradually worsened. In late February 1843 came collapse. "I have foolishly overtasked myself and must abide the penalty," Irving told Sarah Storrow. The inflammation and herpetic lesions that hadn't bothered him since 1822 returned with a vengeance, covering his entire body with a painful rash. Ordered by his doctor to neither read nor write, he glumly put away the pages of his Washington biography. Even the weight of his clothing was agonizing against his skin. Irving retired to his bed, where he huddled naked under light sheets, issuing orders and dictating dispatches.[43]

It had never been this bad. He lost his appetite, and after being bled by a doctor, could barely sit up. Hamilton attended to him diligently, "with incessant assiduity, and with a womans kindness," Irving told his sister approvingly. "I cannot speak too highly of his conduct."[44] Despite his misery, he remained at his post, and ignored his doctor's advice to leave Madrid for the healing waters of a spa.

Over the next month, Irving sent Hamilton to the shops and cafés in the surrounding neighborhoods to gauge public support for Espartero. The news wasn't good; the regent had little support in the Spanish legislature, but rather than fight for his measures against a hostile majority, Espartero took the drastic step of dissolving the body and ordering new elections. Those elections didn't go his way. Facing an increasingly hostile majority in government and a skeptical public, the regent's hold seemed tenuous—and Irving was anxious to see how it played out. To his disappointment, however, he did so without Brevoort and Ames, who left the legation to return home.

By spring Irving began to feel better. He put on his boots and tramped around in a nearby meadow, though even the slightest effort at writing or bookkeeping inflamed his hands so badly he could hardly hold a pen. Hamilton continued to troll for information on the streets and among the diplomatic corps, then wrote dispatches with Irving late into the evening. Espartero continued to flounder. "I fear that the efforts of his enemies will drive him to the wall," Irving said, "and place him in a position wherein he cannot act constitutionally."[45]

He was right about one thing: the regent's support was gone. By early June, there were revolts and uprisings in nearly every region of the country. A clash between Espartero and his opposition was inevitable, and Irving wondered whether Spain could endure. "If he falls," Irving speculated, "matters will very likely be in a state of chaos and anarchy for a time until a new government is formed." Whatever happened, Irving didn't want to miss a moment of it. "I should be loth to leave [my post] in the present critical state of the Country," he wrote.[46]

He didn't have to wait long. On June 21 the regent held a levee at which he assured the diplomatic corps of his loyalty to the queen and to Spain's constitutional monarchy. Later that afternoon, Espartero and his men rode out for Valencia, vowing to suppress the insurrection there and uphold order. "The political affairs of Spain have gone on from bad to worse," Irving wrote in his official account of the day's events.[47]

With the departure of the regent and his guard from Madrid, two opposing armies angled toward the capital. Madrid hunkered down; its gates were closed and guarded, shops were shuttered, and the city remained lit at all hours. "I was advised not to stir out; as one may get involved in tumults, at such times," Irving said. But the longer he watched the troops outside his window on Calle Victor Hugo, the more frustrated he was at being cooped up indoors. "I could not resist the desire to see something of a city in a state of siege, and under alarm," he confessed to his niece. He leapt into his carriage and drove up and down the Prado, craning his neck out the window like an anxious schoolboy to take in all the excitement. "The houses were illuminated from top to bottom," he reported, "groups were gathered about every door: and troops were patrolling in every direction. . . . I never saw Madrid under more striking and picturesque circumstances."[48]

Over the next several days, as troops drilled and cannons boomed near the gates, Irving wandered the streets on foot, peeking in closed shop windows. With the newspapers shut down during the siege, information was at a premium, so he buttonholed passing soldiers and asked for any details on the approaching armies. Looking out his window at night, he saw bayonets glinting under the streetlights and heard the snap of gunfire. "It has been extremely interesting to me," he wrote.

Had his own government known of Irving's reckless behavior during the siege of Madrid, he might have been recalled out of concern for his own safety. Irving seemed unfazed by the violence around him, but he worried that the encroaching armies might mount a direct attack on the palace to kidnap or kill Isabella. He sent a note to the royal family, offering to bring himself and a number of his fellow ministers to the palace to surround the queen and her sisters in a high-ranking human shield. That offer—which would have alarmed the American government had it known of it—was refused.[49]

In late July came word that two of the regent's generals were riding hard with troops for Madrid to intercept the approaching armies. It was only a matter of time before the inevitable clash, but Irving was denied the dramatic ending. "The question is decided," he wrote glumly to interim secretary of state Hugh Legaré on July 22. "The armies met yesterday morning; a few shots were exchanged when a general embracing took place between the soldiery, and the troops of the Regency joined the insurgents."[50] Just like that, it was over; Espartero was finished. Hearing in Seville of the defeat of his armies in Madrid, the fallen regent went into exile in England.

"All is confusion and suspense here," Irving reported. With Espartero gone, Spain fell into the hands of General Joaquin Narváez and his insurgents, who scrambled to cobble together a new government. Irving held out hope for maintaining the constitutional monarchy, but without Espartero, he was ambivalent. He and the Mexican minister had presented themselves to the new regime in a show of recognition of the legitimacy of the new government, but Irving was skeptical of its success. "Most heartily do I wish, for the sake of Spain, that a government may be formed capable of carrying on the affairs of the nation in a durable and prosperous manner," he wrote to the new secretary of state, Abel Upshur, "but I fear there are too many elements of discord in a state of fermentation to permit such an event."[51]

In August Irving dutifully stood in yet another long line with the diplomatic corps in the royal Hall of Ambassadors as Narváez and the members of the new Cabinet addressed the queen. It was their intent, said new prime minister Joaquín López, to negate the need for a regent by formally declaring Isabella of age on October 10,

1843, her thirteenth birthday. Isabella read her scripted response, and the room erupted in cries of "Viva la Reina!" It was the sort of spectacle Irving normally would have enjoyed, but he was disgusted by the sycophantic courtiers and old nobility who now bowed and scraped before the throne. "It was curious," he wrote caustically, "to see Generals kneeling and kissing the hand of the Sovereign, who but three weeks since were in rebellion against her government, besieging her capital and menacing the royal abode where they were now doing her homage."[52]

The only real question now was, Who would have the queen's hand in marriage? The duke of Cadiz remained the leading candidate, Irving told Upshur in an August dispatch, but there was also speculation the Queen Mother was planning to spirit her daughter away to the Basque region and marry her to one of Philippe's sons. Regardless of the queen's choice of husband, Irving concluded, she was certain to make one or some of the factions unhappy, "and her very throne may be shaken in the violent convulsions which are likely to arise."[53]

His legs started to bother him in early September, and his physician again ordered him to kinder climes to help the inflammation in his ankles. This time, Irving didn't resist. Leaving the legation in Hamilton's capable hands, he rode for Paris and the welcoming arms of Sarah Storrow. Hoping to avoid the society that had bogged down his last visit, he begged Sarah not to let anyone know he was coming. "I come as an *invalid*," he warned her. A week later, he collapsed onto the sofa in the Storrows' apartments, his legs still sore and swollen, but happy to be surrounded by family once again.[54]

Against his better judgment, Irving lingered in Paris for nearly eight weeks. Though largely housebound, he found it impossible to tear himself away from Sarah and her daughter. Yet he knew matters required his attention in Madrid. "Questions may arise," he admitted to Ebenezer, "and claims to sovereignty between warring parties in these revolutionary times, in respect to which I wish to take upon myself the responsibility of deciding." Privately he worried that critics would accuse him of abandoning his post. "The archives of the Legation will testify that the business of the Mission has never been neglected," he fussed to Brevoort, and rightly asserted that he had remained at his post against doctor's orders, even at the expense of his health. "I do not pretend to any great skill as a diplomatist," he said finally, "but in whatever situation I am placed in life, when I doubt my skill I endeavor to make up for it, by conscientious assiduity."[55]

At the end of November, with his legs still aching—and worried that physical inactivity was making him fat—Irving set out for Madrid. "This indisposition has been a sad check upon all my plans," he complained to Henry Brevoort. Between the illness and his diplomatic duties, he hadn't written since January. "A year . . . has now been completely lost to me; and a precious year at my time of life," he wrote. "The Life of Washington; and indeed all my literary tasks have remained suspended; and my pen has remained idle."[56]

He arrived in the Spanish capital on December 1. In his three-month absence, the young queen had been formally declared of age. Irving cautiously reminded the diplomatic corps not to be too dazzled by her title. Ultimately, the queen was still only a girl of thirteen, and he thought it a shame that so young a woman had to "exercise the functions of a Sovreign, while her mind is immature; her character unfixed."[57]

There were changes in his legation; with Carson Brevoort's departure came the arrival of Jasper Livingston. Jasper, the son of Irving's former law teacher, Supreme Court justice Henry Brock-holst Livingston, was another well-spoken young gentleman, cut from the same cloth as Hamilton. "I am altogether much pleased with him," Irving said.[58]

The pain in his legs made it increasingly difficult to perform his duties, but Irving pushed on, hosting a dinner in January 1844 for new diplomats and a few select members of the Spanish nobility. The gathering was a success, but it left him exhausted. "If only I could exercise my pen I should be quite another being," he wrote, "as then, besides being agreeably employed, I should be looking forward to an improvement in my pecuniary means."[59] Burnt out, he requested extended leave from his post in early summer.

Late that winter, in a dramatic turnaround, the Queen Mother decided to end her self-imposed exile in France. In a masterfully choreographed ceremony, the queen and her sister were to ride out to meet their mother on the road just beyond the palace at Aranjuez—and the entire diplomatic corps were expected to be there to witness the reunion. At this point, Irving was nearly crippled, barely able to move much beyond his salon and bedroom. Fortunately, the Albuquerques took pity on him, arranging for several teams of horses to carry him to Aranjuez, and securing him a comfortable room in the house where the diplomatic corps would be staying.

On the day of the event, Irving rode out in a carriage with the Mexican minister, then hobbled downhill on foot to get a good look at what he was sure would be a tearful reunion. He was not disappointed—even the sternest of soldiers "absolutely wept like children"—but he had worn himself out. After standing among the ministers to be presented to the queen, he left early and fell into bed.[60]

In a feeble attempt to regain his spirits, he picked up his pen and made a halfhearted attempt at writing. It was no use. "I have to exercise the pen sparingly, as I find literary excitement produces irritation in my complaint," he told Pierre in disappointment. Under Pierre's careful management, Washington's investments were finally beginning to pay dividends, but Washington remained convinced it would never be enough to unshackle him from his pen. "I do not see any likelihood of realizing Sufficient to enable me to return home and be independent of the fagging of the pen," he said. In the meantime, he was determined to keep his government job as long as he could. "If it were not for *diplomacy*," he admitted, "I do not know what would become of us."[61]

Diplomacy proved difficult, however, when his own government failed to provide him with good information. Called before

Prime Minister Luis Bravo in April 1844 to discuss the fracturing relations between the United States, England, and Cuba, Irving could only stammer out vague assurances. He had been caught off guard by the question, and to his annoyance, most of Bravo's intelligence had come secondhand from the French legation. Part of the problem, as Irving had pointed out a year before, was a lack of constancy in the State Department. It was a fair charge, as the Tyler administration had gone through several secretaries of state. Upshur was Irving's third boss at the State Department in two years, following the resignation of Webster and the death of Legaré in 1843. In February 1844 a freak explosion on board the USS *Princeton* killed Upshur, Navy Secretary Thomas Gilmer, and four others. To fill the vacancy at the head of the State Department, President Tyler lured John C. Calhoun, recently resigned from the U.S. Senate, into the secretary's chair.

Irving was a longtime admirer of Calhoun, but he had grown impatient with the revolving door at the State Department and was in no mood to allow Calhoun time to get up to speed on the issues. His first dispatch to Calhoun started in medias res: "Political affairs here wear a tranquil Surface under the domination of martial law," read the dramatic opening line. He described the growing animosity between General Narváez and Prime Minister Bravo, jealousies in court, and more potential suitors for the queen. Irving again demanded timely direction from the U.S. government. His own want of information, he told Calhoun indignantly, made him look dishonest.[62]

The U.S. secretary of state position, however, was only slightly more stable than that of Spanish prime minister. Shortly after Irving's missive to Calhoun, Bravo's ministry collapsed and Narváez was elevated in his place. Narváez wasn't quite the empty suit Irving had considered Bravo, but neither was he the dynamic Espartero. Irving had already seen so many regents and prime ministers wrecked by the system that it was difficult to muster up much enthusiasm for this one. "I am inclined to think General Narváez honest, though limited, in his political views," was the best he could do. "How long he may continue," Irving speculated, "it is impossible to judge; reverses being so frequent and sudden in this government, where danger always keeps on a par with elevation, and where men apparently rise but to fall."[63]

Irving's presence was regularly required at the royal palace for yet another reception, levee, or birthday party. However, in his condition, standing in the long queue of ministers in the Hall of Ambassadors for hours on end was nearly impossible. While he was waiting for the queen at one ceremony, a court attendant took pity on him and steered him toward a statue with a low pedestal where he could sit until the entrance of the royal party. Unfortunately, once the queen arrived, he was expected to stand for several hours while the long lines of courtiers, clergy, and military filed past the royal family. It was too much; his legs on fire, Irving hobbled out of the ceremony early. He was so embarrassed by his premature exit that he sent the foreign minister an apologetic letter. He was more determined than ever to secure from Calhoun the extended leave of absence he needed to recover his health.

Adding to his misery, in May Hamilton decided to leave the legation and return home. To Irving, his secretary's departure was "a perfect bereavement." Hamilton had been his right hand both in diplomatic and personal affairs, and Irving had come to regard the young man as family. He missed him terribly. "There is an inexpressible loneliness in my mansion, and its great saloons seem uncommonly empty and silent," he lamented to Sarah Storrow. "I feel my heart choking me as I walk about and miss Hamilton from the places and seats he used to occupy."[64]

Jasper Livingston had been cleared by the Senate to take over as the legation's secretary, but Irving's original "diplomatic family"— his boys—were gone. The thought made him long for his own family even more, and his heart ached for the hearth at Sunnyside. He was tiring of Spain:

I am wearied and at times heartsick of the wretched politics of this country. . . . The last ten or twelve years of my life, passed among sordid speculators in the United States, and political adventurers in Spain, has shewn me so much of the dark side of human nature, that I begin to have painful doubts of my fellow man; and look back with regret to the confiding period of my literary career, when, poor as a rat, but rich in dreams, I beheld the world through the medium of my imagination and was apt to believe men as good as I wished them to be.[65]

That spring the queen and her mother went to Barcelona for an extended soak in the baths. Isabella suffered from excessively dry skin, which, Irving said, often made her look "mealy," and required her to seek regular treatment. Gossips whispered, incorrectly, that the queen was making secret arrangements to marry one of Philippe's sons. Irving had initially planned to follow, hoping to learn the real story and lounge in a bath or two, but he changed his mind at the last moment, citing the heat, difficulty of travel, and the expense. At the end of June, however, he received two letters from President Tyler for the queen, one congratulating her on reaching the age of majority, the other offering consolation for the recent death of an aunt. Protocol demanded he deliver them as quickly as possible. More than a little annoyed, Irving set out for Barcelona, four hundred dusty miles away.

Irving had visited Barcelona briefly in 1829, on his way from Granada to London, but he had forgotten just how beautiful it was. Set against the Mediterranean, Barcelona was far more lush than the relatively barren Madrid, with fields of grain and olives stretching to the horizon.[66] It offered good walks, lively cafés, and a respectable opera house—all of which Irving immediately enjoyed. Indeed, the city was so pleasant that after delivering his official correspondence to the queen, he decided to linger, abandoning his small hotel room in favor of the large, comfortable *casa* of Don Pablo Anguera, an associate of Henry Van Wart.

Irving liked Anguera's home, with its painted fresco ceilings and fashionable furniture, but during his month in Barcelona, he practically lived at the opera houses. So did his fellow ministers. "Indeed the theatre is the nightly place of meeting of the diplomatic corps and various members of the Court," Irving wrote, "and there is great visiting from box to box." The July weather was hot, but the breezes off the Mediterranean were cool, and the change in climate did Irving good. His legs were nearly healed, and he strolled daily in Las Ramblas, Barcelona's most fashionable public pedestrian street. He even managed to walk several miles from the mountains back into the city after a dinner at the Brazilian consul's.

He was feeling so good, in fact, that when Calhoun wrote in mid-July granting him a two-month leave of absence, Irving had almost forgotten he had requested it. He admitted to Calhoun that he was "nearly recovered," but never one to look a presidential gift horse in the mouth, hinted that he was "still . . . subject to slight returns of it if I indulge too closely in sedentary and mental occupation."[67] Promising to be back at his post by October, he left Barcelona for France.

Irving spent a week with Sarah Storrow—to his delight, she had given birth to her second child only twelve days before his arrival—then traveled to England for an extended stay in Birmingham, where Sarah Van Wart was recovering from a stroke. "I had anticipated a very melancholy meeting with our dear Sister, expecting to find her a mere wreck," he told Catharine, "but was greatly surprised and rejoiced to find her looking as well as when I last saw her." Still, it was hard to watch as his sister, only three years his senior, was pushed around the gardens in a wheelchair. "I doubt of her ever recovering perfectly," he admitted to Catharine.[68]

Three weeks later, Irving was back in Paris, where his skin condition flared again. He sought comfort at the baths, but his illness kept him confined indoors. "I am stagnant, absolutely stagnant," he complained to Livingston, who was still managing their affairs in Spain. Until Irving recovered his health in Paris, Livingston was in charge in Madrid. "It is a great satisfaction to me to think the Legation will be so well represented," he told the young man warmly.[69]

To his credit, Irving continued to work, reading dispatches

from Calhoun and talking with Ashbel Smith, the minister from the Republic of Texas, about the possibility of the United States annexing Texas. While Smith fretted that he considered annexation unlikely, Irving wasn't so sure. "I cannot persuade myself that the Texians consider the case hopeless," he told Calhoun, especially "seeing the encreasing popularity of the question in the United States."[70] In that, Irving was right; the annexation of Texas had become a defining issue of the 1844 U.S. presidential race between Democrat James K. Polk, who was for the annexation, and Whig Henry Clay, who was against it.

By late November, with his legs mostly healed, Irving was back at his post in time to learn of Polk's narrow victory over Clay. While John Tyler and the president-elect had similar views on Spanish relations, Irving's family worried that he would be replaced by a Polk appointee. Irving tried to reassure them of his confidence in Polk. "From all that I can learn he is likely to make a very good president," he wrote. "He is well educated; of highly respectable talents, experienced in public life, and of most unexceptionable private character." Privately, however, he was worried he might be dismissed before he was ready. "If I am spared in office a year or so more," he wrote, "I hope to get my literary concerns in such a state of forwardness as to be able to return home with the means of providing for those dependant upon me."[71]

In the meantime, he still had the job, and he was determined to make the most of it, hosting three diplomatic dinners in a span of five weeks. As a regular stream of guests enjoyed easy conversation over dinner at his large round table, he soon discovered to his surprise that an invitation to dinner at the American minister's was becoming a mark of distinction among the diplomatic corps. "My dinners are well cooked and well served, and I find have a very good name," he reported proudly. "My invitations certainly are always accepted."[72]

Irving's dinners weren't the only hot ticket in Madrid that winter; grand balls were thrown with almost alarming regularity, each more elaborate than the last as the newly empowered—or, in some cases, reempowered—Spanish aristocracy competed to see who could host the most dazzling event. "I am dissipated *officially*," Irving chuckled, "as I have to attend Court fetes of all kinds, and dinner and balls given by personages in office." He found it all rather boring. "I have grown too old or too wise for all that," he wrote. But he thought some good had come of the hectic social schedule; after being thrown together so often, the diplomatic corps had solidified into a tight circle of friends, meeting regularly for card games and private dinners.[73]

To his surprise, both he and the Spanish people were warming to Narváez. Spanish women liked the general for his good looks, Spanish men admired his fiery temper, and Irving thought him "one of the most striking characters; if not the most striking, that has risen to power in Spain during the long course of her convulsions." He was disappointed, therefore, to find Narváez and the crafty Queen Mother at odds, arguing over the role of the clergy in government and almost everything else. "I look on the position of Narváez as perilous in the extreme," Irving wrote, "and I should not be surprised to see him suddenly toppled down by some unlooked for catastrophe."[74]

Irving was determined to resist the countless invitations that poured into the legation, and by late February 1845 he was writing in earnest. "I continue busy with my pen," he said, "and am happy to find that my literary application is not attended with any return of my malady." It was a relief to be writing again—and with each stroke of his pen, he felt the weight of his government job slowly lifted from his shoulders. If recalled by Polk, he could still write for a living, though the thought of doing so alarmed him. "I used to think I would take warning by the fate of writers who kept on writing until they 'wrote themselves down,' and that I would retire while still in the freshness of my powers," he mused to Sarah Storrow, "but you see circumstances have obliged me to change my plans, and I am likely to write on until the pen drops from my hand."[75]

With spring came warmer temperatures and bluer skies, but Irving kept himself shut in his rooms, working on his book. He had

Livingston for company, but while Irving liked the young man, he hadn't warmed to him in the same way he had to Hamilton or Carson Brevoort. "We live pleasantly together because we do not interfere with one another," he said somewhat brusquely. Not that he needed or even wanted the companionship. He had his muse, he explained to Sarah Storrow, and his memories, to fill the quiet moments: "My life has been a chequered one, crowded with incidents and personages, and full of shifting scenes and sudden transitions; all these I can summon up and cause to pass before me, and in this way can pass hours together in a kind of reverie. When I was young my imagination was always in the advance, picturing out the future and building castles in the air, now memory comes in the place of imagination, and I look back over the region I have traveled."[76]

That April Washington Irving turned sixty-two years old. "I reccollect the time when I did not wish to live to such an age," he wrote reflectively, "thinking it must be attended with infirmity, apathy of feeling; peevishness of temper, and all the other ills which conspire to 'render age unlovely.'" Yet, as he wrote to Sarah with the warm April sunshine streaming into his salon, he was feeling good, even optimistic: "Here my Sixty second birthday finds me in fine health; in the full enjoyment of all my faculties; with sensibilities still fresh, and in such buxom activity, that, on my return home yesterday from the Prado, I caught myself bounding up stairs, three steps at a time, to the astonishment of the porter; and checked myself, reccollecting that it was not the pace befitting a Minister and a man of my years."[77]

In late spring, Isabella and her court departed for Barcelona again, but Irving waited behind, uncertain whether he had official permission from the State Department to follow the queen. Irving wanted explicit authorization for two reasons. The first was purely financial. If the State Department formally permitted him to travel with the court, then he could charge all his expenses to the U.S. government. He had paid for his last trip to Barcelona out of his own pocket, and he didn't want to risk shouldering any further expenses he couldn't recover. The second reason was both personal and political: he was trying to ascertain whether he would be retained by the president. "I observe that Mr Polk is beset by heavy office seekers," Irving wrote to Catharine, "and he will have many important political friends to provide for."[78]

According to the gossip, Irving's recall was imminent. He had sent several dispatches to the new secretary of state, James Buchanan—the fifth secretary Irving served under—none of which had been answered. "This silence makes me think that I am being weighed in the balance," he huffed. Despite the uncertainty, Irving held on to the hope that he would be retained, if only so he could continue drawing his government salary. "I would long ere this have resigned my post and returned to my friends," he admitted to Sarah, "but the constant thought of those I have to provide for, cuffs down my pride, and prevents me from sacrificing, to my independence and my inclinations, a post which enables me to keep my little flock at home in decent maintenance."[79]

Diplomatically, there wasn't much new to report, but Irving continued providing Buchanan with regular updates throughout the summer, perhaps to remind him that, for the time being, he was still the minister to Spain, and he was doing his job. Rumors of insurrection continued, as did the bickering between Narváez and the Queen Mother. Without official authorization, Irving was stuck in Madrid while the court remained at Barcelona. He could only watch and listen, relying on regular reports from other diplomats and any gossip he could glean during his daily walks in the Retiro or from his seat in the opera house.

In August an interesting offer crossed his desk when publisher George P. Putnam, the thirty-one-year-old partner in the New York publishing firm of Wiley & Putnam, asked for exclusive rights to publish anything new Irving might be writing. "I have nothing at present that I am prepared to launch before the public; neither am I willing just now that any of my former works should be published separately," Irving told Putnam. "If, hereafter, I can make a satisfactory arrangement . . . with your [publishing] House, I assure you there is none with which I would be more happy to deal."[80]

To his annoyance, his herpetic condition returned in late September. Frustrated and unwilling to wait for formal leave from the State Department, he sought treatment in Paris, providing Buchanan no solid date for his return, but promising to come back "as soon as I find myself in travelling condition." Throwing his trunks and books into a mail carriage, he left so abruptly that his housekeeper cried inconsolably, convinced he was never coming back.[81]

The journey to France was difficult, and Irving relapsed on his arrival in Paris, requiring several weeks of quiet to recover. His plans to return to Madrid by mid-November were delayed by a diplomatic crisis that required his immediate assistance—but not in Spain. The American minister to the Court of St. James's had specifically requested Irving's presence in London to help negotiate the so-called Oregon question.

At issue was a chunk of land between the Continental Divide and the Pacific Ocean that the United States and Britain had cohabited peacefully for more than thirty years, until recently. The United States asserted a claim for the entire territory, extending the northwestern boundary to the 54 degree, 40 minutes line of latitude. Naturally, the British objected, and were trying to push the boundary back to the 42nd parallel, beyond the Columbia River. The two countries had vacillated between war and resolution. President Polk, who had vowed to address the issue as a presidential candidate, hoped to resolve the matter diplomatically, and had sent to the Court of St. James's an American minister who had already proven himself adept at negotiating delicate issues: Louis McLane.

Irving knew the area in question conceptually—he had stared at enough maps while writing *Astoria*—but that wasn't why McLane was calling on him for help. Nor did he need Irving's assistance in crafting a compromise. Polk was prepared to place the border at the 49th parallel. What McLane required was help selling his compromise, which would entail not just politicking but careful conversation and delicate maneuvering among British ministers, aristocrats, and royalty. Like Polk, McLane knew exactly the right man for the job. Irving set out for London in early January, buying the president time to swagger in his December 1845 message to Congress before sending the McLane/Irving team to manage the situation.

To Irving's frustration, communications with Washington, D.C., remained excruciatingly slow. Polk had been in office nearly a year, but Irving had yet to receive any formal notification of whether he would be retained as minister. He had continued to cash his paycheck without complaint, but he was no longer interested in playing games of political patronage. Polk either wanted him, or he didn't; it was as simple as that. Irving was convinced he would be replaced. At the expense of his friendship with Van Buren, he had stood to be counted with the Whigs in 1840, and the Whigs had since been run out of office by Polk and his Democrats. It was only a matter of time, Irving thought.

Actually, the job was probably Irving's for as long as he wanted it. Irving was a competent minister, and his fame made him a popular member of any president's diplomatic corps, regardless of party. But the silence from Washington, D.C., was deafening—and as usual, Irving assumed that quiet on the part of any correspondent only meant bad news for him. If neither Polk nor Buchanan could decide on his current status, Irving would make that decision himself.

"The time having elapsed which I had allotted to myself to remain abroad when I accepted the mission of Envoy Extraordinary and Minister Plenipotentiary to the court of Spain," began Irving's December 12, 1845, letter to Buchanan, "I now most respectfully tender to the President of the United States my resignation of that post." It was a difficult letter to write, but Irving handled it with his typical elegance. "I am actuated by no party feeling, nor any indisposition to aid in carrying out the foreign policy of the present administration," he told Buchanan, "but solely by an earnest desire to return to my country and my friends."[82] It was done.

On a cold morning in early January 1846, Irving traveled by train from Paris to Le Havre. Two days later he was in London, a city that had lost all charm for him. London no longer belonged to Geoffrey Crayon, who had written of its colorful back alleys and lofty spires a generation before. This was now the London of Charles Dickens, with the chimneys and smokestacks of the Industrial Revolution. Irving thought it "smoky smutty and dismal."[83]

His first morning there, Irving had breakfast with John Murray III and McLane's secretary, Gansevoort Melville, an "intelligent and apparently amiable" young man with an interest in literature. The three chatted about copyright law over their toast, and Irving paged through the first ten chapters of a manuscript Gansevoort's younger brother had written about his experiences as a beachcomber in the South Pacific. Irving "was much pleased" with it, Gansevoort reported excitedly, "declared portions to be 'exquisite,' s[ai]d the style was very 'graphic' & prophesied its success."[84] Murray published young Herman Melville's first book, *Typee*, in February. Just as Irving had predicted, it was a success.

Irving's involvement in the Oregon negotiations was hailed by McLane as a "god send," and his confidence in his former right hand, now colleague, was justified. Irving had lost none of his ability to maneuver through English society, and his literary reputation always helped. As they worked, the two ministers turned a blind eye to British newspapers that agitated for war. "We shall eventually get out of all this quarrel without coming to blows," Irving said calmly.[85]

He was right. His presence alone had been enough to get both sides talking again, and in June the Oregon Treaty—which drew the border at the 49th parallel—was ratified by the U.S. Senate, and signed by President Polk. "I have reason to congratulate myself," Irving wrote later, "that, in a quiet way, I was enabled, while in England, to facilitate the frank and confiding intercourse of Mr. McLane and Lord Aberdeen, which has proved so beneficial to the settlement of this question so that . . . my visit to England was not without its utility."[86]

Irving returned to Madrid in early March, stopping briefly in Paris for an emotional good-bye with Sarah Storrow, and was back at his post on the morning of March 7. He had been away for nearly five months.

All he could do now was wait for his replacement to arrive. He had already arranged for the Albuquerques to take over his apartments on Calle Victor Hugo, and was currently living out of his bedroom. Most of his trunks were packed and stacked around him. His health was excellent; his mood bright.

News of Irving's resignation had rocked the diplomatic corps. Dinners were held in his honor nearly every evening, and Irving ate until he was certain he would burst. He requested a private reception with the queen to pay his respects, and as he walked alone through the empty salons toward the queen's chamber, he felt a strange sense of closure. "I felt peculiar interest in this visit from the idea that I should soon cease to tread these halls forever," he wrote. His conversation with the queen was pleasant, though short. "I was quite struck with the change in her appearance," he said. No longer the girlish twelve-year-old he had first seen in 1842, the fifteen-year-old Isabella "had quite a womanly air," he wrote. "Her complexion was improved . . . and she looked quite handsome, or at least," he added, "the benignant express of her countenance persuaded me to think so."[87]

In April Irving learned that his replacement, North Carolina lawyer Romulus M. Saunders, had been approved by the U.S. Senate and was on his way. He couldn't arrive fast enough. "I am getting tired of courts," Irving wrote, "and shall be right glad to throw off my diplomatic coat for the last time." For the moment, it remained on. That spring the United States and Mexico had gone to war over the annexation of Texas, which had joined the Union in December 1845. Mexico was dear to Irving's heart, and he was sick about the conflict. "I am heartily sorry for it as I fear it is but the beginning of troubles that may shake the peace of the world," he said. He wrote a lengthy letter to the new Spanish premier, Xavier Istúriz, expressing his regret at the conflict, committing a slight breach of protocol, as he had not yet received official instructions from the U.S. government on how to proceed in discussions with Spain regarding the matter. Fortunately, his own views were supported in the official dispatch he later received from Buchanan.[88]

At last, in late July Romulus Saunders arrived to replace him. Rough in dress and even rougher in language, Saunders had a friend and ally in Polk, but not in many others; John Quincy Adams had once referred to him as a "venomous reptile."[89] At this point, it didn't matter to Irving. On July 29 he escorted Saunders to present his credentials to the queen and to deliver his own letter of resignation, making a short speech in Spanish as he announced his recall. "I now take leave of Your Majesty," Irving said with a bow, "wishing you, from the bottom of my heart, a long and happy life, and a reign which may form a glorious epoch of the history of this country." He meant every word. He continued to follow Isabella's career with interest, and shook his head in sad understanding when the young queen finally married the duke of Cadiz in October.

"Thus closes my public career," Irving said, hardly believing the words himself. He had been away from Sunnyside for more than four years. "I shall hail with joy," he had written to Kemble on his departure, "the day that I return to nestle myself down there for the remainder of my life."[90]

That day, at last, arrived. On September 19, 1846, Washington Irving stepped off a steamboat at Tarrytown, only two short miles north of Sunnyside. He was home for good.

15

Icon

1846–1859

Is not Time—relentless Time! shaking, with palsied hand, his almost exhausted hour-glass before thee?—hasten then to pursue thy weary task, lest the sands be run ere thou hast finished thy history.

—*A History of New York*, 1809

"ON MY RETURN HOME," Irving wrote to a Spanish acquaintance, "I found my place very much out of order, my house in need of additions and repairs and the whole establishment in want of completion." If he was to spend the rest of his days at Sunnyside, he would make sure it was not only as comfortable as possible, but large enough to contain the ever-expanding inventory of nieces, nephews, and their families. New rooms on the second floor had ample closet space and easy access, while a "picture gallery" with portraits of friends and engravings from his books was created at the rear of the house. Irving also installed a new convenience, a bath-room—which, as its name implied, was simply a room with a bath—with a zinc-lined tub to which hot running water was piped in from behind the kitchen stove.[1]

He was most pleased with the addition of a three-story tower at the northeast corner of the house, with four bedrooms for servants or overflow guests. Irving had dictated his vision for the structure to his patient architect, George Harvey, and workmen labored for seven months, digging stone from the nearby hillsides to use on the building's exterior. With its curving roof and cupola, his tower resembled those of the Alhambra and other Spanish castles. Kemble, though, whose first glance at the tower came from a boat on the Hudson, thought it looked like a pagoda. The name stuck.[2]

So far, Irving had managed to keep costs for recent renovations to Sunnyside under control—"[they] will not be expensive enough to ruin me," he said optimistically—but with his government post resigned, he no longer had a regular source of income. He was still planning to issue an author's revised edition of his works, provided he could find a publisher. Unfortunately, Lea & Blanchard wasn't interested in paying his asking price. Negotiations continued halfheartedly, with Wiley & Putnam and several others hovering nearby in case relations soured. But at the moment, building Sunnyside was much more enjoyable than writing or discussing contracts. "I am growing a sad laggard in literature," Washington admitted to Pierre. "I am too ready to do anything else rather than write."[3]

Fortunately, a number of Washington's investments were slowly paying dividends. In January 1847 Pierre passed on to his uncle the profits from an investment in the Screw Dock Company— "In faith, the Dock deserves its name!" Washington chortled— which were immediately spent on improvements to Sunnyside, including repairs to the kitchen yard, stable, and barnyard north of the house. "I know I am 'burning the candle at both end' this year," he told Pierre sheepishly, "but it must be so until I get my home in order, after which expenses will return to their ordinary channel, and I trust my income will expand, as I hope to get my literary property in a productive train."[4]

With an eye on the bottom line, Pierre continued to push his dithering uncle. "Make all dispatch with the preparation of your uniform edition," he advised, "and then to work to complete your Life of Washington, and take your ease forever after." But even gentle pressure was too much for the sixty-four-year-old Washington's increasingly fragile nerves; within a week, his legs and ankles were inflamed and swollen. While he blamed his condition on standing in wet January weather to oversee final work on the pagoda, the timing of the attack suggests a case of nerves. The condition spread to his face and eyes, and Washington feared he might be stricken blind. "That has passed away," he wrote in relief in mid-February, "and you cannot think what a cause of self-gratulation it is to find out that I am only lame."[5]

Even with the money coming in from his investments, Irving knew he needed a more stable source of income. But he seemed stalled on both his author's revised edition and his George Washington biography. As was now his habit when he needed money and inspiration, Irving opened his trunks and rummaged through abandoned manuscripts. There were a number of incomplete Spanish tales, "which had lain for years lumbering like rubbish," but which, with a little polishing, "will more than pay the expense of my new building."[6]

Skeptical, Pierre encouraged him to keep working on his author's revised edition. "You lost the *Conquest of Mexico* by not acting upon the motto of *Carpe diem*," Pierre scolded, "and I am a little afraid you may let slip the present opportunity for a favorable sale of a uniform edition of your works, by suffering your pen to be diverted in a new direction."[7]

Pierre's lecturing only annoyed Washington. "Don't snub me about my late literary freak," he snapped. "I am not letting my pen be diverted in a new direction. I am, by a little agreeable exertion, turning to account a mass of matter that has been lying like lumber in my trunks for years." For several weeks Washington scribbled at various Spanish chronicles before finally putting them aside. Most were still incomplete, but he felt he had made his point. "I write for pleasure as well as profit," he huffed to Pierre, "but another time will ride my hobby privately, without saying a word about it to anybody."[8]

Pierre apologized, and Washington knew he had overreacted; Pierre, after all, was only looking out for his uncle's financial independence. "Tell him not to be uneasy," he told Pierre's wife reassuringly, and extended an invitation to Pierre to visit him at Sunnyside.

"Tell him I promise not to bore him about literary matters when he comes up," Washington said, "but I want to have a little talk with him about stocks, and rail roads."[9]

For all of Washington's gruffness, he knew Pierre was right; money was an issue. The renovations at Sunnyside were nearly complete. He was delighted with the result—"the additions and alterations have turned out beyond my hopes," he told Sarah—but everything had cost more than he had anticipated. "I am now living at the rate of twice my income," he admitted, "and until I can get my literary property into productive operations I must continue from day to day to grow gradually poorer."[10]

With financial pressure mounting, he still suffered from writer's block. Instead, he tramped around his new farmyard that summer, giving directions to his laborers, and standing for so long that he eventually collapsed with inflamed legs. He retired to Sunnyside's western piazza and sat in his comfortable Voltaire chair, waving at the yachts on the Hudson, dozing over books, and receiving countless guests. "I am a complete rustic," Irving said of himself in the autumn of 1847. "Live almost entirely at home; have not slept but twice from under my own roof for eight months past. . . . I am surrounded, however, by my family of nieces, who are like daughters and most affectionate daughters to me."[11]

Gradually his motivation returned, and he went back to work on his life of George Washington, immersing himself so completely in the project that even offers to discuss his revised editions with interested publishers were ignored. "I have not time to turn these matters over in my mind," he told Pierre, and headed for New York City to bury himself in Astor's library.

His week of research and writing at Astor's stretched to two weeks, then a month, then three. The careful balance of work and New York society, he told his niece, "has had a good effect on me in every way. It has rejuvenated me, and given such a healthful tone to my mind and spirits that I have worked with greater alacrity and success." While his own health was good, Astor's wasn't. "He is very much bowed down and almost helpless," Irving said. "He speaks so low that it is difficult to hear him." On the morning of March 29, 1848, John Jacob Astor, the richest man in America, died at the age of eighty-four.[12]

Irving served as one of Astor's pallbearers, helping lay him to rest in the Trinity Churchyard Cemetery on the west side of Manhattan. Irving was also asked to serve as one of six executors of Astor's will, overseeing the legalities of a fortune that exceeded $20 million. Irving's choice as an executor was based on friendship more than legal ability; out of deference to his late friend, Irving accepted the responsibility—and its generous pay. Up to this point, he had refused any money from Astor; his only profits from *Astoria* came from sales of the book, not from Astor's wallet. That, however, was literature; this was business—and Irving allowed himself to be paid a professional fee for his legal services, receiving $10,592.66 from Astor's estate, more than a quarter of a million dollars today. Irving kept that figure private, but tongues flapped with rumors—and the loudest voice of all was James Fenimore Cooper's. "To-day, J. J. Astor goes to the tomb," Cooper snarled. "Irving is an executor, and report says with a legacy of $50,000. What an instinct that man has for gold!"[13]

Cooper was mistaken, but Irving let him grumble; his affection for Astor was genuine. "I never came under a pecuniary obligation to [Astor] of any kind," he later wrote. "My intimacy with Mr. A was perfectly independent and disinterested. . . . He was altogether one of the most remarkable men I have ever known."[14]

Irving lost another friend later that spring, this one the dearest of all. On May 17 Henry Brevoort died in New York City at age sixty-six. He was only a year older than Irving.

We can only imagine how Brevoort's death affected Irving. There is not a single letter regarding Brevoort's death, or any correspondence in which Irving recalls his friendship with the man he had adored the most throughout his life. In fact, no correspondence at all exists between the dates of May 5, 1848—perhaps the time Irving learned of Brevoort's failing health—and May 30, a week after Brevoort's funeral at which, we know from Philip Hone's diary,

Irving served as a pallbearer. Indeed, the only direct reference we have to Brevoort following Irving's return from Spain in 1846 is an 1848 letter seeking to fill Brevoort's vacant seat on the board of trustees for the Astor Library.[15] Given that the 1838 death of his brother Peter had resonated in Washington's letters for years, as had the marriage and subsequent absence of his niece Sarah Storrow, Irving's silence regarding Henry Brevoort is deafening. It is as if any mention of Brevoort had been purged deliberately from Irving's voluminous correspondence—an undeserved fate for an intimacy that spanned five decades.

By the time of Brevoort's death, Irving had been in New York City for nearly five months. His nieces provided regular updates on work at Sunnyside, and to his disappointment, another problem surfaced that he simply couldn't build around or clear away. The Hudson River Railroad had made its way up the east bank of the Hudson, giving New Yorkers a convenient mode of travel from the city to the upper Hudson valley—and it ran right through Irving's riverfront property, less than one hundred yards from his front door. The scenic vista between his house and the river was ruined, as were the silence and solitude. "If the Garden of Eden were now on Earth, they would not hesitate to run a railroad through it,"[16] Irving groaned. A portion of his precious riverfront property was filled, tracks were laid, and Irving received a settlement of $3,500. Irving and the railroad had an uneasy relationship. He regularly complained about engineers blowing their train whistles as they pointed out Sunnyside to their passengers, but he had to admit that it made commuting to New York City or to Kemble's place in Cold Spring Harbor much more convenient, especially as the station was only a ten-minute walk from Sunnyside.

Irving was involved in another negotiation that summer, with happier results. On July 26, after four months of intense discussions, he and Putnam signed a contract granting Putnam exclusive rights to all of his works, to be published in a uniform author's revised edition. The agreement was an unusual one for its day, in that Irving received regular royalty payments of 12.5 percent of the retail price of every book sold, with a guarantee of $1,000 the first year, $1,500 the second year, and $2,000 annually in years three through five. That gave Irving at least $8,500 over the next five years, an agreement the financially skittish writer found especially attractive. "I trust," he wrote with relief, "through my arrangements with my bookseller and further exercise of my pen in completing works now nearly finished, I shall make my income adequate to my support."[17] That was an understatement; over the first few years of his agreement with Putnam, Irving earned about $9,000 annually, roughly a quarter of a million dollars today.

With contract in hand, Irving had to revise his books—a process he didn't relish. Fortunately, he had made significant headway on A History of New York, and was working regularly on several others. On September 1, only six weeks after signing the agreement, Putnam released A History of New York as the first volume of Irving's Author's Revised Editions.

Knickerbocker hadn't been revised since 1829. Irving had mellowed over the intervening two decades, and for the 1848 edition, he thought Diedrich Knickerbocker should do so as well. Out went the anti-Jeffersonian sentiment that had given Knickerbocker his bite and some of his biggest laughs, but which Irving found both dated and out of step with the more gentlemanly reputation he had cultivated in the forty years since Diedrich's first appearance. He had "softened a good deal that was overcharged," he told Pierre, "had chastened the exaggerated humor of some portions . . . and tempered the rawness of other parts without losing any of the raciness." It wasn't quite the same book, but it didn't matter. After six years of being out of print, a new edition of Diedrich Knickerbocker was available again, and the public devoured it. Critics in particular were delighted with the elegant format. "If any works of our language are worthy of such choice embalming, and such an honored place in all libraries as these volumes are destined to fill," said one critic, "it is those of Washington Irving."[18]

He was a hit all over again; demand sent Knickerbocker back for a second printing in less than six weeks. In the meantime, Putnam had issued the revised edition of *The Sketch Book* to equal acclaim. If Irving hoped the revised editions would help secure his literary reputation, he needed look no further than the reviews for his most popular work. "Washington Irving's name is uppermost in our thoughts when speaking the claims or recounting the successes of American authorship," hailed the *Evening Post*. Another review was more direct: "Few single works have attained a wider influence, or a more enduring fame." Sales of *The Sketch Book* exceeded even Putnam's expectations, with 7,000 copies sold within three months.[19]

From the autumn of 1848 through the spring of 1849, Irving labored at *Columbus, Bracebridge Hall,* and *Astoria* almost as fast as Putnam could publish them. Meanwhile, he continued work on his life of George Washington and the Muhammad biography he had shelved in 1831. Making things even more frantic, Astor's will had not only made him an executor of the estate—a task Irving still struggled with—it had also appointed him one of the lead members of the committee overseeing the establishment of the Astor Library. It was all enormously hard work, and Irving was sagging. "I have had more toil of head and fagging of the pen for the last eighteen months than in any other period of my life," he said, "and have been once or twice fearful my health might become deranged."[20]

He put everything aside to devote the summer months almost exclusively to writing a new volume for the Putnam collection, *Oliver Goldsmith: A Biography,* which Putnam published in August. It wasn't quite a new Irving book—he had expanded a biographical sketch he had written for Galignani in 1825 and revised in 1840—but it was eagerly anticipated and enormously well received. "If there is anybody of whom it could be said that it was his duty to write a Life of Goldsmith, it is Washington Irving," observed the *Christian Review*. "None but a man of genial nature should ever attempt to write the Life of Goldsmith: one who knows how much wisdom can be extracted from folly; how much better for the heart it is to trust than to doubt."[21] Geoffrey Crayon, the critics bubbled, had not lost his touch.

Goldsmith's success, however, came at a price. Irving was exhausted. Putnam, dazzled by the potential profits from another new Irving work within the year, pushed him to complete *Mahomet* as quickly as possible. Irving had none of it. "I . . . am not yet in a mood to take up my pen," he griped to Pierre, "so Mr. Putnam must stay his stomach with Goldsmith a little longer." Despite his grumbling, he managed to complete the first volume in time for Christmas 1849 sales, and Putnam's instincts proved correct; readers were positively giddy with anticipation for Irving's newest book. "The life of Mohammed by Washington Irving!" exclaimed the *United States Magazine*. "What visions of delight flood the mind at the thought!"[22]

The first major biography of the Prophet to be written by an American, *Mahomet* straddles a fine line between fiction and biography—and some critics were uncertain what to make of it. "As a chapter of history it falls below the dignity and weight of the subject," wrote the reviewer in the *Literary World*. "It is painted in water colors, while it should be cast in bronze. . . . But that Washington Irving should have made it interesting as a Fairy Tale . . . is a fault of his genius only, and, our readers will agree, a pardonable one." Irving followed this volume four months later with *Mahomet and His Successors*, another popular success that met with similar head-scratching from critics. "Mr. Washington Irving is a pleasant writer," said the *Christian Observer*, trying its best to remain positive, "but not, we think, a very deep or acute thinker. . . . We do not think that Islamism is a subject altogether adapted to Mr. Irving's cast of mind."[23]

The healthy sales of *Mahomet* and other volumes of Irving's revised editions did not go unnoticed by John Murray III, who already owned the English rights to most of Irving's work and now expressed an interest in publishing the revised editions in London. There was only one problem: Irving's revised editions were already being published in England, albeit illegally, by Henry Bohn, in cheap, briskly selling volumes. Bohn's shady justification for poaching on Murray's English rights was that Irving was an American citizen, and therefore not entitled to the protection of British copyright law. Murray sued Bohn and, in a unique defense, argued that since Irving was of Scottish heritage, he was therefore an Englishman and entitled to British copyright protection. Murray even offered to pay Irving's way to London to testify in court, an offer the writer gruffly declined, though he provided Murray with a detailed Irving family genealogy to help the publisher make his case. Murray and Bohn eventually settled, with Bohn purchasing a number of Irving's British rights from Murray for 2,000 guineas. That was fine by Irving; he had no financial stake in the squabble. Further, had the story been picked up by the American press, he did not want it to appear that he had claimed to be an Englishman. "I have no idea of compromising my character as a native born and thoroughly loyal American citizen in Seeking to promote my pecuniary interests," he warned Murray.[24]

By 1850 Putnam had published most of Irving's literary catalog. *The Alhambra* and *Granada* were the only remaining titles to be released, but after the rapid pace of 1849—when Putnam was releasing the revised editions as quickly as one book a month— Irving was exhausted. "I don't think in the whole course of my literary career I have been such a slave to the pen as for the last eighteen months," he wrote in February. As he feared, his health weakened, and he spent the spring and early summer months trying to shake a fever that left him racked with chills and unable to sleep. For a moment, he feared he might not recover and made out his will. Then, slowly, he regained his strength. "I find I do not rally from any attack of the kind so Speedily as I used to do," he told Sarah apologetically. The revised editions were put aside, and Irving devoted the rest of the year to catching up with loved ones.[25]

Still, finding the time to write letters was difficult. There were lengthy communications from family, friends, and colleagues, but Irving's fame also brought a new kind of correspondence that required his attention: fan mail. As the nation's most famous author, he received bundles of mail from admiring readers, as well as countless manuscripts from published and unpublished writers, each begging for a word of encouragement—or, at the very least, an autograph. "Every letter to be answered is a trifle," he explained wearily "but your life in this way is exhausted in trifles."[26]

For all his complaints, Irving was serious about his correspondence. Many of his letters of 1851 open with an apology for the delay in his response, but he made a point of answering them all as quickly as he could, scrawling thank-you notes, short comments, or words of encouragement to almost every aspiring poet, playwright, and novelist who sent their work. It was then only fitting that *Harper's New Monthly* dubbed Irving, "The patriarch of American Letters" in its April 1851 issue.

Irving eased back into writing that spring, and the revised editions of *The Alhambra* and *Granada* finally made their way into print in the summer of 1851. Putnam's volumes were continuing to earn a small fortune for both publisher and author, but Irving was coming to regard them as a distraction. What he really wanted to do was focus on his George Washington biography. For much of the summer, he remained at Sunnyside, poring over copies of Washington's letters and papers, writing steadily and almost merrily. "I am always happiest when I have a considerable part of my time thus employed," he told Sarah, "and feel reason to be thankful that my intellectual powers continue capable of being so tasked."[27]

His solace was interrupted in mid-September by the death of James Fenimore Cooper. "A shock," Irving said, "for it seems but the other day that I saw him at our common literary resort at Putnam's . . . apparently destined to outlive me, who am several years his senior." Despite their strained relations—which Irving always insisted was all on Cooper's side—Irving remained a fan of Cooper's writing. "His works form an invaluable part of our literature," he told Lewis Gaylord Clark. "When an author is living, he is apt to be judged by his last works. . . . When an author is dead, he is judged by his best works, and those of Cooper excited enthusiasm at home and applause throughout the world." Irving, whom Cooper had labeled a "double dealer" and "below the ordinary level, in moral qualities," graciously agreed to serve as the head of the committee that prepared a memorial and dinner in Cooper's honor.[28]

Delays postponed the Cooper dinner until February 1852, when the event finally took place at Metropolitan Hall in New York, with Irving serving as cochairman alongside William Cullen Bryant and Daniel Webster. Irving was the first to speak and, typically, stumbled through his remarks—"the pangs of delivery were awful," he admitted.[29] He finally turned over the floor to Bryant, who spoke at length on Cooper's life and works, raising eyebrows only when he mentioned "an unhappy coolness that had existed" between Irving and Cooper. That was a story Irving hoped to keep out of the newspapers.

There was no such animosity, either real or imagined, between Irving and another popular American writer, Nathaniel Hawthorne. Irving knew Hawthorne largely through his work—the two had never met—and admired both the man and his books enormously. After receiving an advance copy of *The Wonder Book* from Hawthorne in early 1852, Irving sent his colleague a genuinely appreciative note. "I prize it as the right hand of fellowship extended to me by one whose friendship I am proud and happy to make," he wrote, "and whose writings I have regarded with admiration as among the very best that have ever issued from the American press."[30]

The feelings were mutual. Several months later, Hawthorne sent to Sunnyside a copy of *The Blithedale Romance* with what could only be called a fan letter:

I beg you to believe, my dear Sir, that your friendly and approving word was one of the highest gratifications that I could possibly have received, from any literary source. . . . Pray do not think it necessary to praise my "Blithedale Romance." . . . From my own little experience, I can partly judge how dearly purchased are books that come to you on such terms. It affords me—and I ask no more—an opportunity of expressing the affectionate admiration which I have felt so long; a feeling, by the way, common to all our countrymen, in reference to Washington Irving, and which, I think, you can hardly appreciate, because there is no writer with the qualities to awaken in yourself precisely the same intellectual and heart-felt recognition.[31]

In early 1852 Irving continued work on the Washington biography with a new intensity, but his health was suffering, especially after a fall from a horse. That kind of abuse was hard on a man nearing seventy years, but Irving pressed on. He told Sarah Storrow, "I never fagged more steadily with my pen than I do at present. I have a long task in hand, which I am anxious to finish, that I may have a little leisure in the brief remnant of life that is left to me. However, I have a strong presentiment that I shall die in harness; and I am content to do so, provided I have the cheerful exercise of intellect to the last." He couldn't keep it up for long. "My Life of Washington lags and drags latterly," he complained in May. So, too, was he. Irving's position on the board of trustees for the Astor Library required him to spend much of his time that autumn shuttling between Sunnyside and New York City, and constant travel wore him out. He was ill again with the old "bilous attacks," and his mind was unfocused. "I no longer dare task it as I used to do," he told Sarah Storrow. "When a man is in his seventieth year, it is time to be cautious."[32]

In January 1853 John P. Kennedy, newly installed as President Fillmore's secretary of the navy, invited Irving to Washington, D.C.—a useful diversion, as he planned to plumb the State Department archives for materials for his book. On January 16, after waiting out a heavy snowstorm, Irving was on a train to D.C. "Whom should I see," he wrote, "but Thackery." The English novelist William Makepeace Thackeray, still basking in the success of *Henry Esmond,* was en route to Philadelphia on a speaking tour of the United States. The two writers "took seats beside each other in the cars," Irving wrote, "and the morning passed off delightfully."[33]

Irving's trip to D.C. was less productive than he had hoped. His first visit to Mount Vernon, in the company of some of President Fillmore's family, was more pleasure than business. That same evening he attended a White House reception for the president, where his presence created a sensation. "I had to shake hands with man woman and child who beset me on all sides," Irving groaned, "until I felt as if it was becoming rather absurd." The local press reported Irving's embarrassment with a smile. "[Irving] certainly is the best read man in our country, and deservedly the most esteemed," said a Baltimore newspaper. "The happiness of having pressed his hand will be among the cherished recollections of the hundreds who clustered around him at the President's reception."[34]

Newspapers hailed Irving as "the lion of the literary world," but he found the responsibilities associated with the moniker exhausting. "My good sir, theres not a roar left in me," he wrote to one correspondent in February. "I am the tamest most broken down lion that ever was shewn in a menagerie—not even to be stirred up with a long pole." Any opportunities for research were crammed between social obligations that, even at the White House, were "tedious."[35]

Irving remained in Washington long enough to see Franklin Pierce sworn in as the fourteenth president. As Irving stood on the marble terrace of the Capitol, shivering in the snow beside Mrs. Fillmore, he was struck by the symbolic elegance of the ceremony. "It was admirable to see the quiet and courtesy with which this great transition of power and rule from one party to another took place," Irving wrote. "I . . . have seen the two Presidents arm in arm, as if the sway of an immense empire was not passing from one to the other." He had only chatted casually with Pierce, but he liked what he saw. "He is a quiet, gentleman like man in appearance and manner," he said, "and I have conceived a goodwill for him, from finding, in the course of our conversation, that he has it at heart to take care of Hawthorne, who was his early fellow student." A classmate of Pierce's at Bowdoin College and a close friend since, Hawthorne's active support for Pierce earned him an appointment as consul to Liverpool—"a lucrative post," Irving noted.[36]

Irving bid good-bye to the Kennedys, signed an autograph for Fillmore's starstruck daughter, then headed back to New York. Stepping off the train at the Dearman station, he walked toward Sunnyside, where his nieces were clustered on the piazza, watching for him through a spyglass. "Uncle Wash" was ushered into his parlor and gently lowered into his Voltaire chair. The Squire of Sunnyside was home.

On April 3, 1853, Washington Irving turned seventy years old. His health was satisfactory, but he considered his age pragmatically:

> I have reached the allotted limit of existence—all beyond is especial indulgence. So long as I can retain my present health and spirits, I am happy to live, for I think my life is important to the happiness of others; but as soon as my life becomes useless to others, and joyless to myself, I hope I may be relieved from the burden; and I shall lay it down with heartfelt thanks to that Almighty Power which has guided my incautious steps through so many uncertain and dangerous ways, and enabled me to close my career in serenity and peace . . . in the little home I have formed for myself, among the scenes of my boyhood.[37]

By late May, however, he was ill again, which forced him to abandon work on his biography. "In sober sadness I believe it is high time I should throw by the pen altogether," he said sadly, "but writing has become a kind of habitude with me. . . . It is pretty hard for an old huntsman to give up the chase."[38] But he worried that his abilities might be deteriorating with age. Nervously, he bundled his manuscript pages, handed them to Pierre, and paid Kennedy a visit in Maryland.

For weeks, as Irving and Kennedy lounged in the sun at the latter's country home in Ellicott's Mills, or dallied at tenpins at Berkeley Springs, Pierre patiently read the manuscript at Sunnyside. "Familiar as I am with the story, I have been equally surprised and gratified to perceive what new interest it gains in your hands," he wrote his uncle enthusiastically. "I doubt not the work will be equally entertaining to young and old." Washington was enormously pleased. "I now feel my mind prodigiously relieved," he replied, "and begin to think I have not labored in vain."[39]

Irving had concluded his manuscript with George Washington's inauguration as president, and was convinced the work was finished. He soon decided that it wasn't. On his return to Sunnyside in July, however, he felt that the intensive writing of the past several months had given him a "weariness of the brain." What he really needed, he said, was "a good spell of *literary abstinence*."[40]

Off he went to Lake Champlain and Ogdensburg—the very place he had visited with Judge Hoffman fifty years before on his first real excursion into the wilderness. Where there had been only forest, there were now villages and small towns. "All was changed,"[41] Irving observed wistfully.

Stopping by the riverbank where he had launched a canoe fifty years earlier, old faces and adventures swam before him: "I sat for a long time on the rocks summoning Reccollections of byegone days and of the happy beings by whom I was then surrounded—All had passed away—all were dead and gone; of that young and joyous party I was the sole survivor—they had all lived quietly at home out of the reach of mischance—yet had gone down to their graves—while I, who had been wandering about the world, exposed to all hazards by sea and land—was yet alive. It seemed almost marvelous." There was no sadness in the observation, only quiet acceptance. At seventy, Irving had a healthy respect for his own mortality, and in September 1853 he had chosen a burial site on the southern slope of a hill in Sleepy Hollow Cemetery, overlooking the Old Dutch Church. His interest in the cemetery went beyond the literary; when Tarrytown planners had proposed naming the burial ground "Tarrytown Cemetery" in 1849, Irving had immediately informed them of their error and suggested "Sleepy Hollow Cemetery" instead. It was *his* cemetery, among the very places he had made famous. He had the remains of other family members moved to his chosen site, built an iron railing around it, and marked his burial space next to his mother. He was ready.[42]

Irving settled back into Sunnyside for the winter, overseeing the final touches on a cottage he was building for his gardener, as well as other "unprofitable improvements" to his property. "A pretty country retreat is like a pretty wife—one is always throwing away money in decorating it," he said with a twinkle. "Fortunately, I have but one of those two drains to the purse, and so do not repine." All invitations that winter were refused in favor of the company of his nieces. "How can I tear myself from them?" Irving asked. "Domestic affection forbids it!"[43]

His main diversion in the spring of 1854 was "dipping into town occasionally to pass a few hours at the Astor library, but returning home in the evening." With the speed and convenience of train travel making such trips easy, Irving had become America's first literary commuter.[44] Only now the sign at the train station near Sunnyside no longer read "Dearman." That April the citizens of Dearman had chosen to rename their town in honor of their famous neighbor. From then on, Irving—and today's commuters—would step onto the platform under a station sign reading "Irvington."

By August Irving had begun the process of "toning up" his George Washington manuscript, hiring Pierre to assist him on the project and to steer the book through publication. It had been nearly four years since Putnam had released anything by Irving. The publisher was eager for a new volume, and Irving certainly wanted the money. He collected the stories and essays he had written years earlier for *Knickerbocker* and other magazines. Titled *Wolfert's Roost* as a wink to the former owner of his beloved Sunnyside, the book was published in February 1855. To those readers who hadn't read the stories in their original *Knickerbocker* format, *Wolfert's Roost* was the most coveted of prizes: a new Washington Irving book, full of surprises—including "The Creole Village," in which Irving had coined the timeless phrase "the almighty dollar."[45]

There was little doubt that it would sell well, and positive reviews appeared on both sides of the Atlantic. It was Washington Irving who was being appraised more than the work itself, and reviewers were almost universal in their tributes. "It would not be easy to overpraise this American miscellany," effused the London *Athenaeum*. "There is as much elegance of diction . . . as when Geoffrey Crayon first came before the English world, nearly forty years ago." The *Boston Telegraph* declared unabashedly that the book was "superior to any of his previous works in one respect—that of wide range and variety. . . . It is, in fact, a volume which contains 'representative' papers of all his former works." Some declared it his best work since *The Sketch Book*. It was a better reception than its author had anticipated, and Irving wept as he pored over the overwhelmingly complimentary reviews and warm accolades at Sunnyside.[46]

Shortly after the publication of *Wolfert's Roost*, Putnam issued part one of Irving's *Life of George Washington*, which detailed Washington's career prior to the American Revolution. Irving had little time to read the glowing reviews and letters; Putnam had already advertised part two as available in August, and part three in October. "I have authorized no such statement," Irving snapped to his publisher. "I wish you would make no promises on my behalf but such as I distinctly warrant."[47]

Irving's skittish horse, Gentleman Dick, was partly to blame for his missing Putnam's deadlines. On April 19, as Irving rode Gentleman Dick at Sunnyside, the horse spooked and ran into a tree at a full gallop, throwing the seventy-two-year-old hard to the ground. "My head was pretty well battered," Irving said, "and came nigh being forced down into my chest, like the end of a telescope." Miraculously, he escaped with no broken bones, but the experience laid him up for several days and made breathing painful. It was Gentleman Dick's second offense—months earlier, the horse had run out of control for several miles, with Irving barely clinging to its neck—and Irving finally caved in to the demands of his nervous nieces that he sell his unpredictable steed. "Poor Dick!" Irving wrote sympathetically. "His character was very much misunderstood by all but myself." The event was reported in the newspapers with typical overstatement, and for several weeks Irving wrote letters to panicked friends, assuring them the reports were "as usual, exaggerated."[48]

In September Irving was back at work on volume two of *George Washington*. This installment focused on Washington's service during the American Revolution, and Irving worried he would be unable to do the topic justice. "It is very difficult to give a clear account of a battle," he fretted to Pierre.[49] Reviews for the first volume continued to be positive, and his desk was papered with congratulatory letters from friends and fellow writers encouraging him to complete the first American president's biography.

Irving hadn't planned to write Washington's life story beyond his inauguration. His presidency alone was enough to fill several volumes. It promised to be hard work, but, Irving had to admit, he relished the accolades as well as the idea of ending his career on such a distinguished topic. Why shouldn't the nation's most famous Founding Father be memorialized by the nation's most famous author? He wouldn't just write part of Washington's life; he would write *all* of it.[50]

There was another former president who also required his attention. That autumn Irving received a dinner invitation from Martin Van Buren, from whom he had been estranged for more than a decade. But times—and politics—had changed, and Van Buren generously extended an olive branch to his old friend. "It gives me great pleasure to accept your kind invitation," replied Irving, and he and Kemble joined Van Buren for dinner at Lindenwald, his estate in Kinderhook. Dining with Van Buren brought back a flood of memories for Irving, and not just of their days together in London. They were in the very house in which Irving had written A *History of New York* forty-six years before. His life seemed to be coming full circle.

Irving worked quickly on the second volume of *Washington*; it was ready in time for a Christmas 1855 release. He had scored again; friends and critics rushed to offer praise. "You have done with

Washington just as I thought you would," wrote Prescott admiringly, "and, instead of a cold marble statue of a demigod, you have made him a being of flesh and blood, like ourselves—one with whom we can have sympathy."[51]

Irving accepted the praise gladly; he was already deep into volume three, working so relentlessly that he gave himself throbbing headaches. He worried that he might not finish the task at hand. "I am constantly afraid that something will happen to me," he confided to Pierre. Something larger than his own legacy was compelling him to finish. In a way, Washington Irving was fulfilling an obligation to George Washington, the man who had blessed him as a child. "I have reason to believe he has attended me through life," Irving said of his namesake. "I was but five years old, yet I can feel that hand upon my head even now."[52]

Irving did his best to keep up with the books, manuscripts, and samples of poetry that poured into Sunnyside with alarming regularity, but the task was overwhelming, and the effort was a distraction. "Oh these letters—these letters!" he groaned to Pierre. "They tear my mind from me in slips and ribbons."[53]

One correspondence, however, sparked his interest. It was from his past, a letter from Emily Foster, now fifty-two years old, long married, with five children, asking Irving if he would receive her oldest son at Sunnyside. She and her family, she added, had recently been rereading his books aloud, and "I could see you, your *own self*, as we read, and your very smile," she wrote. "Do tell me about yourself, dear Mr. Irving. You do not know how much and how often I think of you."[54]

"You can scarcely imagine my surprise and delight on opening your letter," Irving replied. "A thousand recollections broke at once upon my mind of Emily Foster, as I had known her at Dresden, young and fair and bright and beautiful, and I could hardly realize that so many years had elapsed since then." He told her of Sunnyside, of his neighbors, and of his "house full of nieces," who, he wrote, in perhaps an intended dig, "almost make me as happy as if I were a married man." But that slight flare-up was all; the old regrets and hurt feelings were gone. He wished her well, and signed off as "Your affectionate friend."[55]

The third installment of *Life of George Washington* appeared in July 1856. Beginning with *Wolfert's Roost* in February 1855, Irving had published four books in eighteen months—and he was already starting another! He confined himself to Sunnyside through the autumn and winter to work on the fourth part of *George Washington*. Unanswered mail littered the tables and floors of his study; he had no time to plow through the endless requests for scraps of his blotting paper, pieces of wood from his trees, or kind words for just-published novels. "When I remind you that I am approaching my seventy-fourth birth day," he said to one friend in March 1857, "that I am laboring to launch the fourth volume of my life of Washington, and that my table is loaded with a continually increasing multitude of unanswered letters which I vainly endeavor to cope with, I am sure you will excuse the tardiness of my correspondence."[56]

It was taking him longer than he had hoped to complete the new volume; his mind was scattered, and he was having problems keeping track of his own narrative. Yet he never stopped writing, driven onward, he joked grimly, by "my mock admonition to Diedrich Knickerbocker not to idle in his historic wayfaring": "Is not Time—relentless Time! shaking, with palsied hand, his almost exhausted hour-glass before thee?—hasten then to pursue thy weary task, lest the sands be run ere thou hast finished thy history." The finger-wagging had its effect; part four of *Life of George Washington* was published in May 1857. "It has been the most wearing and engrossing task that I have had in the whole course of my literary career," wrote a spent Irving, "and, had I been aware how it would have enlarged under my hand, I should hardly have ventured at my time of life, to undertake it."[57]

The work was nearly finished, but Irving could no longer keep up the pace he had maintained for the past two years. He spent the remaining months of 1857 shuffling through the backlog of mail, fulfilling requests for his autograph, and squashing a rumor that he was planning to write a biography of Kit Carson. Among the pile of letters was one from Sarah Storrow, informing him that she would not be able to visit the United States any time soon. "I now give up the hope of seeing much more of you in this world," he responded sadly.[58]

Concerned for his uncle's health, Pierre moved to Sunnyside in early 1858, sleeping in the narrow room upstairs, just off of Washington's bedroom. That winter Washington was suffering from catarrh, a swelling of the mucous membranes that made it difficult for him to breathe, and some nights Pierre lay in the dark listening to his uncle cough in the next room for what seemed like hours at a time. Writing came slowly and only with tremendous effort, and Washington often joked to Pierre that his "harp of a thousand strings" was no longer in tune. "But I cannot complain now if some of the chords should be breaking," he conceded.[59]

Irving spent much of the spring in his Voltaire chair on Sunny-side's western piazza, dozing fitfully and rambling on wistfully about old friends, most now long gone: Allston, Burr, Leslie, Newton. Even Matilda Hoffman and Emily Foster did not escape his thoughts. Buried among his most private belongings were Matilda's Bible and her miniature portrait, and the surviving pages of the anguished letter he had written to Emily's mother thirty years earlier.

To Irving's annoyance, Putnam announced the final volume of *Life of George Washington* for the coming fall without checking with his author first. Putnam was destined for disappointment. Pierre had watched his uncle write for the last few months, and knew his current habits were not conducive to speed. "When in the mood," Pierre noted, "everything came easy; when *not*, the devil himself could not make him write."[60]

Indeed, by fall—about the time Putnam was hoping to have the book at the printer—Irving confessed to Pierre that he had not been writing much, and he wasn't sure that the little he had written was very good. "I have been spell bound," he said, "have taken things to pieces, and could not put them together again."[61] He was still bothered by catarrh and by asthma attacks that kept him awake at night gasping for breath. It was no wonder he could scarcely find motivation to "mount his horse," as he called it, to complete his Washington biography.

His health took a turn for the worse in the middle of October—so much so that newspapers reported Irving had become "dangerously ill." That wasn't quite true, but for several days he had a fever and his head throbbed incessantly. He admitted that in his eagerness to complete his *Life of George Washington*, he had overtasked himself—"the pitcher might have gone once too often to the well," he said. At this point, it was no longer George Washington or Diedrich Knickerbocker driving him onward; it was Washington Irving's own mortality. "I do not fear death," Irving said stoically, "but I would like to go down with all sail set."[62] He was determined to finish—and in November, after several weeks of intense work, he passed several completed chapters to Pierre for review.

As Irving worked, his health worsened. After visiting Sunnyside in late December, a concerned Oliver Wendell Holmes sent him a bottle of Whitcomb's Remedy for Asthma along with some medicated cigarettes to help with his cough. Many nights, Irving refused to retire to bed, worried he would be unable to breathe, and asked Pierre to spend the night talking with him in his bedroom. Pierre was worried. "The fluctuation of feeling from one day to another seems incredible," he wrote.[63]

There were good days—that Christmas, Irving was "full of fun, humor and anecdote." Such days were becoming rarer. Irving was growing increasingly terrified of being left alone in his bedroom at night—the "haunted chamber," he called it—and would either sleep on the sofa in the parlor downstairs, or knock on Pierre's bedroom door in the middle of the night and beg to come in and talk. Despite Washington's deteriorating condition, Pierre thought his uncle was as mentally alert as ever. "He was never more delightful in conversation than during those long evenings," recalled Pierre.[64]

In early March, with his face swollen and his nerves shot, Irving completed the final page of the final volume of his *Life of*

George Washington. Pierre took it from there; his uncle let the book go to print without ever seeing the final proofs. "In better health, I could have given more effect to parts," he said, "but I was afraid to look at the proofs, lest I should get muddling."[65] The work was finished.

On April 3, 1859—a gray, rainy Sunday—Washington Irving turned seventy-six years old. As greetings and bouquets arrived at Sunnyside—"beautiful flowers to a withered old man!" he said—Washington and Pierre sorted through a number of unpublished manuscripts, mostly Spanish tales, still lying at the bottom of a desk drawer. Washington let them be; he was done writing. "Henceforth," he vowed, "I give up all further tasking of the pen." As family gathered around him that afternoon for his birthday dinner, Washington had a violent coughing fit and staggered, gagging, out of the room and up to bed. His nieces sat at the table in stunned silence, tears in their eyes.[66]

The final volume of Irving's *Life of George Washington* appeared on May 10, nearly nine months later than Putnam's announced publication date. The wait was worth it. "You have charmingly shown Washington's dislike of state; and you have hit off John Adams's character in perfection at a single touch," said a letter from historian George Bancroft, who requested an autographed copy.[67] Such accolades were routine; Irving had become practically untouchable. As William Preston explained to Irving that May, in the last letter he would write to his friend of more than forty years, "I have often had an enhanced consideration, when it was known that I had been an acquaintance of Washington Irving; for I don't believe that any man, in any country, has ever had a more affectionate admiration for him than that given to you in America. I believe that we have had but one man who is so much in the popular heart."[68] Like the subject of his last book, Washington Irving had achieved the status of icon.

Rumors of Irving's decline continued to circulate in the newspapers. In June a concerned Gouverneur Kemble made the trip from Cold Spring Harbor to check on Irving at Sunnyside. As Irving entered the parlor to greet him, Kemble fumbled for words. "Why, you are looking . . ." Kemble started.

"Very badly!" Irving laughed.

"But better than I expected to see you!" replied Kemble. The two old friends spent the day together, had dinner, and talked until dark. As Kemble prepared to leave, Irving was choked with emotion. "Good bye and God bless you," he said to his friend for what he knew would be the last time. As Kemble walked away from Sunnyside, Irving burst into tears.[69]

His nights were mostly restless. Pierre sat up with his uncle into the early morning hours, talking, reading aloud, or sitting by watchfully as Washington tossed and turned in bed. In the mornings, he was often confused, sometimes uncertain who he was. Yet there was still some of the old spark of Diedrich Knickerbocker behind the tired eyes. One evening Irving sat in the parlor to read, complaining that he couldn't find anything decent in his library and was thus reduced to reading his favorite author. "What is it?" an intrigued Pierre asked, and Irving held up the book for Pierre to see. It was his own *Life of George Washington*.[70]

In early autumn Irving began playing backgammon and whist, a card game similar to bridge, to keep himself awake as long as possible to avoid the horrors of his bedroom. He slept fitfully, coughing through the night, fighting for breath. In the mornings, he awakened groggily, in a nervous sweat, believing he still had a manuscript to finish. His doctor, John C. Peters, was summoned to administer opium in light doses to try to calm him. His nieces tended to his needs lovingly, but were always on the verge of tears. Irving smiled at them reassuringly. "I am getting ready to go," he said. "I am shutting up my doors and windows."[71]

On November 7 Irving was visited by Theodore Tilton, editor of the New York *Independent,* for what was his final interview with any newspaper or magazine. "He was suffering from asthma, and was muffled against the damp air with a Scotch shawl, wrapped like a great loose scarf around his neck," Tilton reported, "but as he took his seat in the old armchair, and, despite his hoarseness and troubled chest, began an unexpectedly vivacious conversation, he almost made me forget that I was the guest of an old man long past his 'threescore years and ten.'" As Tilton stood to leave that afternoon, he caught sight of a painting of Sir Walter Scott surrounded by literary colleagues. "You should write one more book," Tilton said, motioning toward the canvas, "your reminiscences of those literary friends." Irving shook his head with a grim smile. "Ah, it is too late now! I shall never take the pen again," he replied. "I have so entirely given up writing, that even my best friends' letters lie unanswered. I must have rest. No more books now!"[72]

Monday, November 28, 1859, dawned clear and unseasonably warm, and Irving awoke in such a good mood that Pierre spent several hours in New York City, leaving his uncle in the care of several nieces. That morning Washington walked slowly out to the little brook on his property—his "Little Mediterranean," he called it—but returned home glum, suffering from a shortness of breath. Pierre was back at Sunnyside that afternoon to find Washington chatting in the parlor with family, breathing normally, though in somewhat low spirits. As the family sat down to dinner, the last rays of the winter sunset flooded the dining room at Sunnyside, and Irving bubbled with almost childlike excitement about the beauty of the sunset as it twinkled, then faded, on the Hudson.

Irving napped after dinner, and awoke in time for tea and conversation. He was quiet that evening, almost distant, but gamely participated in several hands of whist in the parlor. Pierre watched his uncle warily; he seemed "heavy, and a good deal depressed." At 10:30 P.M. Washington kissed everyone good night and retired to his upstairs bedroom accompanied by his niece Sarah Irving—Ebenezer's seventh daughter, whom Washington had come to adore as much as the absent Sarah Storrow—who carried the veritable apothecary of medicines Irving needed to take each evening.

Irving stood quietly at the foot of his bed for a moment, as if lost in thought. "Well, I must arrange my pillows for another weary night," he sighed—and then, so quietly that Sarah could barely hear it, whispered, "You cannot tell how I have suffered. When will this end?" With a sob of pain, he clutched at his left side. Gasping for breath, he clawed for the footboard of his bed as he collapsed heavily on the floor. The sound and Sarah's hysterical screams brought the family scrambling up the stairs to the bedroom. Pierre cradled his uncle's head in his lap, but there was no miraculous revival. At seventy-six years old, Washington Irving had suffered a massive heart attack. He was gone.

News of Irving's death traveled rapidly down the Hudson River. The newly installed telegraph sent the ominous message "Washington Irving is dead!" down the wire to newspapers across the country. "Who is there that the tidings did not touch with profound sorrow?" lamented the *Milwaukee Sentinel*.[73] Flags were lowered to half-staff in New York City, and the mayor and common council approved a formal resolution marking his passing and honoring his life and work.

On December 1 Tarrytown and Sleepy Hollow were swathed in black. Mourners stepped off the train platform at Irvington under a black-draped sign, while businesses in Tarrytown shuttered their windows for the day. The courts in New York City closed deferentially, allowing government officials to attend Irving's funeral. At 12:30 P.M., as church bells rang solemnly in New York City, a line of carriages pulled away from Sunnyside, carrying Washington Irving's family, the pallbearers, Dr. Peters, and attending clergymen. Among the eight pallbearers were James Renwick and an emotional Gouverneur Kemble, ready to lay his fellow Lad of Kilkenny to rest.[74]

The service at the Old Dutch Church in Tarrytown was Episcopal—Irving defied his Presbyterian father to the very end—and at the conclusion of the services, Irving lay, as he had requested, in an open casket. More than a thousand mourners filed past to pay their respects. Irving's casket was then placed in a coach at the head of a procession of 150 carriages, which slowly made its way up the hill toward the Sleepy Hollow Cemetery. "It is a thing that lies near my heart," Irving had once said of the cemetery. "I hope, some day or other, to sleep my last sleep in that favorite resort of my boyhood."[75]

A late spell of Indian summer warmed the air that afternoon—an "exquisite" day, Pierre remarked—as hundreds of mourners thronged against the iron fence surrounding Irving's gravesite. As Washington Irving was lowered into the ground, in the spot he had so carefully chosen next to his mother, the sun began to sink in the sky, bathing the Sleepy Hollow hillside in warm, red shadow.

Irving was buried beneath a simple headstone, engraved only with his name and dates of birth and death. There is no epitaph. The shy, private Irving had once again declined to make a public statement. He would leave his legacy for others to discuss and decide.

His friend Longfellow, commemorating Irving in a December 15 speech before the Massachusetts Historical Society, urged his audience to "rejoice in the completeness of his life and labors, which, closing together, have left behind them so sweet a fame, and a memory so precious. . . . We feel a just pride," continued Longfellow, "in his renown as an author, not forgetting that, to his other claims upon our gratitude, he adds also that of having been the first to win for our country an honourable name and position in the History of Letters."[76]

Irving likely would have been embarrassed by such a statement. He hadn't planned to win recognition and acceptance for American writers, and he certainly hadn't intended to become his country's first man of letters. He had only been trying to earn a living. Fifty years earlier, mourning the death of his seventeen-year-old fiancée and facing certain unemployment, he had rocketed out of seemingly nowhere with a book that had given American readers their first real literature, and provided New Yorkers in particular with the first sense of their own history and a character that embodied their very identity. A decade later, with little money and few prospects, he had tantalized American and British readers with elegant tales of English customs, Christmas traditions, and old New York. His most memorable creations—Diedrich Knickerbocker, Rip Van Winkle, Ichabod Crane, the Headless Horseman—owed their existence in no small part to financial hardship and need. Washington Irving and his characters became icons. Almost in spite of himself, the middle-class son of a New York merchant became one of the most famous men in the world.

His literary reputation was hard-earned, carefully cultivated, and intensely protected. As he produced elegantly written tales of the American West, Spanish histories, or Dutch legends, Irving had made it all look easy. In truth, it had always been hard work. Writing, while it flowed from his pen gracefully, rarely flowed easily. Inspiration was a struggle, and he had sometimes suffered long, depressing periods of writer's block. Criticism hurt him terribly. He constantly questioned his abilities, and craved the appreciation and affection of his readers. Yet while Irving had often catered to public tastes, he was also intrepid in exposing readers to his own quirky interests in Spanish history, Moorish castles, and Islamic prophets.

To Irving's surprise, colleagues, readers, and fans were just as eager for his approval. Politicians, writers, actors, artists, and wannabes of every type clamored to be associated with him. A friend to six presidents, he had danced with Dolley Madison in the White House, consoled Martin Van Buren in London, and flattered a young Queen Isabella in Madrid as John Tyler's minister to Spain. John Jacob Astor tapped him to be his personal biographer. Mary Shelley had a crush on him. Edgar Allan Poe flattered him. Sir Walter Scott loved him. Dickens, Longfellow, and Hawthorne adored him. Even those like James Fenimore Cooper who loathed him gave his work their grudging respect.

Irving was also lucky. He had risen to prominence as an American writer at a time when there were few other writers with whom to compete. While skeptics like Poe argued that critics were inclined to be too forgiving of Irving's limitations simply because he was the country's first bona fide writer, what Poe didn't seem to appreciate was that going first meant going it alone. Unlike Poe, Irving had no preeminent American man of letters to flatter and ask for letters of recommendation; he had to fend for himself. Where he lacked guidance, he had improvised, sometimes spectacularly, pulling off a wondrous literary hoax to launch Knickerbocker, intuitively mastering the complex whims of international copyright to protect Geoffrey Crayon on both sides of the Atlantic, and projecting a confident public image that differed from his shy, uncertain, private self—a feat even Poe couldn't pull off.

Yet to Irving, such things were secondary. Ultimately, he had simply been trying to find his way in the world, making the most of his limited talent, moderate ambition, and enormous personal charm. That he had succeeded beyond his expectations—and those of others—delighted him. But Washington Irving had never set out to write for posterity, as Longfellow might argue. Irving, like Shakespeare, wrote for the masses.

Perhaps the most appropriate epitaph, then, was from his own pen, some forty years earlier, as he was on the cusp of international fame with *The Sketch Book:*

> I have attempted no lofty theme, nor sought to look wise and learned, which appears to be very much the fashion among our American writers at present. I have preferred addressing myself to the feeling and fancy of the reader more than to his judgment. My writing, therefore, may appear light and trifling in our country of philosophers and politicians, but if they possess merit in the class of literature to which they belong, it is all to which I aspire in the work.[77]

Acknowledgments

I owe an enormous debt of gratitude to various colleagues, family, and friends who joined me on the six-year journey that resulted in the book you now hold in your hands. Having them with me made the trip that much more enjoyable.

Two of my most important companions have been Jonathan Lyons, literary agent extraordinaire, who believed in this project from the start and whose friendship and advice I value greatly, and Casey Ebro, my tireless and patient editor at Arcade. Her careful ear and skillful pencil were never short of astounding, and her enthusiasm and affection for all things Irving kept us upbeat and focused.

I am indebted to the staff at Historic Hudson Valley, particularly Kate Johnson and Anne Goslin, for their information and conversation, and to Dina Friedman at Sunnyside for providing an insider's look at Irving's home. I appreciate the patience of Sharon Brevoort, who allowed me to pepper her with questions about her ancestors. In London, Helen Trompeteler at the National Portrait Gallery was endlessly helpful. In Washington, D.C., I am thankful for the assistance of Heather Moore at the U.S. Senate Historical Office, Mary Edwards at the U.S. Department of Treasury, and the countless librarians at the Library of Congress.

No biography of Irving would be possible without the hard work of those scholars who have gone before, and I am indebted to the editors of Twayne's thirty-volume *Complete Works of Washington Irving*, a meticulously researched and notated effort that finally puts Irving's letters and papers in a uniform format. Locating these and other volumes required much scouring, and I am grateful for the help of countless small, independent used-book sellers in the United States and abroad.

On a personal level, it is not an exaggeration to say this book could not have been written without the indulgence and encouragement of my colleagues at my "day job," Councilmember Mike Knapp, Joyce Fuhrmann, Josh Bokee, Daniela Moya, and Carmen

Berrios. I am appreciative of the help and support of Richard and Jeannette Seaver, Miranda Ottewell, Jay, Elli, and Bremer Kaprosy, Tiffany Cooke, Tim Sullivan, Rod, Taylor, and Kimberly Barnes-O'Connor, Scott Phillips, Jim Eismeier, Jerry Crute, Doran Butuche, Michael Gaitan, and Laurie Locascio. I am grateful for the love and guidance of my parents, Larry Jones and Elaine and Wayne Miller, and my brother, Cris, whose instant messages were always worth responding to, even when I was swamped.

Most of all, I am eternally indebted to my wife, Barb—my first and best reader, editor, friend, and fan, whose level head and sense of humor kept us grounded even as things went crazy—and our daughter, Madison, who made it all seem so normal. You worked hard for this book, too, and I love you both.

Notes

In citing works in the notes, short titles are used. Works frequently cited are identified by the following abbreviations:

Journals I   Washington Irving. *Journals and Notebooks, Volume I: 1803–1806.* Edited by Nathalia Wright. Vol. 1 of *The Complete Works of Washington Irving.* Madison: University of Wisconsin Press, 1969.

Journals II   Washington Irving. *Journals and Notebooks, Volume II: 1807–1822.* Edited by Walter A. Reichart and Lillian Schlissel. Vol. 2 of *The Complete Works of Washington Irving.* Boston: Twayne, 1981.

Journals III   Washington Irving. *Journals and Notebooks, Volume III: 1819–1827.* Edited by Walter A. Reichart. Vol. 3 of *The Complete Works of Washington Irving.* Madison: University of Wisconsin Press, 1970.

Journals IV   Washington Irving. *Journals and Notebooks, Volume IV: 1826–1829.* Edited by Wayne R. Kime and Andrew B. Myers. Vol. 4 of *The Complete Works of Washington Irving.* Boston: Twayne, 1984.

Journals V   Washington Irving. *Journals and Notebooks, Volume V: 1826–1829.* Edited by Sue Fields Ross. Vol. 5 of *The Complete Works of Washington Irving.* Boston: Twayne, 1986.

LBI   George S. Hellman, ed. *Letters of Henry Brevoort to Washington Irving.* New York: G. P. Putnam's Sons, 1918.

Letters I   Washington Irving. *Letters, Volume I: 1802–1823.* Edited by Ralph M. Aderman, Herbert L. Kleinfield, and Jenifer S. Banks. Vol. 23 of *The Complete Works of Washington Irving.* Boston: Twayne, 1978.

Letters II	Washington Irving. *Letters, Volume II: 1823–1838.* Edited by Ralph M. Aderman, Herbert L. Kleinfield, and Jenifer S. Banks. Vol. 24 of *The Complete Works of Washington Irving.* Boston: Twayne, 1979.
Letters III	Washington Irving. *Letters, Volume III: 1839–1845.* Edited by Ralph M. Aderman, Herbert L. Kleinfield, and Jenifer S. Banks. Vol. 25 of *The Complete Works of Washington Irving.* Boston: Twayne, 1982.
Letters IV	Washington Irving. *Letters, Volume IV: 1846–1859.* Edited by Ralph M. Aderman, Herbert L. Kleinfield, and Jenifer S. Banks. Vol. 26 of *The Complete Works of Washington Irving.* Boston: Twayne, 1978.
PMI	Pierre M. Irving. *Life and Letters of Washington Irving.* 4 vols. New York: G. P. Putnam, 1862.
STW	Stanley T. Williams. *The Life of Washington Irving.* 2 vols. New York: Oxford University Press, 1935.

All conversions from nineteenth-century dollars and English pounds to current American dollars are made using the very helpful online device:

Samuel H. Williamson, "Five Ways to Compute the Relative Value of a U.S. Dollar Amount, 1790–2005," MeasuringWorth.com, 2006.

CHAPTER 1: GOTHAM

1. PMI, 1:15; STW, 2:246–49.
2. PMI, 1:26.
3. Irving to Henry Panton, Sunnyside, 15 February 1850, *Letters IV*, 204.
4. PMI, 1:23.
5. STW, 1:5; Irving to Emily Foster, Paris, 23 August 1825, *Letters II*, 129.
6. PMI, 1:25.
7. Burrows, 296.
8. PMI, 1:27.

9. Burrows, 305.

10. PMI, 1:28.

11. STW, 1:11; PMI, 1:29.

12. Irving to Philip J. Forbes, Sunnyside, 25 October 1852, *Letters IV*, 333–34; PMI, 1:33; Hellman, 14; STW, 1:20.

13. Hellman, 17–18.

14. Irving, "The Author's Account of Himself," in *The Sketch Book*, 8.

15. Tour in Scotland 1817, *Journals II*, 119.

16. Paulding, 29.

17. Ibid., 26, 29.

18. Ibid., 26–27.

19. Warner, 27; PMI, 1:36.

20. Tour in Scotland, *Journals II*, 119.

21. Burrows, 357–58.

22. Brooks, 165–66; Irving, "The Legend of Sleepy Hollow," *Sketch Book*, 274.

23. Brooks, 165; "The Legend of Sleepy Hollow," 273.

24. STW, 1:14.

25. Irving to Mrs. Amelia Foster, [April–May 1823], *Letters I*, 738.

26. Burrows, 333.

27. Tour in Scotland, *Journals II*, 118.

28. See Irving, *Letters of Jonathan Oldstyle*, xxi–xxii.

29. PMI, 1:37.

30. Ibid., 39.

31. Ibid., 42–43.

32. Ibid.

33. STW, 1:26. Also STW, 1:386n22.

34. See *Letters I*, n16.

35. PMI, 1:45.

36. Irving to Mr. and Mrs. William Irving Sr., Johnstown, 2 July 1802, *Letters I*, 3.

37. PMI, 1:46–47.

38. Burrows, 328.

39. *Letters of Jonathan Oldstyle*, 39; STW, 1:388n66.

40. *Letters of Jonathan Oldstyle*, 3–7.

41. Hedges, 17–19.

42. *Letters of Jonathan Oldstyle*, 8.

43. Ibid., 12.

44. Ibid., 18.

45. "Historical Note," *Letters of Jonathan Oldstyle*, 40; PMI, 1:47.
46. See STW, 1:40; *Letters of Jonathan Oldstyle*, 20, 22–26. See also explanatory note 27.1, *Letters of Jonathan Oldstyle*, 47.
47. *Letters of Jonathan Oldstyle*, 30–31.
48. Ibid., 34.
49. PMI, 1:48.
50. New York Journal, 1803, *Journals I*, 9.
51. Irving, *Astoria*, 3.
52. Irving, *Miscellaneous Writings I*, xx.
53. "Textual Commentary, [Contributions to *The Corrector*]," in ibid., 282.
54. "[Contributions to *The Corrector*]," in ibid., 8.
55. STW, 1:41.

CHAPTER 2: TRAVELER

1. PMI, 1:62.
2. Ibid.
3. Irving to Alexander Beebee, Bordeaux, 22 July 1805, *Letters I*, 38; Irving to William Irving Jr., Ship *Rising States*, Mouth of Gironne, at Quarantine, 26 June 1804, *Letters I*, 7–10.
4. Irving to Elias Hicks, 24 July 1804, *Letters I*, 41; Irving to John Furman, Genoa, 24 October 1804, *Letters I*, 111.
5. Irving to Beebee, Nice, 19 September 1804, *Letters I*, 80.
6. Irving to Andrew Quoz?, Bordeaux, 20 July 1804, *Letters I*, 34–35.
7. Irving to Beebee, Bordeaux, 22 July 1804, *Letters I*, 40; Irving to William Irving Jr., Bordeaux, 1 August 1804, *Letters I*, 44.
8. European Journal, 1804–1805, *Journals I*, 72; Traveling Notes, 1804, *Journals I*, 46; PMI, 1:75.
9. Irving to William Irving Jr., Bordeaux, 1 August 1804, *Letters I*, 44; Irving to William Irving Jr., Montpellier, 14 August 1804, *Letters I*, 54; European Journal, 1804–1805, *Journals I*, 65.
10. Irving to William Irving Jr., Montpellier, 14 August 1804; *Letters I*, 58, 66.
11. Irving to William Irving Jr., Marseilles, 27 August 1804; *Letters I*, 70–71
12. European Journal, 1804–1805, *Journals I*, 80–83.
13. Irving to Peter Irving, [Marseilles, 5 September 1804], *Letters I*, 73–74; European Journal, 1804–1805, *Journals I*, 43; Irving to Quoz?, Bordeaux, 20 July 1804, *Letters I*, 33.
14. Irving to William Irving Jr., Nice, 20 September 1804, *Letters I*, 90.

15. Traveling Notes, 1804, *Journals I*, 480; Irving to William Irving Jr., Nice, 20 September 1804, *Letters I*, 93.
16. European Journal, 1804–1805, *Journals I*, 78.
17. Traveling Notes, 1804, *Journals I*, 485.
18. Irving to William Irving Jr., Nice, 20 September 1804, *Letters I*, 93.
19. Irving to John Furman, Genoa, 24 October 1804, *Letters I*, 113; Irving to Beebee, Nice, 27 October 1804, *Letters I*, 86; European Journal, 1804–1805, *Journals I*, 120.
20. Irving to William Irving Jr., Nice, 20 September 1804, *Letters I*, 106.
21. Irving to William Irving Jr., Genoa, 20 December 1804, *Letters I*, 123.
22. Irving to William Irving Jr., Genoa, 30 November 1804, *Letters I*, 119.
23. Ibid., 120.
24. Irving to William Irving Jr., Ship *Matilda*, 25 December 1804 [through January 1805], *Letters I*, 142.
25. Ibid., 145–46.
26. European Journal, 1804–1805, *Journals I*, 150.
27. European Journal, 1804–1805, *Journals I*, 152; Irving to William Irving Jr., Ship *Matilda*, 25 December 1804 [through January 1805], *Letters I*, 148.
28. Irving to William Irving Jr., Ship *Matilda*, 25 December 1804 [through January 1805], *Letters I*, 154; European Journal, 1804–1805, *Journals I*, 162.
29. Traveling Notes, 1804–1805, *Journals I*, 523; European Journal, 1804–1805, *Journals I*, 179–80, 188–90.
30. European Journal, 1804–1805, *Journals I*, 203.
31. European Journal, 1804–1805, *Journals I*, 195; Irving to William Irving Jr., Rome, 4 April 1805, *Letters I*, 173–74.
32. *Journals I*, 228n197; Irving to Elias Hicks, 4 May 1805, Intra. Lago Maggiore, *Letters I*, 182.
33. See European Journal, 1804–1805, *Journals I*, 238–43.
34. Ibid., 262.
35. Irving, "Memoir of Washington Allston," in *Miscellaneous Writings II*, 173.
36. Ibid., 173–74.
37. European Journal, 1804–1805, *Journals I*, 271; "Memoir of Washington Allston," 174.
38. "Memoir of Washington Allston," 175.
39. Ibid.
40. European Journal, 1804–1805, *Journals I*, 276. Likely a paraphrasing of Moore; Irving to William Irving Jr., Rome, 4 April 1805, *Letters I*, 175.

41. Ibid., 175, 176.
42. PMI, 1:139–40. Emphasis in original.
43. Ibid; European Journal, 1804–1805, *Journals I*, 284.
44. European Journal, 1804–1805, *Journals I*, 313.
45. Ibid., 328.
46. Ibid., 337–40.
47. Ibid., 344.
48. Irving, "Verses Written on the Lake of Lucerne," in *Miscellaneous Writings I*, 149.
49. European Journal, 1804–1805, *Journals I*, 393–96.
50. Ibid., 405.
51. See European Journal, 1804–1805, *Journals I*, 407–17; Irving to William Irving Jr., Paris, 31 May 1805, *Letters I*, 189.
52. European Journal, 1804–1805, *Journals I*, 419.
53. Irving to Elias Hicks, Intra. Lago Maggiore, 4 May 1805, *Letters I*, 186–87.
54. Irving to William Irving Jr., Paris, 31 May 1805, *Letters I*, 190.
55. PMI, 1:151.
56. Irving to William Irving Jr., Paris, 31 May 1805, *Letters I*, 192; European Journal, 1804–1805, *Journals I*, 426–27; Irving to Peter Irving, Paris, 15 July 1805, *Letters I*, 196. Emphasis in original.
57. Irving to Beebee, Paris, 3 August 1805, *Letters I*, 203.
58. European Journal, 1804–1805, *Journals I*, 433.
59. Ibid., 445, 448–49.
60. Irving to Peter Irving, London, 20 October 1805, *Letters I*, 206.
61. Irving to William Irving Jr., London, 26 October 1805, *Letters I*, 208. Emphasis in original.
62. Irving to William Irving Jr., London, 26 October 1805, *Letters I*, 208; Irving to Peter Irving, London, 7 November 1805, *Letters I*, 215.
63. Irving to Furman, Genoa, 24 October 1804, *Letters I*, 112.

CHAPTER 3: *SALMAGUNDI*

1. Irving to Peter Irving, London, 7 November 1805, *Letters I*, 215.
2. STW, 1:77; Burrows, 379.
3. Burrows, 274, 416; STW, 1:74.
4. Burrows, 383–84; Homberger, 67.
5. Burrows, 374. Attributed to John Lambert.
6. PMI, 1:165.

7. Ibid., 168.

8. PMI, 1:165; Paulding, 37.

9. PMI, 1:166–67; Paulding, 37.

10. Irving to Gouverneur Kemble, New York, 24 May 1806, *Letters I*, 217–18.

11. Irving to Kemble, New York, 26 May 1806, *Letters I*, 219–20.

12. Ibid.

13. Mary E. Fenno to G. C. Verplanck, December 1810(?), STW, 1:91.

14. Irving to Mrs. Amelia Foster, [April–May 1823], *Letters I*, 739; PMI, 1:173. This story is also repeated by a number of Irving biographers. See STW, 1:77 and Hellman, 46.

15. Paulding, 426; Irving, "Historical Note," in *Salmagundi*, 319; Paulding, 38.

16. *Shorter Oxford English Dictionary*, 5th ed., s.v. "Salmagundi."

17. *Salmagundi*, 67–68.

18. "Table 2, Subeditions and Variant States of 1A," *Salmagundi*, 390–91; *Salmagundi*, 68.

19. PMI, 1:179; Paulding, 38.

20. *Salmagundi*, 72.

21. *Salmagundi*, 96. Emphasis in original.

22. Leary, 14.

23. *Salmagundi*, 152–57, 322. For Dennie's reaction, see PMI, 1:185.

24. *Salmagundi*, 68.

25. Irving to Josiah Ogden Hoffman, New York, 2 February 1807, *Letters I*, 223.

26. Irving to Andrew Quoz, Ship *Matilda*, 1 January 1805, *Letters I*, 169.

27. STW, 1:89.

28. Irving to Mary Fairlie, Philadelphia, 17 March 1807, *Letters I*, 224; *Salmagundi*, 126.

29. Adams, 82.

30. Irving to Fairlie, Philadelphia, 17 March 1807, *Letters I*, 227; PMI, 1:183.

31. Irving to Fairlie, New York, 2 May 1807, *Letters I*, 231–32.

32. Ibid.

33. Cited in PMI, 1:188.

34. Ibid.

35. Irving to Fairlie, Fredericksburg, Virginia, 13 May 1807, *Letters I*, 236.

36. Ibid., 234.

37. Adams, 579.

38. Ibid., 758.

39. Ibid., 794.

40. Ibid., 768.

41. Irving to Fairlie, Fredericksburg, Virginia, 13 May 1807, *Letters I*, 235; PMI, 4:301.

42. McFarland, 75; *Letters I*, 242n3.

43. McFarland, 78; PMI, 1:191.

44. Irving to Mrs. Josiah Ogden Hoffman, Richmond, 4 June 1807, *Letters I*, 238.

45. Ibid.

46. McFarland, 81.

47. Irving to James K. Paulding, Richmond, 22 June 1807, *Letters I*, 239–40.

48. Ibid.

49. Ibid., 239; McFarland, 82–83.

50. Irving to Paulding, Richmond, 22 June 1807, *Letters I*, 239.

51. Irving to an unknown correspondent, [Richmond, summer 1807], *Letters I*, 240; PMI, 1:196.

52. Irving to Kemble, Richmond, 1 July 1807, *Letters I*, 241.

53. Irving to [Fairlie?], Washington City, 7 July 1807, *Letters I*, 244; Irving to Kemble, Richmond, 1 July 1807, *Letters I*, 242.

54. Irving to [Fairlie?], Washington City, 7 July 1807, *Letters I*, 245; McFarland, 85.

55. Irving to [Fairlie?], Washington City, 7 July 1807, *Letters I*, 245.

56. Decision of Burr jury, http://www.law.umkc.edu/faculty/projects/ftrials/burr/Decision.htm.

57. Aderman, 33.

58. *Salmagundi*, 272–77. Emphasis in original.

59. Burrows, 417.

60. Irving to Ann Hoffman, New York, 17 November 1807, *Letters I*, 250–51. Emphasis in original.

61. STW, 1:86. Emphasis in original.

62. Irving to Hoffman, New York, 17 November 1807, *Letters I*, 252.

63. PMI, 1:210–11.

64. Paulding, 38–39.

CHAPTER 4: HOAX

1. PMI, 1:211; Irving, *Salmagundi*, 306.

2. Irving, "The Author's Apology," in *A History of New York*, 3.

3. Peter Irving to Washington Irving, 30 April 1808, PMI, 1:214.

4. See Irving to Joseph Gratz, New York, 30 March 1808, *Letters I*, 254.

5. Irving to Richard McCall?, New York, 18 November 1808, *Letters I*, 258. See *Letters I*, 256n2. Other Irving scholars tend to agree the Irvings were involved in a bit of illicit trade.

6. Notes While Preparing Sketch Book &c, 1817, *Journals II*, 184n39.

7. Irving to Henry Brevoort, Skeenesborough, 9 May 1808, *Letters I*, 255–56.

8. Irving to Mrs. Josiah Ogden Hoffman, Albany, 2 June 1808, *Letters I*, 256–57.

9. PMI, 1:218–19.

10. STW, 1:398n14; PMI, 1:219.

11. Irving to Richard McCall?, New York, 18 November 1808, *Letters I*, 258.

12. Ibid., 260.

13. Ibid.

14. Irving to Mrs. Amelia Foster, [April–May 1823], *Letters I*, 739. Emphasis in original; Irving to Brevoort, New York, 11 June 1808, *Letters I*, 257; Irving to Mrs. Foster, [April–May 1823], *Letters I*, 739.

15. PMI, 1:222–23.

16. Notes While Preparing Sketch Book &c, 195.

17. Ibid.

18. PMI, 1:221–22.

19. Irving to Mrs. Foster, [April–May 1823], *Letters I*, 740.

20. Ibid.

21. Ibid.

22. Ibid.

23. Ibid.

24. Ibid.

25. PMI, 1:231; Notes While Preparing Sketch Book &c, 192.

26. Irving to Mrs. Foster, [April–May 1823], *Letters I*, 739.

27. "The Author's Apology," 3.

28. Irving to Brevoort, Kinderhook, 11 May 1809, *Letters I*, 263–64.

29. Irving to Mrs. Hoffman, Kinderhook, 19 May 1809, *Letters I*, 265.

30. Irving to Sarah Irving, Kinderhook, 20 May 1809, *Letters I*, 267.

31. Irving to Brevoort, Kinderhook, 20 May 1809, *Letters I*, 268–69. Emphasis in original.

32. Irving to Mrs. Hoffman, [June? 1809], *Letters I*, 272; Irving to William P. Van Ness, New York, 24 June 1809, *Letters I*, 270. Emphasis in original.

33. Irving to Peter Irving, [New York, late summer 1809], *Letters I*, 273; PMI, 1:235–36.
34. Irving to Brevoort, Philadelphia, 23 October 1808, *Letters I*, 274. The newly added section detailed Peter Stuyvesant's journey up the Hudson.
35. *A History of New York*, 6; PMI, 1:234–35.
36. Ibid.
37. PMI, 1:235.
38. *A History of New York*, 6–7.
39. Ibid., 7.
40. *A History of New York* (1809 ed.), 527.
41. Ibid., 520, 515, 536.
42. Ibid., 507, 656–57.
43. Ibid., 435.
44. Ibid., 445.
45. Irving to Mrs. Foster, [April–May 1823], *Letters I*, 741.
46. Aderman, 35; PMI, 1:239.
47. PMI, 1:240; Charles Dickens to Irving, 1841, PMI, 3:165.
48. PMI 1:239.
49. Irving to Mrs. Hoffman, Albany, 26 February 1810, *Letters I*, 284; PMI, 1:247.
50. Michael Black, "Political Satire in Knickerbocker's *History*," in *The Knickerbocker Tradition: Washington Irving's New York*, ed. Andrew B. Myers (Tarrytown, N.Y.: Sleepy Hollow Restorations, Inc., 1974), 79.
51. *A History of New York*, 5.
52. PMI, 1:243; Irving to Mrs. Hoffman, Johnstown, 12 February 1810, *Letters I*, 282.
53. Irving to John E. Hall, New York, 26 September 1810, *Letters I*, 290–91.

CHAPTER 5: ADRIFT

1. Irving to Mrs. Josiah Ogden Hoffman, Albany, 26 February 1810, *Letters I*, 284.
2. STW, 1:126.
3. Irving to Mrs. Amelia Foster, [April–May 1823], *Letters I*, 741.
4. PMI, 1:253; Irving to John E. Hall, New York, 26 September 1810, *Letters I*, 291.
5. Irving to Henry Brevoort, New York, 22 September 1810, *Letters I*, 288–89.

6. Notebook of 1810, *Journals II*, 14–15.
7. Irving to Brevoort, City of Washington, 13 January 1811, *Letters I*, 296.
8. Ibid., 297.
9. Ibid.
10. Ibid.
11. Ibid.
12. Irving to Brevoort, Washington, 7 February 1811, *Letters I*, 300.
13. Ibid., 301.
14. Notebook 1818, *Journals II*, 262–63.
15. Irving to William Irving, Washington, D.C., 16 February 1811, *Letters I*, 306.
16. Ibid.
17. Irving to Brevoort, Washington, 5 March 1811, *Letters I*, 308.
18. PMI, 1:279–80.
19. Irving to Brevoort, New York, 8 June 1811, *Letters I*, 322.
20. Irving to Mrs. Foster, [April–May 1823], *Letters I*, 741.
21. Irving to James Renwick, New York, 10 September 1811, *Letters I*, 326–27.
22. Irving to William Irving Jr., [October? 1811], *Letters I*, 333.
23. Irving to Brevoort, New York, 8 June 1811, *Letters I*, 323.
24. Brevoort to Irving, Mackinac, 29 July 1811, *LBI*, 45.
25. Brevoort to Irving, Mackinac, 28 June 1811, *LBI*, 27.
26. Ibid., 30.
27. Ibid., 34.
28. Irving to Brevoort, New York, 17 March 1812, *Letters I*, 335.
29. Irving to Brevoort, New York, 8 July 1812, *Letters I*, 338–40.
30. Irving to Peter Irving, New York, 30 December 1812, *Letters I*, 350.
31. Irving to Renwick, Washington, 24 November 1812, *Letters I*, 343.
32. Irving to Renwick, Washington, 8 December 1812, *Letters I*, 347.
33. Irving to Renwick, Washington, 18 December 1812, *Letters I*, 350.
34. Ibid., 349.
35. Brevoort to Irving, Edinburgh, 9 December 1812, *LBI*, 64–65.
36. Irving, "Biography of Captain James Lawrence," in *Miscellaneous Writings I*, 71.
37. PMI, 1:300.
38. Irving to Brevoort, New York, 2 January 1813, *Letters I*, 354; Brevoort to Irving, Edinburgh, 1 March 1813, *LBI*, 72.
39. PMI, 1:240.
40. Irving to Joseph Delaplaine, New York, 10 August 1814, *Letters I*, 364.

41. Irving to Peter Irving, New York, 30 December 1812, *Letters I*, 351.
42. Irving, "Biographical Memoir of Commodore Perry," in *Miscellaneous Writings I*, 94.
43. PMI, 1:311–12.
44. Irving to Brevoort, Albany, 26 September 1814, *Letters I*, 371; Irving to William Irving Jr., New York, 16 October 1814, *Letters I*, 379.
45. Ibid., 320.
46. Irving to Moses Thomas, New York, 21 October 1814, *Letters I*, 382.
47. Irving, "Defence of Fort M'Henry," in *Miscellaneous Writings I*, 132.
48. Irving to William Irving Jr., [New York, 20 December 1814], *Letters I*, 383; PMI, 1:323.
49. PMI, 1:324–25.
50. *Letters I*, 369n3.
51. Irving to Gulian C. Verplanck, Philadelphia, 21 January 1815, *Letters I*, 387.
52. Irving to Verplanck, Philadelphia, 17 January 1815, *Letters I*, 386.
53. Irving to Oliver Hazard Perry, New York, 21 February 1815, *Letters I*, 390; Irving to Mrs. Foster, [April–May 1823], *Letters I*, 741.
54. Irving to Mrs. Foster, [April–May 1823], *Letters I*, 741–42.
55. Ibid.
56. Ibid.

Chapter 6: Desperation

1. For more on Irving's voyage aboard the *Mexico*, see Irving to Henry Brevoort, Birmingham, 5 July 1815, *Letters I*, 397–98.
2. Ibid., 398.
3. Ibid., 399.
4. Irving to Brevoort, [Birmingham?, 16 July? 1815], *Letters I*, 401.
5. Ibid, emphasis in original; Irving to William Irving Jr., [London, 21 July 1815], *Letters I*, 403.
6. Irving to Jean Renwick, Birmingham, 27 July 1815, *Letters I*, 404.
7. Irving to Brevoort, Liverpool, 23 August 1815, *Letters I*, 418.
8. Chandler, 96.
9. PMI, 1:335.
10. Irving to Brevoort, Liverpool, 19 August 1815, *Letters I*, 415. Emphasis in original.
11. Irving to Brevoort, Liverpool, 23 August 1815, *Letters I*, 417.
12. Ibid.

13. Irving to Ebenezer Irving, [Liverpool, August 1815], *Letters I*, 421.
14. Irving to Sarah Irving, [Liverpool, 21 September 1815], *Letters I*, 423.
15. STW, 1:150.
16. Irving to Brevoort, Liverpool, 17 October 1815, *Letters I*, 425–26.
17. Irving to Ebenezer Irving, [October? 1815], *Letters I*, 427.
18. Irving to Brevoort, Birmingham, 15 March 1816, *Letters I*, 432.
19. Irving to Renwick, Liverpool, 5 April 1816, *Letters I*, 440.
20. Irving to Brevoort, Liverpool, 9 May 1816, *Letters I*, 446–47.
21. Irving to Brevoort, Birmingham, 16 July 1816, *Letters I*, 449.
22. Ibid.
23. Ibid.
24. Ibid., 450.
25. Notes 1815–1821, *Journals II*, 70; Irving to Brevoort, Birmingham, 6 November 1816, *Letters I*, 458.
26. *Letters I*, 455n1.
27. Irving to Sarah Irving, Birmingham, 18 October 1816, *Letters I*, 456.
28. Irving to William Irving Jr., [Liverpool, fall? 1816], *Letters I*, 457; PMI, 1:357.
29. Irving to Brevoort, Birmingham, 9 December 1816, *Letters I*, 462.
30. Irving to Brevoort, Birmingham, 16 July 1816, *Letters I*, 450.
31. Irving to Brevoort, Birmingham, 9 December 1816, *Letters I*, 463.
32. Irving to Brevoort, Birmingham, 29 January 1817, *Letters I*, 467.
33. Irving to Brevoort, Liverpool, 24 March 1817, *Letters I*, 474.
34. Washington Allston to Washington Irving, 9 May 1817, PMI, 1:362.
35. Irving to Allston, Birmingham, 21 May 1817, *Letters I*, 477–78.
36. Irving to Mrs. Amelia Foster, [April–May 1823], *Letters I*, 742.
37. Lacey, 72.
38. Irving to Brevoort, Birmingham, 26 May 1817, *Letters I*, 481.
39. *Journals II*, 93n4.
40. STW, 1:164.
41. Ibid.
42. Ibid; Irving to Brevoort, Liverpool, 7 June 1817, *Letters I*, 483.
43. *Letters I*, 484n1.
44. Irving to Brevoort, Liverpool, 11 July 1817, *Letters I*, 486–87.
45. Ibid.
46. Notes circa 1817, *Journals II*, 169.
47. McClary, xxxi. Ben McClary is also inclined to agree that this was the primary project Irving was pursuing at the time.
48. McClary, xxxii–xlv.
49. Ibid.

50. Irving to Peter Irving, London, 19 August 1817, *Letters I*, 488–89.
51. Irving to Brevoort, Edinburgh, 28 August 1817, *Letters I*, 495.
52. STW, 1:156.

Chapter 7: Determination

1. Irving, "Abbotsford," in *The Crayon Miscellany*, 125.
2. Irving to Peter Irving, [Edinburgh, 26 August 1817], *Letters I*, 491.
3. Tour in Scotland 1817, *Journals II*, 99; Henry Brevoort to Washington Irving, Edinburgh, 1 March 1813, *LBI*, 84.
4. "Abbotsford," 126.
5. Pearson, 147.
6. Ibid.
7. Ibid., 152.
8. Irving's recollection of his 1817 visit to Scott at Abbotsford can be found in "Abbotsford," 125–68.
9. Irving to Brevoort, Edinburgh, 28 August 1817, *Letters I*, 498; "Abbotsford," 572.
10. See Irving to Peter Irving, [Edinburgh, 26 August 1817], *Letters I*, 494n27, for the text of Scott's note.
11. Tour in Scotland 1817, 113.
12. Ibid., 103
13. Ibid., 106.
14. For fragments of Irving's uncompleted Rosalie novel, see Tour in Scotland 1817, 119–27.
15. Irving to Walter Scott, Hawick, 23 September 1817, *Letters I*, 507.
16. Irving to Peter Irving, Edinburgh, 20 September 1817, *Letters I*, 505.
17. Hellman, 101.
18. Irving to John Murray II, Liverpool, 16 October 1817, *Letters I*, 510–11.
19. Irving to Brevoort, Liverpool, 10 October 1817, *Letters I*, 508–9.
20. Irving to Brevoort, Leamington, 7 July 1818, *Letters I*, 527. Emphasis in original.
21. Irving to Mrs. Josiah Ogden Hoffman, Liverpool, 23 November 1817, *Letters I*, 514.
22. PMI, I, 392.
23. Irving to William Irving Jr., Liverpool, 23 December 1817, *Letters I*, 514–15.
24. Ibid., 515.

25. Ibid.
26. V. Markham Lester, e-mail message to author, 28 February 2005.
27. Irving to Brevoort, Liverpool, 30 April 1818, *Letters I*, 524; McClary, 14; Irving to Charles R. Leslie, Liverpool, 8 February 1818, *Letters I*, 519.
28. Irving to Brevoort, Liverpool, 19 May 1818, *Letters I*, 525, 526n1.
29. Irving to Moses Thomas, [3 March 1816], *Letters I*, 520; Irving to Brevoort, Liverpool, 19 May 1818, *Letters I*, 526. Emphasis in original.
30. Irving to Silas Richards, Birmingham, 17 July 1818, *Letters I*, 528. Emphasis in original.
31. So said the *Maidstone Gazette*, quoted in the London *Times* on 30 July 1818. See *Letters I*, 529n1.
32. PMI, 1:396; McClary, 13.
33. PMI, 1:405.
34. Ibid., 406.
35. McClary, 14–15.
36. Ibid., 14n17.
37. Irving to Brevoort, London, 27 September 1818, *Letters I*, 534.
38. Irving to Ebenezer Irving, [London, 13 October 1818], *Letters I*, 535.
39. William Irving Jr. to Washington Irving, New York, 14 October 1818, STW, 1:170–71.
40. Irving to Ebenezer Irving, [London, late November 1818], *Letters I*, 536.

CHAPTER 8: SENSATION

1. PMI, 1:410.
2. STW, 1:172; PMI, 1:411.
3. McClary, 15; Irving to John Howard Payne, [December 1818], *Letters I*, 536.
4. Irving to Ebenezer Irving, London, 1 March 1819, *Letters I*, 539.
5. Irving to Ebenezer Irving, [London, 3 March 1819], *Letters I*, 540.
6. Ibid.
7. Irving to Henry Brevoort, London, 3 March 1819, *Letters I*, 542.
8. Ibid., 543.
9. Irving to Ebenezer Irving, London, 1 March 1819, *Letters I*, 539.
10. Johanna Johnston, *The Heart That Would Not Hold: A Biography of Washington Irving* (New York: M. Evans, 1971), 168–71; McFarland, 157.
11. Irving to Brevoort, London, 1 April 1819, *Letters I*, 545–46; Irving to John Treat Irving, London, 13 May 1819, *Letters I*, 547.

12. Irving to Brevoort, London, 13 May 1819, *Letters I*, 548. Emphasis in original.
13. Irving to Ebenezer Irving, London, 1 March 1819; *Letters I*, 539.
14. Irving, "Prospectus," in *The Sketch Book*, appendix A, 300.
15. *New York Evening Post*, 26 June 1819. See Aderman, 46.
16. Irving to Ebenezer Irving, [3? March 1819], *Letters I*, 542n1.
17. *The Sketch Book*, xxv; PMI, 1:419.
18. PMI, 1:418.
19. Irving to Brevoort, London, 10 July 1819, *Letters I*, 550.
20. Irving to Brevoort, London, 28 July 1819, *Letters I*, 551–52.
21. Irving to Brevoort, London, 2 August 1819, *Letters I*, 553; Irving to Brevoort, London, 16 August 1819, *Letters I*, 557.
22. Irving to Brevoort, London, 16 August 1819, *Letters I*, 557; PMI, 1:431; Irving to Brevoort, London, 12 August 1819, *Letters I*, 555.
23. Ibid., 553.
24. Ibid., 554.
25. Irving to Henry Van Wart, [September? 1819], *Letters I*, 565.
26. Irving to Brevoort, London, 9 September 1819, *Letters I*, 559. Emphasis in original.
27. Ibid, 559–60.
28. Brevoort to Irving, Bloomingdale, 9 September 1819, *LBI*, 110.
29. PMI, 1:422.
30. *North American Review*, September 1819, 348. See *The Sketch Book*, xxviii. Emphasis in original.
31. "Preface to the Revised Edition," in *The Sketch Book*, 3.
32. McClary, 16–17.
33. Irving to Walter Scott, London, 30 October 1819, *Letters I*, 568.
34. "Preface to the Revised Edition," 4–5; Scott to Irving, Abbotsford, 17 November 1819, PMI, 1:439–40.
35. "Preface to the Revised Edition," 6.
36. Irving, *A History of New York*, 76.
37. Irving to John Howard Payne, Portland Place, 28 January 1820, *Letters I*, 574.
38. "Advertisement," in *The Sketch Book*, appendix B, 301.
39. Irving to Ebenezer Irving, [London?, 29 December 1819], *Letters I*, 573.
40. Brevoort to Irving, New York, April 1820, *LBI*, 123–24; *The Sketch Book*, xxviii.
41. "Preface to the Revised Edition," 7.
42. Brevoort to Irving, New York, 9 November 1819, *LBI*, 120; Irving to Brevoort, London, 13 May 1820, *Letters I*, 581.

43. Ibid., 581–82.

44. Ibid.

45. Ibid., 580–81.

46. Irving to Ebenezer Irving, [London, 28 June 1820], *Letters I*, 587.

47. Irving to Brevoort, Paris, 22 September 1820, *Letters I*, 595.

48. Irving to Brevoort, London, 12 August 1820, *Letters I*, 554.

49. Irving to Brevoort, Paris, 22 September 1820, *Letters I*, 595.

50. Irving to William Irving Jr., Paris, 22 September 1820, *Letters I*, 596–97.

51. Brevoort to Irving, New York, November 1820, *LBI*, 128–29.

52. Irving to Brevoort, [October? 1820], *Letters I*, 606–7.

53. PMI, 2:24–26.

54. Irving to John Murray II, Paris, 31 October 1820, *Letters I*, 601.

55. Irving to Charles R. Leslie, Paris, 31 October 1820, *Letters I*, 604; Irving to Leslie, Paris, 19 December 1820, *Letters I*, 611.

56. PMI, 2:20.

57. Irving to Richard Rush, Paris, 28 October 1820, *Letters I*, 600. Emphasis in original.

58. Irving to Brevoort, Paris, 10 March 1821, *Letters I*, 615; PMI, 2:33.

59. PMI, 2:32.

60. Irving to Brevoort, Paris, 10 March 1821, *Letters I*, 614; Brevoort to Irving, New York, 7 May 1821, *LBI*, 137.

61. PMI, 2:38–39.

62. Irving to Brevoort, Paris, 5 April 1821, *Letters I*, 619.

63. Irving to Brevoort, Paris, 14 April 1821, *Letters I*, 624.

64. Brevoort to Irving, New York, 15 June 1821, *LBI*, 143.

65. PMI, 2:48.

66. Irving to Murray, [6 July 1821], *Letters I*, 633; McClary, 36.

67. PMI, 2:52.

68. Irving to Mrs. Thomas W. Storrow, London, 26 August 1821, *Letters I*, 641; Irving to William Harris, [London, 6 August 1821], *Letters I*, 637.

69. Irving to Peter Irving, [September 6, 1821], *Letters I*, 646.

70. PMI, 2:56.

71. Brevoort to Irving, Bloomingdale, 9 September 1819, *LBI*, 112–13; Brevoort to Irving, New York, 15 June 1821, *LBI*, 144; Brevoort to Irving, New York, April 1820, *LBI*, 126.

72. Irving to Ebenezer Irving, Birmingham, 1 November 1821, *Letters I*, 653.

73. Ibid.

CHAPTER 9: RUT

1. Irving to Mrs. Thomas Storrow, Birmingham, 10 December 1821, *Letters I*, 660; Irving to Mrs. Amelia Foster, [April–May 1823], *Letters I*, 743.
2. Ibid.
3. Irving to Ebenezer Irving, London, 29 January 1822, *Letters I*, 661–62.
4. PMI, 2:73.
5. Irving to Charles Wiley, London, 6 March 1822, *Letters I*, 667.
6. STW, 1:206.
7. Irving to Peter Irving, 35 Maddox Street, Hanover Square/London, 24 March 1822, *Letters I*, 672. Multiple versions of this story exist, with Murray paying Irving a final amount ranging from 1,000 to 1,200 guineas. See PMI, 2:76–77; STW, 1:207; McClary, 41–42.
8. Irving, "Horsemanship," in *Bracebridge Hall*, 70; Irving to Peter Irving, Edinburgh, 6 September 1817, *Letters I*, 503.
9. Irving, "The Stout Gentleman," in *Bracebridge Hall*, 56; STW, 1:209; Aderman, 55–57.
10. Aderman, 58–62; Irving to Brevoort, London, 11 June 1822, *Letters I*, 677.
11. Irving to Sarah Van Wart, Mainz, 2 September 1822, *Letters I*, 703.
12. Irving to Van Wart, Heidelberg, 18 September 1822, *Letters I*, 707; Irving to Thomas Moore, Munich, 16 October 1822, *Letters I*, 713.
13. Ibid., 714.
14. Ibid., 717, 719.
15. See Reichart, 67–70.
16. Irving to Thomas Storrow, Dresden, 22 December 1822, *Letters I*, 727; German and Austrian Journal, 1822–1823, *Journals III*, 99; Irving to Charles R. Leslie, Dresden, 15 March 1822, *Letters I*, 735.
17. Reichart, 82; Williams and Beach, 110–11.
18. Irving to Peter Irving, Dresden, 10 March 1823, *Letters I*, 731.
19. German and Austrian Journal, 1822–1823, *Journals III*, 126–27.
20. Ibid., 118.
21. PMI, 4:353. Emphasis in original.
22. Irving to Van Wart, Dresden, 7 March 1823, *Letters I*, 730; Irving to Leslie, Dresden, 15 March 1823, *Letters I*, 736.
23. German and Austrian Journal, 133. Irving's journal entry for this date is transcribed in *Journals III* as "Evening delightful," but the editors acknowledge in a footnote that "Emily delightful" is another possible reading. In fact, the second Dresden journal contains just such a

sentence, though in handwriting that may not be Irving's. Yet the question remains why Pierre or later readers would rub out this particular sentence if it simply discussed the weather. Given the pattern of erasures in this section of Irving's journal, it is more likely that Pierre was making an effort to remove a delicate reference to Emily Foster. See *Journals III*, 133n71, for a discussion of this entry, and Hellman, 47–64, for a longer discussion of Irving's relationship with Emily Foster.

24. Ibid.
25. Ibid., 133–34; Williams and Beach, 126.
26. German and Austrian Journal, 138–40.
27. Williams and Beach, 128–29.
28. German and Austrian Journal, 144. See also Williams and Beach, 129n1.
29. German and Austrian Journal, 145–46.
30. PMI, 4:361.
31. Irving to Mrs. Foster, [April–May 1823], *Letters I*, 737–55.
32. PMI, 4:358; Reichart, 93.
33. PMI, 4:357, emphasis in original; Irving to Mrs. Foster, Dresden, 4 May 1823, *Letters I*, 745.
34. Williams and Beach, 139; German and Austrian Journal, 154.
35. Irving to Mrs. Foster, Hirschberg, 23 May 1823, *Letters I*, 752; Irving to Mrs. Foster, Prague, 8 June 1823, *Letters I*, 763–64; Irving to Mrs. Foster, [Prague, 19? June 1823], *Letters I*, 766.
36. Williams and Beach, 167–68; Irving to Peter Irving, [5 August 1823], *Letters II*, 3; PMI, 4:364.
37. Irving to Peter Irving, [20 August 1823], *Letters II*, 4.
38. Ibid.
39. Irving to John Howard Payne, Paris, 22 November 1823, *Letters II*, 17; Irving to Payne, [Paris, late November 1823], *Letters II*, 22. Emphasis in original.
40. French Journal, 1823–1826, *Journals III*, 256–57.
41. PMI, 2:177; Irving to John Murray II, rue Richelieu No. 89/Paris, 22 December 1823, *Letters II*, 26, emphasis in original.
42. Irving to Murray, rue Richelieu No. 89/Paris, 22 December 1823, *Letters II*, 27.
43. Irving to Payne, Paris, 31 January 1824, *Letters II*, 34.
44. Irving to Leslie, Paris, February 8, 1823, *Letters II*, 37.
45. French Journal, 289–90.
46. Irving to Murray, Paris, 25 March 1823, *Letters II*, 41–42.
47. Ibid. Emphasis in original.

48. French Journal, 316–17.

49. Sanborn, 17; PMI, 2:173.

50. French Journal, 361; McFarland, 245.

51. French Journal, 374.

52. Irving to Murray, [5 August 1824], *Letters II*, 67; French Journal, 378.

53. Irving to Thomas Moore, Brighton, 14 August 1824, *Letters II*, 71–72; Irving to Murray, Sloperton Cottage, Deveiss, 18 June 1823, *Letters II*, 56; *Letters II*, 57n3.

54. Irving to Catharine Paris, Paris, 20 September 1824, *Letters II*, 76.

55. Aderman, 63–68; Irving, *Tales of a Traveller*, xxi; *Westminster Review* 2 (October 1824): 340, 346.

56. Ibid.

57. *New-York Mirror and Ladies Literary Gazette* 2 (25 September 1824): 70. See *Tales of a Traveller*, xxii.

58. French Journal, 392.

59. Ibid., 421; Irving to Paris, Paris, 20 September 1824, *Letters II*, 80.

60. Irving to Pierre P. Irving, Paris, 7 December 1824, *Letters II*, 84.

61. Irving to Brevoort, Paris, rue Richelieu No. 89, 11 December 1824, *Letters II*, 90.

62. Ibid.

63. French Journal, 442.

64. Irving to Payne, Paris, 20 January 1825, *Letters II*, 98–99.

65. French Journal, 453.

66. Irving to Pierre P. Irving, Paris, 29 March 1824, *Letters II*, 106–9.

67. French Journal, 479.

68. *New-York Mirror*, 25 September 1824, cited in STW, 2:294. Whether this is the specific review Irving read is debatable. Nonetheless, the sentiment was the same; French Journal, 480, emphasis in original.

69. PMI, 2:239.

70. See McClary, 76–77; STW, 1:292–93, 464n101.

71. See French Journal, 488; Irving to Thomas W. Storrow, Le Havre, 2 July 1825, *Letters II*, 122.

72. Irving to Pierre M. Irving, [n.d.], *Letters IV*, 709; PMI, 2:14.

73. Irving to Archibald Constable, Paris, 19 August 1825, *Letters II*, 126–27. Emphasis in original.

74. Mary Shelley to Payne, Kentish Town, [1825], Sanborn, 38.

75. Sanborn, 61.

76. Payne to Shelley, London, [late 1825], Sanborn, 73.

77. Shelley to Payne, Kentish Town, 29 June 1825, Sanborn, 77.

78. Shelley to Payne, Kentish Town, [28 July 1825], Sanborn, 83.

79. Shelley to Payne, [29 July 1825], Sanborn, 85.
80. Payne to Irving, Paris, [late 1825], Sanborn, 18–19.
81. French Journal, 510.
82. Irving to Murray, Paris, 19 August 1825, *Letters II*, 127–28; Irving to Emily Foster, Paris, 23 August 1825, *Letters II*, 129.
83. Irving to Storrow, Beycheville, 17 October 1825, *Letters II*, 141.
84. French Journal, 537.
85. French Journal, 546.
86. Irving to Storrow, Bordeaux, 2 December 1825, *Letters II*, 151.
87. French Journal, 555.
88. Irving to Storrow, Bordeaux, 31 October 1825, *Letters II*, 146.

CHAPTER 10: WORKAHOLIC

1. Irving to Alexander H. Everett, Bordeaux, 31 January 1826, *Letters II*, 168; Irving to Thomas W. Storrow, Bordeaux, 3 February 1826, *Letters II*, 171–72.
2. McClary, 82; Irving to John Murray II, Bordeaux, 6 February 1826, *Letters II*, 173.
3. See *Letters II*, 181n3.
4. See Bowers, 5–7; *Columbus*, xxxii.
5. Irving to Charles R. Leslie, Madrid, 21 April 1826, *Letters II*, 195; Columbus, 3–4; Bowers, 6.
6. *Letters II*, 170n5.
7. *Columbus*, xxxviii; McClary, 86–87.
8. Spanish Journal, 1826–1827, *Journals IV*, 14–21.
9. Irving to John Howard Payne, Madrid, 14 April 1826, *Letters II*, 192; Spanish Journal, 1826–1827, 22.
10. Irving to Storrow, Madrid, 15 March 1826, *Letters II*, 187; Irving to Leslie, Madrid, 21 April 1826, *Letters II*, 196.
11. See Spanish Journal, 1826–1827, 32; Irving to Storrow, Madrid, 9 July 1828, *Letters II*, 238; STW, 1:311.
12. Spanish Journal, 1826–1827, 33.
13. PMI, 3:359–60.
14. Irving to Storrow, Madrid, 12 June 1826, *Letters II*, 199.
15. See Spanish Journal, 1826–1827, 37–39.
16. PMI, 2:253.
17. Irving to Storrow, Madrid, 9 July 1826, *Letters II*, 202. See Spanish Journal, 1826–1827, 40; PMI, 2:253.

18. Irving to Storrow, Madrid, 9 July 1826, *Letters II*, 204.

19. See Spanish Journal, 1826–1827, 48–58.

20. Irving to Storrow, Madrid, 26 October 1826, *Letters II*, 211.

21. Irving to Murray, Madrid, 21 December 1826, *Letters II*, 213.

22. Spanish Journal, 1826–1827, 63.

23. Irving to Storrow, Madrid, 3 January 1827, *Letters II*, 218. See journal entries for January 6–8, Spanish Journal, 1826–1827, 64.

24. McClary, 86–88.

25. Spanish Journal, 1826–1827, 71.

26. Irving to Alexander Hill Everett, Seville, 15 April 1829, *Letters II*, 402.

27. See entry for January 31, Spanish Journal, 1826–1827, 68.

28. Irving to Pierre M. Irving, Madrid, 22 February 1827, *Letters II*, 221.

29. Irving to Storrow, Madrid, 26 February 1826, *Letters II*, 222–23.

30. Longfellow, 801. See Spanish Journal, 1826–1827, 73n278.

31. Brevoort to Irving, New York, 1 January 1827, *LBI*, 152–53.

32. Ibid.

33. Irving to Brevoort, Madrid, 4 April 1827, *Letters II*, 225–26.

34. Ibid.

35. Ibid., 226.

36. Brevoort to Irving, New York, 19 November 1827, *LBI*, 165.

37. Irving to Murray, Madrid, 21 December 1826, *Letters II*, 213, and Madrid, 4 April 1827, *Letters II*, 229.

38. See Irving to Murray, Madrid, 29 July 1827, *Letters II*, 242; Irving to Colonel Thomas Aspinwall (Letter 2), [Madrid, 29 July 1827], *Letters II*, 241.

39. Irving to Aspinwall (Letter 1), Madrid, 29 July 1827, *Letters II*, 240.

40. McClary, 94–95.

41. Irving to Aspinwall, Madrid, 8 October 1827, *Letters II*, 251.

42. PMI, 2:268; Irving to Aspinwall, Madrid, 8 October 1827, *Letters II*, 251.

43. Spanish Journal, 1827–1828, 113.

44. Brevoort to Irving, New York, 19 November 1827, *LBI*, 166–67.

45. Spanish Journal, 1827–1828, 121.

46. Brevoort to Irving, New York, 30 April 1829, *LBI*, 190–91.

47. Irving to Brevoort, Madrid, 23 February 1828, *Letters II*, 274.

48. *Southern Review* 12 (May 1831): 246. See *Columbus*, lxxxvii.

49. *North American Review* 28 (January 1829): 103–34. See Aderman, 71–88.

50. Brevoort to Irving, New York, 31 May 1828, *LBI*, 180–81.

51. Irving to Catharine Paris, [ca. March 1828], *Letters II*, 291.

52. Irving to Storrow, Granada, 10 March 1828, *Letters II*, 279; Irving to Antoinette Bolviller, Granada, 15 March 1828, *Letters II*, 280.

53. Irving to Storrow, Granada, 10 March 1828, *Letters II*, 279; Irving to Bolviller, Granada, 15 March 1828, *Letters II*, 282.

54. Irving to Bolviller, Granada, 15 March 1828, *Letters II*, 282–84.

55. See Spanish Journal and Notebook, 1828, *Journals IV*, 155.

56. Irving to Catharine D'Oubril, Seville, 19 April 1828, *Letters II*, 303.

57. Irving to Aspinwall, n.p., [7 May 1828], *Letters II*, 308.

58. Irving to Bolviller, Seville, 20 July 1828, *Letters II*, 321.

59. Irving to Peter Irving, Seville, 2 August 1828, *Letters II*, 327.

60. Irving to Aspinwall, Cadiz, 31 August 1828, *Letters II*, 331.

61. Irving to Prince Dmitri Ivanovitch Dolgorouki, Puerto Sta. Maria, 2 October 1828, *Letters II*, 340.

62. Irving to Murray, November 23, 1828; *Letters II*, 357; Irving to Dolgorouki, Puerto Sta. Maria, 2 October 1828, *Letters II*, 339.

63. Irving to Ebenezer Irving, Port St. Mary's, 16 October 1828, *Letters II*, 343; Irving to Murray, Port St. Marys, 16 October 1828, *Letters II*, 345.

64. Irving to Ebenezer Irving, Port St. Mary's, 16 October 1828, *Letters II*, 343. Emphasis in original.

65. Irving to Murray, Port St. Marys, 16 October 1828, *Letters II*, 344.

66. Irving to Peter Irving, 19 November 1828; *Letters II*, 356; Irving to Peter Irving, 13 December 1828; *Letters II*, 364; Irving to Ebenezer Irving, 19 December 1828; *Letters II*, 364.

67. For more on this agreement, see *LBI*, 190–95.

68. Irving to Aspinwall, Seville, 27 December 1828, *Letters II*, 369.

69. Spanish Journal, 1828–1829, *Journals IV*, 245–46.

70. Irving to Diego Clemencín, [Seville, 8 January 1829], *Letters II*, 371–72.

71. Spanish Journal, 1828–1829, 247–52.

72. Irving to Alexander H. Everett, Seville, 14 February 1829, *Letters II*, 382.

73. Irving to Peter Irving, Seville, 3 March 1829, *Letters II*, 387.

74. Irving to Aspinwall, Seville, 4 April 1829, *Letters II*, 395.

75. Irving to Peter Irving, Seville, 10 April 1828, *Letters II*, 400.

76. Irving to Aspinwall, Cadiz, 31 August 1828, *Letters II*, 330–31.

77. Irving to Peter Irving, Seville, 10 April 1829, *Letters II*, 400.

78. Irving to Murray, Granada, 9 May 1829, *Letters II*, 414–15.

79. See Aderman, 88–90.

80. Irving to Peter Irving, Seville, 29 April 1829, *Letters II*, 410.

81. Irving to Brevoort, [Alhambra, 23 May 1829], *Letters II*, 425; Irving to Peter Irving, Alhambra, 13 June 1829, *Letters II*, 436.
82. Bowers, 107–13; Irving to Edgar Irving, Alhambra, 23 May 1829, *Letters II*, 429.
83. See Irving to Peter Irving, Alhambra, 13 June 1829, *Letters II*, 436–37.
84. Irving to David Wilkie, Alhambra-Granada, 15 May 1829, *Letters II*, 420; Irving to Brevoort, [Alhambra, 23 May 1829], *Letters II*, 426.
85. Irving to Aspinwall, Alhambra, 23 June 1829, *Letters II*, 443.
86. Irving to Aspinwall, Alhambra, 4 July 1829, *Letters II*, 445.
87. Brevoort to Irving, New York, 31 May 1829, *LBI*, 196.
88. Ibid, 197.
89. Irving to Ebenezer Irving, Alhambra, 22 July 1829, *Letters II*, 451; Irving to Peter Irving, Alhambra, 18 July 1829, *Letters II*, 447.
90. Irving to Louis McLane, Alhambra, Granada, 22 July 1829, *Letters II*, 453.
91. Irving to John Wetherell, Alhambra, 18 July 1829, *Letters II*, 448.

CHAPTER 11: POLITICIAN

1. Henry Brevoort to Irving, New York, 6 November 1829, LBI, 205; Irving to Peter Irving, Alhambra, 25 July 1829, *Letters II*, 454–55.
2. Remini, 283.
3. Remini, 283–85.
4. Remini, 283; Irving to Brevoort, Valencia, 10 August 1829, *Letters II*, 462.
5. Irving to Peter Irving, London, 16 October 1829, *Letters II*, 473.
6. McClary, 127–30.
7. Ibid., 130.
8. Irving to Brevoort, London, 1 March 1831, *Letters II*, 593.
9. Irving to William Godwin, Chandos Street, Cavendish Place, 30 January 1830, *Letters II*, 505; Irving to Thomas Moore, Chandos Street, Cavendish Square, 17 November 1829, *Letters II*, 480.
10. PMI, 2:417–18; Irving to Ebenezer Irving, [late October–early November 1829], *Letters II*, 476.
11. Irving to Ebenezer Irving, [London, October 1829], *Letters II*, 476.
12. Irving to Major William B. Lewis, London, 20 November 1829, *Letters II*, 484.
13. Ibid., 485.

14. Ibid., 486.
15. Ibid., 483.
16. Brevoort to Irving, New York, 6 November 1829, *LBI*, 203.
17. Irving to Peter Irving, n.p., 18 December 1829, *Letters II*, 494.
18. Irving to Peter Irving, n.p., [late December 1829–January 1830], *Letters II*, 495.
19. See Irving to Obadiah Rich, [London, 20 February 1830], *Letters II*, 508; Irving to John Howard Payne, 8 Argyll Street [London], 4 March 1830, *Letters II*, 509.
20. PMI, 2:429, 430, 431–32. Emphasis in original.
21. *Quarterly Review*, May 1830. See *Miscellaneous Writings II*, 6–7.
22. Irving to Gouverneur Kemble, London, 18 January 1829, *Letters II*, 501; Brevoort to Irving, New York, 23 March 1830, *LBI*, 208–11.
23. See Irving to Mary Shelley, [28 May 1830], *Letters II*, 525, note.
24. Irving to Peter Irving, n.p., 27 July 1830, *Letters II*, 535. Emphasis in original.
25. Irving to John Murray II, Argyll Street [London], 6 July 1830, *Letters II*, 531.
26. Irving to Murray, Argyll Street [London], 3 August 1830, *Letters II*, 538.
27. Brevoort to Irving, New York, 30 March 1829, *LBI*, 186.
28. See *Letters II*, 545n6.
29. McLane to Levi Woodbury, 30 August 1830, Remini, 285.
30. For an overview of *Companion*'s critical reception, see *Companions of Columbus*, xliv–xlv.
31. Irving to Peter Irving, Birmingham, 3 February 1831, *Letters II*, 586; Irving to Brevoort, London, 1 March 1831, *Letters II*, 592.
32. Irving to John B. Nicholson, London, 18 June 1830, *Letters II*, 528–29; Irving to Peter Irving, 6 June 1831, *Letters II*, 605. See also *Letters II*, 605n2 and STW, 2:329.
33. Brevoort to Irving, Paris, 30 June 1831, *LBI*, 235.
34. Irving to Stephen Pleasanton, Legation of the United States, London, 8 July 1831, *Letters II*, 617.
35. Irving to Louis McLane, London, 30 August 1831, *Letters II*, 647–48.
36. Irving to McLane, London, 14 September 1831, *Letters II*, 654; Irving to Edward Livingston, London, 22 September 1831, *Letters II*, 657.
37. Sanderlin, 92.
38. McFarland, 187.
39. Ibid., 190.

40. McClary, 155–56.
41. Irving to Colonel Thomas Aspinwall, Birmingham, 4 October 1831, *Letters II*, 660.
42. Irving to Murray, Birmingham, 4 October 1831, *Letters II*, 661.
43. Irving to Aspinwall, Sheffield, 14 October 1831, *Letters II*, 662. Emphasis in original.
44. Irving to Aspinwall, Sheffield, 18 October 1831, *Letters II*, 663.
45. Irving to Aspinwall, Sheffield, 22 October 1831, *Letters II*, 663–64.
46. Ibid., 664.
47. Irving to Murray, Sheffield, 22 October 1831, *Letters II*, 665.
48. McClary, 160.
49. Irving to Murray, Granada, 9 May 1829, *Letters II*, 414–15.
50. Irving to Murray, Barlborough Hall, Chesterfield, 29 October 1831, *Letters II*, 670.
51. Ibid., 671.
52. Irving to Peter Irving, n.p., 6 November 1831, *Letters II*, 672.
53. See Irving to Catharine Paris, Newstead Abbey, 20 January 1832, *Letters II*, 683.
54. Irving, "Newstead Abbey," in *The Crayon Miscellany*, 177.
55. Irving to Charles Leslie, Newstead Abbey, 9 January 1831, *Letters II*, 678–79. Emphasis in original.
56. Irving to Peter Irving, Newstead Abbey, 20 January 1831, *Letters II*, 680.
57. McClary, 167.
58. Irving to William Cullen Bryant, Newstead Abbey, 26 January 1832, *Letters II*, 687.
59. Irving to James Renwick, Newstead Abbey, 26 January 1832, *Letters II*, 688–89, emphasis in original; Irving to Pierre P. Irving, 6 February 1832, *Letters II*, 690.
60. Irving to Bryant, London, 6 March 1832, *Letters II*, 694.
61. Irving to Pierre P. Irving, London, 6 February 1832, *Letters II*, 689.
62. Remini, 224–25.
63. Irving to McLane, London, 22 February 1832, *Letters II*, 693.
64. Irving to Peter Irving, London, 6 March 1832, *Letters II*, 696.
65. Ibid., 695.
66. Ibid., 696.

CHAPTER 12: FRONTIERSMAN

1. See Irving to Peter Irving, [New York, 30 May 1832], *Letters II*, 703; Irving to James Watson Webb, New York, 20 June 1832, *Letters II*, 706.

2. *New-York Mirror* 9, no. 40 (9 June 1832): 386.
3. STW, 2:338n76, emphasis in original; Irving, "A Tour on the Prairies," in *The Crayon Miscellany*, 6–7.
4. See *Letters II*, 701n1.
5. Irving to Peter Irving, [New York, 30 May 1832], *Letters II*, 703.
6. *New-York Mirror* 9, no. 40 (9 June 1832): 386, emphasis in original; STW, 2:33.
7. Ibid., 2:32–33.
8. Irving, *Salmagundi*, 262; Irving to Peter Irving, [New York, 30 May 1832], *Letters II*, 703.
9. Henry Brevoort to Irving, Fontainebleau, 28 July 1832, *LBI*, 253.
10. All quotes and accounts of the Irving dinner are taken from the 9 June 1832 edition of the *New-York Mirror*, pp. 386–87, 390–91.
11. PMI, 2:492, emphasis in original; Brevoort to Irving, Fontainebleau, 28 July 1832, *LBI*, 253.
12. Irving to Peter Irving, Washington City, 18 December 1832, *Letters II*, 736–37.
13. These figures include the so-called outer boroughs, before the 1898 consolidation. Brevoort to Irving, New York, 19 November 1827, *LBI*, 167–68; STW, 2:30–31; "A Tour on the Prairies," 8.
14. See Irving to Peter Irving, Washington, 16 June 1832, *Letters II*, 705.
15. Ibid.
16. *New-York Mirror* 9 (23 June 1832): 401–3. See Aderman, 94–96.
17. PMI, 3:20–21; Irving, *The Alhambra*, xxxiv.
18. Irving to Peter Irving, Philadelphia, 21–28 June 1832, *Letters II*, 707.
19. Irving to Peter Irving, New York, 9 July 1832, *Letters II*, 709.
20. Irving to Peter Irving, Washington City, 18 December 1832, *Letters II*, 733–34.
21. Ibid.
22. American Journals, 1832, *Journals V*, 48.
23. Irving to Catharine Paris, Independence, Missouri, 26 September 1832, *Letters II*, 726.
24. Irving to Paris, St. Louis, Missouri, 13 September 1832, *Letters II*, 723.
25. Irving to Paris, St. Louis, Missouri, 13 September 1832, *Letters II*, 723; Irving to Paris, Fort Gibson, Arkansas, 9 October 1832, *Letters II*, 727; American Journals, 1832, 75.
26. Ibid., 86–89.
27. Irving to Paris, Cincinnati, 2 September 1832, *Letters II*, 717.
28. "A Tour on the Prairies," 10–11; *The Crayon Miscellany*, xxxiii.
29. *Journals V*, 127.

30. Irving to Peter Irving, Washington City, 18 December 1832, *Letters II*, 735; "A Tour on the Prairies," 63.
31. "A Tour on the Prairies," 102.
32. Irving to Peter Irving, Washington City, 18 December 1832, *Letters II*, 735.
33. Irving to Paris, Montgomery's Point, Mouth of the Arkansas, 16 November 1832, *Letters II*, 731; American Journals 1832, 136–49.
34. Irving to Paris, Montgomery's Point, Mouth of the Arkansas, 16 November 1832, *Letters II*, 731–32.
35. Remini, 195.
36. Irving to Peter Irving, Washington City, 18 December 1832, *Letters II*, 736; PMI, 3:45. Emphasis in original.
37. Remini, 241.
38. Irving to Peter Irving, Washington City, 18 December 1832, *Letters II*, 736.
39. Irving to Martin Van Buren, Washington, 2 January 1833, *Letters II*, 742; Irving to Gouverneur Kemble, Washington, 4 January 1833, *Letters II*, 744.
40. Irving to Paris, Washington, 23 January 1833, *Letters II*, 750.
41. Irving to Peter Irving, New York, 1 April 1833, *Letters II*, 756–57.
42. Irving to Peter Irving, [Washington, ca. December 1832], *Letters II*, 740.
43. Remini, 250.
44. Irving to Josiah Quincy, New York, 3 April 1833, *Letters II*, 757.
45. Irving to Peter Irving, New York, 1 April 1833, *Letters II*, 756.
46. Irving to Peter Irving, New York, 15 April 1833, *Letters II*, 758.
47. Irving to Van Buren, Washington, 5 October 1833, *Letters II*, 774.
48. Irving to Peter Irving, New York, 28 October 1833, *Letters II*, 780.
49. Irving to Peter Irving, n.p., 24 November 1833, *Letters II*, 781.
50. Irving to Pierre M. Irving, New York, 15 September 1834, *Letters II*, 798.
51. Ibid.
52. Ibid., 799.
53. Irving to Pierre M. Irving, New York, 29 October 1834, *Letters II*, 802.
54. See Brooks, 420.

CHAPTER 13: SUNNYSIDE

1. Irving to Peter Irving, n.p., 24 November 1824, *Letters II*, 804.
2. Irving to Colonel Thomas Aspinwall, New York, 2 February 1835,

Letters II, 807; Irving to Aspinwall, New York, 8 March 1835, *Letters II*, 811.

3. Irving to Peter Irving, n.p., 11 April 1835, *Letters II*, 818.

4. Irving, "Introduction," in *The Crayon Miscellany*, 8.

5. *Western Monthly Magazine* 3 (June 1835): 329–37. See Aderman, 103–7; PMI, 3:67; *Crayon Miscellany*, xxxi.

6. McClary, 171; Irving to Aspinwall, New York, 20 May 1835, *Letters II*, 823.

7. *Southern Literary Messenger* 1 (July 1835): 646. See Aderman, 108.

8. Irving to Peter Irving, n.p., 11 April 1835, *Letters II*, 818.

9. Irving to John Pendleton Kennedy, New York, 9 June 1835, *Letters II*, 830.

10. Irving to Peter Irving, New York, 8 July 1835, *Letters II*, 835; Johnson, 5.

11. Irving to Aspinwall, New York, 15 July 1835, *Letters II*, 836–37.

12. McClary, 172. Emphasis in original; Irving to Peter Irving, New York, 8 July 1835, *Letters II*, 835.

13. *Crayon Miscellany*, xlvii.

14. Irving to Peter Irving, [26 September 1835], *Letters II*, 842.

15. Irving, *The Adventures of Captain Bonneville*, 5.

16. See Irving to George Harvey, New York, 23 November 1835, *Letters II*, 844–46; Irving to Peter Irving, New York, 24 November 1835, *Letters II*, 846.

17. Ibid.

18. See *Letters II*, 848n1–3.

19. Irving to Peter Irving, New York, 25 December 1835, *Letters II*, 847.

20. PMI, 3:87.

21. Irving to Major James H. Hook, New York, 27 March 1836, *Letters II*, 865.

22. Aderman, 109–10; Irving to Pierre M. Irving, Tarrytown, 12 December 1836, *Letters II*, 884.

23. Ibid.; PMI, 3:91.

24. Irving to Pierre M. Irving, Tarrytown, 12 December 1836, *Letters II*, 884.

25. PMI, 3:98; Irving to Ebenezer Irving, n.p., 10 January 1837, *Letters II*, 889.

26. Irving to Sarah Paris, The Roost, 11 January 1837, *Letters II*, 891.

27. See PMI, 3:102–3.

28. Irving to Alexander H. Everett, London, 2 October 1830, *Letters II*, 553.

29. For the complete text of Irving's response to the *Plaindealer*, see *Letters II*, 891–95. For a discussion of the *Plaindealer*'s attack, see PMI, 3:102–11.

30. Irving to Martin Van Buren, New York, 6 February 1837, *Letters II*, 896.

31. Irving to Aspinwall, New York, 29 March 1837, *Letters II*, 904.

32. *Adventures of Captain Bonneville*, xxvii; *Monthly Review, New and Improved*, ser. 2 (June 1837): 279–90. See Aderman, 110–11.

33. *Adventures of Captain Bonneville*, xxvii.

34. *New York Review* 1 (October 1837): 439–40. See Aderman, 111–12.

35. Irving to Gouverneur Kemble, Greenburg, 28 September 1836, *Letters II*, 875; Irving to Van Buren, New York, 6 February 1837, *Letters II*, 896, emphasis in original.

36. See *Letters II*, 921n7.

37. Irving to Van Buren, Tarrytown, 22 August 1837, *Letters II*, 913–14. Emphasis in original.

38. Irving to Kemble, New York, 10 January 1828, *Letters II*, 918.

39. Ibid.

40. Irving to Catharine Paris, Wolferts Rest, 22 March 1838, *Letters II*, 925; Irving to Kemble, New York, 12 March 1838, *Letters II*, 923; Irving to Kemble, Wolfert's Rest, 2 June 1838, *Letters II*, 929.

41. PMI, 3:126–27.

42. Irving to Van Buren, New York, 30 April 1838, *Letters II*, 926.

43. Irving to Ebenezer Irving, Washington, 7 October 1833, *Letters II*, 774.

44. Irving to Sarah Van Wart, Greenburgh, 22 September 1838, *Letters II*, 937.

45. Irving to Van Wart, Greenburgh, 1 December 1838, *Letters II*, 943.

46. PMI, 3:136.

47. Irving to William H. Prescott, New York, 18 January 1839, *Letters III*, 5; Irving to Pierre M. Irving, Madrid, 24 March 1844, *Letters III*, 708.

48. "Letter of 'Geoffrey Crayon' to the Editor of the Knickerbocker Magazine," *Knickerbocker Magazine*, March 1839. See Irving, *Miscellaneous Writings II*, 100.

49. STW, 2:106; Henry Wadsworth Longfellow to G. W. Greene, Cambridge, 23 July 1839. See *Miscellaneous Writings I*, lxix. Emphasis in original.

50. See Irving to the Reverend Robert Bolton, Greenburg, 27 May 1839, *Letters III*, 16; Irving to Van Buren, Greenburgh, 2 July 1839, *Letters III*, 18.

51. Irving to Edgar Allan Poe, Greenburgh, 6 November 1839, *Letters III*, 24–25.

52. See *The Letters of Edgar Allan Poe*, 1:121, in *Letters III*, 25n4.

53. Edgar Allan Poe to N. C. Brooks, Philadelphia, 4 September 1838, STW, 2:101–2.
54. Irving to William H. Prescott, Greenburgh, 21 January 1840, *Letters III*, 36; Irving to Lewis G. Clark, [before 10 January 1840], *Letters III*, 32–33.
55. Irving to Van Buren, Tarrytown, 13 January 1840, *Letters III*, 34; Irving to Kemble, 4 February 1840, *Letters III*, 39.
56. See Irving to Kemble, New York, 5 February 1840, *Letters III*, 43.
57. Irving to Van Wart, Greenburgh, 4 May 1840, *Letters III*, 53.
58. Irving to Kemble, Greenburgh, 31 October 1840, *Letters III*, 58.
59. Irving to Van Wart, Greenburgh, 25 November 1840, *Letters III*, 61–62.
60. Irving to Van Wart, n.p., [early December 1840], *Letters III*, 65.
61. Irving to Mssrs. Lea & Blanchard, New York, 25 February 1841, *Letters III*, 77.
62. Irving to Van Wart, Greenburgh, 19 January 1841, *Letters III*, 72.
63. Irving to Charles Storrow, Greenburgh, 8 November 1840, *Letters III*, 60; Irving to Sarah Storrow, n.p., [May 3, 1841], *Letters III*, 88.
64. George Ticknor, *Life of William Hickling Prescott* (Boston, 1864), pp. 187–88. See Irving, *Biography of the Late Margaret Miller Davidson*, xxxvii; Irving to Sarah Storrow, Hell Gate, 11 July 1841, *Letters III*, 125–26.
65. Ibid., 127, emphasis in original; Irving to Joseph C. Cabell, Sunnyside Cottage, near Tarrytown, 8 May 1841, *Letters III*, 90–91.
66. Transcribed by Irving in his 25 May 1841 letter to Sarah Storrow. See *Letters III*, 100–101.
67. Irving to Charles Dickens, Sunnyside Cottage, 25 May 1841, *Letters III*, 105–7.
68. Irving to Sarah Storrow, New York, 3 October 1841, *Letters III*, 162; Irving to Storrow, Sunnyside, 19 November 1841, *Letters III*, 167.
69. See Irving to Storrow, Sunnyside, 29 October 1841, *Letters III*, 164. Emphasis in original.
70. PMI, 3:184–85.
71. PMI, 3:182–85.
72. Charles Dickens, "As the Literary Guest of America," in *The World's Famous Orations, Great Britain, Volume II*, ed. William Jennings Bryan. (New York: Bartleby.com, 2004), http://www.bartleby.com/268/4/15.html.
73. Irving to Ebenezer Irving, New York, 10 February 1842, *Letters III*, 180.

74. Irving to Ebenezer Irving, n.p., 16 February 1842, *Letters III*, 181.
75. Ibid., 181, 183.

Chapter 14: Minister

1. Irving to Ebenezer Irving, n.p., 17 February 1842, *Letters III*, 184.
2. Irving to Ebenezer Irving, Washington, 16 March 1842, *Letters III*, 192. Emphasis in original.
3. See Irving to Hugh S. Legaré, New York, 28 March 1842, *Letters III*, 199; Irving to William C. Preston, New York, 28 March 1842, *Letters III*, 200; Irving to William C. Rives, New York, 28 March 1842, *Letters III*, 200; Irving to John Tyler, New York, 28 March 1842, *Letters III*, 201; Irving to Daniel Webster, New York, 28 March 1842, *Letters III*, 202; Irving to Webster, New York, 2 April 1842, *Letters III*, 202–3. Emphasis in original.
4. See Irving to Messrs. Lea & Blanchard, Sunnyside, 26 February 1842, *Letters III*, 186–87; Irving to Lea & Blanchard, New York, 10 March 1842, *Letters III*, 189–91.
5. Kaplan, 134; Irving to Philip Hone, New York, 4 April 1842, *Letters III*, 206; Irving to Catharine Paris, Ship *Independence*, 10 April 1842, *Letters III*, 211.
6. Irving to Paris, London, 3 May 1842, *Letters III*, 213–14; Irving to Paris, The Shrubbery, 7 May 1842, *Letters III*, 217.
7. Irving to Paris, London, 3 May 1842, *Letters III*, 213.
8. Irving to Paris, The Shrubbery, 7 May 1842, *Letters III*, 216; McClary, 179–80.
9. Irving to Paris, The Shrubbery, 7 May 1842, *Letters III*, 218.
10. Ibid., 219–20.
11. Irving to Sarah Van Wart, Paris, 8 June 1842, *Letters III*, 233.
12. Irving to Paris, Paris, 10 June 1842, *Letters III*, 237.
13. Irving to Mary Irving, Madrid, 3 August 1842, *Letters III*, 267.
14. Irving to Paris, Paris, 7 July 1842, *Letters III*, 244.
15. Irving to Henry Brevoort, Paris, 1 July 1842, *Letters III*, 241–42; Irving to Paris, The Shrubbery, 7 May 1842, *Letters III*, 220–21; Irving to Sarah Storrow, Bordeaux, 16 July 1842, *Letters III*, 247.
16. Bowers, 138–42; Irving to Paris, September 2, 1842, *Letters III*, 307–14.
17. Ibid., 313–16.
18. See Irving to Webster, Legation of the United States, Madrid, 2 August 1842, *Letters III*, 264.

19. Irving to Paris, Madrid, 3 August 1842, *Letters III*, 270–71; Irving to Sarah Storrow, Madrid, 4 August 1842, *Letters III*, 276–77.

20. Irving to Paris, Madrid, 3 August 1842, *Letters III*, 272.

21. Ibid.

22. Irving to Storrow, Madrid, 12 August 1842, *Letters III*, 282.

23. Irving to Ebenezer Irving, [October? 1842], *Letters III*, 369.

24. Irving to Charlotte Irving, Madrid, 16 September 1842, *Letters III*, 331.

25. Irving to Storrow, Madrid, 10 September 1842, *Letters III*, 326; Irving to Storrow, Madrid, 11 September 1842, *Letters III*, 328.

26. See Irving to Storrow, Madrid, 26 September 1842, *Letters III*, 336–39.

27. Irving to Julia Grinnell, Madrid, 30 September 1842, *Letters III*, 343.

28. Irving to Storrow, Madrid, 5 November 1842, *Letters III*, 372; Irving to Ebenezer Irving, [October? 1842], *Letters III*, 369.

29. Irving to Storrow, Madrid, 12 November 1842, *Letters III*, 394; PMI, 3:251.

30. Irving to Webster, Legation of the United States, Madrid, 5 November 1842, *Letters III*, 375.

31. Ibid., 376–77.

32. Irving to Pierre M. Irving, Madrid, 17 November 1842, *Letters III*, 403; Irving to Storrow, Madrid, 12 November 1842, *Letters III*, 394.

33. Irving to Webster, Legation of the United States, Madrid, 11 November 1842, *Letters III*, 390.

34. "Critical and Miscellaneous Writings of Sir Walter Scott," *Graham's Magazine* 21 (October 1842): 218–19.

35. For details, see Irving to Pierre M. Irving, Madrid, 12 November 1842, *Letters III*, 391–93.

36. Irving to Pierre M. Irving, Madrid, 12 November 1842, *Letters III*, 393.

37. Irving to Helen Irving, Madrid, 12 November 1842, *Letters III*, 391.

38. Irving to Catharine Irving, Madrid, 15 November 1842, *Letters III*, 399.

39. Irving to Paris, Madrid, 20 November 1842, *Letters III*, 407.

40. Irving to Paris, Madrid, 10 December 1842, *Letters III*, 429; Irving to Storrow, Madrid, 12 December 1842, *Letters III*, 434–38.

41. Ibid., 437.

42. Irving to Storrow, Madrid, 5 January 1843, *Letters III*, 449.

43. Irving to Storrow, Madrid, 24 February 1843, *Letters III*, 486; Irving to Paris, Madrid, 4 March 1843, *Letters III*, 488.

44. Irving to Paris, Madrid, 25 March 1843, *Letters III*, 497.
45. Irving to Webster, Legation of the United States, Madrid, 24 May 1843, *Letters III*, 528.
46. Irving to Storrow, Madrid, 17 June 1843, *Letters III*, 539; Irving to Paris, Madrid, 21 June 1843, *Letters III*, 541.
47. Irving to the Secretary of State, Legation of the United States, Madrid, 22 June 1843, *Letters III*, 546.
48. Irving to Storrow, Madrid, 14 July 1843, *Letters III*, 556.
49. Ibid., 557; Irving to Storrow, Madrid, 18 July 1843, *Letters III*, 559. See also Irving to Paris, Madrid, 10 August 1843, *Letters III*, 577.
50. Irving to Legaré, Legation of the United States, Madrid, 22 July 1843, *Letters III*, 563.
51. Irving to Storrow, Madrid, 23 July 1843, *Letters III*, 565; Irving to the U.S. Secretary of State, Legation of the United States, Madrid, August 3, 1843, *Letters III*, 574.
52. Irving to Paris, Madrid, 10 August 1843, *Letters III*, 581.
53. Irving to the Secretary of State, Legation of the United States, Madrid, 19 August 1843, *Letters III*, 591.
54. Irving to Storrow, Madrid, 6 September 1843, *Letters III*, 603; Irving to Paris, Versailles, 18 September 1843, *Letters III*, 608–9.
55. Irving to Ebenezer Irving, [Paris], 30 September 1843, *Letters III*, 612; Irving to Brevoort, Bordeaux, 26 November 1843, *Letters III*, 618.
56. Ibid., 617.
57. Irving to Paris, Madrid, 20 January 1844, *Letters III*, 658.
58. Irving to Storrow, Madrid, 20 December 1843, *Letters III*, 633.
59. Irving to Storrow, Madrid, 7 January 1844, *Letters III*, 644.
60. Irving to Paris, Madrid, 23 March 1844, *Letters III*, 704–5.
61. Irving to Pierre M. Irving, Madrid, 24 March 1844, *Letters III*, 708; Irving to Storrow, Madrid, 27 April 1844, *Letters III*, 735.
62. Irving to John C. Calhoun, Legation of the United States, Madrid, 23 April 1844, *Letters III*, 730.
63. Irving to Calhoun, Legation of the United States, Madrid, 6 May 1844, *Letters III*, 739–42.
64. Irving to Storrow, Madrid, 15 May 1844, *Letters III*, 747.
65. Irving to Storrow, Madrid, 18 May 1844, *Letters III*, 751.
66. See Irving to Paris, Valencia, 10 August 1829, *Letters II*, 465.
67. Irving to Calhoun, Legation of the United States, Barcelona, 14 July 1844, *Letters III*, 800.
68. Irving to Paris, The Shrubbery, Edgbaston, 30 August 1844, *Letters III*, 814; Irving to Paris, Paris, 15 September 1844, *Letters III*, 816.

69. Irving to Jasper Livingston, Paris, 25 September 1844, *Letters III*, 818–20.
70. Irving to Calhoun, Paris, 16 October 1844, *Letters III*, 822.
71. Irving to Storrow, Madrid, 6 December 1844, *Letters III*, 842–43.
72. Irving to Storrow, Madrid, 18 January 1845, *Letters III*, 869.
73. Irving to Storrow, Madrid, 31 January 1845, *Letters III*, 874; Irving to Storrow, Madrid, 18 January 1845, *Letters III*, 870.
74. Irving to Paris, Madrid, 19 February 1845, *Letters III*, 889–90.
75. Irving to Storrow, Madrid, 27 February 1845, *Letters III*, 899–900.
76. Irving to Storrow, Madrid, 27 March 1845, *Letters III*, 924.
77. Irving to Storrow, Madrid, 3 April 1845, *Letters III*, 929.
78. Irving to Paris, Madrid, 22 April 1845, *Letters III*, 949.
79. Irving to Storrow, Madrid, 10 May 1845, *Letters III*, 961.
80. Irving to George P. Putnam, Madrid, 13 August 1845, *Letters III*, 1020–21.
81. Irving to James Buchanan, Paris, 1 October 1845, *Letters III*, 1030. See Irving to Paris, Paris, 1 November 1845, *Letters III*, 1031.
82. Irving to Buchanan, Paris, 12 December 1845, *Letters III*, 1038.
83. Irving to Storrow, London, 7 January 1846, *Letters IV*, 4.
84. See Hershel Parker, ed., "Gansevoort Melville's 1846 London Journal," *Bulletin NYPL* 69 (December 1965): 646–47. See *Letters IV*, 6n8.
85. Irving to Storrow, London, 2 February 1846, *Letters IV*, 9; Irving to Storrow, London, 17 January 1846, *Letters IV*, 7.
86. Irving to Pierre M. Irving, [Madrid, late July 1846], *Letters IV*, 85.
87. Irving to Paris, Madrid, 16 March 1846, *Letters IV*, 27.
88. Irving to Paris, Madrid, 25 April 1846, *Letters IV*, 54; Irving to Sabina O'Shea, Madrid, 4 June 1846, *Letters IV*, 65.
89. See *Letters IV*, 45n2.
90. Irving to Paris, [Madrid, early August 1846], *Letters IV*, 89; Irving to Gouverneur Kemble, New York, 5 April 1842, *Letters III*, 209.

CHAPTER 15: ICON

1. Irving to Sabina O'Shea, Sunnyside, 18 September 1847, *Letters IV*, 151; Johnson, 33.
2. Irving to Gouverneur Kemble, Sunnyside, 8 July 1847, *Letters IV*, 139.
3. Irving to Sarah Storrow, Sunnyside, 18 October 1836, *Letters IV*, 97; Irving to Pierre M. Irving, n.p., [31 December 1846], *Letters IV*, 109.

4. Irving to Pierre M. Irving, Sunnyside, 6 January 1847, *Letters IV*, 109–10.

5. PMI, 4:16; Irving to Helen Dodge Irving, Sunnyside, 14 February [1847], *Letters IV*, 113.

6. Irving to Pierre M. Irving, n.p., [April? 1847], *Letters IV*, 132.

7. PMI, 4:14.

8. Irving to Pierre M. Irving, [Sunnyside, 14 April 1847], *Letters IV*, 125–26; Irving to Pierre M. Irving, Sunnyside, 15 April 1847, *Letters IV*, 128–29.

9. Irving to Helen Dodge Irving, Sunnyside, 30 April 1847, *Letters IV*, 131.

10. Irving to Storrow, Sunnyside, 6 June 1847, *Letters IV*, 133–36.

11. Irving to O'Shea, Sunnyside, 18 September 1847, *Letters IV*, 151.

12. Ibid.; Irving to Storrow, Sunnyside, 18 October 1846, *Letters IV*, 98.

13. Madsen, 268; See STW, 2:210.

14. Irving to Henry R. Schoolcraft, Sunnyside, 10 November 1851, *Letters IV*, 274.

15. Irving to John Dix, New York, 30 December 1848, *Letters IV*, 187.

16. PMI, 4:37.

17. Irving to Storrow, Sunnyside, 17 July 1848, *Letters IV*, 178.

18. See PMI, 4:42, 43.

19. Ibid., 46, 47

20. Irving to Storrow, Sunnyside, 5 July 1849, *Letters IV*, 198.

21. See PMI, 4:56.

22. Irving to Pierre M. Irving, n.p., 21 September 1849, *Letters IV*, 202; "Washington Irving," *United States Magazine and Democratic Reviews* 21 (December 1849): 492.

23. *Literary World* 5 (22, 29 December 1849): 537–38, 560–61; "Lives of Mahomet and His Successors," *Christian Observer* 162 (June 1851): 378–79.

24. See Irving to John Murray III, Sunnyside, 19 August 1850, *Letters IV*, 218–19; McClary, 191–95; Irving to Murray, Sunnyside, 22 September 1850, *Letters IV*, 222.

25. Irving to O'Shea, Sunnyside, 24 February 1850, *Letters IV*, 206; Irving to Storrow, Sunnyside, 18 July 1850, *Letters IV*, 211.

26. Irving to J. S. Lyon, Sunnyside, 27 November 1847, *Letters IV*, 158; PMI, 4:80.

27. Irving to Storrow, Sunnyside, 6 May 1851, *Letters IV*, 251.

28. Irving to Rufus W. Griswold, Sunnyside, 18 September 1851, *Letters*

IV, 260; Irving to Lewis Gaylord Clark, Sunnyside, 6 October 1851, *Letters IV*, 261–62.

29. Irving to John P. Kennedy, Sunnyside, 20 December 1853, *Letters IV*, 457.

30. See Irving to Storrow, Sunnyside, 6 May 1851, *Letters IV*, 252; PMI, IV, 86; Irving to Nathaniel Hawthorne, Sunnyside, 29 January 1852, *Letters IV*, 294.

31. Hawthorne to Irving, 16 July 1852, STW 2:205–6.

32. Irving to Storrow, Sunnyside, 13 January 1852, *Letters IV*, 291; Irving to Storrow, Sunnyside, 29 May 1852, *Letters IV*, 307–8.

33. Irving to Catharine Irving, Baltimore, 17 January 1853, *Letters IV*, 351.

34. Irving to Catharine Irving, Washington, 23 January 1853, *Letters IV*, 360. See *Letters IV*, 363n3.

35. Irving to Catharine Irving, Washington, 23 January 1853, *Letters IV*, 363n3; Irving to Daniel Lord, Washington, 3 February 1853, *Letters IV*, 364–65; Irving to Sarah Irving, Washington, 16 February 1853, *Letters IV*, 373.

36. Irving to Storrow, Sunnyside, 28 March 1853, *Letters IV*, 385; Irving to Helen Dodge Irving, Washington, 28 February 1853, *Letters IV*, 378; Irving to Storrow, Sunnyside, 28 March 1853, *Letters IV*, 385.

37. Irving to Storrow, Sunnyside, 28 March 1853, *Letters IV*, 386.

38. Irving to Mary E. Kennedy, Sunnyside, 27 May 1853, *Letters IV*, 407.

39. PMI, 4:153; Irving to Pierre M. Irving, Ellicott's Mills, 8 July 1853, *Letters IV*, 1853.

40. Irving to Storrow, Sunnyside, 29 July 1853, *Letters IV*, 422. Emphasis in original.

41. Irving to Mary E. Kennedy, Sunnyside, 8 September 1853, *Letters IV*, 432.

42. Irving to Storrow, Sunnyside, 19 September 1853, *Letters IV*, 436; Irving to Lewis G. Clark, [27 April 1849], *Letters IV*, 192.

43. Irving to Elizabeth Kennedy, Sunnyside, 11 November 1853, *Letters IV*, 452.

44. Irving to Kennedy, Sunnyside, 21 February 1854, *Letters IV*, 464.

45. Irving to Helen Dodge Irving, Cassilis, 26 June 1853, *Letters IV*, 416. See Irving, "The Creole Village," in *Wolfert's Roost*, 27.

46. PMI, 4:187; See STW, 2:226.

47. Irving to George P. Putnam, [March? 1855], *Letters IV*, 530.

48. Irving to John P. Kennedy, Sunnyside, 23 April 1855, *Letters IV*, 532;

Irving to Storrow, Sunnyside, 27 June 1855, *Letters IV*, 541; Irving to John P. Kennedy, Sunnyside, 23 April 1855, *Letters IV*, 532.

49. PMI, 4:196.

50. Ibid., 195.

51. Ibid., 204.

52. Ibid., 209. See *National Intelligencer*, 23 March 1857. This article was also reprinted widely after Irving's death.

53. PMI, 4:209.

54. Ibid., 217.

55. Irving to Emily Fuller, Sunnyside, 2 July 1856, *Letters IV*, 589–90.

56. Irving to Charles Lanman, Sunnyside, 2 March 1857, *Letters IV*, 609.

57. See Irving to Frederick S. Cozzens, Sunnyside, 22 May 1857. See also Irving, *A History of New York*, 216; Irving to Charles A. Davis, Sunnyside, 2 June 1857, *Letters IV*, 626.

58. Irving to Storrow, Sunnyside, 4 August 1857, *Letters IV*, 623

59. PMI, 4:239.

60. Ibid., 253. Emphasis in original.

61. Ibid., 252.

62. Ibid., 255.

63. Ibid., 265.

64. Ibid., 265, 268.

65. Ibid., 276.

66. Ibid., 279; Irving to Kennedy, Sunnyside, 11 May 1859, *Letters IV*, 688.

67. PMI, 4:282.

68. William C. Preston to Irving, Charlottesville, 11 May 1859. See PMI, 4:286.

69. PMI, 4:290.

70. Ibid., 296.

71. Ibid., 333.

72. Ibid., 319, 322.

73. See "Washington Irving," *Milwaukee Sentinel*, 1 December 1859.

74. PMI, 4:327–29; Irving's eight pallbearers were Kemble, Cogswell, Renwick, Col. James A. Hamilton, Col. James Watson Webb, Henry Shelton, Esq., and Messrs. George T. Morgan and Nathaniel B. Holmes. See Edmund Clarence Stedman, "The Death and Burial of Washington Irving," *New York Tribune*, 2 December 1859.

75. Irving to Ebenezer Irving, [Madrid, fall 1842], *Letters III*, 440.

76. "Address on the Death of Washington Irving," Longfellow, 800–802.

77. Irving to Brevoort, London, 3 March 1819, *Letters I*, 543.

Selected Bibliography

Adams, Henry. *History of the United States of America during the Administrations of Thomas Jefferson*. New York: Literary Classics of the United States, 1986.

Aderman, Ralph M., ed. *Critical Essays on Washington Irving*. Boston: G. K. Hall, 1990.

Bowers, Claude G. *The Spanish Adventures of Washington Irving*. Cambridge: Riverside Press, 1940.

Brooks, Van Dyke. *The World of Washington Irving*. New York: E. P. Dutton, 1944.

Burrows, Edwin G. and Mike Wallace. *Gotham: A History of New York City to 1898*. New York: Oxford University Press, 1999.

Chandler, George. *An Illustrated History of Liverpool*. Liverpool, England: Rondo, 1972.

Hedges, William L. *Washington Irving: An American Study, 1802–1832*. Baltimore: Johns Hopkins Press, 1965.

Hellman, George S. *Washington Irving, Esquire*. New York: Alfred A. Knopf, 1925.

Homberger, Eric. *The Historical Atlas of New York City: A Visual Celebration of Nearly 400 Years of New York City's History*. New York: Henry Holt, Owl Books, 1998.

Irving, Washington. *The Adventures of Captain Bonneville*. Edited by Robert A. Rees and Alan Sandy. Vol. 16 of *The Complete Works of Washington Irving*. Boston: Twayne, 1977.

————. *The Alhambra*. Edited by William T. Lenehan and Andrew B. Myers. Vol. 14 of *The Complete Works of Washington Irving*. Boston: Twayne, 1983.

————. *Astoria; or, Anecdotes of an Enterprize beyond the Rocky Mountains*. Edited by Richard Dilworth Rust. Vol. 15 of *The Complete Works of Washington Irving*. Boston: Twayne, 1976.

————. *Bracebridge Hall; or, The Humourists: A Medley by Geoffrey Crayon, Gent*. Edited by Herbert F. Smith. Vol. 9 of *The Complete Works of Washington Irving*. Boston: Twayne, 1977.

————. *A Chronicle of the Conquest of Granada*. Edited by Miriam J. Shillingsburg. Vol. 13 of *The Complete Works of Washington Irving*. Boston: Twayne, 1988.

————. *The Crayon Miscellany*. Edited by Dahlia Kirby Terrell. Vol. 22 of *The Complete Works of Washington Irving*. Boston: Twayne, 1979.

—————. *A History of New York.* Edited by Michael L. Black and Nancy B. Black. Vol. 7 of *The Complete Works of Washington Irving.* Boston: Twayne, 1984.

—————. *A History of New York; Washington Irving: History, Tales and Sketches.* Edited by James W. Tuttleton. New York: Literary Classics of the United States, 1983.

—————. *Letters of Jonathan Oldstyle, Gent./Salmagundi.* Edited by Bruce I. Granger and Martha Herzog. Vol. 6 of *The Complete Works of Washington Irving.* Boston: Twayne, 1977.

—————. *The Life and Voyages of Christopher Columbus.* Edited by John Harmon McElroy. Vol. 11 of *The Complete Works of Washington Irving.* Boston: Twayne, 1981.

—————. *Life of George Washington.* Edited by Allen Guttman and James A. Sappenfield. Vols. 19–21 of *The Complete Works of Washington Irving.* Boston: Twayne, 1982.

—————. *Mahomet and His Successors.* Edited by Henry A. Pochmann and E. N. Feltskog. Vol. 18 of *The Complete Works of Washington Irving.* Madison: University of Wisconsin Press, 1970.

—————. *Miscellaneous Writings, Volume I: 1803–1859.* Edited by Wayne R. Kime. Vol. 28 of *The Complete Works of Washington Irving.* Boston: Twayne, 1981.

—————. *Miscellaneous Writings, Volume II: 1803–1859.* Edited by Wayne R. Kime. Vol. 29 of *The Complete Works of Washington Irving.* Boston: Twayne, 1981.

—————. *Oliver Goldsmith: A Biography/Biography of the Late Margaret Miller Davidson.* Edited by Elsie Lee West. Vol. 17 of *The Complete Works of Washington Irving.* Boston: Twayne, 1978.

—————. *The Sketch Book of Geoffrey Crayon, Gent.* Edited by Haskell Springer. Vol. 8 of *The Complete Works of Washington Irving.* Boston: Twayne, 1978.

—————. *Tales of a Traveller by Geoffrey Crayon, Gent.* Edited by Judith Giblin Haig. Volume 10 of *The Complete Works of Washington Irving.* Boston: Twayne, 1987.

—————. *The Voyages and Discoveries of the Companions of Columbus.* Edited by James W. Tuttleton. Vol. 12 of *The Complete Works of Washington Irving.* Boston: Twayne, 1986.

—————. *Wolfert's Roost.* Edited by Roberta Rosenberg. Vol. 27 of *The Complete Works of Washington Irving.* Boston: Twayne, 1979.

Johnson, Kathleen Eagen. *Washington Irving's Sunnyside.* Tarrytown, N.Y.: Historic Hudson Valley Press, 1995.

Kaplan, Fred. *Dickens: A Biography*. Baltimore: Johns Hopkins University Press, 1998.

Lacey, Louis, ed. *The History of Liverpool from 1207 to 1907: Some Notes*. Liverpool: Lyceum Press, 1907.

Leary, Lewis. *Washington Irving*. Pamphlets on American Writers, no. 25. Minneapolis: University of Minnesota, 1963.

Lester, V. Markham. *Victorian Insolvency: Bankruptcy, Imprisonment for Debt, and Company Winding Up in Nineteenth-Century England*. New York: Oxford University Press, 1995.

Longfellow, Henry Wadsworth. *Poems and Other Writings*. Edited by J. D. McClatchy. New York: Literary Classics of the United States, 2000.

Madsen, Axel. *John Jacob Astor: America's First Multimillionaire*. New York: John Wiley & Sons, 2001.

McClary, Ben Harris, ed. *Washington Irving and the House of Murray*. Knoxville: University of Tennessee Press, 1969.

McFarland, Philip. *Sojourners*. New York: Atheneum, 1979.

Myers, Andrew B., ed. *A Century of Commentary on the Works of Washington Irving*. Tarrytown, N.Y.: Sleepy Hollow Restorations, 1976.

Paulding, William Irving. *The Literary Life of James K. Paulding*. New York: Charles Scribner, 1867.

Pearson, Hesketh. *Sir Walter Scott: His Life and Personality*. New York: Harper & Brothers, 1954.

Reichart, Walter A. *Washington Irving and Germany*. Ann Arbor: University of Michigan Press, 1957.

Remini, Robert V. *The Life of Andrew Jackson*. New York: Penguin Books, 1988.

Sanborn, F. B., ed. *The Romance of Mary Wollstonecraft Shelley, John Howard Payne and Washington Irving*. Boston: Bibliophile Society, 1907.

Sanderlin, George. *Washington Irving: As Others Saw Him*. New York: Coward, McCann & Geoghegan, 1975.

Smiles, Samuel. *A Publisher and His Friends: Memoirs and Correspondence of the Late John Murray with an Account of the Origins and Progress of the House, 1768–1843*. 2 vols. New York: Charles Scribner's Sons, 1891.

Warner, Charles D. *Washington Irving*. Port Washington, N.Y.: Kennikat Press, 1968.

Williams, Stanley T., and Leonard B. Beach. *The Journal of Emily Foster*. New York: Oxford University Press, 1938.

Wills, Garry. *James Madison*. New York: Times Books, 2002.

Index

Abbotsford, 158–159

Abbotsford and Newstead Abbey (Irving), 319

Aberdeen, Lord, 272–273, 275, 346

abolitionist movement, 301

Adams, John, 5

Adams, John Quincy, 233, 257, 265, 269

Adventures of Captain Bonneville, The (Irving), 327–328

adventure stories, 6

Agapida, Fray Antonio (pseudonym), 258, 272, 357

agrarian reform, 105

Albuquerque, Cavalcanti de, 348–349

Alhambra, 251, 260

Alhambra, The (Irving), 284, 285, 287, 289, 296–297, 390

Allston, Washington, 39–41, 131, 144, 168, 169–170, 171

Almodóvar, Count, 349, 351

American Citizen (newspaper), 18–19, 26

American public, reception of Irving by, 98, 291–295, 310–311, 334

American Revolution, 2, 13

Ames, Hector, 347, 358

Analectic (magazine), 116–118, 119, 124, 125

Anderson, John, 7–8, 11, 40

André, John, 12

Andrews, John, 286–287

appearance, 30, 47, 267

Ariosto, Ludovico, 6

Aspinwall, Thomas, 245–246, 255, 256, 261, 280, 281, 289, 317, 320–321, 327

Astor, John Jacob, 4, 52, 85, 111, 191, 293, 313–315, 323, 324, 345, 383–384

Astoria (Irving), 314–315, 320, 321, 323–324

Astor library, 387

Azendai (Payne), 216

bachelorhood, 87–88

Ballston Springs, 17–18

Bancroft, George, 403

bank failures, 329

bankruptcies, 166–167, 231

Barcelona, Spain, 369–370, 373–374

Barlow, Joel, 109

Barrow, John, 151

Battle of Waterloo, 127–130

Bean, Jesse, 303

Benson, Egbert, 120

Bentley, Richard, 324, 327

Bethune, Joanna, 52

bias, in storytelling, 6

Biddle, Nicholas, 46

Biography and Poetical Remains of the Late Margaret Miller Davidson (Irving), 337–338

Black Hawk (chief), 302

Black Hawk War, 302

Blackwood, William, 155–156

Blennerhassett, Harman, 66–67, 68
Bohn, Henry, 388–389
Bolivian mine investment, 227, 230, 234, 261
Bologna, Italy, 43
Bonneville, Benjamin Louis Eulalie du, 322, 323, 324, 327
Bracebridge Hall (Irving), 197, 198, 202–205
Bradford & Innskeep, 124
Brent, Robert, 108
Brevoort, Carson, 345, 349, 365
Brevoort, Henry Jr.
    business dealings of, 25, 79–80, 85, 113–114, 132–133, 243–244, 320
    on *Columbus*, 249
    correspondence with, 91, 92, 112–113, 276–277, 294, 295, 349, 365
    death of, 384–385
    in Europe, 273
    as Irving's literary agent, 113, 118, 176, 177–180, 183, 196–197, 247, 248, 256
    on Jeffrey, 155
    marriage of, 164–165
    as one of the Lads, 53, 55
    relationship between Irving and, 110–111, 120–121, 138–139, 142–143, 171, 195–196, 244–245
    reunion between Irving and, 274
    on William Irving, 199
Britain. *See also* London
    Irving in, 128–132
    strained relations between U.S.

and, 104–105, 375–376
    trade negotiations between U.S. and, 265, 266, 269–270, 272, 274, 275
British West Indies, 265, 269–270, 272–273
Broadway, 52–53
Brockedon, William, 151
Brown, Charles Brockden, 12, 21
Brussels, 48
Bryant, William Cullen, 258–259, 286–287, 326
Buckram, Dick (pseudonym), 25
buffalo hunting, 305–306
bullfights, 237
Burns, Robert, 111–112
Burr, Aaron, 5, 13, 18, 19, 21, 25–26, 27, 34, 66–70, 72–73
    business climate, 13–14
    business investments
        Bolivian mines, 227, 230, 234, 261
        land speculation, 320, 323, 324–325, 329–330, 345
        losses in, 312, 323, 336
        steamboat venture, 191–193, 196, 198
        successful, 381
Byron, Lord, 99, 117, 131, 132, 137, 150, 151–152, 164, 184, 193, 219, 285

Cabell, Joseph, 38–39, 41, 42–45, 46, 339
Caine, George, 81
Calhoun, John C., 105, 269, 307, 309, 367, 370
Calliopean Society, 14

Campbell, Archibald, 103
Campbell, Thomas, 103, 117, 131, 144, 149, 154, 159
Canada
  British West Indies and, 270
  illegal trade with, 79–80
Canning, George, 151, 275
career
  indecision about, 132–133
  in law, 12–14, 16–17, 56–57, 84, 85–86
  writing as, 12, 124–125, 148, 172–173, 175–176, 249–250
Carey & Lea. See Carey, Lea & Carey
Carey, Lea & Blanchard. See Carey, Lea & Carey
Carey, Lea & Carey, 253, 255, 256, 258, 275, 287, 312, 318, 319, 321, 324, 327–328, 338–339, 345–346, 353
Carson, Laura Elizabeth, 164
Carvills, the, 255–256
Cass, Lewis, 348
Catskills, 298–299
character traits, 24–25
Charles II (Payne), 217, 218, 219–220
Cheetham, James, 18, 22, 26–27
Cheves, Langdon, 105
Childe Harold's Pilgrimage (Byron), 150, 164
childhood, 1–12
cholera epidemic, 299
Christmas story, 185–186
Chronicle of the Conquest of Granada (Irving), 239, 253, 254, 256, 258–260, 261, 272, 357, 390
Church, Edward, 191

Cipher Letter, 67
Citizen of the World (Goldsmith), 9
Civil War, 307
Clark, Lewis Gaylord, 333, 334, 358
Clark, William, 301–302
Clay, Henry, 67, 116, 163, 165, 296, 309, 342
Clinton, George, 110
Cogswell, Joseph, 345
Colburn, Henry, 203, 289
Colden, Mary, 16
Coleman, William, 18, 22, 27
Coleridge, Samuel Taylor, 99, 137, 152
Columbus, Christopher, 233, 235, 236–237
Columbus biography. See Life and Voyages of Christopher Columbus
commerce, 13–14
Companions of Columbus (Irving), 274, 275–276
Constable, Archibald, 156, 184–185, 228, 236
Constitution. See U.S. Constitution
Continental Congress, 4
Cooper, James Fenimore, 202–203, 219, 301, 315, 316–317, 384, 390–391
Cooper, Thomas, 52, 56, 82, 114, 297–298
copyright issues, 61, 76, 147–148, 182, 335–336, 388–389
Corrector (newspaper), 26
Crawford, William, 110
Crayon, Geoffrey (pseudonym), 178, 190–191, 194–195, 222, 248, 296–297, 317, 333–334

Crayon Miscellany, The (Irving), 317, 319, 320–321
critics' reviews
  of *Abbotsford and Newstead Abbey*, 319
  of *Adventures of Captain Bonneville*, 328
  of *Alhambra*, 297
  of *Astoria*, 324
  of *Columbus*, 248–250
  of *Companions*, 275–276
  of *Crayon Miscellany*, 321
  of *History of New York*, 98–99
  Irving's response to, 326–327
  of *Life of George Washington*, 403
  of *Mahomet*, 388
  negative, 222–224, 291, 325–326, 328, 334, 357–358
  of *Oliver Goldsmith*, 387
  of *Tour on the Prairies*, 318–319, 325–327
  of *Traveller*, 222–224
  of *Wolfert's Roost*, 397

Dana, Richard Henry, 183
Daveiss, Joseph, 67
Davidson, Margaret Miller, 337–338
Decatur, Stephen, 119, 121, 125–126, 132
"Defense of Fort McHenry" (Key), 122–123
Delaplaine, Joseph, 119
Democrat-Republicans, 18–19
Dennie, Joseph, 61
Der Freischütz (Weber), 207, 208–209
Dickens, Charles, 99, 186, 339–340, 340–342, 377

Disraeli, Benjamin, 236, 240
D'Israeli, Isaac, 150, 151, 189
Don Juan (Byron), 184
"Don Juan" (Irving), 338
D'Oubril, Pierre, 236
Dresden, 206–215
drinking, 53
Dunlap, William, 21–22
Duval, A. V. P., 216

Eddy, Thomas, 52
Edinburgh, Scotland, 155
Edinburgh Review (periodical), 150, 155, 204–205
education, 1, 5–8, 10–14
Elements of Mechanics, The (Renwick), 285, 286
Ellsworth, Henry, 300, 301, 303–305
England. *See* Britain
erythema multiforme, 201–202
Espartero (regent of Spain), 350–351, 356, 360, 361–363
esta obra, 78–79, 81, 84, 86, 89. *See also History of New York, A*
European travels, 28–50. *See also specific countries*
Everett, Alexander Hill, 233–234, 236, 237, 238, 249, 253, 257, 262
Everett, Edward, 346

Fairlie, Mary, 62–66, 72, 79, 81–82, 114, 298
family business
  bankruptcy of, 166–167
  hardships facing, 79–80, 105, 139–140, 142

Irving's role in, 102–103, 115, 135–138, 163
Peter's role in, 84, 133–135
success of, 101
Federalists, 4, 18–19, 64
federal tariffs, 307, 309–310
Felston, Cornelius, 341
Fenno, John, 17
Fenno, Maria. *See* Hoffman, Maria
Ferriere, Jean, 29
Fessenden, Thomas, 61
First Bank of the United States, 105, 107, 110
Fiske, Jonathan, 11, 12
Force Bill, 308–309, 310
Forsyth, John, 313
Foster, Amelia Morgan, 207–208, 215
Foster, Emily, 208–214, 215, 399–400
Foster, Flora, 208, 209–210, 212, 213–214
Foster family, 207–215, 220
France, 29–34, 45–47, 104–105.
See also Paris, France
Franklin, Benjamin, 12, 20
Frederic I (king), 206–207

Genoa, 34–35
George IV (king), 274
Germany, 206–207
ghost stories, 12, 15–16
Gifford, William, 220–221
Godwin, William, 183, 267
Goldsmith, Oliver, 9, 337
Gotham, 74–75
Graham, Isabella, 52

Granada, 250–252, 260–262.
See also Chronicle of the Conquest of Granada

Hall, John Nalder, 101, 252, 254
Hamilton, Alexander, 4, 5, 13, 17, 18, 34, 105
Hamilton, Alexander Jr., 345, 349, 358, 361, 368
Hamilton, James, 307
Hamilton, Walter, 151
Harvey, George, 320, 321, 322, 380–381
Hawthorne, Nathaniel, 391–392
Hell Gate, 321–322
Henderson, Josiah A., 11
herpes simplex virus, 201–202
Highland Grange, 103–104
Highlands, 15
History of New York, A (Irving), 113, 140, 144
new editions of, 114, 137, 168, 171, 195, 218, 386
publicity for, 92–95
reception of, 95–101
Scott on, 118–119
writing of, 89–92
Hoffman, Ann, 62, 75, 81–82, 83
Hoffman, Charles Fenno, 292–293
Hoffman, Josiah Ogden, 16–17, 19, 23–24, 56–57, 62, 64, 85–86, 294, 325
Hoffman, Maria, 16–17, 27, 90, 91, 208
Hoffman, Matilda, 75, 83–89, 139, 209
Holmes, Oliver Wendell, 402

homosexual behavior, 55, 88, 171
Hone, Philip, 291, 292, 293, 321
honorary degrees, 271–272, 310
Hudson River, 15–16
Hudson River Railroad, 385

Indian orations, 113
Indian Removal Act (1830), 300
Indian tribes, 112–13, 300, 302, 303, 305
Irving, Ann (sister), 80–81
Irving, Catharine (sister), 7, 17–18, 352, 359
Irving, Ebenezer (brother), 13, 14, 171–172, 291
  family business and, 102–103, 134, 136, 138–140
  finances of, 165–166, 253
  as financial consultant, 268
  as Irving's literary agent, 248
  as one of the Lads, 53–54
  political appointment for, 336–337
  Sketch Book and, 176–177
  at Sunnyside, 340, 343
Irving, John Treat (brother), 6, 13, 14, 57, 262, 268, 294, 331
Irving, Oscar (nephew), 299
Irving, Peter (brother), 14, 19, 25–26, 57, 347–348
  business investments of, 174–175, 191–193, 196, 198, 225, 227
  death of, 331–332
  esta obra and, 78–79
  family business and, 102–103, 128, 131, 133–136, 139–140, 142, 166–167
  finances of, 165–166

financial support of, 268
  health problems of, 134–135, 136, 137, 250, 329
  as one of the Lads, 53
  at Sunnyside, 323, 325
  travels with, 140–141, 191–192
Irving, Pierre Munro (nephew), 2, 53, 55, 76, 209, 238–239, 241, 245, 314–315, 345, 353, 366, 381–383, 394–395, 402–403
Irving, Pierre Paris (nephew), 223, 225
Irving, Sarah (mother), 1–2, 3, 126, 128, 144–145, 201
Irving, Sarah (niece), 405–406
Irving, Washington
  Abbotsford and Newstead Abbey, 319
  The Adventures of Captain Bonneville, 327–328
  The Alhambra, 284, 285, 287, 289, 296–297, 390
  appearance of, 30, 47, 267
  appointment of, as secretary of legation to the Court of St. James's, 262–266, 268–270, 272–273, 275
  Astoria, 314–315, 320, 321, 323–324
  bachelorhood of, 87–88
  Biography and Poetical Remains of the Late Margaret Miller Davidson, 337–338
  Bracebridge Hall, 197, 198, 202–205
  on brotherhood, 227
  business investments of, 191–193, 196, 198, 227, 230, 234, 261,

312, 320, 323–325, 329–330, 336, 345, 381

celebrity status of, 98–99, 101, 205, 291–295, 300–301, 302, 334, 393

character of, 24–25

as chargé d'affairs in London, 276–277

childhood, 1–12

Chronicle of the Conquest of Granada, 239, 253, 254, 256, 258–260, 261, 272, 357, 390

Companions of Columbus, 274–276

as conversationalist, 56

The Crayon Miscellany, 317, 319, 320–321

death of, 405–407

education, 1, 5–8, 10–14

European travels of, 28–50

finances of, 102–103, 114, 132–133, 192–193, 196, 224–225, 230–231, 234, 238–239, 242–243, 256, 268, 312, 319–320, 322–323, 353, 383

health problems, 201–202, 205, 332, 360–361, 364, 365, 366, 370, 375, 381–382, 389, 401, 401–405

A History of New York, 89–101, 113, 114, 118–119, 137, 140, 144, 168, 171, 195, 386

homesickness of, 257, 261, 368–369

honors bestowed on, 256–257, 271–272, 310

influence of, as writer, 267

law career of, 12–14, 16–17, 56–57, 84–86

legacy of, 407–409

"The Legend of Sleepy Hollow," 187–188, 190

Legends of the Conquest of Spain, 320–321

Life and Voyages of Christopher Columbus, 236–242, 244–250, 255, 256, 275, 357–358

Life of George Washington, 270–272, 340, 342, 360, 382, 383, 390, 392, 394–403

literary debut of, 19–23

literary reputation of, 268, 275–276, 408

as lobbyist for family business, 105–110, 115

Mahomet, 280–281, 388

Matilda Hoffman and, 75, 83–89, 139, 209

military career of, 121–125

as minister of Spain, 342–343, 344–379

Oliver Goldsmith, 387–388

patriotism of, 119–120, 121, 244, 316

political views of, 65, 301, 330

pseudonyms of, 19–20, 25, 59, 92, 178, 190–191, 258–259, 272, 296–297, 317

reaction of, to negative reviews, 222–224, 226

relationship between father and, 2–3

return of, to U.S., 50, 290–300, 380–381

Irving, Washington (*continued*)
  "Rip Van Winkle," 169, 178, 190, 298
  The Sketch Book, 176–195, 387, 409
  Tales of a Traveller, 219–223
  A Tour on the Prairies, 316–319, 325–327
  Western frontier trip by, 300–307
  Wolfert's Roost, 396–397
Irving, William (father), 1–3, 8
  death of, 73–74, 201
  disapproval of, 13
  as disciplinarian, 10
  disposition of, 2
  political views of, 4
  relationship between Washington and, 2–3
Irving, William Jr. (brother), 3, 13, 14, 28, 42, 53, 136
  aid to Irving by, 171–173
  business deals of Peter and, 193
  death of, 199–200, 201
  political career of, 120, 123, 163, 165
  relationship between Irving and, 174, 199
Isabella II (queen), 349–352, 355–356, 358–359, 363–364, 365, 369, 373, 378
Italy, 34–44

Jackson, Andrew, 257, 262–265, 269, 272, 276, 296, 307–312
Jay, John, 5
Jefferson, Thomas, 12, 18, 25, 61, 96–97

Jeffrey, Francis, 155, 204–205
"John Bull" (Irving), 187
Johnson, Samuel, 6
Johnstown, New York, 15–16, 17–18, 80–81

Kemble, Charles, 216, 218
Kemble, Gouverneur, 53, 54–56, 75, 111, 273, 298, 336, 403–404, 406
Kemble, John, 153
Kemble, Peter Jr., 53, 75–76, 111
Kennedy, John Pendleton, 310, 392, 394
Kent, James, 18, 293
Key, Francis Scott, 122–123
Kilmaster, Ann, 1, 5
Knickerbocker, Diedrich (pseudonym), 92–94, 98, 100, 190–191, 333–334, 386
Knickerbocker, Herman, 108
Knickerbocker Magazine, 333–334, 336, 338

Lads of Kilkenny, 53–56, 75–76, 111
Lady of the Lake (Scott), 157
La Jeunesse de duc Richelieu (Duval), 216
land speculation, 320, 323, 324–325, 329–330, 345
Latrobe, Benjamin, 108, 300, 304
Latrobe, Charles, 298
law career, 12–14, 16–17, 56–57, 84
Lay of the Last Minstrel (Scott), 157
Lea & Blanchard. *See* Carey, Lea & Carey
Lea & Carey. *See* Carey, Lea & Carey

Lea, Carey & Blanchard. *See* Carey, Lea & Carey
"Legend of Sleepy Hollow, The" (Irving), 187–188, 190
legends, local, 15–16
Legends of the Conquest of Spain (Irving), 320–321
Leggett, William, 325–327
Leo (pope), 236
Leslie, Charles, 131, 170, 194, 198–199, 234, 245
Lewis, Meriwether, 301
Lewis, Morgan, 25
Life and Voyages of Christopher Columbus (Irving), 256
abridged version of, 255, 275
errors in, 248
plagiarism charge and, 357–358
publication of, 245–248
reception of, 248–250
writing of, 236–242, 244–245
Life of Byron (Moore), 267–268
Life of George Washington (Irving), 270–272, 340, 342, 360, 382, 383, 390, 392, 394–403
literary criticism, 118
literary debut, 19–23
literary reputation, 268, 275–276, 408
literary tastes, 6–7
"Little Man in Black, The" (Irving), 76
Liverpool, 127–132, 143–144, 163
Livingston, Edward, 276
Livingston, Henry Brockholst, 16
Livingston, Jasper, 365, 368, 370, 373
Livius, John, 207–209
Lockhart, Anne, 278

Lockhart, John G., 222, 278, 279, 319, 321
Lockhart, Sophia, 278
London, 48–49, 264–273, 275, 377
Longfellow, Henry Wadsworth, 242, 334, 407
Longworth, David, 57, 59, 60, 61, 76
Loreto, Italy, 43
Louis-Philippe (king), 348, 350, 356
Lowndes, William, 105
Lucerne, Switzerland, 44
Lyttleton, Lady, 194–195

Madison, Dolley, 105–107, 109
Madison, James, 5, 104, 105, 106, 107, 109
Madrid, 234–235, 236, 247, 250. *See also* Spain
Mahomet (Irving), 280–281, 388
Manhattan, 4–5, 8. *See also* New York
Maria Christina (queen mother), 350, 366, 374
Marmion (Scott), 149, 157
Married and Single (Payne), 216
Marseilles, 31
Marshall, John, 69, 71
Masterson, Henry, 13, 16
Matilda (ship), 35–37
Matthews, Arthur, 271–272
McCall, Richard, 53, 54
McComb, John, 52
McLane, Louis, 262–266, 268, 272–273, 275, 276, 296, 308, 311–313, 375–377
Medwin, Thomas, 218
Melville, Gansevoort, 377
Melville, Herman, 377

Mercer, John, 38, 46

Merry, Anthony, 66

Merwin, Jesse, 90

Milan, Italy, 43–44

Miller, John, 151, 185, 188

Minstrelsy of the Scottish Border (Scott), 156

Mitchell, Samuel, 78

Moore, Thomas, 195, 196, 206, 267–268, 271, 273, 297

Morier, John P., 207

Morning Chronicle (newspaper), 19–23, 25–26

Morse, Samuel, 270

Mount Pleasant, 54–55

Muhammad, 117, 247

Murray, John, 163–164, 184, 188–191, 193–194, 197, 198, 217–221, 225, 234
    business negotiations with, 274, 279–284, 285–286, 317–318, 319, 320–321
    Columbus and, 245–246, 252
    disagreements between, 235–236, 258–259
    financial difficulties of, 240–241, 280
    initial meeting with, 149–152
    problems with, 202–203
    relationship between Irving and, 253, 254, 266–267, 347

Murray, John III, 286, 377, 388–389

Myers, George, 227

Naples, Italy, 38–39

Napoleon, 30, 105, 116, 126, 127–129, 130, 197

Napoleonic Wars, 13

Narváez, Joaquin, 363–364, 367–368, 372, 374

Native Americans, 112–113, 300, 302, 303, 305

naval biographies, 117–118

Navarette, Martin Fernández de, 233, 235, 241, 257–258

Netherlands, 47–48

Newton, Gilbert Stuart, 170, 171, 294, 299

New York
    business climate in, 13–14
    as Gotham, 74–75
    growth of, 295–296
    identity of, 100
    political campaigns in, 64–65
    return of Irving to, 290–300
    social scene in, 51–54
    yellow fever outbreak in, 11–12

New York aristocracy, 4

New York Evening Post (newspaper), 18–19, 27, 77, 92–95, 178, 180, 182, 387

New-York Mirror (newspaper), 201, 223, 226, 292, 297, 334

New York politics, 4–5

Nice, 31–33

Nicholas, Charles, 82, 103

Non-Importation Act and Embargo, 79–80, 104–105, 110, 113, 115

Nullification Crisis, 307–310

Ogden, Henry, 53, 54

Ogden, Thomas, 23–24

Oldstyle, Jonathan (pseudonym), 19–23

Oliver Goldsmith (Irving), 387–388
Ordinance of Nullification, 307–310
Orgeon Treaty, 375–376, 377
Orlando Furioso (Ariosto), 6
Osage Indians, 303
Oswegatchie travels, 23–25
Oxford University, 271–272

P. & E. Irving and Company, 103,
    110, 115, 133–140, 142, 147, 163,
    166–167. *See also* family business
Paine, Thomas, 12
Paris, Daniel, 7, 18
Paris, France, 45–47, 215–216, 221
Paris, Sarah Sanders (niece), 299,
    325, 332, 337, 338.
    See also Storrow, Sarah
Parliamentary Act (1825), 269
parodies, 96–97
passports, 30–31
patriotism, 119–120, 121, 244, 316
Patterson, Elizabeth, 116
Paulding, James Kirke
    friendship of Irving and, 9–11, 53,
      55, 91, 92, 115, 262, 291, 331
    marriage of, 142
    Salmagundi and, 57–58, 59, 60–61,
      70–71, 76, 77
Paulding, William Irving, 55
Pawnee Indians, 303, 305
Payne, John Howard, 175, 186–187,
    197, 216–217, 225, 228–230, 234
Peel, Robert, 346
Perry, Oliver, 125
Philadelphia, 5, 63–64
philanthropy, 52
Philipse, Frederick, 103

physical appearance, 30, 47, 267
Pierce, Franklin, 393
Pilot, The (Cooper), 219
Pioneers, The (Cooper), 203
pirated copies, 183–184
plagiarism charges, 357–358
play adaptations, 216–217, 218
Poe, Edgar Allan, 319, 334–335,
    408
political activities, 105–110
political appointments, 163, 165,
    172–173, 262–263, 296, 330–331,
    342–343
political aspirations, 100–101
political campaigns, in New York,
    64–65
political satire, 96–97
political views, 65, 301, 330
political writings, 26–27
Polk, James K., 371, 374, 375–376
Porter, David, 53, 121
Pourtales, Albert-Alexandre de, 298,
    300, 304, 305
Powell, Peter, 170
Pragmatic Sanction, 349–350
Prescott, William Hickling, 332–333
presidential elections
    1800, 18–19
    1804, 25–27
    1840, 337
    1844, 371
Preston, William C., 145–146, 155,
    160–163, 306–307
pseudonyms, 19–20, 25, 59, 92, 178,
    190–191, 258–259, 272, 296–297,
    317
public persona, 88–89, 194, 329

publishing business, 147–148, 149, 163–164

Putnam, George P., 374–375, 385–386, 389, 401

Quarterly Review, 254, 255, 280

Real Academia de la Historia, 256–257

religion, 3

Renwick, James, 131, 136, 137–138, 142, 285, 286, 291, 292, 406

Renwick, Jean, 111–112

Repository of the Lives and Portraits of Distinguished Americans, 119

Representative (newspaper), 236, 240

Republicans, 61, 64

reviews. *See* critics' reviews

Revolutionary War, 2

Rich, Obadiah, 234–235, 236–237, 247, 252

Richeleieu (Payne), 217, 218, 234

Riley, Isaac, 81

"Rip Van Winkle" (Irving), 169, 178, 190, 298

Rob Roy (Scott), 158, 159

Rogers, Samuel, 271

Romaine, Benjamin, 5–6, 7, 10–11

Romantic poetry, 132

Rome, 39–42

Roost. *See* Sunnyside Cottage

Royal Literary Fund, 271

Royal Society of Literature, 271

Rush, Richard, 175, 194–195

Salmagundi (periodical), 57–63, 65, 70–71, 73–76, 77, 112, 218, 293

Salzburg, 206

Sanders, Sarah. *See* Irving, Sarah

Santa Claus, 185

Saunders, Romulus M., 378, 379

schooling. *See* education

Scotland, 160–161

Scott, Sir Walter, 99, 117, 131, 137, 149–150, 153, 188–189, 197–198, 319, 357

   death of, 279

   friendship with, 160, 162, 184–185

   health problems of, 278–279

   meeting with, 154–160

Second Bank of the United States, 329

Second Barbary War, 125–126

Secretary of Legation position, 262–266, 268–270, 272–273, 275

Select Reviews (magazine), 115, 116

Serna, Francisco de la, 260

Seville, Spain, 252

Shelley, Mary, 220, 228–230, 267, 273–274

Sketch Book of Geoffrey Crayon, The (Irving), 176–191, 387, 409

   British publication of, 183–187, 188–190

   essays in, 178, 180–181, 183, 185–186, 187, 189–190

   publication of, 177–178

   reception of, 176–180, 182, 183, 188

   success of, 181–182, 190–191, 195

slavery, 301, 310
Sleepy Hollow, 11, 47–48, 168–169
Sleepy Hollow Cemetery, 395–396, 406–407
Smith, Ashbel, 371
Smith, Robert, 109
smuggling, 79–80
"Song of Marion's Men" (Bryant), 287, 326
South Carolina, 307–310
Southey, Robert, 246
Spain. See also Madrid
　　Irving as Minister of, 342–343, 344–379
　　political unrest in, 349–351, 355–356, 359, 360–363
Spy, The (Cooper), 202
Stael, Madame de, 42, 82
St. Louis, Missouri, 301
Storm, Hall, 33, 34
Storrow, Sarah (niece), 338, 339, 348, 352–353, 364, 370, 401.
　　See also Paris, Sarah Sanders
Storrow, Thomas Wentworth, 191, 216, 239, 240, 242, 247, 337
storytelling, bias in, 6
Stratford-upon-Avon, 285
Sunnyside Cottage, 320–324, 327, 328–329, 334, 339, 340, 380–381, 383, 385, 396
Swallow Barn (Kennedy), 310
Swift, Jonathan, 99
Switzerland, 44–45

Tales of a Traveller (Irving), 219–223
Tarrytown, 11–12

Tarrytown home. See Sunnyside Cottage
Texas, 371
Thackeray, William Makepeace, 392
theater
　　atmosphere of, 10
　　attendance by Irving at, 9–10
theater reviews, 20–22
Thomas, Moses, 115, 116, 122, 124, 137, 148, 163–164, 169, 203, 222
Tickler, Toby, 26
Tilton, Theodore, 404–405
Tintern Abbey, 131–132
Tompkins, Daniel, 62, 121–122, 123–124
Tour on the Prairies, A (Irving), 316–319, 325–327
trade negotiations, between U.S. and Britain, 265, 266, 269–270, 272, 274, 275
trade restrictions, 79–80, 104–105, 130–131
Trumbull, John, 51–52
Tyler, John, 342, 344, 367, 369
Typee (Melville), 377

United States
　　return of Irving to, 290–300
　　rifts between North and South in, 307–308
　　trade negotiations between Britain and, 265, 266, 269–270, 272, 274, 275
Upshur, Abel, 363
U.S. Constitution, ratification of, 4

Vail, Aaron, 330
Van Buren, John, 284–285, 311
Van Buren, Martin, 19, 262, 265, 269, 272, 276–278, 284–285, 288–289, 308, 310, 311, 313, 327, 329–331, 336–337, 398
Vanderlyn, John, 46–47
Van Ness, Cornelius, 262
Van Ness, John Peter, 107
Van Ness, William P., 89
Van Ness manor, 311
Van Tassell property, 299–300, 306, 312, 320
Van Wart, Henry, 91, 128, 146–147, 166, 168, 216
Van Wart, Sarah (sister), 128, 347, 370
Van Wart, Irving, 216
Verplanck, Gulian, 179, 308
Victoria (queen), 346
Vienna, 206
Voyages and Discoveries of the Companions of Columbus (Irving), 275–276

Wallis, Severn, 357
War of 1812, 104, 114, 117–118, 119–122, 125, 130, 131, 133, 298
Washington, D.C., 108, 115, 296, 308, 344–345, 392–393
Washington, George, 2, 4–5
Washington biography. See Life of George Washington
Waverly (Scott), 156, 157
Webb, James, 290

Webster, Daniel, 308, 309, 342, 354–355, 356–357
Wellington, Duke of, 128
Western frontier, 24–25, 300–307
West Point Foundry Association, 298
Whig party, 337, 376
"Widow and Her Son, The" (Irving), 161–162
Wiley, Charles, 202
Wilkins, Martin, 56
Wilkinson, James, 66, 67, 69–70
Willes, William, 170
William IV (king), 274
Wirt, William, 163
Wolfert's Roost. See Sunnyside Cottage
Wolfert's Roost (Irving), 396–397
Woman of the Cliffs, 12
Woodbury, Levi, 275
Wordsworth, William, 132
World Displayed, The, 6–7
writer's block, 205, 215, 217, 276, 353–354
writing
    deciding on, as career, 172–173, 175–176
    lack of interest in, 103–104
    as nonviable career path, 12, 124–125, 148, 249–250

Ximinez, Mateo, 251, 260

yellow fever, 8, 11–12

Zurich, 44–45